Transatlantic Passages

Edited by

PAULA RUTH GILBERT and MILÉNA SANTORO

Transatlantic Passages

Literary and Cultural Relations

between Quebec and Francophone Europe

McGill-Queen's University Press

Montreal & Kingston · London · Ithaca

ISBN 978-0-7735-3787-3 (cloth)
ISBN 978-0-7735-3790-3 (paper)

Legal deposit fourth quarter 2010
Bibliothèque nationale du Québec

Printed in Canada on acid-free paper

This book has been published with the help of a grant from the Canadian Federation for the Humanities and Social Sciences, through the Aid to Scholarly Publications Program, using funds provided by the Social Sciences and Humanities Research Council of Canada.

McGill-Queen's University Press acknowledges the support of the Canada Council for the Arts for our publishing program. We also acknowledge the financial support of the Government of Canada through the Canada Book Fund for our publishing activities.

Library and Archives Canada Cataloguing in Publication

Transatlantic passages : literary and cultural relations between Quebec and Francophone Europe / edited by Paula Ruth Gilbert and Milena Santoro.

Includes bibliographical references.
ISBN 978-0-7735-3787-3 (bound).
ISBN 978-0-7735-3790-3 (pbk.)

1. Québec (Province)–Relations–Europe, French-speaking. 2. Europe, French-speaking–Relations–Québec (Province). 3. Québec (Province)–Civilization–European influences. 4. Québec (Province)–Intellectual life. 5. Canadian literature (French)–Québec (Province)–History and criticism. I. Gilbert, Paula Ruth II. Santoro, Miléna

FC2919.T74 2010   303.48'271404   C2010-903268-3

This book was designed and typeset by studio oneonone in Sabon 10/13.5.

Paula wishes to dedicate this volume to her fellow traveler, Dr Michael Randy Gabel, and to her vagabonding daughter, Meredith Gilbert Lewis, Esq.

Miléna wishes to dedicate this volume to the memory of her father, Dr Bruce Andrews. Although he passed away in 2007, his love, encouragement and intellectual inspiration will never be forgotten.

Contents

III The Theatrical Space of Exchange

IV Franco-European Immigrant Voices in Quebec

V Contemporary Art Forms and Popular Culture

Acknowledgments

The editors would like to acknowledge the fine work of all the contributors to this volume and the inestimable support of the editorial team at McGill-Queen's University Press.

This project has been a labor of love, and we feel privileged to have been able to work together in a consistent spirit of collaboration and friendship. Indeed, although the initial idea may have been Miléna's, our combined enthusiasm and visions have made this multi-faceted book so much more than the sum of its individuals. With many of its thematics and inspiration springing directly from our own transatlantic crossings, exchanges, and mutual interests, we truly feel that this volume reflects a "passage" we have shared together and a connection we have joyously poured onto the page.

We particularly wish to thank our families and close friends for the many ways in which they enable us to pursue our passions.

Permissions

We gratefully acknowledge the following individuals and entities for permissions for the following text and images:

Dalkey Archive Press (USA) and The Mercury Press (Canada) for permission to reprint excerpts of Gail Scott's *My Paris*.

Monique Proulx for permission to translate "Le Temps, Monsieur/ Time, Sir."

Les Écrits des forges for permission to reprint and translate poems from Nicole Brossard's *Je m'en vais à Trieste*.

Taylor & Francis Ltd, www.informaworld.com, for permission to reproduce a previously published portion of Jane Moss's contribution to this volume.

Bonnie Baxter, for the photographs and artwork included in her article and the splendid cover image, PARIS, from her *Jane's Journey* series, 2008 (Atelier du Scarabée, Val-David, Québec; www.bonniebaxter.com).

François Morelli, for the four photographs of his installations and work in progress as part of *Home Wall Drawing. L'art de manger* (2004).

Julius Baltazar, Jacques Clauzel, Denise Desautels, Hélène Dorion, Jacques Fournier, Jean-Luc Herman, Bernard-Gabriel Lafabrie, and Paul Litherland for the images included in Alisa Belanger's article for this volume.

Hugues Léveillée, on behalf of Les Éditions Conception/Robert Charlebois, for the opportunity to reprint and translate Robert Charlebois's hit song "Ce soir je chante à l'Olympia/Tonight I'm Singing at the Olympia."

Transatlantic Passages

Introduction
On *"Passages," Passeurs,* and *Passeuses* in Paris and Montreal

PAULA RUTH GILBERT

MILÉNA SANTORO

The arcade is a street of lascivious commerce only; it is wholly adapted to arousing desires. Because in this street the juices slow to a standstill, the commodity proliferates along the margins and enters into fantastic combinations ... The flâneur sabotages the traffic. Moreover, he is no buyer. He is merchandise.
Walter Benjamin, *The Arcades Project* 42

3. Rain. Earlier cranked up the varnished horizontal wood-slat outer blind or "store" ... People straight as pokers at the bus stop below. Or rushing carrying baguettes ... Some leaning forward. To examine suits in windows of exclusive men's shop. Across street. Then lying back on divan by rice-paper screen. By roxy-painted night-table. With Walter Benjamin's 1000-page volume – *Paris, Capitale du XIXe siècle* – on it. Left by previous studio occupant. Cover photo of ornate decorative balcony. Topped by mirror reflecting the glass-and-iron ceiling of one of those labyrinthine 19th-century passages or arcades. They used to forge through buildings. The labyrinth the shape of ancient utopias.
Gail Scott, *My Paris* 8

Place and time are essential elements of who we are. Our identity is shaped by the architectures of our experiences, be they spatial, temporal, intellectual, material, or spiritual. In the citations above from Benjamin, a German-born theorist, and Scott, a contemporary Anglo-Québécois feminist writer, it is clear that Paris is a powerful locus of desire and of being. Just as Benjamin found in Paris the fuel for his reflections on modernity, so Scott, a contemporary *flâneuse,* finds in Benjamin's *Arcades Project* a structuring principle for her own postmodern text, a first-person narrative where the subject is never that of a verb but is rather expressed in infinitives, gerunds, and accumulated sentence fragments that convey her vision of an outsider's encounter with and passage through what remains an enduring nineteenth-century Parisian cityscape.

Like Benjamin and Scott, we too have found inspiration and an intellectual grounding in our fascination for the language and culture of certain cities and regions. On the one hand, we draw on nineteenth-century Paris and urban planning and design, *les magasins de nouveautés/de luxe, les passages*/the arcades, *les grands magasins*, catacombs, sewers, cemeteries, the metro, railway stations, *la flânerie/le flâneur/la flâneuse* in the streets of Paris, Balzac, Flaubert, Baudelaire, Haussmann, Zola, Walter Benjamin, phantasmagoria, spectacles, "temples" of capitalism, commerce, commodification, objectification, gender relations, the bourgeoisie, and all that characterizes the "Old World" of nineteenth-century Europe. On the other hand, we have also been drawn to the "New World" of Montreal and Quebec, the social, economic, and cultural revolution that the Québécois embarked upon beginning in the 1960s (often termed the Quiet Revolution), and their rapid entry into the technological age, represented by such achievements as the construction of the Montreal metro with its underground shopping emporia, its deployment of artworks and architecture, its underground city shaped by the cold winter climate. How do all of these seemingly disparate ideas inform and expand our chosen metaphors of "*passages*," *passeurs*, and *passeuses*? How does the individual and collective movement/passing of people through subterranean and street-level passageways – in both time and space and at once permanent, transient, ambiguous, and liminal – connect with their intellectually critical ideas, influences, literary "production," creative impulses, and visual depictions? In what ways are such passages common to individuals on both sides of the Atlantic, or to those having made the transatlantic voyage? These questions inspire and undergird the framework of our volume, *Transatlantic Passages: Literary and Cultural Relations between Quebec and Francophone Europe*.

In the spirit of Walter Benjamin's montage vision of nineteenth-century Paris, *Das Passagen-Werk* (translated as *The Arcades Project*; the German literally means "Factory of Passages/Alleyways"), our collection of essays aspires to offer a critical and creative exploration in English of the often neglected links, transfers, and cultural commerce between Francophone Europe and Quebec. As a central, structuring, and suggestive metaphor, the notion of "passage" suggests and links ideas of movement, transaction, and architecture, along with more figurative places and modes of exchange, including literature, music, and indeed, all art forms that communicate amongst themselves and with a potential public. Etymologically, the word "passage" has been used since the Renaissance for both an architectural space and a fragment of literature or music. More recently, "passage" has gained currency in art, with reference to cubism in particular, to describe "tight brushwork to link objects in separate spatial plains."[1] Of course, in earlier times, the link between the Old World and the New was maintained by "booking passage" on a ship, and indeed, for many generations of young adults from North America, the European tour or study abroad remains a "rite of passage," an essential experience to the construction of a mature, cosmopolitan cultural identity. Passages, then, characterize and structure our lives even as they build our characters. They connect us even as they lead us, unfolding in time and space and informing our view of the world's possibilities.

We cannot pretend to imitate the great, multi-layered work of Benjamin whose "montage of emblematic images, texts, and objects from different layers of the past" sought to "develop a dialectical historical vision in which the perspectives of the past and present would mutually inform each other, making visible the continuities and breaks between them" and whose project functioned "as a kind of historiographic equivalent of the arcade, a passageway cut through the nineteenth century, with dozens of windows proffering to the viewer a vast range of historical perspectives" (Trumpener 319–20). Nevertheless, we too aspire to present a structured montage of linked images – windows, if you will – offered by each essay and creative piece and that together form a panorama of exciting and illuminating transatlantic voyages, both physical and intellectual, that cultural critics have not as yet systematically mapped with regard to the French-speaking Western Hemisphere.[2] We hope this montage will offer glimpses of how the "past and present ... inform each other" in the reflections and creative work of writers, artists, and scholars who share a certain understanding and experience of transatlantic passages.

By way of introducing our volume, then, we would like to explore briefly underground (catacombs, sewers, cemeteries, metros, and underground malls) and street-level (arcades/passages, shopping malls, streets, and *grands magasins*) metropolitan passages and spaces in Montreal and Paris, and the ways in which their conception and construction form and frame the urbanites (*flâneurs/flâneuses*) who participate in the concomitant structures of commodification. To quote Gilles Marcotte, founder of a research group devoted to "Montréal imaginaire" that published several anthologies including explorations of the links between Montreal and Paris, "in the world we live in today, most human questions pass through the city."[3] A comparison of the passages that characterize Paris and Montreal will permit us to address transatlantic convergences and differences on concepts or issues that include urban "limits," time, gender, climate, and consumerism. As *flâneuses* ourselves, we move both individually and collectively from France/Paris and francophone Europe in transatlantic passages toward Quebec/Montreal, from the nineteenth-century to the "New World" of the 1960s and back again, with an eye on the horizon of more contemporary exchanges between France and Quebec, embodied by individual creative voices and specific cultural phenomena.

Flânerie in Paris

For Benjamin, considered by some to be the "father" of Cultural Studies, nineteenth-century Paris "constituted a veritable laboratory of social change, and in that laboratory the *flâneur* served as both an emblem of the city and a surrogate for the writer in that city" (Ferguson 80) – whether the triumphant, analytical, and successful *artiste-flâneur* of Balzac, the dispossessed, dislocated, alienated, and exiled drifter-*flâneur* of Flaubert, or the ambivalent, ambiguous, and yet totally modern *flâneur* of Baudelaire. According to Ferguson, "[m]ore than any other urban type, the *flâneur* suggests the contradictions of the modern city, caught between the insistent mobility of the present and the visible weight of the past ... *Flânerie* ... is a social state that offers the inestimable, and paradoxical, privilege of moving about the city without losing one's individuality. At once on the street and above the fray, immersed in a [sic] yet not absorbed by the city, the flâneur resolves a conflict in a seductive image of independence justified by experience, of a knowledge rendered credible by the self-sufficiency of the knower" (80). The *flâneur* – since no *flâneuse* was allowed or even acknowledged at the time – wanders through the "city of arcades ... [and] street-galleries" where Paris assumes a "structure that makes it the ideal backdrop" for him (Benjamin 17) and where his gaze can seek refuge in a crowd: "The crowd is the veil through which the familiar city is transformed for the *flâneur* into phantasmagoria" (Benjamin 21).[4] For Benjamin, this urban stroller "abandons himself to the phantasmagoria of the marketplace" (14).

This last point noted by Benjamin contradicts the assertion that only men could be *flâneurs* in nineteenth-century Paris, essentially because women could not safely walk around the city alone (and maintain any sort of a good reputation) and because as weak and fragile beings, they could be too easily seduced by the temptations of the market place, rather than being able to remain somewhat aloof and observe the city in all of its commercial glory. Clearly, men could be equally seduced as they passed by. Beginning in the 1820s, one ideal site for a stroll – especially for the increasingly powerful bourgeoisie of both sexes – was the arcade, the covered passageway, "a city, a world in miniature ... a place of refuge" (from *The Illustrated Guide to Paris*, 1852, as quoted in Benjamin 32), where one could be protected from inclement weather, gaze at objects of luxury craftily and sumptuously displayed in shop windows, and sensually pass the time away by playing a game of *lécher la vitrine*: "The arcade is posed as the site and perfect emblem of the emergence of the culture of the 'commodity,' a culture of movement and dislocation in which the eye and the mind are increasingly solicited, and threatened, by an unprecedented range of stimuli masquerading as the utopia of the New" (Prendergast 5). But if the arcade was "an ultramodern marketplace, a showpiece of metropolitan culture ... and, for window-shopping flâneurs ... a primeval fairyland of consumer wishes, where the collective desires of early industrial society were embodied in the material form of commodities" (Trumpener 321), it also functioned in other important ways and as an essential part of other urban metaphors: "The arcade was at once city street and subterranean passage; along with the metro tunnels, sewer system, and catacombs, it formed a ghostly underground counterpart to Haussmann's new Paris of grand avenues and monuments. The arcade stood as the threshold between these two cities" (Trumpener 321).

As we have seen, Benjamin explored this important metaphor of the "passage" as central to an understanding of Paris in the nineteenth century. With his own fascination for entrances and exits – into and out of the arcade, the shop, the metro, the railway station, the catacombs, the sewer system (Prendergast 30) – he clearly linked the "passages," and by extension those who passed though them, to other subterranean structures: "By day, the labyrinth of urban dwellings resembles consciousness; the arcades (which are galleries leading into the city's past) issue unremarked onto the streets. At night, however, under the tenebrous mass of the houses, their denser darkness protrudes like a threat, and the nocturnal pedestrian hurries past ... But another system of galleries runs underground through Paris: the Métro, where at dusk glowing red lights point the way into the underworld of names ... [T]hey have all thrown off the humiliating fetters of street or square, and here in the lightning-scored, whistle-resounding darkness are transformed into misshapen sewer gods, catacomb fairies" (84). We have here a confluence of metaphors of passages, passing, and the *passeurs* and *passeuses* walking through these spaces that are also phenomena and symptoms of the psyche. The subterranean passages which provoked both fear (see Hugo's *Les misérables*) and fascination (see the night-time photography done by Nadar of the metro), the underworld of the sewers with their morbid commodification of death (see the organized boat trips in the sewers and the staged and displayed bones and skulls in the Catacombs photographed by Nadar), the Cimetière Père Lachaise in its enduring literary popularity – all of these urban locales stress the rapidly increasing speed (enshrined in the new railway stations) and ephemerality of urban life as it moved from the nineteenth to the twentieth century. They also represent what Benjamin calls "the enthronement of the commodity" (18), the growth of capitalism, commerce, exchange values, consumerism, and the spectacles (phantasmagoria) of European bourgeois living.

But "passages," with their passers-by, are not situated solely underground. They also exist in above-ground locations – at street level, in department stores (Zola's "temples" of consumerism). If the *passeur* and the *passeuse* can seek refuge in the crowd as the veil through which the city is transformed into phantasmagoria for these *flâneurs*, then "[t]his phantasmagoria in which the city appears now as a landscape, now as a room, seems later to have inspired the décor of department stores, which thus put flânerie to work for profit. In any case, department stores are the last precincts of flânerie. … The flâneur plays the role of scout in the marketplace" (Benjamin 21). He – and in post-modern times, she – moves back and forth from individual passer-by to part of a collective separated from, beneath, or on the street: "Streets are the dwelling place of the collective. The collective is an eternally unquiet, eternally agitated being that … experiences, learns, understands, and invents as much as individuals do within the privacy of their own four walls … More than anywhere else, the street reveals itself in the arcade as the furnished and familiar interior of the masses" (Benjamin 423).

Passages to Montreal

Transformed into intellectual, literary, and artistic ideas and influences – emigrating first by boat, then by air, later to England through that engineering marvel of a subterranean passage, the Chunnel, and even more recently via media such as film and video, the Internet, and other global exchange networks – the architecture, urban designs, commodity fetishes, and "passages" themselves have moved through space and time from nineteenth-century Paris across the Atlantic to land on the shores of the New

World. If Paris was, in Benjamin's words, the "capital of the nineteenth century," Montreal was in its own right a capitalist metropolis in the same period, with the preponderance of all of Canada's wealth and power concentrated in the hands of the inhabitants of its "Golden Square Mile" by the turn of the century. This wealth grew largely out of the strategic positioning of Montreal as a hub for commerce, transported by both rail and boat via the St. Lawrence Seaway. Indeed, the Victoria Bridge, the first to span the river, was opened in 1860 to link Montreal's rail network with the Grand Trunk system from New England. Like Paris, Montreal acquired a sewer system commensurate with its metropolitan expansion (its population doubled between 1845 and 1870,[5] and more than doubled again between 1891 and 1911[6]) during the latter half of the nineteenth century, and its horse-drawn tramway system began operations in 1861. If the Paris metro opened in 1900 for the city's landmark World Exhibition (along with the Grand and Petit Palais, those "temples" of artistic commodification, whose function was similar to that of the Eiffel Tower that showcased the glory of French engineering in 1889), plans were proposed for a similar system in Montreal as early as 1910, once again showing the circulation of the idea of the modern metropolis on both sides of the Atlantic.[7] As one historian of the Montreal metro puts it: "The wheeled object is a symbol of modernity that no self-respecting large city can do without" (Deglise 37).

For a variety of economic, structural, and political reasons, Montreal's metro was not built until mid-century, with the official inauguration of its first twenty stations and twenty-two kilometres not occurring until the fall of 1966, less than a year before Expo '67, which would put Montreal on the map and demonstrate Quebec's rapid modernization to the world. Montreal was thus only the eighth city in North America to have a metro, but, more interestingly, it was the first to have, as the historian Fabien Deglise puts it, "created at the same time, in its commercial and economic center, an indoor city" (39). The vision for this indoor city of metro lines and commercially exploitable "passages" is credited to the urbanist Vincent Ponte, hired by the Canadian Northern Railroads (CNR), and who, in turn, hired architects Henry Cobb et Ieoh Ming Pei (who later designed the controversial Louvre Pyramid), in order to design and build the Place Ville-Marie,[8] its forty-five storey cruciform shape and name both recalling the earliest colonial settlement built by missionaries in the part of the city now called Old Montreal. With as much shopping space underground as office space above (Hustak 33), Place Ville-Marie launched in 1962 the wave of construction that would result in one of the largest urban underground networks of passageways in the world, now measuring some thirty kilometres in total, through which half a million people pass daily (Deglise 135).

Unlike the Paris metro, Montreal's system was always conceived of as a place for commercial consumption, as well as for public transportation. Given its harsh winter climate and summer humidity, Montreal's subterranean network linking shopping centers, entertainment complexes, office buildings, and transportation hubs (both rail and bus stations are connected to the metro system) made and continues to make city life more enjoyable year-round. Moreover, by contrast with much of the Paris network, Montreal's metro was also conceived of as a place to display public art and innovative architecture, with the work of over seventy artists and architects represented in Montreal's sixty-five stations (Clairoux n.p.). Still, Montreal's system owes much to its Parisian predecessor and European roots: not only did Montreal mayor Jean Drapeau choose the French model of rubber-tired trains for his city's system in the 1960s, but he hired the French RATP (Régie autonome des transports parisiens) as engineers on the project, and then named many of the stations after people or places in Europe, with an emphasis on the early explorers and settlers of New France (Clairoux 65–110). The choices for station names in honor of such historic figures and European reference points clearly echoes the naming patterns of the Paris metro and street system.

As Marc Augé puts it in *Un ethnologue dans le métro*: "So many stations, so many situations or personalities recognized, remembered, magnified: the train threads its way through history at an accelerated speed; untiringly, it shuttles back and forth without stopping, between the great men, the important places and the grand monuments ... Taking the metro in some ways is tantamount to celebrating the cult of our forebears" (Augé 33). While this recollection of history, and almost exclusively men's role in it, is true of both the Paris and Montreal metro systems, it is also true that Montreal, by contrast with Paris and in large part due to the more contemporary construction of both the metro and the city, is also a place where the past is ephemeral, constantly being razed, erased, replaced, or undermined by the modern and the new. One literal example of this is the complex called the *Promenades de la cathédrale*, an underground shopping mall built in the eighties beneath what had been a sinking downtown Anglican church that was ultimately saved from destruction. As Deglise puts it: "A church basement transformed into a temple of consumerism, the story is certainly far from banal, except ... in Montreal's indoor city which has in the end spent the last forty years cultivating paradoxes but also a pronounced taste for fragmentation and incongruity" (Deglise 70).

The promenades evoked by the name of this engineering and architectural phenomenon, in addition to the notion of the heterogeneity of its position and vocation, bring us back to the notion of *flânerie* in the utopian spaces of the urban labyrinth, for that is indeed as much at the heart of the Montreal underground experience as it was and still is in that of the Paris arcades and "passages," and most especially in the more recent phenomenon of commercial "shopping malls" in newer or redesigned Paris metro stations. In his essay, "Flâner rue Notre-Dame, en 1862," in response to the observations of Hector Fabre, a nineteenth-century Montreal lawyer who ultimately became Canada's first diplomat in Paris, Gilles Marcotte asserts: "The *flâneur* made the city itself his world, and the city, so conceived, refused limitation by borders of any sort, and especially not national ones. To stroll rue Notre-Dame is to bear the contradiction of the universal, of diversity in the very heart of what, by its name, essentially invokes the origin, the original. It is also, in this name that suggests the mission and vocation of New France, to maintain the contradiction of gratuity, of the absence of a mission" (Marcotte 102).

In his analysis of Fabre's wanderings and nostalgia at the spectacle of a Montreal cityscape changing before his eyes, Marcotte highlights well both the importance of the aesthetic experience of *flânerie*, which is essentially gratuitous, and the universality of the urban particularism the *flâneur* observes. This is the experience that links Paris and Montreal, or any modern metropolis, even though nineteenth-century critics were quick to affirm that "the *flâneur* can be born anywhere; he only knows how to live in Paris."[9] This "passage" from a particular cityscape to a universal human experience is remarkably similar to what Marc Augé has termed the "law of the metro," which: "inscribes the individual journey within the comfort of a collective ethic, and it is in this that it is exemplary of what one could call the ritual paradox: it is always experienced individually, subjectively; only singular trajectories give it reality, and yet it is eminently social, the same for all, according to each person that minimum of collective identity by which a community is defined" (Augé 54). If the structures of street-level existence, alleyways, and subterranean passages in Paris and Montreal form a cityscape viewed, traversed, and consumed by millions of passengers and passersby every day, then, despite their past and present differences, these two cities can be seen as homologous urban frameworks, creating a sense of community due to the fact that their inhabitants, their *passeurs* and *passeuses*, share a space and time in their multiple individual trajectories, and are equally seduced by the phantasmagoria of commerce, fetishism, commodification – in short, by modernity. This is the sense of belonging of which Roger Fournier writes in *Moi, mon corps, mon âme, Montréal, etc.*: "I am walking slowly on Sherbrooke Street, between the old three or four storey houses that are in the process of being demolished, and I feel a marvelous lucidity. All around me are cars, unfamiliar pedestrians, trees, concrete, moving steel. Everything rumbles, rolls, crashes, rises into the sky in greyish petals. Belonging. I belong to millions of tons of concrete and moving steel" (178).

Charting our *lieux de passages*

The various features of city life in France and Quebec that we have outlined here, by the same token, are but one manifestation of an ongoing, evolving relationship between peoples and individuals, who share a history, a language, material culture, and travel patterns that create a network of "passageways," influences, and points of reference defying oceans and epochs. It is this network that we have tried to open up, using the metaphor of "passages" and the concrete example of urban experiences in Paris and Montreal, and upon which the remainder of this volume will expand, since, as we both believe, "the page is a shop window, [and] urban strolling [is] a reading" ["[l]a page est une vitrine, la marche urbaine, une lecture"] (LaRue and Chassay 260).

Comprised of scholarly articles, interviews, and "passages" by internationally recognized writers and creative artists, this interdisciplinary cultural and literary studies volume covers: historic(al) and contemporary "passages"; parallel cultural phenomena and movements, along with the artistic, literary, and socio-cultural figures who embody them; cityscapes; cinema; art; photography; literature of all genres, including popular forms such as hardbound or internet-based comic art; music; and other spectacles that show influence, confluence, collaboration, and the transfer of ideas across the Atlantic. The scope of this collection, along with its inclusion of original creative works (most offered for the first time in English translation), make this project a unique and compelling Francophone extension of the burgeoning field of Anglophone transatlantic regional studies, as well as to the various disciplines represented by its outstanding roster of leading academic and creative contributors.

We have divided the collection into five distinct and yet linked sections which – at the risk of "pushing" our metaphor of "passages," arcades, and the exchange value of ideas even further – we envision as five distinct and yet linked "emporia" of influences within which are congregated displays of luxurious intellectual goods. Section I investigates "Women's History and Passages across the Atlantic." Section II focuses on "European Cultural Influences on Quebec Writers." For Section III we present "The Theatrical Space of Exchange." Section IV highlights "Franco-European Immigrant Voices in Quebec," while Section V brings the volume into today's world with its analyses of "Contemporary Art Forms and Popular Culture."

In keeping with the opening epigraph from Gail Scott's *My Paris,* we continue to privilege this author and her post-modern "conversation with Walter Benjamin" by using excerpts of this work as epigraphs to all of the sections of this volume. Scott is a Montreal-based novelist, short story writer, translator, and essayist, whose writings and translations have been nominated for prizes such as a Lambda award and a Canadian Governor General's award. Her work is resolutely modern and feminist, yet, as she shows us in *My Paris,* she is acutely aware of the need to be in dialogue with other authors, writing in other times, places, and languages. She is an exemplary incarnation of the kind of *passeuse* this volume showcases, a *flâneuse* who contemplates identity and difference, language, age, gender, and the importance of place, space, commodification and the ephemera of culture to our urban experiences. The passages we have chosen from her work all reflect or evoke the myriad themes and intellectual exchanges and "passages" explored by our contributors.

Just as the name of the modern architectural landmark of the Place Ville-Marie deliberately evokes the first settlement of what would later become Montreal, so our first section, "Women's History and Passages across the Atlantic," is rooted in history, in particular women's history, given their important yet often neglected transatlantic passages. Like Benjamin, we affirm modernity's links with the past, by starting with Patricia Smart's historical study, "A Place for the Spirit: Canada as Dream and Reality in the Autobiographical Writings of the Women of New France." At the origins of the rich autobiographical tradition in Quebec literature are the writings of four women, all members of religious orders, who played major roles in the New France of the seventeenth-century that they crossed the ocean to help found. Taken together, their memoirs provide a woman-centered view of transatlantic migration, narrated with a down-to-earth quality and even a humor that contrasts with the heroic and tragic tone of male-authored texts. Overall, these autobiographical accounts attest to the fact that for all of these women authentic selfhood (and even sainthood) was attained through openness to the other: a configuration of self, alterity, and the divine made possible by the space of what would become Canada.

In the following piece, "Time, Sir," the award-winning Québécois writer Monique Proulx offers us a fascinating glimpse into her understanding of the difference in the concepts of time and history between Quebec and France. A finalist for a 2008 Governor General's Award for her novel *Champagne*, Proulx originally wrote this essay for a French radio program. We offer it here for the first time in English translation, because it captures perfectly not only the layered nature of cultural perceptions and influences, but also the disorientation of a modern literary *flâneuse* on the streets of Paris where so much has remained unchanged since the nineteenth century.

In her essay on "French and Quebec Feminisms: Influences and Reciprocities," Chantal Maillé, of Montreal's Simone de Beauvoir Institute, explores the political and theoretical links that formed between French and Québécois women during the second wave of feminism. She first analyzes the influence of the feminist writings of de Beauvoir and of French post-colonial thinkers in France on Québécois feminists, and then uses specific issues or catalysts such as the veil, parity and the Global March of Women [*La marche mondiale des femmes*] to reflect on the parallel trajectories and divergences of French and Québécois feminisms. Maillé's perspective as a sociological and political analyst complements the focus on literary exchanges and influences that has characterized much of the work on such transatlantic feminist connections to date.[10]

It seems fitting to conclude this section devoted to women with a selection of poems from *Je m'en vais à Trieste* by the internationally acclaimed Québécois poet, essayist, novelist, and feminist theorist, Nicole Brossard. These poems paint the memories of powerful visual images of places in France and francophone Europe, from the perspective of a French-speaking Québécois *flâneuse* whose gaze moves backward and forward in time and space, noting the weight of gender, past and present traumas, and the promise of the next generation in her *lieux de passage*: "three centuries or one only in the stretch / of the future it comes to the same" (59). Brossard, whose work has twice received Canada's Governor General's prize among many other awards, has, like Proulx and Scott, an emblematic cosmopolitan creative voice, displaying in her practice the power of alterity and the spatial or temporal interconnectedness of experiences in the formation of an identity challenged by the reality of global travel.

The epigraph from Gail Scott's *My Paris* with which we open Section II, "European Cultural Influences on Quebec Writers," highlights, in its references to Balzac, the European intertexts visible in writings by Quebec authors that the contributors to this part of the volume all explore. In "Writing beyond Redemption: Hubert Aquin and Mordecai Richler in Postwar Paris," Patrick Coleman draws comparisons between the two writers, one francophone and one anglophone, who both traveled to Paris in the early fifties. Coleman looks at the kind of contacts they made, how they envisioned writing as a profession, what inspired and frustrated them, and how this may reveal significant similarities and differences in the cultural horizons of writers from both of Montreal's linguistic communities in this pre-1960s moment. Karen McPherson escorts us into another region of francophone Europe, Switzerland, in her essay, "*Des châteaux en Suisse? Switzerland in the Quebec Imagination: Aquin and Brossard.*" She approaches Nicole Brossard's 2007 novel, *La capture du sombre*, as a return journey to the Switzerland of the Quebec imagination, first inscribed emblematically in Hubert Aquin's 1965 novel, *Prochain épisode*. By looking closely at how the world is mapped out in the writings of these two major Quebec writers, she also marks some of the changes to Quebec "identity" as well as to "the current state of the world" ["l'état présent du monde"] (Brossard, *La capture du sombre* 18) effected across the forty-three intervening years between the two literary transatlantic passages. By way of echoing the thrust of McPherson's essay, we include here additional poems from *Je m'en vais à Trieste*, whose title evokes James Joyce's European trajectory, in which Brossard offers more personal impressions of her travels in France, where she encounters both literary influences and "an excess of life" (129).

We then return to the work of Gail Scott with an essay by Lorna Irvine, "*Chez Nous*: Gail Scott's *My Paris*," in which she reads Scott's "generically slippery" text both horizontally and vertically, exploring the connections between Scott's narrator/*flâneuse* and Benjamin. For Irvine, Scott's contemporary street-walker understands the deeply unconscious control of gender and the profound effects of language use. She creates evocative disjunctions within and among conventional oppositions: present and past; rich and poor; male and female; self and other; actor and spectator; writer and reader; stasis and change; black and white; nineteenth and twentieth centuries. An additional passage from Scott's *My Paris* is included here to illustrate the observations and juxtapositions that Irvine analyzes in her essay on the author.

The remainder of Section II continues to explore salient examples of transatlantic passages, intertexts, and influences. Karen Gould's "Transatlantic Reading in the Works of France Théoret" considers the act of reading and the role of French and European intertexts in two of Théoret's novels, *Laurence* (1996) and *Huis clos entre jeunes filles* (2000). In Théoret's historical novel, *Laurence*, the act of reading and reflecting on Victor Hugo's *Les misérables* becomes a pivotal narrative moment and psychological indicator, as it fuels the protagonist's desire to become an intentional reader and learner in her new urban environment, Montreal. In her semi-autobiographical novel, *Huis clos entre jeunes filles*, Théoret again integrates the act of reading into the thematic substance of her narrative by incorporating the discovery of a World War II novel, *La vingt-cinquième heure*, written by a lesser-known Roumanian writer, Virgil Gheorghiu. Théoret's transparent use of powerful transatlantic intertexts in both novels positions the act of reading as a key site of psychological refuge, cultural resistance, and female self-discovery. Her intertexts also establish important links to European culture and history that extend the reach of her novels beyond the personal, local, and historical contexts of modern Quebec. Patrice Proulx expands even further the scope of such transatlantic crossings in her essay, "Literary Border Crossings: Reconceptualizing Montesquieu's *Lettres persanes* in Lise Gauvin's *Lettres d'une autre* and Chahdortt Djavann's *Comment peut-on être français?*" Proulx compares two contemporary narratives – the first by a Québécois and the second by an Iranian writer living in France – that both use structural and thematic elements from Montesquieu's eighteenth-century epistolary novel to focus on issues of migration and national identity. Just as Gauvin's protagonist Roxane poses the question of "comment peut-on être Québécois(e)," Djavann's novel recounts the story of a young Iranian woman, also named Roxane, who must adapt to a new life in Paris. In giving voice to what is essentially a minor character in Montesquieu's novel, both of these contemporary writers are demonstrating how influence can be translated into inspiration in the passage from one culture and epoch to another.

We conclude the second section with another literary "passage" or "souvenir" by the Montreal novelist and poet, Louise Dupré. A professor of literature, Dupré has maintained her scholarly career even while producing a prize-winning body of poetry, fiction, and dramatic texts, including the recent play, *Tout comme elle*, which was staged by the French-born Canadian director Brigitte Haentjens and received the 2005–06 Critics' Prize from the *Association québécoise des critiques de théâtre*. In her "France in the Heart of the Eastern Townships," Dupré remembers her Catholic schooldays in Quebec when she was introduced to the literature of France by one of the French nuns who were her teachers – twentieth-century avatars of the missionaries discussed by Patricia Smart in Section I. For Dupré, this transformative encounter with French culture was the point of departure in an ongoing intellectual journey enriched by transatlantic influences, exchanges and appreciation.

We stroll onto the stage in Section III, "The Theatrical Space of Exchange." Opening, once again, with an evocative excerpt from Scott's *My Paris*, we move to an essay by Louise Forsyth, "Marie Cardinal, Translator of Myths and Theatre: The Words to Say Difference." Exiled from her homeland of Algeria, Cardinal spent her adult life shuttling between France and Quebec. Her work, published between 1962 and 2001, comprises novels, essays, and drama, particularly translations and adaptations of Greek tragedies. Forsyth analyzes the significance of the theme of exilic identity in Cardinal's writing, and reminds us of one example of a successful transatlantic career made in the passage from Europe to Quebec. In an original overview of theatrical transfers made in the opposite direction, Jane Moss, in her "(Post)Colonial Performances: Nationalist and Post-nationalist Quebec Theater in Europe," discusses the varying successes in the past four decades of Quebec playwrights and their plays in France. Focusing on the playwrights Carole Fréchette, Larry Tremblay, and espeically Daniel Danis, Moss pays particular attention to their deployment of language, theatricality, and narrativity, within the context of the contemporary debates about *littérature-monde*. She concludes by affirming that since the transatlantic passages of post-nationalist Quebec plays depend on their distinctiveness and alterity, to efface those differences would be to undermine the appeal of these postcolonial performances.

Moss's analysis of the language question in particular resonates in interesting ways with this section's epigraph by Gail Scott, as does the contribution of Michel Cochet, "Michel Cochet on Larry Tremblay: An Auto-Interview." Cochet is a French actor and theatre director who created his own troupe in 1997, La Compagnie du Zouave, with the goal of putting on plays by contemporary authors. He has staged a number of plays by Quebec playwrights, including those by Larry Tremblay, and his meditations on successful theatre and the "Quebec touch" in this piece are a testimony to the excitement and innovation such transatlantic exchanges and "translations" can generate.

Section IV, "Franco-European Immigrant Voices in Quebec," presents both actual and imagined passages from francophone Europe to Quebec, while making additional stops in other francophone regions. After yet another compelling excerpt from Scott's *My Paris*, the section's first essay by Mary Jean Green connects Benjamin, Scott, and *la flânerie* with another nomadic writer, Régine Robin. In "From *Flâneuse* to Cybernomad: Roaming the World with Régine Robin," Green shows how Robin creates a transatlantic exchange between two facets of her own persona, represented by her two emails tagged .fr and .ca, due to her dual residency in both France and Quebec. Robin's bi-cultural writings offer a unique understanding of comparative immigrant experiences in both France and Quebec, rooted in her real life status and history as a Jew in France and as a French immigrant in Montreal. Indeed, a substantial number of Québécois novels feature protagonists who cross the Atlantic as immigrants coming to Montreal, as travelers visiting France, as soldiers going to fight in wars in Europe, or as other kinds of exiles and wanderers. Susan Ireland's essay, "Transatlantic Crossings in the Work of Alice Parizeau and Naïm Kattan," examines two such narratives situated in the mid-twentieth century, a key period in the history of both Europe and Quebec. In Parizeau's *Côte-des-Neiges*, the female protagonist, accompanied by her husband, goes to France in search of a cure for her depression, but is forced to return to Quebec at the beginning of World War II; in Kattan's trilogy, *Adieu Babylone*, *Les fruits arrachés*, and *La fiancée promise*, the narrator also leaves Paris for Montreal in the postwar period. Ireland's essay thus focuses on the ways in which such transatlantic crossings shape the characters' identities and inform their vision of Québécois society.

Another immigrant in Quebec, the Swiss-born film editor Werner Nold, has given us a revealing interview for this volume, "From Europe to Quebec Cinematic History." Nold joined the National Film Board of Canada in 1961, and since that time has served as film editor on many groundbreaking and historic projects, including *Pour la suite du monde*, *La vie heureuse de Léopold Z.*, *La gammick*, *Le temps d'une chasse*, and, perhaps most famously, the *Games of the XXI Olympiad*. Nold has received both the Queen Elizabeth II Jubilee Medal and the Order of Canada. His work as a film editor has more recently been honored with a tribute by filmmaker Jean-Pierre Masse, *Werner Nold, cinéaste-monteur*. Nold and Masse have also completed a second project, *Le montage selon Werner Nold*, in order to preserve the memory and craft of this exceptional and exemplary figure in Quebec cinema. His compelling narrative of arrival in Montreal and of participating in the birth of Quebec's national cinema offers an autobiographical dimension to this section devoted to literary and literal passages from the Old World to the New.

We conclude this fourth section with an essay by Rachel Killick, "Three *Demoiselles sauvages* in Search of Other Worlds: Corinna Bille and Gabrielle Roy in the Films of Léa Pool." Like Nold, director Léa Pool was born in Switzerland. Her films, with their notions of distance, alterity, and estrangement, and their preference for temporary sojourn over permanent settlement, have been located both by critics and by Pool herself in the interstitial fragilities and fertilities of a plural yet singularly solitary identity, at once and never completely, francophone-Swiss, Polish-Jewish, and Montreal-Québécois. Killick's essay proposes an examination of this complex encounter made manifest in Pool's 1991 *La demoiselle sauvage*, a film version of Swiss author Corinna Bille's short story of the same name, and in her 1998 documentary on the life and work of Franco-Manitoban Gabrielle Roy. Killick focuses on the permutations and significance of the *demoiselle sauvage* figure, including both Roy and Pool herself as further embodiments of the paradigm; on the contrasting topographies and differing spatial environments which shape the transcontinental destinies of all three figures; and on Pool's concomitant transmutation of the "other world" of literature from the written page to the audio-visual universe of film. The essay assesses the strength and importance of Pool's cinematic contribution to such intercultural and inter-generic "passages" between the two francophone cultures of Switzerland and Quebec.

Our fifth and final section concerns "Contemporary Art Forms and Popular Culture." Here, our chosen passage by Gail Scott evokes elements of contemporary culture, including television and popular singers. Artistic collaboration is at the heart of the section's opening essay and photographic journey, "Riopelle and Me: *Impression passagère,*" by American-born, Quebec-based multi-media artist Bonnie Baxter. This essay is about Baxter's artistic and personal connection with celebrated Québécois artist Riopelle, and the way that their careers criss-crossed across the Atlantic and converged for a decade of important and productive collaboration. For Riopelle and Baxter, experience with the formal French atelier printing method made their own experimental daring possible. Riopelle led a nomadic existence among homes in Quebec and France, where he was nicknamed the "peerless trapper" in reference to his Quebec origins, but also to his prodigious talent. The encounter of Riopelle's drive and inspiration with Baxter's talent and willingness to experiment with traditional forms and techniques resulted in several extraordinary series of prints. Baxter has since moved on to other methods of printmaking, but her most recent series of artwork, *Jane's Journey* – from which our cover jacket borrows – takes a look back at this period of transatlantic inspiration and other passing impressions. The semi-autobiographical Jane is a malleable figure drawn from the childhood readers, *Dick and Jane*. Her figure is a "base" metal, a raw, wild point of color, in the "precious" domesticated landscape of Paris, among others. As imagined and embodied by Baxter, she is a distinctively North American nomadic presence, observing and channeling the spaces and influences she encounters.

Another Quebec multi-media and performance artist, François Morelli, works in Montreal but travels frequently to Europe and France in particular for his installations. He chronicles and photographs one series of these installations in "Crossings: *In Situ* Art in Transit." The project of *Home Wall Drawing: L'art de manger*, which had at its heart the notion of barter, was conducted in twenty-two residences across France from 28 January to 26 April 2004. Morelli's proposal was to make a stamp design mural in people's homes in exchange for sharing a favorite home-cooked meal. *Home Wall Drawing: L'art de manger* attempts to decompartmentalize artistic activity even as it questions the "elite" status of the art object as much in its creation as in its reception and exhibition. The *in situ* nature of Morelli's graphic installations serves to put art in relation to its context, a context that in this case offers a perfect illustration of the transatlantic connections being made among individuals as well as contemporary institutions.

The critical essay that follows, "A Quiet Evolution: Artist's Books in Quebec and France (Beausoleil, Dorion, Desautels)," offers Alisa Belanger's groundbreaking analysis of artist's books as a notoriously difficult-to-define genre that blurs disciplinary boundaries but that has proven to be particularly fertile ground for promoting intellectual and aesthetic passages between Quebec and Francophone Europe. Belanger examines the ways in which Quebec writers have used artist's books as a creative outlet in France, Belgium, and Switzerland since the early 1990s, to which her selection of accompanying photographs bears moving witness. She focuses on the collaborations between European artists and the acclaimed Québécois poets Claude Beausoleil, Denise Desautels and Hélène Dorion, demonstrating how their interactions allow for the development of non-hierarchical transatlantic exchanges between the creative individuals involved.

Music also forms a consistent, frequent, and popular method for the exchange and transmission of cultures. In "*La Chanson québécoise: Not the Same Old (French) Song*," Brian Thompson chronicles the rising international profile of the Quebec tradition of *chansonniers*: many of these Québécois singers, starting with Félix Leclerc, had first to be recognized in France before they were taken seriously in Quebec. These *chansonniers* played an important role in the Quiet Revolution, helping to make the Québécois conscious of their own language, culture and identity, in parallel with the recognition of regional languages and cultures in France, promoted by similar singer-songwriters performing in Occitan, Breton, and Alsatian. The transatlantic cross-fertilization and collaboration on musical comedies like *Starmania* and *Notre-Dame de Paris* later made certain artists household names in the other country (sometimes also more so than at home); collaborations between music festivals in France and Quebec have furthered this musical commerce. Despite the distinct and yet linked musical traditions in Quebec and France/francophone Europe, performing in Paris – and especially at one of its famous concert venues – retains a certain prestige, as exhibited in the translation of "Ce soir je chante à l'Olympia"/ "Tonight I'm Singing at the Olympia," by the modern-day Quebec *chansonnier*, Robert Charlebois. Charlebois, best known perhaps for songs such as "Lindberg" and "Je reviendrai à Montréal," is a popular and populist Quebec author, composer, musician, performer, and actor whose seminal contribution to the musical landscape has been recognized by his being named Officer of the Order of Canada and an Officer of the *Ordre national du Québec*, the highest distinction given by the Government of the province.

Figures like Charlebois remind us that any study of "transatlantic passages" would not be complete without a solid understanding of the exchange of popular culture – the only culture known by most of today's youth. We end our volume, therefore, with Guy Spielmann's "(Not so) Separate but Unequal: On the Circulation of Popular Culture Items between France and Quebec." While international exchanges of "high" cultural productions tend to be self-selecting and relatively limited in distribution, the circulation of items belonging to popular culture is as massive as it is surreptitious, especially given that items are often modified to fit the target culture in the most unobtrusive manner, and without explicit reference to the original. A common feature of this type of exchange is its radically asymmetrical character, such that the very term, "exchange," becomes questionable. Does this situation apply to exchanges between two cultures that are not completely distinct because they share a common heritage and a common language, like the Québécois and the French? To answer this, Spielmann examines a variety of pop culture genres, especially BD (*bande dessinée*/comics), television, and internet productions. In the case of BD, the fact that native Québécois BD are rare, and that virtually none make it to the European market would initially support the hypothesis of a "neo-colonial," asymmetrical cultural circulation. However, recent examples from new media, such as the popular animated Internet vignettes of *Têtes à claques*, allow Spielmann to suggest a more complex system of exchange where a diversity of factors must be considered, including the "popular" or "artistic" cultural status of creative works, economics, and especially the unique cultural and linguistic relationship between France/ francophone Europe and Quebec.

Even though the passages in this volume document and explore an extensive array of exchanges, influences, and movement of intellectual, artistic, and human capital between European countries like France or Switzerland and Quebec, we recognize that, because of its pioneering nature, this volume only begins to chart the richness of the field of Francophone transatlantic studies. Indeed, while a few of the essays that follow highlight parts of Francophone Europe outside of metropolitan France and areas of Quebec outside of Montreal, we can only concur with Gilles Marcotte's affirmation, cited earlier, that "in the world we live in today, most human questions pass through the city" ("Montréal et ses romanciers" 317), which, at least in this study of transatlantic passages, means Paris and Montreal. Most of the articles that follow thus focus on these two urban centers, precisely because Paris has long remained a draw for intellectuals, writers, and artists from many regions and of many cultures, just as Montreal has become a multi-ethnic metropolis and preferred locus for creative endeavours of all sorts. In fact, while we have included here examinations of a large number of literary, artistic, musical, visual, and popular-culture figures, the list is by no means exhaustive. We are not forgetting, for example, the works and trajectories of Mavis Gallant, Anne Hébert, Marie-Claire Blais, Marguerite Duras, Jacques Poulin, Michel Tremblay, Robert Lepage, and Nancy Huston, among many others who have lived, travelled, and worked on both sides of the Atlantic. Some of these authors and their transatlantic passages have already been studied elsewhere, but, by and large, much remains to be discovered and explored, both in terms of individuals whose life works and thought have had an international dimension and in terms of the cultural domains and tendencies in which they have participated and which they have helped to create.

In *Transnational Connections: Culture, People, Places*, urban anthropologist Ulf Hannerz reminds us that "cultures, in the plural, as packages of meanings and meaningful forms, distinctive to collectivities and territories, [are] … obviously affected by increasing interconnectedness in space. As people move with their meanings, and as meanings find ways of traveling even when people stay put, territories cannot really contain cultures" (8). Our *lieux de passages*, mapping the *flânerie* of our varied *passeurs* and *passeuses*, should therefore be seen as an open framework for further studies, which, much in the spirit of *The Arcades Project* of Walter Benjamin, can lead down endless avenues of reflection on the constantly evolving and interacting cultures and peoples of the Francophone Atlantic world.

Notes

1 "Passage," *Wiktionary*, Web, 1 June 2009, http://en.wiktionary.org/wiki/passage.

2 The field of transatlantic studies is much more developed in English, with reference to the connections among English-speaking communities and countries on both sides of the Atlantic. The only systematic attempt to extend this field of study to Francophone elements is the three- volume encyclopedia edited by Bill Marshall, *France and the Americas: Culture, Politics and History. A Multidisciplinary Encyclopedia* (Santa Barbara, Denver and Oxford: ABC/Clio, 2005). This encyclopedia, part of ABC/Clio's "Transatlantic Relations" series, deals with France's links with the New World, and thus does not focus solely on Quebec, nor does it deal fully with what Marshall terms "the gray area of francophone Belgium and Switzerland" (xxii) in the transatlantic relationships it attempts to describe. Frédéric Bastien's introductory essay on "France and Canada," however, does offer an excellent historical overview of political and diplomatic relations between the two countries, including France's direct relations with successive provincial governments in Quebec (Marshall 9–16).

3 Gilles Marcotte, "Montréal et ses romanciers," quoted in *Montréal en prose 1892–1992*, 318. All translations are the authors' unless otherwise indicated.

4 Wikipedia defines phantasmagoria this way: "A modified type of magic lantern was used to project images onto walls, smoke, or semi-transparent screens, frequently using rear projection. The projector was mobile, allowing the projected image to move on the screen, and multiple projecting devices allowed for quick switching of different images. Frightening images such as skeletons, demons, and ghosts were projected" (*Wikipedia, The Free Encyclopedia*, n.d.,Web, 1 June 2009). The concept of phantasmagoria expanded more broadly and deeply, however, throughout the nineteenth century in France and later, as developed by Benjamin. In effect, it became associated with a changing and incoherent series of apparitions or

phantoms, as in a dream. It came to stand for a sense of the imaginary, appearance, phantom, mental image, or spectacle of modern, commodified life, a series of objects turned into commodities via fetichism. For Benjamin (whose reflections intersected with or inspired those of Marx, Adorno, and since then, Derrida), in his "Paris, Capital of the Nineteenth Century: Exposé of 1939," "new forms of behavior and the new economically and technologically based creations … enter the universe of a phantasmagoria … Thus appear the arcades; … thus appear the world exhibitions, whose link to the entertainment industry is significant. Also included in this order of phenomena is the experience of the flâneur, who abandons himself to the phantasmagorias of the marketplace … As for the phantasmagoria of civilization itself, it found its champion in Haussmann and its manifest expression in his transformation of Paris … [H]umanity will be prey to a mythic anguish so long as phantasmagoria occupies a place in it" (14–15).

5 Gilles Marcotte, "Flâner rue Notre-Dame, en 1862," 97.

6 Paul-André Linteau, *Brève histoire de Montréal* 89.

7 For a brief recap of the history of plans for a Montreal subway system, see Deglise, *Montréal souterrain*, 36–9, and also Clairoux, *Le métro de Montréal : 35 ans déjà*, 11–23.

8 Deglise, 26–7, 57–66.

9 "Le Flâneur à Paris," *Paris, ou le livre des cent-et-un* (Paris: Ladvocat, 1831) 6, cited in Ferguson 82.

10 See, for example, Karen Gould's *Writing in the Feminine: Feminism and Experimental Writing in Quebec* (Carbondale: Southern Illinois University Press, 1990); Bénédicte Mauguière's *Traversée des idéologies et explora-*tion des identités dans les écritures de femmes au Québec (1970–1980) (New York: Peter Lang, 1997); and Miléna Santoro's *Mothers of Invention: Feminist Authors and Experimental Fiction in France and Quebec* (Montreal: McGill-Queen's University Press, 2002).

Works Cited

Augé, Marc. *Un ethnologue dans le métro*. Paris: Hachette, 1986.

Benjamin, Walter. *The Arcades Project*. Trans. Howard Eiland and Kevin McLaughlin. Cambridge and London: The Belknap Press of Harvard University Press, 2004.

Brossard, Nicole. *La capture du sombre*. Ottawa : Leméac éditeur, 2007.

– *Je m'en vais à Trieste*. Ottawa: Écrits des forges, 2003.

Clairoux, Benoît. *Le métro de Montréal : 35 ans déjà*. Montreal : Editions Hurtubise HMH, 2001.

Deglise, Fabien. *Montréal souterrain : Sous le béton, le mythe*. Montreal : Héliotrope, 2008.

Ferguson, Patricia. *Paris as Revolution: Writing in the 19th-Century City*. Berkeley: University of California Press, 1994.

Fournier, Roger. *Moi, mon corps, mon âme, Montréal, etc.* Montreal: *La presse*; Paris: Albin Michel, 1974.

Hannerz, Ulf. "Introduction: Nigerian Kung Fu, Manhattan *Fatwa*." *Transnational Connections: Culture, People, Places*. London: Routledge, 1996. 1–13.

Hustak, Alan. *Downtown Montreal*. Montreal: Véhicule Press, 2002.

LaRue, Monique, and Jean-François Chassay. *Promenades littéraires dans Montréal*. Montreal : Québec/Amérique, 1989.

Linteau, Paul-André. *Brève histoire de Montréal*. Montreal: Boréal, 1992.

Marcotte, Gilles. "Flâner rue Notre-Dame,

en 1862." *Écrire à Montréal*. Montreal:
Boréal, 1997. 95–104.

– "Montréal et ses romanciers." *Montréal en prose 1892–1992*. Montreal: L'hexagone, 1992. 317–18.

Marshall, Bill, ed. *France and the Americas: Culture, Politics and History. A Multidisciplinary Encyclopedia*. 3 vols. Santa Barbara, Denver and Oxford: ABC/Clio, 2005.

"Passage." *Wiktionary*. Web. 1 June 2009. http://en.wiktionary.org/wiki/passage.

"Phantasmagoria." *Wikipedia, The Free Encyclopedia*. n.d. Web. 1 June 2009. http:// en.wikipedia.org/wiki/Phantasmagoria.

Pike, David L. *Subterranean Cities: The World beneath Paris and London, 1800–1945.* Ithaca: Cornell University Press, 2005.

Prendergast, Christopher. *Writing the City: Paris and the Nineteenth Century*. Oxford: Blackwell, 1995.

Scott, Gail. *My Paris.* 1999. Champaign, IL: Dalkey Archive Press, 2003.

Trumpener, Katie. "Through the Arcades." *Modern Philology* 91. 3 (February 1994): 319–25.

Women's History and Passages across the Atlantic

.

---

97. Raining. Entering café lit by giant geometric teardrops. Suspended from ceiling. Smaller wall versions. Over curly-pawed tables. Pretty but unheated. So sitting far from window. R arriving almost simultaneously. *Le Nouvel Obs* in hand. On cover *Fifteen Leading Intellectuals*. Derrida. Lyotard. Deleuze. Etc. All worriedly reflecting on growing entrenchment of Right. Which Right they having spent lives striving to philosophically defeat. By *en principe* displacing. Deferring. Huge Western *I*. Casting unecological shadow. Over earth. Malheureusement issue not including Kristeva. Weil. Arendt. Irigary. [sic] Buci-Glucksmann. Collin. Wittig. Nor any other woman.

   Maybe women too busy with 1000 little details. To be seen as *truly* philosophical. I ironizing to R. Nodding at several pointed bras. Under well-pressed sweaters. À la mode again. The shape of women's silhouettes. Expressing something of epoch. Crinoline for imperialist expansion. Or "sadistic" bloomers (B saying). At out-set of suffragettes. R agreeing feminine. In Paris. Considered dangerous. Therefore requiring effort to contain. Through discipline of hyper-female roles. Albeit he protesting men *also* wearing perfume. Carrying purses. Then smiling fake embarrassed. With pleasant friendly mouth. Of guy from Winnipeg.

Gail Scott, *My Paris* 105–6

interesting.

A Place for the Spirit: Canada as Dream and Reality in the Autobiographical Writings of the Women of New France

PATRICIA SMART

Canada was described to us as a place of horror, people [in France] called it the sub-urbs of hell, and said that a more contemptible society did not exist. Our experience is the opposite, for we find here a Paradise ...

[L'on nous figurait le Canada comme un lieu d'horreur; on nous disait que c'était les faubourgs de l'enfer, et qu'il n'y avait pas au monde un pays plus méprisable. Nous expérimentons le contraire, car nous y trouvons un Paradis...]
Marie de l'Incarnation, Letter to her brother (4 September 1640)[1]

... what God had not willed in Troyes, He would perhaps bring to pass in Montreal.

[... peut-être ce que Dieu n'avait pas voulu à Troyes, Il le voudrait à Montréal].
Marguerite Bourgeoys, *Memoirs* (1697)

At the origins of the autobiographical tradition in Quebec literature are the writings of four women, all members of religious orders, who played major roles in seventeenth-century New France. Two of these women were born in France: Marie de l'Incarnation, the great mystic and foundress of the Quebec Ursuline order, and Marguerite Bourgeoys, the colony's first teacher, who came to New France as a layperson but later founded the un-cloistered order of the Congregation of Notre Dame to ensure the conti-nuity of her work and mutual support for the women who had joined her in her mission. Marie's writings include her spiritual autobiography of 1654[2] and a voluminous correspondence;[3] Marguerite Bourgeoys is the author of a volume of memoirs, composed in 1697 at the age of 78.[4] The two others – Sisters Jeanne-Françoise Juchereau de Saint-Ignace of the Hos-pitalières de Saint-Augustin and Marie Morin of the Hospitalières de Saint-Joseph – are the Canadian-born authors, respectively, of the *Annales* of the Hôtel-Dieu of Quebec (1636–1716)[5] and of Montreal (1659–1725).[6] Their *Annales*, written primarily as records of the history of their communities, rely on oral history as well as on documents conserved within the com-munity to recount the migration from France to the New World as experienced by their founding members. Juchereau's *Annales* in particular is a layered work: it quotes at length from the written account of the early years by Mère Marie de Saint-Bonaventure (Marie Forestier), one of the three Hospitalières de Saint-Augustin (Augustinian) sisters who emigrated along with Marie de l'Incarnation and two other Ursulines in 1639, and it was completed and prepared for publication by another member of the order, Marie-Andrée Duplessis de Sainte-Hélène, who was born in France but emigrated to Quebec in 1702, at the age of fifteen.

With the exception of the spiritual autobiography and the letters of Marie de l'Incarnation, these accounts are much closer to the traditional definition of memoir than they are to autobiography. Their aim is to record historical events, and their authors rarely indulge in the expression of personal feelings or individual reflexions. Often, particularly in the *Annales*, the "we" that narrates them seems to be the collective voice of the community, distilled from the individual voices of all the members whose stories have been passed on from generation to generation. Written either for younger sisters of the religious communities or for readers in France whose support had to be enlisted for the missionary venture, they are often edifying in tone and intent, and present an idealized view of reality. Taken together, though, they provide a woman-centered view of migration from France to Canada, narrated with a down-to-earth quality and even a humor that contrasts with the heroic and tragic tone of the male-authored Jesuit *Relations*.

Although many of the women's religious orders in France were founded as non-cloistered teaching or nursing orders in the sixteenth century or earlier, by the early seventeenth century the reforms of the Catholic Counter-Reformation had imposed strict rules of *clausura* or cloistering on them. As Elizabeth Rapley explains, this regulation, formalized by the Council of Trent in 1615, came at a time of spiritual effervescence, when many women were caught up in the mysticism that had swept through Europe during the Counter Reformation and were experimenting with new forms of religious life. The Council, however, saw female religious above all as virgins who must be sealed off from the world, reducing female sanctity to a single characteristic: chastity. According to the new regulations, the walls of women's monasteries must be "high enough to close off any view, either from within or from without. The entrances were to be locked and double-locked, [and] spaces where the nuns came close to the outside world – the parlor, the church – were to be protected by narrow-meshed grilles."[7] No men were allowed to enter the cloister, not even priests; nor were mature women, who were seen as worldly and therefore as objects of temptation. Rapley mentions that when Marie de l'Incarnation entered the Ursuline monastery in Tours in 1631 at the age of 31, all fifty-eight of the other nuns in the convent were under the age of sixteen. Such an emphasis on radical separation from the world at an early age made for submissive nuns, treated as children by their bishops, women who tended to regard the world outside the convent walls as corrupt and dangerous – a view borne out by reality in the case of the Augustinian nun Mère Jeanne de Sainte-Marie, a beautiful young woman who had entered the convent for protection after being kidnapped and raped by a nobleman (Juchereau 32).

The challenge to the practice of cloistering posed by New France came less from any awareness of its injustice to women than from the necessities of the colonial venture. Like all the other colonizing nations in the New World, France wanted to create a country in its own image. But unlike the others, it saw the native peoples not as enemies to be exploited or exterminated, nor even primarily as trading partners, but rather as "barbarian brothers to be brought into the circle of the family and civilized by the Gospel" ["un frère qu'il devait retrouver dans la barbarie et ramener dans le cercle de la famille, en le faisant rentrer par l'Évangile dans la civilisation"].[8] The missionary aim made France unique as well in having women in the New World not only in the traditional roles of wife and mother, but as active and central partners in the colonial enterprise, which was seen as "a work of spiritual maternity" ["une œuvre de maternité spirituelle"].[9] By the 1630s the Jesuit missionaries had become aware that the Indian boys and men they were attempting to educate would fall back into "barbarianism" unless their women were also educated into the French way of life. Because of the rules of the cloister, there was no question of inviting French nuns to emigrate; but in his *Relation* of 1634 the Jesuit superior Paul Le Jeune made an impassioned plea for some generous laywomen to offer their services to the colony as teachers and hospital workers. A year later, he comments with amazement on the huge response he has received – not from laywomen, but from within the convents of France:

There are so many of these who write to us, and from so many convents, and from various orders in the Church of the strictest discipline, that you would say they are competing to see who can be the first to mock the difficulties of the sea, the mutinies of the ocean and the barbarism of these countries.

[Il y en a tant qui nous écrivent et de tant de monastères, et de divers ordres très réformés en l'Église, que vous direz que c'est à qui se moquera la première des difficultés de la mer, des mutineries de l'Océan et de la barbarie de ces contrées.][10]

The written accounts of Marie de l'Incarnation and the other nuns who would emigrate to Canada give an idea of the excitement generated within the convents at the possibility of a missionary vocation. Surprisingly, for these women who sought union with God through the total abnegation of self, the vast and forbidding expanses of the New World represented not an escape from the cloistered way of life but an extreme and exotic extension of it. Jeanne-Françoise Juchereau writes for example of the founding mothers of her community that:

they were convinced that they could only satisfy their zeal and fulfill their vocation in Canada by following the Barbarians into the woods as the missionary fathers did; taking pleasure in living hidden from the world, unknown, in complete separation and total abnegation of all things, entirely abandoned to the care of Providence; and finally, expecting and hoping to find nothing loveable except God in this country of the cross.

[Elles ... se persuad[aient] qu'elles ne pourraient satisfaire leur zèle et remplir leur vocation pour le Canada, qu'en suivant les barbares dans les bois, comme font les Missionnaires; se faisant un plaisir de vivre cachées, inconnues au monde, privées de toutes les consolations de la terre, dans une séparation générale et un dénuement parfait de toutes choses, entièrement abandonnées au soin de la Providence; et enfin ne cherchant et n'espérant trouver que Dieu seul aimable dans ce pays de croix] (Juchereau 12).

The chance for sacrifice and even martyrdom stoked the fires of imaginations already attuned to excess by the baroque sensibilities of their era and practiced in the discipline of self-mortification. Marie de l'Incarnation wrote to her spiritual director in 1635:

I envisage the hardships, both on the sea and in the country, I envisage what it is to live with Barbarians, the danger of dying there of hunger or cold, the many occasions when one might be seized ... and I find no change at all in the disposition of my spirit [j'envisage tous les travaux tant de la mer que du pays; ce que c'est d'habiter avec des Barbares; le danger qu'il y a de mourir de faim, ou de froid; les occasions fréquentes d'être prise; [et] je ne trouve point de changement dans la disposition de mon esprit] (April 1635, *Corr.* 27).

And the three Augustinian nuns who would emigrate with her and two other Ursulines in 1639, far from being deterred by the rumors they had heard that the Indians were *mangeurs d'hommes* [cannibals], "thought only of their desire to sacrifice themselves for God, and ... encouraged each other by heroic stories, considering themselves exiles for the glory of God" ["elles ne s'occupaient alors que du désir de se sacrifier pour Dieu, et ... s'encourageaient l'une l'autre par des motifs héroïques, se regardant comme des exilées pour la gloire de Dieu"] (Juchereau 12). These rumors were more than idle imaginings; Marie de l'Incarnation had received letters from Jesuits telling of their near escapes from death at the hands of the Indians, and the Jesuit *Relations* of the 1640s contained lurid descriptions of captives of the Iroquois who had been eaten, as well as of the torture and execution of Isaac Jogues and several other Jesuits. By 1659, at the height of the Iroquois raids on Montreal, Marie Morin reports that the three Hospitalières de Saint-Joseph preparing for their voyage to that city paid little attention to the material things that would be needed in their new life, "thinking only of abandoning everything" ["ne pensant ... qu'à se dépouiller et ne rien apporter de la maison"]. Others in the community looked after the practical details, "not wanting these victims to have any thoughts other than that of their immolation, of preparing themselves to suffer martyrdom by the Iroquois" ["ne voulant pas que ces victimes eussent d'autres pensées que celle de leur immolation, se préparant dans leur esprit à souffrir le martyre par les Iroquois"] (Morin 86). Morin mentions the pain felt by the members of the French order at seeing three of their best novices depart for Canada, "which had the reputation of being a lost country for which even the best people felt horror" ["qui passait pour un pays perdu pour qui les gens de bien même avaient de l'horreur"] (Morin 87).

While these women had dreamed of great and dramatic sacrifice, the hardships of the day to day reality that awaited them in Canada must have come as a surprise to them. Some of the details of this reality are captured in the diary of Mère de Saint-Bonaventure (Marie Forestier), quoted in Juchereau's *Annales*, which notes that, when their ship was delayed after its arrival at Tadoussac in July 1639, the six nuns, the Ursuline patron Mme de la Peltrie and six Jesuits prevailed upon the captain of a small codfishing boat to find room for them aboard his vessel. "Nothing seemed difficult to us as long as it brought us closer to our loveable place of habitation," she writes:

So we got onto the boat and found a place for ourselves on the upper deck, as the rest of the boat was full of cod, which filled the entire boat with quite a bad odor. For several days and nights we suffered a great deal. Lacking bread, we were obliged to scrape up crumbs from the baggage hold, which contained more rat droppings than biscuit; we picked through them to find bits that were edible, and ate them with pieces of dried cod that were raw, as we had no means of cooking them. We were also given a sort of plant, very hard, that grew on the rocks beside the river. When one is very hungry, all of these things taste good.

[rien ne nous paraissait difficile pourvu qu'il nous procurât l'entrée de cet aimable séjour. Nous passames donc dans la barque, où il n'y avait que le tillac pour nous loger, tout étant plein de morue, qui rendait une assez mauvaise odeur. Pendant quelques jours et quelques nuits que nous y restâmes, nous souffrimes beaucoup de nécessité. Le pain nous ayant manqué, on fût obligé de ramasser les miettes de la soûtte, où il y avait plus de crottes de rats que de biscuit; nous primes la peine de les éplucher pour en avoir un peu, que nous mangions avec de la morue sèche toute crue, n'ayant pas de quoi la faire cuire. On nous donna aussi d'une sorte de passe pierre fort dure, que l'on trouvait sur le bord du fleuve. Tout cela était bon pour des personnes de grand appétit.] (Juchereau 17)

In Quebec, the Hospitalières de Saint-Augustin sleep for the first few weeks on branches brought in from the woods, which turn out to be "so full of caterpillars that we were covered in them" ["si remplies de chenilles, que nous en étions toutes couvertes"] (Juchereau 20). Their first patients are Algonquin Indians infected with smallpox, and they use up all their own linen, even the wimples and cuffs from their habits, to dress the ulcers on their bodies. Nights are spent washing the bedding, which the French women of the colony refuse to touch for fear of contagion. Before the end of the first winter, all three nuns have fallen ill from exhaustion. In what is certainly a pre-feminist observation, Mère Bonaventure describes the state of the hospital, which has been looked after by the Jesuits during the nuns' absence, on the return of the first of the nuns to get well: "She found a *ménage d'homme* [an example of men's housekeeping], that is, everything was filthy and in disorder: the linens were thrown in all directions, rotten and spoiled, and everything was so full of dirt that she had a terrible time trying to get things clean again" ["elle trouva un ménage d'homme, c'est-à-dire fort malpropre et en désordre: le linge était de tous côtés pourri et gâté, et tout était si plein d'ordure qu'elle eut bien de la peine à nettoyer"] (Juchereau 24).

Having set out for New France with the goal of transforming it into a more spiritual image of the France they had left behind, a place in which the native peoples would be granted the "privilege" of being assimilated into the fold of the Catholic religion and French culture, these women encountered instead a radical otherness of climate, geography and culture. Many of their accounts contain vivid descriptions of the extreme cold of Canadian winters and tell of the new kinds of food to which they gradually became accustomed. (The traditional French-Canadian dish of *fèves au lard* obviously had its origins at this time, when pork and beans were among the few staples available). Writing to a close friend in Tours at the end of her first year in New France, Marie de l'Incarnation is enthusiastic about the fact that they have survived so well in spite of their extreme poverty, strenuous living conditions and the unfamiliar food:

We spent the winter as sweetly as in France; and, although we were crammed together in a tiny hole where there was no air, we weren't sick at all, and never have I felt so strong. If in France we only ate pork fat and salted fish as we do here, we would be ill and we'd have no voice; [but] we are very healthy and we sing better than you do in France. The air is excellent; indeed, this is an earthly Paradise where crosses and thorns arrive so lovingly that the more one is pierced, the more one's heart is filled with sweetness.

[Nous avons passé cet hiver aussi doucement qu'en France; et quoique nous soyons pressées dans un petit trou où il n'y a point d'air, nous n'y avons point été malades, et jamais je me sentis si forte. Si en France on ne mangeait que du lard et du poisson salé comme nous faisons ici, on serait malade et on n'aurait point de voix; nous nous portons fort bien et nous chantons mieux qu'on ne fait en France. L'air est excellent, aussi est-ce un Paradis terrestre où les croix et les épines naissent si amoureusement que plus on est piquée, plus le cœur est rempli de douceur.] (4 September 1640, *Corr.* 109–10)

The account of the following winter contained in the *Annales de l'Hôtel-Dieu de Québec* reveals the brutal reality behind Marie's somewhat idealized account of the living conditions of these nuns. More exposed than the Ursulines because of their hospital work to the raging epidemic of small-pox that was sweeping through the Algonquin community, two of the tiny group of Hospitalières de Saint-Augustin are gravely ill and coughing blood by the winter of 1641, and their only food is bread, pork, peas, and a few plums and grapes, none of which the sick nuns can tolerate. The sisters spend fifty francs of their meager savings on a "scrawny calf that wasn't worth two *écus* [the equivalent of three francs], but our need for making broth was so desperate that we'd have paid even more for it" (Juchereau 31). A servant sent to the country to find eggs returns at the end of the day with only one egg, by now frozen, with which the sick nuns profess to be delighted. By March, Mère Jeanne de Sainte-Marie (the nun who had been kidnapped in France) is dead at the age of 28. Mère Bonaventure writes of her: "One could say that she experienced nothing but bitterness in Canada, and yet she expressed great joy about the privilege of dying here. She had been here for less than eight months; her weak constitution was unable to stand the rigor of the climate for even a year" ["On peut dire qu'elle n'a ressenti que de l'amertume dans le Canada, quoiqu'elle ait témoigné une joie particulière d'y mourir. Il n'y avait pas huit mois qu'elle y était, son faible tempérament n'ayant pu supporter la rigueur de ce climat seulement une année"] (Juchereau 32).

Marie Morin's description of the conditions in which the Hospitalières de Saint-Joseph sisters lived is even more detailed. She too speaks of their food – small quantities of wheat, pork, peas, beans and salted eel, with pumpkin for dessert – and concludes that "the love of penance and holy poverty added seasoning to these foods and made them taste good" ["Ce qui le faisait trouver bon avec l'amour de la pénitence et sainte pauvreté qui asaisonnait le tout et le faisait trouver de bon goût"] (Morin 102–3). Morin writes that "the cold of this country can only be understood by those who have suffered from it." [[le froid] de ce pays ne peut être compris que par ceux qui le souffrent"]. For more than twenty-eight years, she says, the Hospitalières lived in a house with more than two hundred holes in it, with wind and snow filling not only their cells but the stairway, the attic and the chapel. The first act of the morning was to take shovels and brooms and get rid of the snow blocking the doors and windows. No food was free of the danger of freezing: bread had to be roasted on the fire before each meal, water and wine placed on the table for drinking would be frozen within fifteen minutes, and food served hot would be cold and almost frozen by the time one had finished eating (Morin 104).

Only the mystic Marie de l'Incarnation writes of the spiritual dimensions of Canadian nature. For her, the attraction of Canada was precisely that it represented the space of "admirable nothingness" she had always yearned for. "It's true that in Canada the senses do not sustain one; the spirit detaches itself from nature in the pure crosses that are found here" ["Il est vrai, les sens ne soutiennent point en Canada; l'esprit laisse la nature dans les pures croix qui s'y retrouvent"], she writes (30 August 1642; *Corr.* 151). And elsewhere: "Did you know that hearts here have quite different feelings than they do in France? Not sensual feelings, as there are no objects here that flatter the senses; but completely spiritual and divine feelings, for here God wants the heart stripped of all things ... We see ... here a sort of necessity of becoming a saint; either you die, or you assent to it" (24 August 1641; *Corr.* 122); later adding: "to truly live the Canadian vocation it is necessary to die to everything; if the soul doesn't force itself to do this, God will bring it about and will mercilessly crush our nature until it is reduced to this death ... It is impossible for me to express to you what it costs one to reach this point ... But it must be reached, and one must not envisage the possibility of living in this land of blessings except with a new spirit" ["Pour bien goûter la vocation au Canada, il faut de nécessité mourir à tout; et si l'âme ne s'efforce de le faire, Dieu le fait lui-même, et se rend inexorable à la nature, pour la réduire à cette mort ... Je ne puis vous dire ce qu'il en coûte pour en venir là ... Car enfin, il faut en venir là, et il ne faut pas penser de pouvoir vivre dans cette nouvelle terre de bénédiction qu'avec un esprit nouveau"] (15 September 1641, *Corr.* 140–1).

In spite of (or perhaps because of) the hardships they endured, it is clear that New France offered these women a space of freedom and self-realization unavailable to them in seventeenth-century France. Marguerite Bourgeoys would found an uncloistered order open to women of all classes and financial means, devoted to teaching and counseling the girls and women of the Montreal region, especially the poor, at a time when such a thing was impossible in France. And cloister itself, while it remained precious and essential for the other orders, was necessarily relaxed somewhat in Canada. All of these nuns were forced to fight against the ecclesiastical authorities at various points in the development of their communities, in order to convince them that their situation in Canada was different from that of religious communities in France and required different rules. Marie de l'Incarnation realized within a few years of her arrival that the Quebec Ursulines needed their own constitution: "We need one that is specific to this country, not only because we have our own rules, but because there are things that cannot be dealt with in the French manner: the climate, the food and other circumstances are entirely different" ["il nous en faut encore une particulière pour ce pays, comme nous y avons aussi des règlements particuliers, d'autant qu'il y a quelque chose qui ne s'y peut pas accommoder à la façon de France: le climat, les vivres et autres circonstances y sont entièrement différentes"], she wrote to her son (30 August 1644; *Corr.* 229). By 1647 they would have that constitution, which, among other things, allowed all members of the order to speak briefly and show affection to their native pupils, unlike non-teaching members of the community in France, who were allowed no contact with students.[11] Many years later, all of Marie's legendary diplomatic skills would be required in order to prevent Bishop Laval from modifying that constitution. "He has given us eight months or a year to think about it," she wrote to her superior in Tours in 1661. "But, my dear Mother, the affair is already thought out and the resolution all made: we will not accept it unless at the extremity of obedience" ["Il nous a donné huit mois ou un an pour y penser. Mais, ma chère Mère, l'affaire est déjà toute pensée et la résolution toute prise: nous ne l'accepterons pas si ce n'est à l'extrémité de l'obéissance"] (13 September 1661; *Corr.* 653).

The Hospitalières de Saint-Joseph, founded in 1634 in France as a non-cloistered *confrérie* or lay association devoted to nursing, were forced to accept *clausura* in 1659, the same year that three members of the order set sail for Montreal. The three arrived in Montreal committed to cloister, but not to wearing a religious habit or to taking solemn vows, both of which were imposed on them in 1672 after a twelve year battle with Bishop Laval and Abbé de Queylus, the superior of the Sulpicians, who now owned the properties of the entire island of Montreal. And the nuns of the Hôtel-Dieu de Québec fought with Laval's successor, Bishop Saint-Vallier, for over a decade and were eventually forced to capitulate (in 1701) to his insistence that they follow French practice and extend their apostolate from the simple care of the sick to that of what we would today refer to as "street people."[12]

Certainly the fearful view of the corrupt "outside world" that many of the nuns had held in France was transformed by the Canadian experience. All of the writers describe an atmosphere of fervor and devotion that animated the entire society of New France, at least in the early years. Juchereau mentions the pious widow of one of the governors, Mme Daillebout, who decides not to return to France after his death in 1660 because "belonging entirely to God, she judged that she would be better off here, especially since at that time in New France one breathed nothing but devotion" ["Étant déjà toute à Dieu, elle jugea qu'elle le servirait plus parfaitement ici, d'autant plus aisément qu'en la Nouvelle France on ne respirait alors que la dévotion"] (Juchereau 82). In her letters of the 1640s, Marie de l'Incarnation constantly compares the atmosphere of the Canadian mission to that of the early Christian Church. "We see in our primitive Church, the zeal and the ardor of the early Church members who were converted by the apostles" ["nous voyons dans notre primitive Église, le zèle et l'ardeur de la primitive Église convertie par les apôtres"], she writes in 1640 (4 September 1640; *Corr.* 104). A year later, she refers to "our new Church; ... one sees in it a completely new spirit which breathes a mysterious something of the divine that delights my heart" ["notre nouvelle Église; ... on y voit un esprit tout nouveau qui porte je ne sais quoi de divin, qui me ravit le cœur"] (15 September 1641; *Corr.* 139). The analogy with the early Church is present as well in all of the other texts, and – even taking into account the tendency to idealize that characterizes most of them – it points to the existence of an extraordinary sense of community among the early inhabitants of New France. In 1659, according to Juchereau, "Fervour was growing daily among the Savages, and Our Lord was pouring his graces so abundantly on Canada that all lived in a simplicity, a good faith and a unity that was very close to what we admired in the early Christians" ["La ferveur croissait tous les jours parmi les Sauvages, et N.S. versait si abondamment ses grâces sur le Canada que l'on y vivait dans une simplicité, une bonne foi et une union qui approchait fort de celle que l'on admirait dans les premiers chrétiens"] (Juchereau, 104). Marie Morin is even more glowing in her account of the early years in Ville Marie (Montreal). She describes a society united by the danger of the Iroquois raids, living in an atmosphere of openness and conviviality, free of the scorn for independent single women that characterized French society and grateful to the women who have come to offer medical services to their community:

All of them lived as saints, in a piety and spirituality such as one finds today only among the best nuns and priests. Those who hadn't heard Mass on a workday were regarded by the others almost as excommunicated, unless they had reasons as strong as those required today from those who miss Mass on Sunday. All the working men went to the first Mass of the day, held before daybreak in the winter and at 4 a.m. in the summer ... and all the women went to another, at 8 a.m. ... Nothing was locked in those days, neither houses nor chests nor basements; everything was open and nothing was ever stolen. Those who had enough goods helped those who had less, without waiting to be asked … When impatience had made someone speak harshly to his neighbor or someone else, the person would not go to bed without asking forgiveness on his knees. And one never heard any mention of the sin of impurity, which was considered with horror even by the least devout. In all, this dear Montreal in its early days (that is to say in approximately its first 32 years) was an image of the primitive Church.

[Aussi vivaient-ils en saints, tous unaniment, et dans une piété et religion envers Dieu telles que sont maintenant les bons Religieux. Celui d'entre eux qui n'avait pas entendu la sainte messe un jour de travail passait parmi les autres quasi pour excommunié à moins qu'il n'eût des raisons et empêchements aussi forts qu'on en demande aujourd'hui pour s'exempter du péché mortel aux jours de fêtes et dimanches. On voyait tous les hommes de travail à la première messe, qui se disait avant le jour pendant l'hiver et dans l'été à 4 heures du matin … et toutes les femmes à une autre, qui se disait à 8 heures … Rien ne fermait à clef en ce temps, ni maison, ni coffre, ni caves, &c., tout était ouvert sans rien perdre. Celui qui avait des commodités à suffisance en aidait celui qui en avait moins, sans attendre qu'on lui demanda … Quand l'impatience avait fait parler durement à son voisin ou autre, on ne se couchait point sans lui en faire excuse à genoux. On n'entendait pas seulement parler du vice d'impureté, qui était en horreur même aux hommes les moins dévots en apparence. Enfin, c'était une image de la primitive Église que ce cher Montréal dans son commencement et progrès, c'est-à-dire pendant 32 ans ou environ.] (Morin 96)

To arrive at any conclusions regarding the gender specificity of these texts, it would be necessary to read them alongside the Jesuit *Relations*, a comparison that I suspect would reveal significant differences, particularly regarding relations with the native peoples. While both the Ursulines and the Augustinians came to Canada because of the Jesuit influence and worked closely with the Jesuits after they had arrived, their teaching and nursing duties (and the more sedentary role required of them as women) led them to a different relationship with their native charges than that of the priests. Unlike the Jesuits, who often express disapproval of Indian ways and discouragement about the possibility of converting them, the nuns typically exhibit respect, affection and admiration for the exemplary Christianity of their converts. And while the Jesuits saw themselves as "soldiers of Christ," whose task was to subject the Amerindians to the laws of Christ,[13] the nuns threw themselves with humility and joy into learning the native languages and discovering cultural differences. Small wonder, then, that the native communities seem welcoming and docile, grateful, as Marie says, that "for the love of their nation we left our country and through pure charity we are dressing and feeding their daughters as if they were our own" ["Ils étaient ravis de ce que pour l'amour de leur nation nous avions quitté notre pays, et que par une pure charité nous vêtions et nourissions leurs filles comme si elles nous appartenaient"] (4 September 1640; *Corr.* 108).

Marie de l'Incarnation frequently (and favorably) compares her native charges to the French Catholics she has left behind. "I have never seen any French girls as ardent to be instructed or to pray to God as our seminarians," ["je n'ai point vu des filles en France ardentes à se faire instruire ni à prier Dieu comme le sont nos séminaristes"], she writes to Paul Le Jeune (March 1640; *Corr.* 93) and to her son, describing a religious procession of Indians and French settlers: "I assure you that I have never seen a procession in France where there was so much order and where it seemed there was so much devotion" ["je vous assure que je n'ai point vu en France de procession où il y eût tant d'ordre et en apparence tant de dévotion"] (30 August 1650; *Corr.* 398). For her, the poverty and simplicity of the Indians is far preferable to the civilized ways of the French, and her sense of the native superiority over the French in matters of the spirit indicates a respect for cultural difference unusual for her time. "O my dear Sister! What a pleasure to find oneself with a large group of Savage women and girls, whose poor clothing, which is only a bit of skin or a piece of an old blanket, doesn't smell as good as those of the Ladies of France! But the candor and simplicity of their spirit is so delightful that it can't be described" ["O ma chère Sœur! Quel plaisir de se voir avec une grande troupe de femmes et de filles Sauvages dont les pauvres habits qui ne sont qu'un bout de peau ou de vieille couverture, n'ont pas si bonne odeur que ceux des Dames de France! Mais la candeur et la simplciité de leur esprit est si ravissante qu'elle ne se peut dire"] (4 September 1640; *Corr.* 108). And, to her Superior in Tours: "We have here Savage *dévots* and *dévotes*, as you have polite ones in France: the difference is that, while they are not as subtle or refined as some of yours, they have a childlike honesty that clearly shows they are souls newly reborn and washed in the blood of Jesus Christ. When I listen to the good Charles Montagnez, Pigarouich, Noel Negabamat, and Trigalin, I wouldn't leave the place to hear the best preacher in France" ["Nous avons ici des dévots et des dévotes Sauvages, comme vous en avez de polis en France: il y a cette différence qu'ils ne sont pas si subtils ni si raffinés que quelques-uns des vôtres; mais ils sont dans une candeur d'enfant, qui fait voir que ce sont des âmes nouvellement régénérées et lavées dans le Sang de Jésus-Christ. Quand j'entends parler le bon Charles Montagnez, Piga-rouich, Noel Negabamat et Trigalin, je ne quitterais pas la place pour entendre le premier Prédicateur de l'Europe"] (15 September 1641; *Corr.* 139). Explaining her work to her son, she makes it clear that the educative process is not aimed at "Frenchifying" the Indian girls: "Are our Savages as perfect as I make them out to be? As for their customs, they lack French politeness: I mean to say the ability to give compliments and to act as the French do. We have not aimed at instilling such things in them, but rather at instructing them well in the commandments of God and the Church [and] in all the other religious activities" ["Si nos Sauvages sont si parfaits come je vous le dis? En matière de mœurs, il n'y a pas la politesse française: je veux dire en ce qui regarde un compliment et façon d'agir des Français. On ne s'est pas étudié à cela mais à leur bien enseigner les commandements de Dieu et de l'Église [et] toutes autres actions de religion"] (26 August 1644; *Corr.* 221).

Gradually, however, the nuns come to recognize the irreconcilable cultural differences that block their project of large-scale conversions, and begin to shift their focus to educating and caring for the French settlers. The realities of Iroquois violence and the death of many of the converted Indians by smallpox are early signs of what will be the ultimate failure of the missionary project. Marie de l'Incarnation accepts the defeat of their mission with sorrow but also with equanimity, fortified by her belief that the Ursulines were called to New France also to ensure the spiritual health of the French community in North America. In 1653, she writes that she feels privileged to work with the French as well as the Indians, for "the Son of God gave himself equally for the souls of both"; and besides, "without the education we give the older French girls, they would be worse than the Savages within six months" ["les âmes des uns et des autres ont également coûté au Fils de Dieu. Sans l'éducation que nous donnons aux filles Fran-çaises qui sont un peu grandes, durant l'espace de six mois ou environ, elles seraient des brutes pires que les Sauvages"] (September 1653; *Corr.* 507). Still, in the final years of her long life, it is her native pupils that Marie thinks of as her greatest joy and satisfaction: "They are the delights of our hearts, and because of them we find a sweetness in our day to day work that we wouldn't exchange for an Empire" ["Ce sont les délices de nos cœurs qui nous font trouver dans nos petits travaux des douceurs que nous ne changerions pas à des Empires"] (27 September 1670; *Corr.* 903).

Overall, these autobiographical accounts attest to the fact that for all these women authentic selfhood (and even sainthood) was attained through a configuration of self, alterity and the divine made possible by the space of New France. While they look back with affection on the sweetness and ease of their lives in France, they refuse to exchange the challenging spirituality of the Canadian space they have created for a return to such comfort. To do so is regarded not only as a weakness but a betrayal, as in the case of two Augustinian nuns who decide to return to France in 1649 after several exhausting months spent caring for the large numbers of Hurons who have taken refuge in Quebec following the death of Brébeuf and his companions. The other seven members of the community support them and remain on cordial terms with them in the following years, realizing that they have reached such a state of frustration that they will only be a burden on the community if they remain. But there is a veiled criticism of them in the *Annales* account: one of the two is described as having had "great weaknesses of mind" ["de grandes faiblesses d'esprit"] ever since her terrifying experience of crossing the Atlantic, and the other of having had unrealistic expectations of the New World: "[She] had never imagined Canada as she found it: she had convinced herself she would be leading a life as sweet as the one she had left behind, and she never succeeded in getting used to the ways of this country" ["[Elle] ne s'était jamais figuré le Canada tel qu'elle le trouva: elle se flattait de mener ici une vie aussi douce que celle qu'elle avait quittée, en laissant son ancienne Maison; elle ne pût s'accommoder aux manières du pays"]. The annalist, Marie Forestier, wonders at the fact that after their return to France these nuns never expressed pangs of conscience about their action, which, she states, "I don't want to describe as an infidelity" ["je ne veux pas taxer d'infidélité"], though clearly wishing that she could indeed describe it as such (Juchereau 75–6). The Hospitalières de Saint-Joseph as well have already developed a strong attachment to their new space within a year of their arrival in Montreal. When, in 1660, they receive the devastating news that their beloved founder La Dauversière has died and that they are therefore without financial support, they are encouraged by their Sulpician advisors to return to France and promised that they will be given their choice of which convent in the French order they prefer to live in. However, after much reflection and prayer, they decide that in spite of their destitute state they will "live and die in this dear country and land of Ville Marie, in the confidence that divine providence would provide for them" ["vivre et mourir dans ce cher pays et terre de Ville Marie, dans la confiance que sa sainte providence pourvoirait à leurs besoins"] (Morin 107).

On numerous occasions in her correspondence, Marie de l'Incarnation insists on her attachment to Canada, most beautifully perhaps in a letter of 1655 where she writes that "it seems to me that nothing under heaven could shake me or detach me from my centre, which is how I think of Canada" ["il n'y a rien ce me semble sous le ciel, qui soit capable de m'ébranler ni de me faire sortir de mon centre, c'est ainsi que j'appelle le Canada"] (*Corr.* 569). Some years later, in response to a friend in the Ursuline community in Tours who has obviously been speculating on whether she might some day choose to return to France, she states, "You are right to believe that I want to die in this new Church: I assure you that my heart is so attached to it that, unless God removes it, it will not let go either in life or in death" ["Vous avez raison de croire que j'ai envie de mourir en cette nouvelle Église: car je vous assure que mon cœur y est tellement attaché, qu'à moins que Dieu ne l'en retire, il ne s'en départira ni à la vie ni à la mort"] (19 August 1664; *Corr.* 734). Finally, a letter written by Marie less than two years before her death to an Ursuline friend in France captures beautifully the paradoxical gifts that Canada has offered to all of these nuns. In it, she speaks of the rigors of the previous winter, the worst she has seen since her arrival in the New World, and of what they have meant in terms of spiritual possibilities:

All our water pipes were frozen, and at first we melted snow to have water for ourselves and our animals; but we needed such a large amount that we had to decide to send our oxen down to the river for it, and they were almost destroyed by attempting to navigate the steep and slippery mountain. There was still ice in our garden in June: all our beautiful fruit trees and grafts were dead. The whole country suffered the same devastation ... Only the trees bearing wild fruit were spared; in this way God, by depriving us of delicacies and leaving us the necessities, wants us to remain in our mortification and do without the sweetnesses we were looking forward to. We're used to it after thirty-one years in this country; we've had time to forget the sweetnesses and delights of old France.

[Tous nos conduits d'eaux ont gelé, [et] au commencement nous faisions fondre la neige pour avoir de l'eau, tant pour nous que pour nos bestiaux; mais il en fallait une si grande quantité que nous n'y pouvions suffire. Il nous a donc fallu résoudre d'en envoyer quérir au fleuve avec nos bœufs qui en ont été presque ruinés à cause de la montagne qui est fort droite et glissante. Il y avait encore de la glace dans notre jardin au mois de Juin: nos arbres et nos entes qui étaient de fruits exquis en sont morts. Tout le pays a fait la même perte ... Les arbres qui portent des fruits sauvages ne sont pas morts; ainsi Dieu nous privant des délicatesses, et nous laissant le nécessaire, veut que nous demeurions dans notre mortification, et que nous nous passions des douceurs que nous attendions à l'avenir. Nous y sommes accoutumées depuis trente et un ans que nous sommes en ce pays, en sorte que nous avons eu le loisir d'oublier les douceurs et les délices de l'ancienne France.] (1 September 1670; *Corr.* 877–8)

All of the autobiographical texts under consideration find expression in this image of nuns in a garden, grafting shoots to provide new beauty in an austere climate and yet accepting with serenity the destruction of their efforts by nature, aware of the sufferings of others and strong in their faith and optimism. Unlike France, with its "sweetnesses and delights," Canada has forced these women to focus only on what is *essential*, and in this sense – thanks largely to their own courage, perseverance and hard work – it has proved to be the "place for the spirit" they had dreamed of in France.

Notes

1 All translations are the author's, unless otherwise indicated. Abbreviations in parentheses after the quotations are identified in the reference notes.

2 Marie de l'Incarnation, "La Relation de 1654," *Écrits spirituels et historiques (Tome II: Québec)*. Quebec: Les Ursulines de Québec, 1985.

3 Marie de l'Incarnation – *Correspondance* (Nouvelle édition par Dom Guy Oury), Solesmes, Abbaye Saint-Pierre, 1971 (*Corr.*).

4 *Les écrits de Mère Bourgeoys: autobiographie et testament spirituel* (Montreal: Congrégation de Notre-Dame, 1964) (*Écrits*). See also *Marguerite Bourgeoys: textes choisis et*

présentés par Hélène Bernier Montreal, Fides (Coll. "Classiques canadiens"), 1958 (*MB*).

5 Mères Jeanne-Françoise Juchereau de St-Ignace et Marie-Andrée Duplessis, *Les annales de l'Hôtel-Dieu de Québec 1636–1716* (Québec: L'Hôtel-Dieu de Québec, 1939) (Juchereau).

6 Ghislaine Legendre, ed., *Histoire simple et véritable: Les annales de l'Hôtel-Dieu de Montréal, 1659–1725* by Marie Morin (Montreal: Les Presses de l'Université de Montréal, 1979) (Morin).

7 Elizabeth Rapley, *A Social History of the Cloister: Daily Life in the Teaching Monasteries of the Old Regime* (Montreal: McGill-Queen's University Press, 2001), 113.

8   Dom Albert Jamet, "Introduction," *Les annales de l'Hôtel-Dieu de Québec 1636–1716*, ii.

9   Jamet, "Introduction," iii.

10 Le Jeune, *Relation* de 1635, in Thwaites (ed.), *The Jesuit Relations and Allied Documents: Travels and Explorations of the Jesuit Missionaries in New France 1610–1791*, Vol. VII, 257.

11 See Claire Gourdeau, *Les délices de nos cœurs* (Quebec, Septentrion, 1994), 41–3.

12 See Leslie Choquette, "'Ces Amazones du Grand Dieu': Women and Mission in Seventeenth-Century Canada," *French Historical Studies* 17.3 (Spring 1992): 627–55, for an excellent overview of the history of all these orders in France and in Canada.

13 See Natalie Zemon Davis, *Women on the Margins: Three Seventeenth Century Lives* (Cambridge, MA, and London: Harvard University Press, 2003), 116–21, on the contrast between Marie and the Jesuits.

Works Cited

Bourgeoys, Marguerite. *Les écrits de Mère Bourgeoys: autobiographie et testament spirituel*. Montréal: Congrégation de Notre-Dame, 1964.

– *Marguerite Bourgeoys: textes choisis et présentés par Hélène Bernier*. Montreal: Fides (Coll. "Classiques canadiens"), 1958.

Choquette, Leslie. "'Ces Amazones du Grand Dieu': Women and Mission in Seventeenth-Century Canada." *French Historical Studies* 17. 3 (Spring 1992): 627–55.

Davis, Natalie Zemon. *Women on the Margins: Three Seventeenth Century Lives*. Cambridge, MA, and London: Harvard University Press, 2003.

Gourdeau, Claire. *Les délices de nos cœurs*. Quebec: Septentrion, 1994.

Jamet, Dom Albert. "Introduction." *Les annales de l'Hôtel-Dieu de Québec 1636–1716*. By Jeanne-Françoise Juchereau de St-Ignace and Marie-Andrée Duplessis.

Juchereau de St-Ignace, Mère Jeanne-Françoise and Marie-Andrée Duplessis. *Les annales de l'Hôtel-Dieu de Québec 1636–1716*. Quebec: L'Hôtel-Dieu de Québec, 1939.

Marie de l'Incarnation. "La relation de 1654." *Écrits spirituels et historiques (Tome II: Québec)*. Quebec: Les Ursulines de Québec, 1985.

– *Correspondance* (Nouvelle édition par Dom Guy Oury). Solesmes: Abbaye Saint-Pierre, 1971.

Morin, Marie. *Histoire simple et véritable: Les annales de l'Hôtel-Dieu de Montréal, 1659–1725* (édition critique par Ghislaine Legendre). Montreal: Les Presses de l'Université de Montréal, 1979.

Rapley, Elizabeth. *A Social History of the Cloister: Daily Life in the Teaching Monasteries of the Old Regime*. Montreal: McGill-Queen's University Press, 2001.

Thwaites, Reuben Gold (ed.). *The Jesuit Relations and Allied Documents: Travels and Explorations of the Jesuit Missionaries in New France 1610–1791*, Vol. VII. New York: Pageant Book Company, 1959.

Time, Sir

MONIQUE PROULX

You're coming from the place to which I'm returning. Just now, you're leaving what I prepare to go back to. An immense territory, almost untouched, upon which the shadow of winter is already outlined. I know that you are a man. The hotel's registry also offers, as a bonus, your phone number and email address, but I won't take advantage of them. Tomorrow afternoon, or later if you are restless by nature, you will sit down in this armchair where I sit writing you. Is this *bergère* armchair an authentic Louis XV or Louis XVII, or a shameless counterfeit? Probably, like me, you know nothing of these cabinet makers' distinctions. Time in our country breaks off abruptly some years back, leaving only the scent of melamine on our furniture and our memories.

I'm dazed, Sir.

This isn't my first stay here. My twentieth, perhaps. Each time, I bring home the same precious commodities: wine in countless bottles that I will have to preserve from the avidity of the customs officers, and betaine citrate. Isn't it wonderful, and admirably logical, that a civilization should portray itself as well by its pharmacology as by its gastronomy, one hand patching up what the other breaks down? But that's not what this is about.

My topic is time, Sir.

Like you, I'm sure, I have been a devoted tourist. I did my best, with enthusiasm even, to see what there was to see and retain some bits of it. Even now I can affirm that the Duke of Chaulnes's microscope, mid-eighteenth century, lies dormant at the Museum of Arts and Crafts and that the Sorbonne began its birth in 1253 to accommodate sixteen poor students. I saw the *Mona Lisa* in person, of course, and the *Raft of the Medusa*. I criss-crossed galleries and alleys, breathed in the historic scents of each old stone raised along my path. You've done as much, Sir, if not more. Of course, we didn't manage to see everything. That would take lifetimes, in this country teeming with so many ancient treasures. But we have the impression of having been honest visitors, and of still being so, scrupulously tallying up artistic objects and famous places to fill in our map of the past.

The past. For it is indeed in this way that we see things: the past in this corner, the present in that one. The past, silently gathering dust next to the present, which quivers with life, the one and the other forever parallel.

All this collapsed not ten days ago, Sir.

I was coming back towards this hotel, my pied-à-terre every time I stay here. I was walking on the rue de Buci, where you yourself will walk, with the joyous nonchalance that the neighborhood calls for, stopping in front of the shellfish vendor to taste ahead of time the oysters and crabs that I was going to gorge on later that night, rummaging around in the little bookshop next door, when I fell upon this postcard that I'm leaving within your reach, in front of the authentic Louis XV armchair (that is, unless it's a counterfeit). At first glance, this image is insignificant. It shows one side of the house, on rue de Buci in fact, where Rimbaud stayed. Directly across from the shellfish vendor, ten paces from our hotel.

Rimbaud.

I know, the famous humans that this city has lodged are legion. An entire tourists' pilgrimage has built up around the buildings where they briefly took up residence, and yet never before, Sir, never was I one of the nostalgic ones who point their cameras at ghosts.

But there, on the rue de Buci, coming back towards the hotel, stunned by this postcard that I'm leaving in your care, something is happening. The walls have more cracks, the houses are dirtier, the pavement more worn, but it's exactly the same neighborhood, the same PRESENT space. And look: Rimbaud just walked out of number 14 rue de Buci, too thin in his gleaming frock coat, his expression cheeky, terribly young and sure that the world is his oyster. He takes a few jaunty steps on the pavement, crosses over to the merchant who has installed himself in the shellfish vendor's place, and as he is poor and starving, he steals an apple and a loaf of bread and skips off to meet his destiny. Poor and starving, yes, but already at the peak of his genius and on the brink of forever revolutionizing poetry before exiling himself for good as a small, greedy bureaucrat who will sell guns.

Do you understand, Sir, what I'm trying to say? There is no past. There is nothing but a series of present moments, endlessly hammered together, overlapping one another to form a sort of ribbon. There is nothing but this uninterrupted ribbon that extends before and behind us. Yesterday it was Rimbaud who was walking on rue de Buci; tomorrow it will be you. But where is the frontier, Sir, between his space and yours? Where then is this frontier at which we can say: this belongs to the present, and that to the past?

Since that moment, I have been dazed with vertigo. Since then, everywhere in this country, I feel the immense, pulsing continuum that encompasses and precedes me; I am no longer able to detach myself from this infinite lineage of which I am the temporary result. The day before yesterday, near the University of Bordeaux, I felt Michel de Montaigne's absence like that of a family member who had perhaps wandered away for a time, a few hours, a few centuries. Last week, at the castle of Ray-sur-Saône, I was rendered speechless in front of a gigantic, living lime tree, planted in 1604 by the chatelaine. And my friends, who had to wrest me away, understood nothing of my emotion. It's because they're from here, immersed since birth in the vestiges of yesterday, blinded by habit.

But us, Sir.

In America, the universe was born at the same time as we were, isn't that so? We see nothing around that reminds us of the human ribbon from which we come because the Native peoples did not leave tangible monuments. It is why we are so fresh, so young, so creative. So ignorant.

And so impressionable, maybe, when reality opens like a swing door.

Once the door is open, we have to accept the sight of what's piled up behind it. Generations pulsating, from Poitou and Champagne in my case, of course, and also from Lorraine, since Jehan d'Arc, the Maid's brother, supposedly passed on his genes to one of my maternal great-grandmothers, but starting farther away, much farther away and more far-flung, since there is nothing human and alive that is not connected in this measureless web. Even to our home, Sir. The plunge into the past carries on in our time, counting backwards, at the heart of our old mountains sculpted by glaciation, of our freshwater lakes that swell the primitive veins of the earth.

Do you understand my vertigo?

Time, Sir.

Do you see to what extent we are links, notes both minute and complementary in the colossal symphony? Do you see how time solders us each to the next, smoothing out our sharp edges, our precious identities? Sit back in our armchair, and listen. Listen well. Do you hear Rimbaud's steps stop for one instant beneath our window, as if to give us a sign, a fraternal sign of recognition?

Montreal, December 2003.
Translated by Galen Bascom with Miléna Santoro

French and Quebec Feminisms: Influences and Reciprocities

CHANTAL MAILLÉ

Introduction

In this text, we aim to explore the nature of links woven between Quebec and French feminisms from the beginning of feminism's second wave. We will examine the influence of feminist writings by Simone de Beauvoir and by various postcolonial thinkers in France on 1960s and 1970s Quebec feminism, and on specific groups such as the *Front de libération des femmes du Québec*. We wish to think about parallel trajectories of French and Quebec feminisms through the observation of founding events such as the publication of Simone de Beauvoir's *Second Sex* and the more recent rise of postcolonial feminist analysis in French. These questions will be examined through the lens of exchanges that have been generated between French and Quebec feminists, allowing us to draw conclusions on the state of these relationships in the current feminist era.

A Recent History of Quebec Feminism: From French Influence to the Establishment of a French Feminist Network

One cannot discuss the exchanges between French and Quebec feminisms without locating them in terms of pre-existing power relations between France and Quebec and acknowledging the creation of feminist networks specific to *francophonie* over the past twenty years. These networks make it possible to access decentralized multilateral exchanges in which links of influence are no longer exclusively from France to other constituencies of *francophonie*. Recently, the 2008 event *Du dire au faire, l'égalité entre les hommes et les femmes dans l'espace francophone*, held in Quebec City in preparation for the 12th *Francophonie* Summit, has allowed feminists from Africa, Europe, Asia, and America to work around a common agenda. Other examples of transnational feminist cooperation within *francophonie* include the World March of Women, initiated by the Quebec women's movement, and the five conferences on francophone feminist research held between 1993 and 2008 in Quebec City, Dakar, Toulouse, Ottawa and Rabat.

Beyond these fieldwork projects that have given concrete meaning to the idea of truly transnational exchanges between various francophone feminist networks, what are the characteristics of the theoretical production of this "*francophonie* feminism"? We can easily note the specific complexity of the relationships between French and Quebec feminisms. Quebec is seen as a model for organized feminism, with its own network of women's groups lacking any comparable counterpart in France. The Quebec women's movement functions beyond the dynamics of unequal exchange that can be observed in the field of feminist socio-political analysis. This movement is characterized by its original, context-specific practice, which is not so deeply anchored in theoretical debates; it was not particularly influenced by French organized feminism, which is much less structured than its Quebec equivalent (Maillé, *Cherchez la femme* 90–1). However, in the field of socio-political analysis, one cannot deny the hegemonic position of French feminist theory vis-à-vis Quebec feminism, and the fact that Quebec francophone academic feminism has developed largely around French feminist theoretical production. Theoretical perspectives developed by Simone de Beauvoir, Christine Delphy, Geneviève Fraisse, Colette Guillaumin, and Nicole-Claude Mathieu that explore gender relations, motherhood, work, and broader societal issues have been widely used and integrated into the works of Quebec feminists, largely because of the absence of a body of original theoretical production within Quebec feminism.

In the field of literary feminism, however, we can observe a different dynamic, as a genuinely Quebec-specific body of theoretical production was developed around authors such as Nicole Brossard, Madeleine Gagnon and Marie-Claire Blais, to name a few. In the following pages, we propose an analysis of the relations between French and Quebec feminism in the socio-political field.

What Impact for *The Second Sex* in Quebec?

In order to better understand the key moments of exchange between Quebec and French feminisms, we propose to go back in time to one particular founding moment: the publication of Simone de Beauvoir's *Second Sex* in 1949. According to the co-authors of *L'histoire des femmes au Québec*, the publication of *The Second Sex* went virtually unnoticed (433), largely due to the lethargy of the Quebec women's movement in the wake of its victorious struggle for women's right to vote in 1940. In a collection of texts published to commemorate the fiftieth anniversary of *The Second Sex* edited by Cécile Coderre and Marie-Blanche Tahon, we find writings that offer new reflections on *The Second Sex*'s impact on Quebec society, and on women in particular. Marie-Josée des Rivières and Geneviève Thibault write that the cultural gap that divided *The Second Sex* from those who identified not yet as *Québécoises* but instead as French Canadian appeared huge in 1949. The book was placed on the *Index Librorum Prohibitorum* ("List of Prohibited Books," abolished in 1966 by Pope Paul VI) by the Catholic Church and garnered little attention. Yet des Rivières and Thibault write that "in 1950, the French-Canadian press mentioned the publication of an essay discussing the 'woman question,' as it was then called. The article, unique in its style, was signed by Madeleine de Calan and published in a periodical entitled *Liaison* ... In a predictable manner, the columnist's prose attempted to suppress the revolutionary aspect of the book through ironic trivialization. Belying its calm appearances, the conservative rhetoric of the article made clear De Calan's concern" (23).

For Des Rivières and Thibault, women were not insensitive to Beauvoir's ideas, and the legend surrounding the book spread, largely by word-of-mouth. Artists such as Madeleine Ferron have spoken of the great measures to which women intellectuals went in the 1950s, defying the taboo of index in order to circulate Beauvoir's book and the ideas it presented. These actions on the part of women, according to des Rivières and Thibault, were the mode by which, in less than a decade, *The Second Sex* would become the "occult bible" of many academics and union leaders, supporters of *Refus global* and activists from Action catholique – all of whom read the book without openly admitting that they had done so (23).

During the 1960s, as Quebec was experiencing its "Quiet Revolution," Beauvoir's essay became the encyclopedia on the condition of womanhood for many Quebec women. In 1964, Quebec women's magazine *Chatelaine* published a special issue marking the fifteenth anniversary of the book and, in one article, asked one hundred women the following: "what has been the influence of Simone de Beauvoir's thought on your evolution?" The editorial reiterated claims around egalitarian feminism; *Chatelaine*'s editor-in-chief, Fernande St-Martin, evidently shared de Beauvoir's views. The tone of her editorial attempted to mobilize women and made clear the prolific influence of *The Second Sex*. It also attested to the deep political transformations that many women experienced upon reading the book (des Rivières and Thibault 23–4).

Des Rivières and Thibault then analyze the responses to de Beauvoir's book in the decades that followed. Specifically, they mention the feminist magazine *La vie en rose*'s 1984 special issue in honor of the 35th anniversary of the book, which focused on Simone de Beauvoir. Quebec writer Denise Boucher wrote, "I love you, Simone de Beauvoir; you are my intellectual mentor." Hélène Pednault, a feminist activist, also affirmed that "I could not have made it without Simone de Beauvoir" (25).

More analyses confirm the considerable impact of Simone de Beauvoir's book on Quebec feminism. In Montreal, the 1978 founding, with de Beauvoir's permission, of the feminist Simone de Beauvoir Institute at Concordia University was yet another example of her profound influence. In her essay "La double postérité du *Deuxième sexe*" (2001), Diane Lamoureux writes that both the radical and reformist branches of Quebec feminism have been influenced by Simone de Beauvoir's work; "in a certain way, these two currents of thought have reclaimed their affiliation with Simone de Beauvoir and *The Second Sex*, without imperialism or annexationism" (36).

Lamoureux continues:

For the founders of the Quebec Women's Federation or the researchers for the Bird Commission and the Conseil du statut de la femme report *Pour les Québécoises: Égalité ou indépendance*, *The Second Sex* often represented the point of departure for their feminist activism ... For those radical feminists who would go on to found the Front de libération des femmes or the Centre des femmes, those who would be central to the Théâtre des cuisines, the Comité de lutte pour l'avortement libre et gratuit or the Centre de santé des femmes, those who would run magazines and become prominent within intellectual circles – what appealed foremost to them about *The Second Sex* was de Beauvoir's link between women's emancipation and the transformation of social structures, her support for reproductive control but not at the expense of heterosexual abstinence, and her insistence on women's autonomy. For them, more than a manifesto in favor of sex equality, *The Second Sex* was fundamentally a plea for liberation and freedom, something too precious to be abandoned to liberalism. It was about women becoming themselves and exploring new horizons. (36–7)

Lamoureux writes that Simone de Beauvoir would become the intellectual reference of some Quebec feminists by default, as there were no other feminist analytical grids available. She cites *Le manifeste des femmes québécoises*, published in 1971 by women loosely affiliated with the Front de libération des femmes du Québec (FLF), whose authors mention the lack of theoretical instruments with which to think through women's oppression (41).

Quebec Feminism: Between Colonial and Postcolonial Analyses

The Quebec context for 1960's feminism, with the founding of major feminist organizations such as Fédération des femmes du Québec (FFQ) and the formation of an impressive network of small radical groups such as the Front de libération des femmes du Québec (FLF), was deeply influenced by one particular political account: that of Quebec's national oppression, which led to the project of Quebec independence. The most leftist political faction in Quebec's feminism of the 1960s – the FLF, rather than the FFQ – had largely integrated references to colonialism into its analysis. The literature of Franz Fanon and Albert Memmi nurtured the reflections of *Nègres blancs d'Amérique* and "Speak White," and many militant Quebec feminists derived inspiration from those authors' works.

The use of colonialism as a metaphor through which to reflect on women's oppression rested on an analysis of Quebec society as a terrain upon which Anglo-Saxon colonial domination was exercised – a legacy of the conquest of New France. This analysis obfuscated, in the process, the reality of indigenous dispossession and colonial anti-Native racism. The Quebec movement for national liberation built itself upon, among other things, postcolonial theorists such as Frantz Fanon (1970), and specific writings such as Albert Memmi's *Portrait du colonisé* (1957), a political work reflecting the colonial realities of African countries in the late 1950s and early 1960s – the so-called "decolonization period." In this vein, the title of Pierre Vallières's famous work, *Nègres blancs d'Amérique* [*White Niggers of America*] suggested that Quebec's national oppression and that of blacks in the United States existed on the same continuum. Within a discourse of national oppression, the status of francophone Québécois was seen as comparable to that of Algerians struggling for independence from France, or of black Americans during the civil rights movement – thereby erasing fundamental distinctions regarding the existence of political rights and representative parliamentary institutions across the three contexts. The discourse thus became one of "decolonizing" Quebec and emptying it of West Island "Rhodesians" (Lamoureux, *L'amère patrie* 116).

An entire subset of 1960s Quebec feminists identified with the women's double oppression analysis, wherein oppression was understood through the questions of both gender and nation (Maillé, *Cherchez la femme* 38). The Front de libération des femmes du Québec is noteworthy in feminist history partly for its famous slogan: "No national liberation without women's liberation; no women's liberation without national liberation." The collective's 1970 text "Nous nous définissons comme esclaves des esclaves" articulated a strong intersection of feminism and national liberation, and also demonstrated an analysis wherein gender and class intersect: "Our movement is part of the Quebec people's struggle for national liberation. We belong to a class society, made up of the exploited and the exploiters. We see ourselves as slaves of slaves. We believe that women will be able to free themselves only within a global liberation struggle for all of society. This freedom will only be possible with the full participation at all levels of the women who comprise half of the Quebec population" (466).

Intersectionality against the Universal Woman

The 1960s and 1970s correspond to the emergence of a wide movement, aimed at integrating perspectives on race, class, and difference with gender analysis within feminist currents that used English as their primary language of communication. This era constitutes a moment of re-founding for feminism's bases. In Quebec, the issue would only emerge twenty years after it erupted in other parts of the continent. Our hypothesis is that this disparity in the integration of perspectives on the intersectionality of oppressions is linked to the dominance of a discourse built on the universal woman within French feminism. Such a discourse prevailed until the beginning of the twenty-first century, when a new postcolonial literature began to circulate in French. Chandra Talpade Mohanty (1998) wrote of the paradigmatic changes that occurred in feminist theory during the 1970s, inspired by international movements for racial equality and the struggles of gays and lesbians, and borrowing from methods inspired by Marxism, psychoanalysis, deconstructionism and poststructuralism. For Mohanty, these changes made it possible to revisit the myth of women's universal condition, in which women's roles as colonial and imperial actors are occluded and their positions remain confined to passive citizens. If such an analysis of the intersections between gender, race and class rapidly became the norm within feminist knowledge production published in English, the situation is quite different for French feminism, which has been relatively closed to debates on the intersectionality of oppressions (Maillé, "Migrations" 2). Although much literature has discussed the articulation of race or class with gender (for example, the works of Nicole-Claude Mathieu), gender remains the first and founding oppression and the matrix for all other oppressions, and the idea of a women's class comprised of all women, remains central and always located within an articulation of *nous, les femmes* [we women]. Difference, when discussed in French feminism, makes reference almost exclusively to the feminism of *différence* – an entirely separate analysis resting on the acknowledgement not of differences amongst women, but of an essential difference between women and men that is constitutive of a *nous les femmes* identity. In the context of Quebec, a feminism of difference has made and continues to make reference to that French current. Quebec feminists have not yet found a way to articulate the differences amongst women that operate as political forces of conflict within Quebec society (Maillé, "Migrations" 3). This has meant that, until very recently, the quest for a Quebec feminist identity has been largely determined by a vision of a Quebec society historically divided according to cleavages between anglophone and francophone women, between Catholic and Protestant. Consequently, narratives of Othered women, whether First Nations, Jewish or Black, have been positioned at the outermost periphery of that process and vision.

In the French feminist milieu, a number of recent publications have opened a new debate around postcolonial feminism. In their work *Les féministes et le garçon arabe*, Nacira Guénif-Souilamas and Éric Macé denounce the republican feminism that has flourished in France in the context of the debate on the veil. In 2005, the periodical *Les cahiers du genre* published a special issue on the overlap of racist and sexist domination, in which other political experiences and theoretical contributions, notably those of Black feminism, were discussed. The journal *Nouvelles questions féministes* (NQF) launched two issues in 2006, *Sexism and Racism: The French Case* and *Sexism, Racism and Postcolonialism*, which both invite reflection on the overlap of different systems of oppression for women against the backdrop of the controversy surrounding the veil and the simultaneous development of postcolonial approaches to French feminism. For the NQF authors responsible for these issues, the multiple questions generated by a postcolonial perspective may be summarized into one single overarching theme: how has the colonizing West built, and continued to build, the colonized or racialized Other? These writings attest to the decompartmentalization with regards to borders that is now beginning in postcolonial theory, as its circulation grows within the francophone world despite a limited prevalence in Quebec.

Postcolonial feminists' work has been at the forefront in questioning many second wave feminist narratives, formulating analyses of race, ethnicity and national identity through which to reflect on women's oppression. These works, located within the continuity of innovative work produced by an older generation of feminists on the intersections of gender relations with race and class, simultaneously constitute a rupture in the theorization and understanding of power relations. One element that has nurtured postcolonial feminisms has been the denunciation of the discursive imperialism of certain manifestations of second wave Western feminism and concomitant victimizations of "other" women. The voices of third world women and the circulation of their ideas at the international level have revealed firsthand understandings of the conditions of oppression for diverse groups of women who have been historically marginalized from second wave feminist discourses. This process, while difficult, has forever changed the various faces of feminism by forcing the recognition of women's heterogeneous experiences. The writings of third world feminists have denounced the white gaze of Western feminists with respect to women from "other" (non-Western) cultures, interrogated the implicit perception of Western norms and values as universal, and challenged the relegation of the actions of non-Western feminist movements to the realm of the invisible. Third world feminists' contributions to the definition of a new feminism have been multifaceted: they have produced original analyses of their oppression, redefined themselves as subjects of these analyses, and paved the way to thinking about difference between Western and third world women in non-hierarchical terms. The starting point for these contributions has been a critical discourse in response to a certain form of Western feminism, criticized for its amnesia with regards to colonial history and its tendency to reproduce colonial models of domination.

Conclusion

French feminism has recently expressed a newfound openness to postcolonial analysis, but such an analysis is still lacking in the Quebec context. In 2009, what is the status of postcolonial theory within Quebec feminism? From victims of colonialism to instruments of colonial oppression, Québécois feminists have yet to fully integrate a broader critique of their practices of domination into their understanding of feminism. While such a critique would invariably add new dimensions to feminist analyses, Quebec feminists still have an alibi with which to evade the inevitable questioning of the nature of these practices: the idea that they live in Quebec, in a culture that has historically defined itself as minoritary and colonized rather than acknowledging its affiliation with white imperialist Western culture. In this manner, the legacy of the national question has made it possible for Quebec feminism to escape the difficult task of examining power relations amongst women and avoid an important moment of truth in this regard, despite initiatives that attest to a willingness to move in that direction. At the same time, we might also interpret this distancing from postcolonial feminism on the part of Quebec feminists as an emancipatory sign, one that challenges the domination of French feminism. In addition to gaining its autonomy from feminism in France, Quebec feminism has everything to win in revisiting its conceptualization of *nous les femmes* in order to let other realities – such as the power relations and status inequalities that exist between women – emerge.

Translated by Margaret Leitold

Works Cited

Benelli, Nancy, Christine Delphy, Jules Falquet, Christelle Hamel, Ellen Hertz and Patricia Roux, eds. *Sexisme et racisme: Le cas français.* Spec. issue of *Nouvelles questions féministes* 25.1 (2006): 1–160.

– *Sexisme, racisme et postcolonialisme.* Spec. issue of *Nouvelles questions féministes* 25.3 (2006): 1–168.

Coderre, Cécile, and Marie-Blanche Tahon, eds. *Le deuxième sexe. Une relecture en trois temps, 1949–1971–1999.* Montreal: Éditions du remue-ménage, 2001.

Collectif Clio. *L'histoire des femmes au Québec depuis quatre siècles.* Montreal: Le jour éditeur, 1992.

Des Rivières, Marie-Josée and Geneviève Thibault. "*Le deuxième sexe*: Témoignages de Québécoises de trois générations." *Le deuxième sexe: Une relecture en trois temps.* Eds. Cécile Coderre and Marie-Blanche Tahon. Montreal: Éditions du remue-ménage, 2001. 21–33.

Falquet, Jules, Emmanuelle Lada and Aude Rabaud, eds. *(Ré)articulation des rapports sociaux de sexe, classe et "race."* Spec. issue of *Cahiers du CEDREF* (2006): 1–220.

Fanon, Frantz. *Les damnés de la terre.* Paris: Maspero, 1961.

Fougeyrollas-Schwebel, Dominique, Éléonore Lépinard and Eleni Varikas, eds. *Féminisme(s): penser la pluralité.* Spec. Issue of *Cahiers du genre* 39 (2005): 1–272.

Front de libération des femmes du Québec. "Nous nous définissons comme esclaves des esclaves." *La pensée féministe au Québec: Anthologie (1900–1985).* Eds. Micheline Dumont and Louise Toupin. Montreal: Éditions du remue-ménage, 2003. 464–70.

Guénif-Souilamas, Nacira, and Éric Macé. *Les féministes et le garçon arabe*. Paris: Éditions de l'aube, 2003.

Lalonde, Michèle. "Speak White." *Écrivains contemporains du Québec*. Eds. Lise Gauvin and Gaston Miron. Montreal: L'hexagone/Typo, 1998.

Lamoureux, Diane. *L'amère patrie: Féminisme et nationalisme dans le Québec contemporain*. Montreal: Éditions du remue-ménage, 2001.

– "La double postérité du *Deuxième sexe*." *Le deuxième sexe: Une relecture en trois temps*. Eds. Marie-Josée des Rivières and Geneviève Thibault. Montreal: Éditions du remue-ménage, 2001. 35–50.

Maillé, Chantal. *Cherchez la femme: Trente ans de débats constitutionnels au Québec*. Montreal: Éditions du remue-ménage, 2002.

– "Féminisme et mouvement des femmes au Québec: Un bilan complexe." *Globe: Revue internationale d'études québécoises* 3.2 (2000): 88–105.

– "Migrations." *Recherches féministes* 15.2 (2002): 1–8.

– "Réception de la théorie postcoloniale dans le féminisme québécois." *Recherches féministes* 20.2 (2007): 91–111.

Mohanty, Chandra Talpade. "Feminist Encounters: Locating the Politics of Experience." *Feminism and Politics*. Ed. Anne Phillips. New York: Oxford University Press, 1998. 254–72.

Spivak, Gayatri. "Can the Subaltern Speak?" *Marxism and the Interpretation of Culture*. Eds. Cary Nelson and Lawrence Grossberg. Champaign: University of Illinois Press, 1988. 271–313.

Vallières, Pierre. *Nègres blancs d'Amérique*. Montreal: Éditions parti-pris, 1968.

Je m'en vais à Trieste (excerpt)

NICOLE BROSSARD

———————————

Le Petit Pont
5 June 1995

fatigue among the green
of Paris. French flag. Jet lag.
Soldiers in Bosnia a Canadian flag
an American song
Notre-Dame-de-Paris *smiling around*
Shakespeare & Co.
being alone left on a chair
as silence in a tourist's mouth (15)

RER/Roissy-Saint-Michel
11 June 1995

we are several
with an excess of memory to dream about
watching the sun at
twilight follow its course future and graffiti (16)

Santorini
1995

between translated from American or English
in French we close our books
feel for our passports
gulp a coffee while watching the sea

from the depths of memory and so tomorrow morning
in the distance other volcanoes (26)

National Library of France
26 September 1997

a great ambition for knowledge
all these trees of methodology and learning
outside my small-scale body
absorbs the shadow the architecture
a faraway garden frozen in the passion
of the northern summer (44)

Deauville
31 May 1998

knotted parasols
cascading with colors in the distance
the lapping of voices
the meaning of life slightly displaced
in the landscape from hour to hour
the luxury of emptiness or surplus
of anguish like a s(h)ellfish (54)

Beach/Deauville
1 June 1998

trotting horses at low tide
at the edge of the horizon
what becomes of life
between the dressing rooms of Marlon Brando
and of Gina Rowlands
where do the devoted children go, destined
to disappear in the sand
their bodies partially tanned
such peace time here and there time for mortars (55)

Luxembourg Garden
27 May 1998

palm trees and rosebushes
violets and palms
scattered chairs and all will end
conversation the embrace
three centuries or one only in the stretch
of the future it comes to the same
when the body wonders
breathless between vowels
near perfect melancholy (59)

RER, return from Verona
14 October 2001

ad 1: the plane. ad 2:
a cloud of fire
then the dust 1 of death
the dust 2 of the Bible and the Koran
in one's mouth and eyes
no blood only dust
while walking in the smell of the fallen sky
every day at the same time
New York has the eyes of men and of chaos
killers' gazes slashing words
making morning fall, slashing
and slash again
the words you have in mind
for all of that if you go through it is quite real
farther on there are some women
their eyes of life hidden in the pain
the endless reflection of the weave (120)

Toulouse
30 March 2002

walking along the Garonne
Le sexe sur le bout de la langue
I move at the speed of elation
a lesbian flavor on my mind
rue des Gestes
again a flick of the tongue
a moist thought
at the root of a perennial us (130)

Paris
24 May 2002

on the way to the *Petit théâtre du rond-point*
the wings seem old like a president
look at all that the gilding
a white toy dog look carefully
Paris in the slow pallor of words
urban pigeons gables on history (140)

Translations by Miléna Santoro, except "Le Petit Pont,"
in English in the original.

SECTION II
European Cultural Influences on Quebec Writers

10. Today might try and find one of those old 19th-century passages. B likening to ghost stepping right through city blocks. They're *everywhere* S saying. Curved arm gesturing. To the left bank. To the right. Brown eyes ironic. Regarding my desire. For her beloved Paris. Where she has hidden. Thrown pavés, paving stones. Been a city worker. Fine profile turning this way or that. Always seeking new streets to step down. As if a walk were a caress.

But passages are not streets. The peculiar light of their aging glass-and-iron roofs. In prime conferring lineage of greenhouse. Replete with palms. Parrots. Mirrors. Moist alleys of desire. Kind of *locus classicus* of B's strange Paris history. I now consuming daily. Lying back on divan. With fresh bread from bakery. Coffee. After raising outer store or shutter. And looking down on traffic. Volume earlier falling open. At allusion to favourite Balzac heroine: *Girl with Golden Eyes*. In some oriental get-up. Guarded by duenna. In absence of marquise. So girl incapable of making contact with handsome young Tom. Who stalking her in Tuileries. Before marquise finding out. And killing her. Allusion not far from anecdote about ancient Chinese puzzle. Representing hachured parts of human form. Prefiguring cubism. Which puzzle fashionable under Second Empire. Reign of terror and indifference. According to B.

Gail Scott, My Paris 14

Writing beyond Redemption: Hubert Aquin and Mordecai Richler in Postwar Paris

PATRICK COLEMAN

Although they were born in Montreal only fifteen months and just a few miles apart, Hubert Aquin (1929–1977) and Mordecai Richler (1931–2001) belonged to worlds that barely overlapped. Aquin's family was francophone, Catholic, and modestly middle-class. The young Hubert's neighbors in what had until recently been the village of Ahuntsic, like his classmates at the Collège Sainte-Marie and later at the Université de Montréal, either belonged to the French-Canadian bourgeoisie or aspired to it. Richler belonged to a family of poor Galician Jews who adopted English as their New World language and lived in the crowded tenements of the Mile End district. His fellow students at Baron Byng High School and at Sir George Williams University were mostly poorer, and while they came from a variety of backgrounds, few if any were francophone Montrealers. The few Anglophones the young Aquin did meet were members of the WASP hunting and fishing elite, customers of his father, who managed the sports equipment section of the Omer de Serres department store. The French Canadians Richler knew were local kids he and his buddies occasionally fought in the streets, and perhaps some dealers in the scrap-metal business that employed his father. It is therefore very unlikely that either youth knew anything much about the kind of life the other lived, or about the kind of cultural background and intellectual ambitions that led each of them to go to Paris in the autumn of 1951. Nor was it any more likely that their paths would cross in the cultural capital of Europe, since Aquin went there to study on a graduate fellowship while Richler was going to live the garret life of the bohemian writer. Yet, the coincidence of their settling in Europe at the same time is a suggestive starting point for literary-historical reflection, especially since the first extended works of fiction they would publish were written there in 1952 and focused on the same theme: that of personal and collective redemption.[1] In this essay, I suggest that we can gain new insight into the early careers of these two writers by looking at the different meanings they gave to the Paris they experienced and imagined, and by comparing the preoccupations and the publishing history of Aquin's long story "Les rédempteurs" ("The Redeemers") and Richler's novel *The Acrobats*.

While their backgrounds were very different, Aquin and Richler arrived in Europe with some of the same personal baggage. Both came from families with strong mothers who elicited strongly ambivalent feelings in their sons.[2] Both identified with their fathers, but at the same time were ashamed of them. Richler enjoyed his father Max's unpretentious earthiness, but hated seeing him exploited by the relatives who kept him in a menial position. Aquin admired his father Jean's expertise with guns (he would later commit suicide with a rifle inherited from him), but was distressed at the obsequiousness he displayed towards the English-speaking clients who called him "John." Both young men were also emerging from strongly religious backgrounds into convictions of unbelief, and despite the important differences between the Catholicism and the Judaism they rejected, their thinking continued to be marked by similar notions of purity, authenticity, and redemption. As they arrived in Paris, then, Aquin and Richler were looking for new and more enabling sources of authority, even as they suspected that any such authority would prove to have feet of clay. And yet, they could not give up the idealistic expectations that gave them their moral energy. While looking to resolve this tension, the young writers clung to what was authentic in what they had: the lucid acknowledgment of defeat.

While this diagnosis is somewhat speculative, it would explain why neither Aquin nor Richler was much taken by the heroic image of the French Resistance, or by the aura of de Gaulle. The Paris they celebrated in their writings in or about this period was a city of rich cultural life, but it was not the political city of the Liberation. The only passage in Aquin's *Journal* to address French politics is a meditation on its *grande défaite* in 1940. Reflecting on Jean Guéhenno's *Journal des années noires*, Aquin's judgment is harsh: "France was really and truly defeated; after four years of occupation it was partly won over to the new order" ["La France a vraiment été défaite; après quatre ans d'occupation elle était en partie gagnée à l'ordre nouveau"]. The Liberation had changed nothing: "Ten years of foreign, let's say Russian, occupation, and France will be absorbed like Hungary, Romania ..." ["Dix ans d'occupation étrangère, russe par exemple, et la France sera assimilée comme la Hongrie, la Roumanie ..."]. Its fate can only be avoided by intervention by a power from above: "Only one thing can save it: a nationalist dictatorship like that of Yugoslavia" ["Une seule chose peut la sauver: une dictature nationaliste à l'exemple de la

Yougoslavie"] (*Journal* 98–9).[3] It is also significant that while Aquin devotes many pages of his journal to French writers, notably Julien Green and Julien Gracq, whose descriptions of a haunted inner life resonated with his personal experience, he ignores Malraux, he only cites Camus in relation to artistic creativity, not political action, and he does not mention Sartre at all except in his reading lists.

Malraux was one of Richler's early heroes, along with other political writers of the 1930s such as Auden and Orwell, yet *The Acrobats* is not set in the postwar Paris of the victorious Allies, but in Franco's Spain. The Valencia depicted in the novel is still scarred by the defeat of the Republicans and is filled with refugees from other defeats. These include a German colonel wanted for war crimes and Chaim, an American Jew who is stateless because he gave away his passport to help a camp survivor get to Brooklyn, but who instead of going to the newly established Israel cannot seem to tear himself away from the company of other victims, including the colonel who hates him.[4] There is a brief reference to the Normandy invasion, but far from calling up any image of heroism, André, the young painter-protagonist of the novel, deflates such rhetoric by focusing on a village in ruins and a boot with a bullet hole in it (*Acrobats* 67). Defeat is more vivid as well as more authentic than victory.

And yet, there are important differences between the two writers in the ways they develop the insights of defeat. The writers Richler admired had not been spectators looking on from a distance, or worse, passive victims, but had participated actively and honorably in the struggle. The memory of their actions, and the art they produced, provided Richler with inspiration that was all the more authentic in that it remained untainted by the triumphalism, or the later compromises, of victory. In later years, Aquin would seek similar inspiration from the story of the Canadian Patriot Rebellion of 1837, but he never quite managed to be enabled by its example, perhaps because it produced no lasting works of literature. Whatever the case, Aquin's accounts of French life do not indicate he found in contemporary Paris a model for the writer's relationship to his historical era as energizing as Richler's. Indeed, he seems not to have looked for one in the contemporary world at all. What fascinated him instead in his first years in Paris was the history of the early Church, about which he read a great deal. He does not discuss his reading in detail, but one can speculate that he found something appealing in the story of an oppressed minority's triumph over a hostile empire. The Church Fathers Aquin studied in Paris with Henri-Irénée Marrou used a more sophisticated version of the militantly ecclesiastical language employed by the Quebec clergy of his era, a language certainly congenial to a young man who only the previous year had been a delegate to a world congress of Catholic youth. The brilliance of Augustine and Jerome was also such that even as he abandoned religious belief Aquin could still identify with them as intellectual leaders. On the other hand, their struggles belonged to a world much more remote than that of the left-wing writers of the 1930s. In the latter case, there was just enough historical distance to give Richler a fantasy space to explore his own identity while remaining grounded in the world around him. Aquin's interest in late antiquity may have been rooted in a deeper collective as well as personal imaginative need, but it was more academic and more abstract.

The same paradoxical combination of intensity and abstraction characterizes Aquin's European experience as a whole. In this regard, it has some of the pathos of the *rendez-vous manqués* of other mid-twentieth century young French-Canadians with the *mère patrie*. Instead of empowering them, the encounter with a Paris more alien than they hoped only reinforced the inferiority complex hidden beneath their extravagant ambitions.[5] A striking but to my knowledge unremarked feature of Aquin's journal is that while he lists the many books he read and the many theatrical performances he attended, he records not a single encounter with an actual Parisian. To be sure, he made enough contacts in the city to get some freelance work assisting with radio broadcasts designed for the Canadian market, and he interviewed a number of French writers for the Montreal weekly *L'autorité*. But with the exception of Michel van Schendel (who immigrated to Canada in 1952 and who would later work for him at Radio-Canada) he does not seem to have established a real connection with anyone of a nationality other than his own. He had relationships with several women, but they were all French-Canadian students like him. Aquin's accounts of his romantic involvements suggest that part of the problem was psychological. The journal records in affecting detail the torments of his longings and misunderstandings, many of which seem to have stemmed from the disproportion between the romantic dramas played out in his own mind and the reality of the woman herself. A peculiar feature of the published journal reinforces this impression of disembodiment. As coincidence would have it, all four of Aquin's significant female friends or lovers had first names beginning with M, and with very few exceptions it is by this single initial that the journal refers to them all.[6] The settings in which these relationships are played out – streets, cafés, hotels, or parks – are equally devoid of distinguishing features. The vagueness of Aquin's

Paris stands in sharp contrast with the geographical precision and vividness of his Switzerland.[7]

Given his limited fluency in French, it is more natural that Richler should remain an outsider in Paris, but in some ways he was more imaginatively connected to the city than was Aquin. One reason was that he had a more enabling literary model in the already-mythic "lost generation" of American writers who had settled there in the 1920s. If Auden and Malraux were his political touchstones, Hemingway and Fitzgerald symbolized the creative potential of expatriate life in Paris. By contrast, the most famous of French-Canadian literary expatriates, Octave Crémazie, had died poor and poetically unfulfilled. The English-language tradition also had a more immediate exemplar in Richler's friend Mavis Gallant, whose determination to pursue an independent writing career he admired, and who had preceded him in leaving Montreal for Europe.[8] At the same time, the potentially debilitating effects of having to compete with eminent predecessors were forestalled by Richler's ironic acceptance that he, and the other postwar English-speaking writers he met in France, was a latecomer to the scene. While setting their sights high in emulation of their heroes, their delusions of grandeur were held in check by what Richler called "a sense of the ridiculous." Indeed, this was the title he gave to the recollections he published about his Paris years. Appropriately enough, they took the form of a modest essay subtitled "Notes on Paris and After" rather than of an extended memoir.[9]

Still, it is significant that Richler wrote an essay commemorating his Paris experience whereas Aquin did not. However ironically he viewed his situation, Richler did have a positive example to challenge him, and self-deprecation did not affect the single-mindedness with which he worked on his writing. Although the milieu in which he lived was composed largely of English-speaking expatriates, it was focused as much on the production as on the consumption of culture. Richler read important new writers such as Beckett and Genet (unmentioned, interestingly, by Aquin), but he was more preoccupied with the practicalities of writing and publishing, in the first instance with the little avant-garde magazines that sought to renew the modernist tradition of anglophone literary life in Paris. The rooms Richler could afford being less comfortable than Aquin's university housing, he spent much of his time in cafés, and certainly more on the streets than in libraries or theatres. His friendships were more varied in terms of nationality, and so were his female companions.[10] In these respects, Richler's Paris experience, contrary to what one might have thought, was in some respects more grounded in the reality of the place than Aquin's. Certainly he could feel that, even before he published, he was already living an actual artist's life.

By contrast, Aquin's journal pictures in vaguer terms the life he would like to live, if only he could make truly productive contact with the world outside his own mind. Part of the problem was that Aquin set out on too many paths, each of which seemed to promise the realization of his considerable intellectual potential. Political science, philosophy, the aesthetic foundations of the novel – at one time or another he read widely in them all, in school and out, always in preparation for a work, and a career, that never quite got defined. One must add that he was not helped as much as he could have been by his cultural environment. The French university system was not one in which a foreigner who had not come up through the tight system of elite *lycées* and *grandes écoles* could make much headway, or find a helpful patron. The publishing world was equally impenetrable to an outsider without *relations*. Even the members of the existentialist and other avant-gardes worked within intimate networks of patronage. Thus it is not surprising that when he finished "Les rédempteurs" in the early spring of 1952, he was rejected by all three of the Paris publishers (Grasset, Gallimard, and José Corti) to whom he submitted it. At the same time, the journal account of his quest is striking for the way it presents Aquin's initiative as a series of isolated gestures. There is no mention of possible recommenders or intercessors. Nor does Aquin suggest he tried to make personal contact with editors or sought counsel on his submission strategy. Corti, for example, was Gracq's publisher and ran a very personal enterprise, but Aquin does not recount any attempt at conversation with him. Aquin may indeed have been ambivalent about the whole idea of publication – as soon as December 1952, he would declare that the work to be "a youthful peccadillo" ["un péché de jeunesse"] (*Journal* 144) – but one wonders whether his diffidence explains or is explained by the absence of any means, external as well as internal, of engaging in a sustained way with the literary institution. Whatever the case, he reacted to rejection neither by persisting on the path he had chosen, energized by adversity, nor by seeking a way to make his work more marketable, but by retreating into a series of abortive projects (including rewriting the story as a play, as yet unpublished, entitled "Le Prophète") that allowed him to continue thinking of himself as a writer without putting that self-image to the test.[11]

Richler, on the other hand, was nothing if not committed to a writing career. Yet, he also benefited from a more favorable conjunction of institutional circumstances. As an English-language writer, he could not, of course, publish in France – unless he wrote pornography for the tourist trade, a thriving business that offered good money and, unlike writing a doctoral thesis, was considered by his circle to be compatible with literary seriousness ("Sense" 55). Nor did Richler consider publishing in Canada. He looked to New York and more especially to nearby London. As it happened, one of Richler's Paris friends, an English writer named Michael Sayer, had contacts in the London publishing world. Sayer introduced Richler to Joyce Weiner, an agent there, and in the summer of 1952 she agreed to represent him. There was no such thing as a literary agent in Paris. Serious French writers and publishers did not like to think of themselves in the crass terms of the marketplace; the brokering of new talent proceeded on a more discreet basis.[12] Over the next decade, Weiner would played an key role in getting Richler's work into print and in advising him on revising it to suit the publishers' needs. The time was in fact ripe for someone like Richler to break into the London scene. The literary scene was being shaken up by a generation of assertive new writers from lower-class backgrounds, the so-called "angry young men." The publishing world was also being energized by new players like the brash young André Deutsch, who had scored a big success by acquiring the rights to Norman Mailer's *The Naked and the Dead* when other, more hide-bound firms had passed on what became a huge bestseller. Deutsch was on the lookout for other new talent, even if it was still raw. He was willing to take a chance on *The Acrobats*. Just as important, Richler was willing to listen to what his agent and his publisher said was needed to bring his book to market in Britain (including substantial cuts and a toning down of its sexual frankness), and subsequently to secure publication in the United States. The novel appeared in both countries in 1954. Richler worked hard, but he was also luckier than he was later willing to acknowledge, when having achieved commercial success he railed against the Canada Council and other forms of government support for the arts.[13]

If we approach Aquin and Richler's first major works from the perspective of their Paris experiences, it may seem strange that the hero of "Les rédempteurs" survives his tribulations, including the temptation of suicide, and ventures forth with the woman he loves, while the nihilistic protagonist of *The Acrobats* almost invites his own murder by a jealous rival. A closer look, however, reveals a more complicated picture, since both texts displace rather than directly depict the authors' hopes and fears. Aquin's story, which has the starkness of an allegorical fable, is set in Edom, a country associated in the Bible with Jacob's dispossessed brother Esau (Gen 36:8–9). Tension between doubles or enemy brothers will become a hallmark of Aquin's fiction, but, curiously, his Edom is not portrayed in relationship to Israel. It exists in isolation. Its people are depressed, their energy sapped by a pervasive sense of guilt and pollution whose origins are never explained. What few details we learn about the main characters of the story suggests that sexual difficulties lie at the root of the problem. The hero, Héman, enjoys physical intimacy with Élisha, but a kind of moral lassitude makes it a fuller connection difficult. His brother Kenaz also loves Élisha and is despondent at his failure to win her for himself. Kénaz's depression is aggravated by his inability, or unwillingness, to respond to the advances of his friend Aram, whose unrequited longing thus mirrors his own. Like the other inhabitants of Edom, therefore, Kénaz and Aram find themselves drawn to the prophet Sheba,[14] who proposes that the people of the city commit collective suicide. Only this radical action will redeem them from their sins and, even more important, spare their descendants the burden of existence altogether. Curiously, Sheba speaks as if all humanity is included in the sacrifice, but nothing is said about any other cities. The city authorities of Edom make a feeble attempt to silence Sheba, but the prophet's message spreads like wildfire, and soon even those who are reluctant to die are swept along by his acolytes to the place of execution. When the ritual is concluded, Sheba hangs himself. Yet he dies unsatisfied, because he has failed to take everyone with him: Héman and Élisha had slipped away from the crowd. They are pursued by a Kénaz determined that no one should escape the fate to which he himself is driven. In the end, however, it is Héman who kills his brother, and he and Élisha survive to become a new Adam and Eve, whose "embrace will populate the world" ["étreinte peuplera le monde"] (143).

This new beginning is hardly a happy one, however, since that same embrace "will restore uninterrupted continuity to dissatisfaction" ["rendra à l'insatisfaction sa continuité ininterrompue"] and ensures that "the fateful and burdensome work of humanity will keep on going as far as us" ["l'oeuvre fatale et lourde de l'humanité se poursuive jusqu'à nous"] (143). For all the effort expended to shed a yearning for redemption that is really only destructive and pointless self-sacrifice, Aquin's characters are not really free. The need for redemption persists beyond the exposure of its destructive effects. Why this should be so the story does not say, but one wonders whether the answer lies in the author's unresolved attitude toward what exists beyond Edom. The internal enemy brother has been eliminated, but what of the external one? If Héman and Élisha are really the only people left on earth, there should not be a problem. But if they are only pretending to be alone, then their false consciousness could well be crippling. Aquin has created a new first couple whose names and background derive from another, pre-existing story, one whose literary (not to say religious and cultural) power Aquin can parody but cannot quite confront. In this respect, "Les rédempteurs" anticipates the dynamic that energizes, but also undermines, Aquin's later novels.

Ritual immolation and dubious redemption are also central to Richler's *Acrobats*. The novel is set in the Spanish city of Valencia in the days leading up to the festival of San José. The celebrations culminate in the ceremonial burning of *fallas*, huge figures of straw and papier-mâché made by local clubs, often in the shape of people they wish to mock, and first paraded around the streets. The festival is a striking variation on a custom found in almost every culture: a symbolic sacrifice designed to relieve social stresses and renew community solidarity. The key word, of course, is *symbolic*. Looking back at Aquin's story, one wonders why none of the characters propose a symbolic rather than a literal sacrifice (a shift reflected in the Genesis story of Abraham and Isaac). At the very least, a single person might have been made to serve as a scapegoat.[15] The answer would seem to be that the condition Aquin depicts is one of de-symbolization. It is precisely the collapse of any distance between the literal and the symbolic, of any room for creative "play" in the social system, which leads to paralysis and despair.

Richler's hero faces precisely the opposite problem: he is surrounded by a profusion of symbols, but they are hollow ones, no longer anchored in material reality. The *fallas* are supposed to embody the vitality and subversive spirit of the people, but in Franco's Spain they are carefully controlled by the police and transformed into an attraction for tourists looking for colorful customs. Richler's hero, the painter André Bennett, is of mixed English and French Canadian blood, but far from embodying in his person a union of these two groups according to the scheme of Hugh MacLennan's *Two Solitudes* (1945), he is a rootless wanderer, alienated from himself. Consumed with guilt because his lover Irene died from a botched abortion, he, too, seeks redemption but despairs of finding anything other than deception or illusion. He tries to keep faith with leftist political ideals but is discouraged by their inability to produce genuine change and their distortion by opportunists. He would like to love the prostitute Toni, who adores him and would herself like to be "saved" by him in a material sense, but

cannot overcome the feeling that he is only a player in a hackneyed romantic plot. In the end, he can only escape artifice through death. He allows
himself to be killed by his rival for Toni's affections, the ex-Nazi colonel
Kraus, who is as much an exile as he is. Kraus has friends in the local government, but much of his power comes from what others more cowardly
or spineless than he project onto him. André is no exception, and he dies
just as the *fallas* are being set on fire at the culmination of the festival.

The hero's death, however, is not an image for the author's own creative
despair. On the contrary, it marks the end of a mistaken quest for redemption that, far from freeing him from the ghosts of his religious and cultural
past, had only replaced them with other empty ideals. Richler later wrote
about his experience of the *fallas* that "those flames in Valencia consumed
… a host of personal devils. The most wintry of my Canadian baggage as
well as some of the more stultifying Jewish injunctions I had grown up
with … I was a free man" (*Images*, 23).[16] What Richler experienced in the
festival was a display of gratuitous excess which liberated him from the
earnestness of the quest for redemption. The novel that arose from this
experience may be an awkward one, heavily indebted to literary models
such as Malcolm Lowry's *Under the Volcano* (Craniford), but it is also the
working-through of this basic insight.

Although Aquin and Richler's first forays into the publishing world took
place under very different circumstances, their careers would take another
parallel turn in the second half of the decade, after they left France. Both
found that writing plays for television gave them a means of creative expression and a way to earn a living: Richler in England, where he also worked
on film scripts, and Aquin in Montreal, where he found a staff job at Radio-
Canada. Yet, here, too, institutional differences played an important role.
The rapidly expanding British television industry (state-sponsored and commercial) was open to Canadian (and blacklisted American) talent. Richler
again benefited from relationships with other North American expatriates.
For Richler, working in British media was an extension of his Paris experience, except that the "sense of the ridiculous" gave way to pride in
mastering the demands of a medium unknown to the literary idols he had
emulated there. In France, the rigidly controlled RTF (the state radio and
television authority) had little room for freelancers from the francophone
world, but by the time Aquin returned to Montreal in 1954, his closest friend,
Louis-Georges Carrier, had begun an influential career at Radio-Canada.
Aquin and Carrier had been classmates at the Collège Sainte-Marie, where
theatrical productions of a modern and sophisticated kind exceptional in

their day had been an important part of their education. Ultimately, one might say, it was by moving into the new medium of television even more than by traveling to Paris that Richler and Aquin found (at least for a few years) a sustaining environment, one that gave them the space they needed to achieve creative maturity.

The purpose of this essay has been to show the historical as well as literary interest of comparing the careers of French and English-language writers from the same city and yet very different cities that was (were) the Montréal/Montreal of the 1950s. But one might ask: whose literature and whose history? A first flowering in the 1960s of what was called "comparative Canadian literature," illustrated notably by the work of Philip Stratford, was attacked in the following decades as a tendentious enterprise of cultural nation-building by francophone Quebec intellectuals, many of whom were engaged in a nation-building effort of their own (Blodgett). More recently, literary critics within Quebec have sought to integrate anglophone writers there into a new conception of *littérature québécoise*, sometimes in a post-nationalist spirit, sometimes intent on assigning them a role in a revised national narrative at odds with pan-Canadian identity claims.[17] No doubt, there will always be a degree of competition between the different histories in which writers like Richler and Aquin are made to feature, but the premise of this essay is that these histories need not be exclusive of each other. What is crucial is that the individual stories of which they are composed be grounded in as comprehensive an understanding of their multiple contexts as the critic can achieve, while acknowledging the limits of his or her resources and imaginative identifications. Reading more than one story should remind us there will be always more than one story to tell.

Notes

1 Before *The Acrobats*, Richler had written another novel, entitled *The Rotten People*, which he judged unsatisfactory and never published. A full study of his early career, and of Aquin's, would have to take account of letters and other unpublished materials. The differences in the degree to which such materials have been published posthumously, made available in publically accessible archives, and discussed (or not) in biographical studies would make another interesting story in comparative Canadian literary history. This essay is based on published sources only.

2 For details on Richler's relationship to his parents, see Kramer. For Aquin, see Maccabée-Iqbal. However, the available accounts of Aquin's relationship to his mother are oddly elusive.

3 All translations are the author's, unless otherwise indicated. With his friend André Raynaud, later a distinguished economist, Aquin would later visit

Yugoslavia to study its system of self-management, but his initial enthusiasm faded in the light of political realities there.

4 The history of Richler's ambivalent attitude to Zionism is traced in detail by Kramer. Here, Chaim seems to illustrate Richler's skepticism about "redemptive" hopes.

5 For memorable fictional illustrations of this paradigm, see Michel Tremblay's *Des nouvelles d'Édouard* (1984) and Anne Hébert's *L'enfant chargé de songes* (1992), both set in the early postwar period.

6 Sometimes this is Aquin's doing, but in other cases it reflects an editorial decision. Since some of these women had spoken publicly about their relationships with Aquin prior to the publication of the journal and some of the details were also being published in another volume of the same edition of Aquin's works (*Itinéraires*), and since by the time the journal was published, the events recorded in the Paris notebooks were forty years old, it is not clear why the editor, Bernard Beugnot, not only maintained but reinforced the vagueness of the references. Or perhaps, given the similarity of the accounts, it was no longer possible to determine with certainty who was who. There is an odd mixture of prurience and coyness in biographical writings and testimonies about Aquin's life.

7 See Karen McPherson's essay in this volume.

8 Richler had met Gallant in Montreal and was inspired by her initiative.

9 It must be said, however, that the essay is marked by Richler's satisfied awareness that he had found a degree of success that had eluded some of his talented friends

10 However, the woman who became his first wife, Catherine Boudreau, was a Franco-Ontarian he met during a visit back to Montreal in 1952.

11 At some point around this time, Aquin submitted "Les rédempteurs" to the newly founded Montreal publishing house L'hexagone, but withdrew it in 1955. The work finally came out in volume 5 of the *Écrits du Canada français* (1959), but a later cryptic complaint (*Point de fuite*, 129n.) about its appearing only as an "extended short story" ["nouvelle allongée"] suggests that the published version may be shorter than the original text (the manuscript is privately held and has not been made available to scholars).

12 Only in recent years have agents emerged as part of the Paris publishing scene, and this development has caused considerable dismay among cultural observers.

13 Kramer offers full and fascinating details of these early years, and he points out the contradictions in Richler's later stance.

14 Like the Elisha of the second book of Kings, the Sheba of Genesis 10:28 is a man, but the potential for gender ambiguity in these biblical names is surely relevant to any reading of the story.

15 Perhaps coincidentally, the theme of scapegoat sacrifice had been revived to disturbing effect a few years earlier in Shirley Jackson's short story "The Lottery" (1948). Aquin would probably not have read it, but it might have been known to Richler.

16 Curiously, this book does not include any images of the Valencia festival.

17 For a sample of recent approaches, see Biron et al.; Moyes and Lane-Mercier.

Works Cited

Aquin, Hubert. *Journal 1948–1971*. Ed. Bernard Beugnot. Montreal: Bibliothèque québécoise, 1992.

– *Point de fuite*. Ed. Guylaine Massoutre. Montreal: Bibliothèque québécoise, 1995 [first pub. 1971].

– "Les rédempteurs." Ed. Claudine Potvin. In *Récits et nouvelles: Tout est miroir*. Ed. François Poisson, with the collaboration of Alain Carbonneau. Montreal: Bibliothèque québécoise, 1998 [first pub. 1959].

Blodgett, E.D. *Five-Part Invention: A History of Literary History in Canada*. Toronto: University of Toronto Press, 2003.

Craniford, Ada. *Fiction and Fact in Mordecai Richler's Novels*. Lewiston, NY: Edwin Mellen, 1992.

Histoire de la littérature québécoise. Ed. Michel Biron, François Dumont, and Élisabeth Nardout-Lafarge; with the collaboration of Martine-Emmanuelle Lapointe. Montreal: Fides, 2007.

Images of Spain. Photographs by Peter Christopher; text by Mordecai Richler. New York: W.W. Norton, 1977.

Kramer, Reinhold. *Mordecai Richler: Leaving St. Urbain*. Montreal and Kingston: McGill-Queen's University Press, 2008.

Maccabée-Iqbal, Françoise. *Desafinado: Otobiographie de Hubert Aquin*. Montreal: VLB, 1987.

Massoutre, Guylaine. *Itinéraires d'Hubert Aquin*. Montreal: Bibliothèque québécoise, 1992.

Richler, Mordecai. *The Acrobats*. New York: G.P. Putnam's Sons, 1954.

– "A Sense of the Ridiculous" [1968]. In *Notes from an Endangered Species and Others*. New York: Knopf, 1974.

Textes, territoires, traduction: (dé)localisations/dislocations de la littérature anglo-québécoise. Eds. Lianne Moyes and Gillian Lane-Mercier. *Québec Studies* 44 (2007–08).

Des châteaux en Suisse? Switzerland in the Quebec Imagination: Aquin and Brossard

KAREN McPHERSON

In Nicole Brossard's most recent novel, *La capture du sombre*, a woman writer from Quebec has been invited to spend time in a castle in Switzerland owned by Tatiana Beaujeu Lehmann, a retired editor who asks of her guest in return only "some conversations and reflections on the present state of the world" ["quelques conversations et réflexions sur l'état présent du monde"] (18).[1] The narrator expresses her desire to write a book in a language not her own: "As a stranger, I want to plunge into the landscape of a provisional world where meaning pushes meaning aside as I pass through" ["Comme une étrangère, je veux plonger dans le paysage d'un monde provisoire où le sens écarte le sens au fur et à mesure de mon passage"] (5). Yet from the beginning, the reader of this novel has the sense of passing through a familiar landscape. Long before the sentence near the end of the novel that explicitly evokes Hubert Aquin's *Prochain episode* ("One calm moment before Beirut goes down in flames in the middle of the Lake and of the *présent recomposé*" ["Un moment tranquille avant que Beyrouth coule en flammes au milieu du Lac et du présent recomposé"] [125]), we are unquestionably – though not exclusively – in the Switzerland of Aquin's fiction. The language that opens Brossard's novel uncannily echoes the reflections, the fire and water, the play of surfaces and depths, the ramblings and driftings that mark the opening passages in *Prochain épisode*. Furthermore, the evocation, in each work, of a suspension of conventional time that makes possible the imagination of the writing project that the book itself represents encourages us to read Brossard's novel alongside Aquin's.[2]

If we understand *La capture du sombre* (2007) as a return journey to the Switzerland of the Quebec imagination inscribed emblematically in Aquin's 1965 novel, we may begin to identify some of the changes to Quebec identity as well as to "the present state of the world" effected across the forty-three intervening years between the two literary transatlantic passages.

In English we build castles in the air whereas the French (in an expression that dates back to the thirteenth century) speak of *des châteaux en Espagne* [castles in Spain] to refer to unrealistic projects spun from dreams and fantasies. Conceived in opposition to the world of concrete objects, facts, and deeds, a castle in Spain is a cherished impossibility.[3] To speak of castles in Switzerland, however, is to blur the boundaries between fact and fiction. There are in fact hundreds of very real stone and mortar castles in Switzerland. Indeed, this Alpine nation is very literally a country of "castles in the air." So is it a real geographical locus or is it a fantasy realm? It seems that Switzerland has been vividly inscribed in the Western imagination as both. How do the country's famous neutrality and insularity play into its symbolic appeal? It is easy to understand how this place of lofty retreat from the world lends itself to the imagination and creativity of the solitary artist with the uninterrupted quiet and the rarefied mountain air fostering the introspective life. But the picture postcard beauty may also signal an unreality associated with shallow surfaces, lies, and deceptions. The neutral haven might be a place of refuge, a step aside from the world's geopolitical systems. But it may just as readily mark and conceal a deep rootedness and complicity in those same systems. Beneath the clean white snowscapes and beyond the polished facades lies a Switzerland of sheltered money, international deals, and radical conspiracies.[4] As the spy story embedded in Aquin's novel suggests, neutral Switzerland is a deceptively blank page on which to write the political script.

Switzerland also has distinct literary significance. This lofty retreat appealing to the romantic imagination provides an ideal setting for works like Lord Byron's "Prisoner of Chillon," Thomas Mann's *Magic Mountain*, Ernest Hemingway's *A Farewell to Arms*. The country is a celebrated destination for writers, a place that many pass through and where some make their final resting place.[5] A place of both writers and literary heroes, Switzerland distills its identity from the encounter of the real and the fictional. Indeed, it is a place where writers become literary heroes and literary heroes attempt to become writers. And it is this compelling literary geography that both Aquin and Brossard are exploring.[6]

But Switzerland in the Quebec imagination may have a more particular significance. Even as the transatlantic relationships between Europe and her former colonies are often ambivalent, bringing up anxious questions of origin, identity, and affiliation, the relationship between Quebec and French-speaking Switzerland seems capable of short circuiting some of those tensions. To the Quebecois, *la Suisse romande* may represent a European not-France, a place of origin (in general terms) that is also specifically not *the* place of origin. And the French-speaking Canadian must certainly feel some affinity for the francophone citizen of the multilingual Swiss Federation. As Aquin suggested in both *Prochain épisode* and his essays in *Point de fuite*, there is potentially fruitful common ground between the two nations in their shared minority status and sovereignty issues.

Aquin's Switzerland

We know that Aquin was drawn personally, politically, and esthetically to Switzerland. As Sylvie Jeanneret noted, it was "a country of predilection for [him]" (42); he made numerous trips there and even tried to move there in 1966. One could argue that the country resonates in singular fashion with Aquin's temperament and his novelistic project. Certainly that land of mountains and glacial lakes composes a world of mirrors and a confusion of heights and depths that seem a natural landscape for fiction, not to mention for someone in a volatile psychological state. Jeanneret remarks that as a country that "encourages well-being, rest and reverie" (46), Switzerland "represents a space that defines itself as against: anti-action, anti-revolution, even anti-heroicising" (47). The man of action, the revolutionary hero, seeking a way out of a Montreal mental hospital, may be drawn to Switzerland but will also find it to be "an impossible place" (52). Yet, Switzerland does appear to enable Aquin to link European literary traditions and revolutionary movements with his own Quebec-centered project. He accomplishes this through the use of what Maurice Cagnon called "spatial palimpsests" (82), the layering and doubling of places and their meanings in the novel. In fashioning fictional spaces out of afterimages and overlays, Aquin is momentarily able to imagine Canada and Switzerland superimposed. He sees "as one both Montreal and Lausanne, both revolutionary Cuba going down in flames and the sun setting" (Cagnon 82). Fredric Jameson's version of Cagnon's "palimpsests" [82] is his idea of "provisional allegorical frameworks" (220). According to Jameson, such frameworks allow Aquin to realize "a host of geographical substitutions" (221) and "[open] the text up to multiple interpretive temptations" (220). He goes on to explain how these substitutions complicate Aquin's project: "Swiss neutrality comes to figure as one possible Utopian image of an independent Québec – with its hydroelectric riches – ideally distanced from the struggle of the world system all around it. Yet this ideal image is problematized by the Cuban framework. Will Québécois independence be a respected enclave within protective mountain ranges, or the embattled blockade of a revolutionary island?" (221). Jameson insists upon "the allegorical hesitation [that] dramatizes the struggle of political interpretations of the Québec of the 1960s" (221). The "idealized" yet "problematized" image of an independent Quebec is reflected in the ambiguous image of a Cuba that "goes down in flames in the middle of Lake Geneva" ["coule en flammes au milieu du lac Léman"] (5). Does Switzerland offer escape or imprisonment? Is this a place where a revolution can begin or where it is extinguished?

Brossard's Switzerland

La capture du sombre opens with a first-person narrator describing her desire to write a book in a language that is not her own: "Since yesterday, something has slipped into my thoughts and modified the course of time so that for a reason as yet unknown to me I have the desire to write a book slowly in a language that is not my own" ["Depuis hier, quelque chose s'est glissé dans mes pensées qui a modifié le cours du temps de manière à ce que j'aie, pour une raison qui m'est encore inconnue, envie d'écrire lentement un livre dans une langue qui ne serait pas la mienne"] (5). In the first five pages of the novel, this narrator is not identified or situated. Rather, she articulates her desire in ways that allow the reader to assimilate her to the author of *La capture du sombre* as well as to that author's many narrative avatars. Phrases like "since yesterday" ["depuis hier"] and "modify the course of time" ["modifier le cours du temps"] clearly connect her to earlier Brossardian narrators who have in turn, in texts like *Elle serait la première phrase de mon prochain roman*, been fluidly and intimately and in ludic fashion associated with the novelist herself.[7] The text makes clear that the narrating "I" is the being that comes into being with the voice that is telling: "As a stranger, I want to plunge into the landscape of a provisional world where meaning pushes meaning aside as I pass through ... I am everywhere where I am" ["Comme une étrangère, je veux plonger dans le paysage d'un monde provisoire où le sens écarte le sens au fur et à mesure de mon passage. ... Je suis partout où je suis"] (5). This last sentence, a refrain throughout the novel, is a persistent reminder of how language comes to construct and situate subjects. However, even as the opening passages of the novel compel us to keep in mind the errant tendencies of the first-person pronoun, we do begin to identify this initial narrator in subsequent sections with a woman writer named Anne who has been invited to spend time in a castle in Switzerland, that *provisional world* where she is undertaking to write a book in a language that is not her own.

The first-person narrator further explains that she is writing this book "in order not to be gentle and to see the horizon of conflagration coming" ["pour ne pas être douce et pour voir venir l'horizon des incendies"] (5). Brossard's writings have long been focused on the horizon, but that horizon has tended to figure future possibilities and an inscription, albeit sometimes fleeting or fragile, of hope. In *La capture du sombre* the focus is somewhat different. Anne seeks to explore the encroaching darkness, to penetrate into the places of obscurity and danger that have come to accompany her realization that "there is darkness on the horizon" ["il y a du noir à l'horizon"] (8). She has used up the vocabulary for describing such darkness in her own language: "Now I need other words for all this dark of nature and civilization that is coming" ["Il me faut maintenant d'autres mots pour tout ce sombre de nature et de civilisation qui vient"] (8). The subject is dark; the future looks bleak. But writing in the language of another may offer a means to try to capture (and perhaps in this way disarm) that dark threat.

It is nonetheless important to note that the *langue étrangère* in the novel is not merely an elaboration on familiar Brossardian ideas about language and its relationship to the writing subject. True, this novel participates in the *intra*textuality of the Brossardian corpus, a writing of resonances and echoes that highlights the creative potential of translation. But this is also one of the most explicitly *inter*textual of Brossard's novels and that "language of the other" in which the story is being told is hauntingly familiar: in addition to Hubert Aquin's *Prochain épisode* and *Neige noire*, we feel the imposing presence of Blais's *Soifs* tetralogy, Hébert's *Le torrent* and *Les fous de Bassan*, Ouellette-Michalska's *La maison Trestler*. It is as if this text were drawing on, one might even say staging, other authors' narrative explorations of the dark.[8]

Brossard's novel of course does much more than merely revisit Aquin's Switzerland: her intertexts are myriad and varied and the drama played out in *La capture du sombre* takes place on a global stage.[9] But there is a Quebec story to be gleaned from these transatlantic passages. I would argue that the Swiss connection encourages a reading back to and through Aquin's *Prochain épisode*, and that a writing of Switzerland that follows so closely in Aquin's textual footsteps is also a rewriting of Quebec four decades later.[10]

The traces of *Prochain épisode* in *La capture du sombre* indeed urge us to explore some of the ways in which Brossard's novel absorbs and redirects the Aquinian paradox (Jameson's idealized yet problematized national allegory). What does a 21st-century Quebec woman writer have to say to the depressed and imprisoned revolutionary writer of 1965? Beyond the shared literary landscape, the many instances of intertextuality, and the parallelism of the phenomenon of a Quebec writer setting a novel in Switzerland, there is one striking textual pivot that compels the reader to read Brossard's novel in dialogue with Aquin's. This is the enigmatic figure of K in *Prochain épisode*. K, the narrator's lover and fellow conspirator, motivates the lyrical strains of that narrative as the narrator waxes nostalgic and poetic, referring to "K's sadness" ["la tristesse de K"], her "leonine hair" ["chevelure léonine"], "twilight locks" ["cheveux crépusculaires"], "amber skin" ["peau ambrée"], "great dark eyes" ["grands yeux sombres"] (37, 25, 33, 28, 27, 37). Imagining their encounter, he calls out to his beloved: "We stretched out naked under the cool sheets, voluptuously overwhelmed by one another, in the punctual splendor of our poem and the dawn" ["(N)ous nous sommes étendus sous les draps frais, nus, anéantis voluptueusement l'un par l'autre, dans la splendeur ponctuelle de notre poème et de l'aube"]. He laments finding himself now "lying alone on a blank white page" ["couché seul sur une page blanche"] (28). He relives in memory and in highly eroticized language an initial scene of lovemaking on "a certain June 24th":

I remember, what triumph in us that night! ... Tonight I can still feel the moist taste of your wild kisses on my lips. On your bed of chalky sands and on your alpine juices, I go down at full speed, I stretch out along the groundwater, I occupy everything; I penetrate, absolute terrorist, into every pore of your spoken lake: I swamp it with a single spurt, I am already overflowing the line of your lips and I flee, oh ! how suddenly I flee swift as lightning on the ocean, I flee on every breaker, shaken by the impulsive wave! I topple you, my love, on this bed suspended above a national holiday.

[Ce soir-là, je me souviens, quel triomphe en nous ! ... Ce soir encore, je garde sur mes lèvres le goût humecté de tes baisers éperdus. Sur ton lit de sables calcaires et sur tes muqueuses alpestres, je descends à toute allure,

je m'étends sur une nappe phréatique, j'occupe tout ; je pénètre, terroriste
absolu, dans tous les pores de ton lac parlé: je l'inonde d'un seul jet, je
déborde déjà au-dessus de la ligne des lèvres et je fuis, oh ! comme je fuis
soudain, rapide comme la foudre marine, je fuis à toutes vagues, secoué
par l'onde impulsive ! Je te renverse, mon amour, sur ce lit suspendu
au-dessus d'une fête nationale ...] (68, final ellipses in original)

Addressing his beloved directly, the narrator recounts their nights of con-
summated passion in terms that draw this scene again and again into
metaphorical relationship with both his writing project and his dreams of
revolution. K is thus at the very center of all the action.

Reading Brossard's novel with echoes of Aquin in one's ear, one cannot
help but recognize in the figure of Kim an avatar of K. In this novel of multiple voices and points of view, Kim stands out as a slightly fugitive focal
point both in the action and in relation to other central characters, especially her brother Charles and her friend and lover June.[11] In relation to
these others, Kim seems always to be pulling toward some geographically
distant and as yet undefined future. She dreams of leaving the village to get
far away from the brother whose violent tendencies frighten her:

I need to go toward the North, to be reborn silhouette in space, without
any bearings. I want the day and the night on every surface of their
twenty-four hours, in my eyes, on my body. It does not matter to me
what I will become in the midst of the immensity of the Great North !

[J'ai besoin d'aller vers le Nord, de renaître silhouette dans l'espace, sans
point de repère. J'ai envie du jour et de la nuit sur toute la surface de
leurs vingt-quatre heures dans mes yeux, sur mon corps. Peu m'importe
ce que je deviendrai au milieu de l'immensité du Grand Nord !] (21–2)

But at the same time, like K in *Prochain épisode*, we find Kim inscribed in
a key scene of lovemaking that reveals her privileged position in the story.
The scene of Kim and June making love inscribes lesbian desire in recog-
nizably Brossardian terms:

Fragments of audible time settle in between Kim and June ... Then
another arm, a slim waist, another arm, an embrace, a silky hand,

another hand, an endlessly smooth *horizon*. Later the deep, slow surrender, the miraculous plunge into the depths of self with honeywoven words hidden *under tongue* or suspended *between the lips* ... Kim's body is at the center of all stories. Kim's life the only viable scenario.

[Des parcelles de temps sonore s'installent alors entre Kim et June ... Puis un autre bras, une taille fine, un autre bras, une étreinte, une main soyeuse, une autre main, *un horizon* qui n'en finit pas d'être lisse. Plus tard, c'est l'abandon grave et lent, la chute miraculeuse au fond de soi avec des mots emmielés cachés *sous la langue* ou suspendus *entre les lèvres* ... Le corps de Kim est au centre de tous les récits. La vie de Kim, seul scénario viable.] (44–5, my emphases)

It is perhaps here that *La capture du sombre* most clearly shows us the distance that has been covered between 1965 and 2007, between the Quebec of Hubert Aquin and that of Nicole Brossard. The occupying, penetrating, inundating male lover, *absolute terrorist*, has yielded the stage to a scene of women's shared desire: "an endlessly smooth horizon." The individuals are no longer distinct; personal pronouns and possessive adjectives are absent as bodies come together: "another arm, a slim waist, another arm." The two women flow into one another in the "deep, slow surrender" of desire and passion. No longer "I topple you, my love, on this bed suspended above a national holiday," but now "the miraculous plunge into the depths of self with honeywoven words hidden under tongue or suspended between the lips."[12]

If Brossard's novel draws our attention to some of the ways in which Quebec has, since Aquin, been marked by changing geopolitical realities and by a rich Quebec literary tradition, the literary intertexts that inscribe the voices of Quebec women writers signal one of the most significant changes marking this passage from the Quiet Revolution to the 21st century: an awakening to gender questions and an opening up of textual spaces to women's celebratory and contestatory voices. Admittedly, even without the passage of decades, the gender difference between the two authors makes for a very different Quebec.[13] But Aquin's enigmatic K (more cipher than character) may also be seen as anticipating the fact that a central character remained to be developed before the Quebec story could be brought to any kind of, even conditional, conclusion.

Next Episodes

Somewhere in the middle of *Prochain épisode* the narrator/writer imagines a conclusion beyond the ending:

[this book] fits the very form of my future: in it and through it I explore my indecision and my improbable future. It is turned globally toward a conclusion that it will not contain since that conclusion, beyond the text, will follow the final period that I will place at the very bottom of the last page.

[(ce livre) épouse la forme même de mon avenir: en lui et par lui, je prospecte mon indécision et mon futur improbable. Il est tourné globalement vers une conclusion qu'il ne contiendra pas puisqu'elle suivra, hors texte, le point final que j'apposerai au bas de la dernière page.] (89)

In the final passages of the book, again writing in the future tense, he reiterates and elaborates: "No, I won't finish this unpublished book: the last chapter is missing … When the fights are over, the revolution will go on; only then will I perhaps find the time to put a final period on this book" ["Non, je ne finirai pas ce livre inédit: le dernier chapitre manque … Quand les combats seront terminés, la révolution continuera de s'opérer; alors seulement, je trouverai peut-être le temps de mettre un point final à ce livre"] (166-7). At this point K is gone, almost without a trace but for her final message that contained this indication: "I am leaving tonight for the north" ["Je pars ce soir pour le nord"] (152). And the narrator persists in imagining a future when he will emerge "victorious over [his] story" ["vainqueur de [son] intrigue"] (which is to say having killed H de Heutz, the next but unachievable episode in the plot) in order to "rush toward you, my love, and close my narrative with an apotheosis. All will finish in the secret splendor of your belly peopled with Alpine juices and eternal snows" ["me précipiter vers toi, mon amour, et clore mon récit par une apothéose. Tout finira dans la splendeur secrète de ton ventre peuplé d'Alpes muqueuses et de neiges éternelles"] (167).

It could be argued that Brossard also comes to Aquin's conclusion (that is, to a pivotal penultimate and inconclusive moment) but there is a significant difference. Brossard's Aquinian conclusion occurs not at the end of her novel but in the penultimate section called *The Level of the Water* [*Le niveau de l'eau*]. On the last page of this section, the narrator Anne evokes a future in terms that let us know we are still in Aquin's world: "Tomorrow I would go back into the castle to dive again into the complex and ancient world of Tatiana Beaujeu Lehmann and the daily life of an archaic and global village" ["Demain, je rentrerais au château pour replonger dans le monde complexe et ancient de Tatiana Beaujeu Lehmann et de la vie quotidienne d'un village archaïque et globale"] (125). This narrator will return to the castle, the village, the ancient world, and will accomplish, once again, the Aquinian gesture par excellence – figured by the verb *replonger* [dive again] followed so closely by the reference to Tatiana, whose family name, Lehmann, bears the echo of Lac Léman, the French name for Lake Geneva. Then in the next and final paragraph comes another Aquinian image with the twinning of fire and water: "The morning light would soon melt into that of the great fountain. A first glimmer of dawn wet with serenity" ["La lueur du matin allait bientôt se fondre à celle du grand jet. Une première lueur d'aube mouillée de sérenité"] (125). We are thus fully prepared for the closing phrase: "One calm moment before Beirut goes down in flames in the middle of the Lake and of the *présent recomposé*" ["Un moment tranquille avant que Beyrouth coule en flammes au milieu du Lac et du présent recomposé"] (125). This is both Aquin's starting point (Cuba goes down in flames [*Cuba coule en flammes*]) and the moment of Brossard's redirection of that story. Beirut is a very different revolutionary marker from Cuba[14] and the addition of the *présent recomposé* suggests the double gesture of the evocation. Neither a *passé composé*, nor the conditional of the preceding paragraph that inscribes a future encased in the past, this imagined *présent recomposé* is a *present* that is already past and yet still (with the *avant que* [before] that precedes it) stretching into a future.[15] And it is this fragile between-time, this tentative conclusion, that marks not only a crossroads in the journeys of Aquin and Brossard and their narrators but also Brossard's intentional recomposition of the present that was Aquin's future.

But *La capture du sombre* does not end there. In the final section of the novel called *Apprendre à sortir d'un paysage* [*Learning to Leave a Landscape*], Brossard steps beyond the Switzerland of her and Aquin's earlier imaginings. Five years have passed and the narrator has moved squarely into the future of Aquin's (and her own) "livre inédit" ["unpublished book"].

Of course Aquin did not stop there either. At the end of *Prochain episode* the narrator looks ahead not only to that next episode, a revolutionary future where he will emerge "victorious over [his] story" but also to an idealized final chapter where he shall "rush toward you, my love, and close my narrative with an apotheosis. All will finish in the secret splendor of your belly peopled with Alpine juices and eternal snows" ["me précipiter vers toi, mon amour, et clore mon récit par une apothéose. Tout finira dans la splendeur secrète de ton ventre peuplé d'Alpes muqueuses et de neiges éternelles"] (167). And yet, in Aquin's literary production, what follows this first novel hardly resembles that imagined apotheosis. Instead of that final exalting episode, we find in the three novels that follow a number of *next* episodes. Instead of the splendor of those "eternal snows," Aquin's subsequent writings bring us finally, in 1974, to the dark snows of his last novel, *Neige noire*.[16] And while in *Prochain épisode* the north that beckoned to K was only a city in Belgium or northwestern Germany,[17] by the time we get to *Neige noire* the journey has taken Aquin's protagonists far to the north, to the Svalbard archipelago of Norway above the Arctic circle and to a dark tale of a honeymoon voyage that culminates in the woman's murder. Many of the details surrounding Kim's projected journey north to Svalbard in Brossard's novel are so reminiscent of the dark tale of *Neige noire* that the reader finds herself once again reading Brossard and Aquin in palimpsest.[18] Abundant intertextual references position *La capture du sombre* as a return not only to *Prochain épisode* but to *Neige noire*. And it seems clear that the grim scenario of *Neige noire* is the same darkness that Brossard's narrator sets out to capture.

If we read the project of Kim's journey to Svalbard against the scenario of *Neige noire*, however, we first note essential differences, among them the fact that unlike the voyage that culminated in Sylvie's murder, Kim's voyage represents her liberation from sexual violence. Furthermore, her departure, envisioned as a retreat into separation and solitude, turns out to have been ultimately a move towards relationship and community. At the end of the novel, we learn that Kim and June spent two years together in Svalbard, where June finished her film called *Apprendre à sortir d'un paysage*, before they returned to Switzerland. We find them in the novel's final chapter sipping tea with Anne and Tatiana and watching the northern lights.

It is tempting to consider the passage through the north as part of the apprenticeship that helps Brossard's female characters step out of the *impossible landscape* of Aquin's Switzerland. In the end, the narrator notes that

Tatiana had quickly understood that the landscape no longer belonged to us. She was slowly preparing to leave that place ... The landscape had begun to fail me as well. It was eluding my thoughts and my desires. I would not be able to continue much longer to talk about this scenery that we would all soon be leaving behind.

[Tatiana avait tôt compris que le paysage ne nous appartenait plus. Elle se préparait lentement à sortir des lieux … À moi aussi le paysage avait commencé à faire défaut. Il se soustrayait à mes pensées et à mes désirs. Je ne pourrais plus continuer longtemps à parler de ce décor dont nous allions bientôt tous sortir.] (128)

But ultimately what will it mean to step out of this landscape? What kind of vision is this? The north evoked at the end of Brossard's novel contains both a stark vision of a dystopian future under the shadow of the threat of global war and planetary destruction (summed up in the reference to the fact that "*[t]he war is still raging over the Northwest Passage*" [in English in the original]) and the seeds of a more utopian vision associated with the gathered women watching the northern lights ("We could still, with our dazzled eyes, embrace the darkness of the nights of the Northern Hemisphere" ["Il nous était encore possible d'étreindre de nos yeux éblouis le noir des nuits de l'hémisphère Nord"] [140]). In that final scene of women gathered to watch the aurora borealis there is the suggestion of a darkness made into or out of light: "the capture of the dark" [*la capture du sombre*].

The closing words of the book could have been written by Aquin: "I dare not write: I am petrified fossil in the position of combat" ["Je n'ose pas écrire: je suis figée fossile dans la position du combat"] (140). But we cannot ignore how the previous sentence ("I am everywhere where I am" ["Je suis partout où je suis"]), a refrain that is pure Brossard, might suggest a way out, or around, or through, allowing us to read some Brossardian hope into the insistent Aquinian ambiguity of that final declaration.[19]

Author's note:

I am grateful to the graduate students with whom I had the pleasure of exploring *La capture du sombre* in my 2007 seminar on the Contemporary Quebec Novel. Their perceptive questions and observations enhanced my understanding of Brossard's novel. I also want to acknowledge the work of Giulio Bonacucina, a student in my 2008 graduate course "Écrire l'Amérique," whose seminar paper on the literary *topos* of Switzerland in the novels of Aquin and Brossard nicely complements my own work on these novels.

Notes

1 All translations are the author's.

2 In Aquin: "Cuba goes down **in flames** in the middle of Lake Geneva while I **sink** into **the depths** of things. Encased in my sentences, I **glide**, a phantom, into the neurotic **waters** of the river and in **my drifting** I uncover the underside of surfaces and **the inverted image** of the Alps … I have **time** to **ramble** in peace … No distraction can be substituted for the **clockwork** precision of **my obsession**" ["Cuba coule **en flammes** au milieu du lac Léman pendant que je **descends** au **fond** des choses. Encaissé dans mes phrases, je **glisse**, fantôme, dans **les eaux** névrosées du fleuve et je découvre, dans **ma dérive**, le dessous des surfaces et **l'image renversée** des Alpes … j'ai **le temps** de **divaguer** en paix … Nulle distraction ne peut donc se substituer à **l'horlogerie** de **mon obsession**"] (5).

In Brossard: "I look often at the time on my **watch**. Sometimes I happen to catch there in the luminous **depths** of the watchface the **reflection** of my eyes. Since yesterday, something has **slipped** into **my thoughts** and modified **the course of time** … A way of **avoiding** short circuits in my mother tongue, perhaps also of **fleeing** … I want **to plunge** into the landscape of a provisional world … I am also writing this book in order not to be gentle and to see the horizon of **conflagration** coming" ["Je regarde souvent l'heure à **ma montre**. Il m'arrive d'y surprendre dans le fin **fond** lumineux du cadran **le reflet** de mes yeux. Depuis hier, quelque chose **s'est glissé** dans **mes pensées** qui a modifié **le cours du temps** … Une manière d'**éviter** des courts-circuits dans ma langue maternelle, peut-être aussi de **fuir** … je veux **plonger** dans le paysage d'un monde provisoire … J'écris aussi ce livre pour

ne pas être douce et pour voir venir l'horizon des **incendies**"] (5).

3 Some etymologies attribute the expression to the fact that there *were* virtually no castles in the countryside in Spain at the time of the Moorish conquest.

4 The seat of international diplomacy and law (the Geneva Convention) was also the headquarters of revolutionary organizations like Algeria's Front de Libération Nationale (FLN).

5 Non-Swiss writers buried in this literary Valhalla include Greene, Borges, Joyce, Rilke, Hesse, and Nabokov.

6 The Switzerland inhabited by their protagonists evokes and shares the literary landscapes inscribed in the travels and works of Balzac, Byron, Hesse, Kafka, Borges, Musset, Rousseau, Simenon, Necker, de Staël, Constant, Ramuz, Rilke, Hugo, and others.

7 "Depuis hier" sends us back to *Hier*; "modifier le cours du temps" has echoes of *Le désert mauve* and *Baroque d'aube*. For a discussion of these two Brossardian syntagmas see my analyses in *Archaeologies* (213–15, 172, 265) and *Incriminations* (176–8).

8 The presence of so many intertexts from twentieth-century Quebec literature might further argue for reading Brossard's literary sojourn in Switzerland as reflecting on Quebec literary history.

9 Brossard's 2007 *La capture du sombre* is set in the present moment, clearly recognizable in references to the activities of the lawyer Laure who pores over articles about September 11th (27) and who "plunges into the analysis of each word of the Patriot Act" ["se plonge dans l'analyse de chaque mot de l'Acte du Patriote"] (13). This contemporary context invites us to read the novel as documenting Nicole Brossard's twenty-first century.

10 As I will suggest in the next section,

the pivotal figure of Aquin's K (assimilated by Patricia Smart in one of the earliest critiques of the novel to the province itself, "Kébec" [Smart, 1973]) and her avatar Kim in Brossard's novel further justify such a reading.

11 Furthermore, one is tempted to see a (bilingual) connection between the name of Kim's lover (June) and Aquin's persistent references to "a certain *June* 24th" ["un certain 24 *juin*"].

12 The signs of lesbian desire are inscribed in "under tongue" ["sous la langue"] (recalling Brossard's so-named 1987 volume of lesbian erotic poetry) and in the felicitous choice of the word *emmielé* (that I have translated as *honeywoven*) which carries both the sweetness of honey (*miel* in French) and the echoes of the near homonym *emmêlé* (tangled or knotted).

13 Patricia Smart identified this disparity as early as 1987 in her article in *Canadian Literature*. For a more elaborate analysis of the place of women's writing in Quebec literary tradition see also her 1988 book *Écrire dans la maison du père*. Her 2001 article "When 'Next Episodes' Are No Longer an Option" also suggests a move beyond the Aquinian paradigms.

14 It would be interesting to explore further the significance of replacing Cuba (in the 1965 text) with Beirut (in the 2007 text).

    The conditional of the preceding paragraph is also beckoning towards a future while already past, but grammatical convention compels us to read that future as circumscribed within that past intentional moment. The *présent recomposé* suggests the tantalizing possibility of reconstructing the present moment in an as yet unrealized future.

15 René Lapierre makes this point most convincingly in his description of

Aquin's last novel: "More than any other Aquinian novel, *Neige noire* belongs to silence, to violence, and to the sacred. But far from being an apotheosis, this novel represents, rather, the final instance of a dissolution of the novelistic that, ever since *Prochain épisode,* has been moving in the direction of the total collapse of speech" (151).

16 "During this time, K was somewhere in the Hanseatic fog in Antwerp or Bremen" ["Pendant ce temps, K se trouvait quelque part dans la brume hanséatique à Anvers ou Brême"] (153).

17 Both novels include a filmmaking project, an implication of incest, and a scene of lesbian lovers.

18 One also notes the provocative form of the final sentence with its ambiguous colon. It is unclear whether the narrator is in fact *petrified* ["figée"] and therefore cannot write or whether the narrator dares not write the phrase, *I am petrified* ["je suis figée"], a more equivocal affirmation. The emphasis on the act of writing as capable of constructing a reality recalls and echoes Brossard's celebrated declaration that "To write I am a woman is full of consequences" ["Écrire je suis une femme est plein de conséquences"]. Many of the essays in the 2005 collection edited by Louise H. Forsyth explicitly address Brossard's relationship to the act of writing. See especially Forsyth's own introductory essay, "To Write: In the Feminine Is Heavy with Consequences."

Works Cited

Aquin, Hubert. *Neige noire*. Ottawa: Le cercle du livre de France, 1978 [1974].

– *Point de fuite*. Montreal: Le cercle du livre de France, 1971.

– *Prochain épisode*. Édition critique établie

par Jacques Allard. Montreal: Bibliothèque québécoise, 1995 [Ed. Pierre
Tisseyre 1965].

Brossard, Nicole. *La capture du sombre*.
Ottawa: Leméac éditeur, 2007.

– *Elle serait la première phrase de mon
prochain roman. She Would Be the First
Sentence of My Next Novel*. Toronto:
Mercury Press, 1998.

Cagnon, Maurice. "Palimpsest in the Writings of Hubert Aquin." *Modern Language
Studies* 8.2 (Spring 1978): 80–9.

Forsyth, Louise, ed. *Nicole Brossard. Essays on Her Works*. Toronto: Guernica
Editions, 2005.

Jameson, Fredric. "Euphorias of Substitution: Hubert Aquin and the Political Novel in Quebec." *Yale French Studies* 65
(1983): 214–23.

Jeanneret, Sylvie. "La Suisse, lieu impossible. Les autres mondes dans *Prochain
épisode* du Québécois Hubert Aquin."
*Variations: Literaturzeitschrift der Uni-
versität Zürich* June 2001: 41–52.

Lapierre, René. *L'imaginaire captif : Hubert Aquin: essai*. Montreal: L'hexagone,
1991.

McPherson, Karen. *Archaeologies of an
Uncertain Future: Recent Generations
of Canadian Women Writing*. Montreal:
McGill-Queen's University Press, 2006.

– *Incriminations: Guilty Women / Telling
Stories*. Princeton, NJ: Princeton University Press, 1994.

Smart, Patricia. *Écrire dans la maison du
père: L'émergence du féminin dans la
tradition littéraire du Québec*. Montreal:
Québec/Amérique, 1988.

– *Hubert Aquin, agent double. La dialectique de l'art et du pays dans* Prochain
épisode *et* Trou de mémoire. Montreal:
PUM, 1973.

– "When 'Next Episodes' Are No Longer an
Option: Quebec Men's Writing in a Post-
feminist, Postnationalist Age." *Québec
Studies* 30 (fall–winter 2000–01):
28–43.

– "Woman as Object, Women as Subjects,
and the Consequences for Narrative:
Hubert Aquin's *Neige noire* and the
Impasse of Post-modernism." *Canadian
Literature* (summer/autumn 1987):
168–78.

Je m'en vais à Trieste (excerpt)

NICOLE BROSSARD

RER/Roissy-Paris
5 March 1996

wet limbs offered and withheld
of plane trees and passersby
some graffiti like children doubled over
bright-colored words that labor
from below to help us escape gravity's grasp (19)

Toulouse
Notre-Dame Dalbade
One morning in 1996

no doubt the man by himself holds
the noise of the sea at arm's length
by knee blows
claps of storm sounds painful blows
in his rocker's, dreamer's chest
no doubt he is playing
the mad organist thief of pink morning (21)

Lyon
December 1999

strolling eating in Lyon
always with a poem on the tip of the tongue
strolling in Lyon and its cold

before Christmas and the decorations strolling
in the gray of thoughts and of the old
images of war and of the bourgeoisie
strolling while thinking of Louise Labé
strolling cannibal devouring the poem
and the carnival moment
strolling while speaking in the gloom
the solitude of the poem (81)

Paris
RER, 10:10, 2001

in October the vegetation covers up
the graffiti again. In Drancy
the world is wrapped in vines and perennials
Africa settles into the gaze of women
in the time for a stop
the continent has fled
in a parked car (119)

Place des Vosges
24 March 2002, 12:15

there is always an excess of life
that makes us lose
balance
eyes riveted by the first buds
you like a sponge absorbing April
its equatorial heat
under the palm and skin, life (129)

Translations by Miléna Santoro

Chez Nous: Gail Scott's *My Paris*

LORNA IRVINE

I knew, when I decided to write about Gail Scott's wonderfully evocative *My Paris*, that I had a difficult task in front of me. Scott's work, like that of the writer Walter Benjamin, whom Scott greatly admires, cannot be casually summarized nor, I might add, comprehensively analyzed. It is generically slippery. The author calls this text a novel. Yet the unnamed narrator's diary-like entries do not add up to what we usually think of as a story, nor do the references to friends and acquaintances, identified only by single capital letters, establish conventional characters. In her essay "A Visit to Canada," Scott tells us that, while she wants to write stories, she is not at all interested in constructing traditional, linear plots. Like Gertrude Stein, whose initials she shares, she experiments with language and grammar and, while recognizing the importance of past and present communities (Spaces 75), believes conventional history to be patriarchal. Her focus is on the gaps, the spaces, that such history glaringly reveals. Here, Scott argues, resides the feminine, the voice of which can necessarily be represented only in the sparsest of language. As well, if women are to find a speaking and a seeing suited to their own needs, all genres of literature – poetry, journal entries, theory and so on – necessarily must participate in the constructing of the female story. They must evoke the specificities of space and time, paying particular attention to the author's own experience, captured by Scott in the repetition of the expression *chez nous*, usually a reference to Canada in general, but sometimes to Scott's own background, for instance in Montreal or in the west of Canada. Thus the references to her "scraggly North American look" (33) situate her as an outsider in Paris. At other places, *chez nous* implies the smallness of the late twentieth-century world, where all of us are necessarily implicated, for example, in the conflict in Bosnia. Throughout *My Paris*, references to the weather in Bosnia empha- size such connections.

Scott's texts, and *My Paris* in particular, are dense, frequently requiring vertical, as well as horizontal reading and, as the opening of this text demonstrates, including visual images as well as words. Textual boundaries are thus complicated, denying generic specificity to a particular work. Furthermore, Scott's writing seems always in progress. For example, in the summer 1994 edition of *Books in Canada*, the author published "There's No Such Thing as Repetition," a reference to Gertrude Stein. It is designated a short novel (it's two and a half pages in length, thus raising questions about its categorization as a novel), and is written in Paris. In the introduction, the author, who shortly merges with the unnamed central character of the novel, mentions earlier twentieth-century writers such as Hemingway, Stein, Baldwin, and Proust and, in the novel, adds to these names references to nineteenth-century novels of Paris, and to major thinkers such as Marx and Wittgenstein. The overwhelming presence of the conflict in Bosnia reminds the narrator and thus the reader of the significance of world events on people not directly involved, making of the *chez nous* more or less the whole world. Language and memory carry traces of the past and haunt the various Parisian spaces that the late twentieth-century observer seeks to represent. The observed Paris is also a "projection" of the character's own Quebec culture (*chez nous*), influencing her awareness of racism "and other crimes of indifference" (9); she mentions, for example, the Montreal shooting of Anthony Griffin by a policeman acquitted by an all-white jury. Such juxtapositions surely aim for emotional illumination. There is also horizontal movement. The main character walks the streets of Paris; for her, as for Walter Benjamin, whose name does not appear in this piece but who suffuses *My Paris*, walking turns her into a *flâneuse*, continuing, with a difference, into the late twentieth century, a mode of observation used by Benjamin to connect himself, a man of the early twentieth century, with a disappearing nineteenth century.

Scott also packs in references that reappear in *My Paris*, to the traces of wars and revolutions, to the squalid lives of the contemporary poor, but also, in sharp contrast, to Paris's art, to the romanticized beauty of the Seine. She experiments with the voice of the narration, telling her readers that "the narrator can no longer be a single notion" because a work of art must absorb the reader "into the vortex of the author's vision" (11). Such seduction confuses narrative boundaries and complicates critical objectivity, confusions demonstrated, for example, in Jorge Luis Borges's parable, "Borges and Myself," which begins: "The other one, the one called Borges, is the one things happen to. I walk through the streets of Buenos Aires and stop for a moment, perhaps mechanically now, to look at the arch of an entrance hall, and the grillwork on the gate; I know of Borges from the mail and see his name on a list of professors or in a biographical dictionary." And so the parable continues, ending with the statement: "I do not know which of us has written this page" (*Labyrinths* 246–7).

The fickleness of categories is demonstrated in *My Paris* where an opening section, "Narrator on Author," introduces the author who, the narrator tells us, displays a postcard of a "Saltimbanque" – a circus performer, a wandering acrobat. This card draws attention to wandering, performance, the visual, and so on, all themes in *My Paris*. Most important, the equation of narrator and author connects them in the ensuing text; both inhabit the Parisian "faux-deco studio" where the narrator lives. The other opening piece is a picture of naked female mannequins modeling laced and unlaced boots. The one closest to us wears a wild wig of dark hair, while another, bending over with her back to us, has her hair carefully coifed in a dark roll. In the center of the picture the image of a live woman dressed in shorts and a top and sporting short dark hair smiles coyly. The words sprinkled around suggest Parisian window displays; thus are introduced commerce and female bodies, the latter seen in pieces, demonstrating Scott's conviction that "many women have a sense of being already fragmented. Alienated by male fictions" (*Spaces* 62). Scott is clearly recalling here the gendered nature of commodification and consumption that became increasingly evident, as noted by Benjamin, from the nineteenth century onwards.

As the journal entries begin in *My Paris*, the narrator temporarily situates herself in an extended literary tradition: "Like a Heroine from Balzac. I am on a divan" (11). In this room is a 1,000-page volume, Walter Benjamin's *Paris, Capital of the Nineteenth Century*, the intertextual use of which profoundly affects the movement, images and philosophy of the daily diary that the narrator keeps. Like Benjamin, she creates illuminating contrasts and concordances through juxtaposition; unlike him, she mostly paraphrases the ideas of other writers rather than directly quoting. She often refers to Benjamin's work:

Waking today wondering why B. In montage method he using for huge Paris history. Juxtaposing *Les noms des rues*, Paris street names section. On *Prostitution* chapter. It making perfect sense to abut *Mode* and *Passages*, arcades … On second look. It not *Les noms des rues de Paris*, Paris street names. But simply *Les rues de Paris*, Paris streets. Juxtaposed on *Prostitution* chapter. Association banal to point of prurient. Given it implying. Any (female) walker. Possibly on way to sexual market. Which banality seemingly contesting. Alleged objectivity of history-montage method. Wherein author saying nothing. Only endlessly ... conjuncting. Facts and anecdotes. For purpose of shocking unconscious knowing. Into realm of conscious recognition.

But can unconscious. Be trusted. (27)

Here, Scott's method is dramatically illustrated. Her contemporary "street-walker" understands the deeply unconscious control that gender has, as well as the profound effects of language. Space illustrates gendering; the narrator returns from her walks to an apartment with curved walls as pale as eggshells. The dining table is round. Scott also demonstrates the performative nature of gender and sexual orientation, avoiding Cartesian ways of thinking, describing cross-dressing, "sexual bi-ambivalence" (46), transsexuality and so on.

One can quickly get lost in the avenues opened up in this novel. Let me turn, then, to a particular internal narrative that I'll introduce by way of a reference to Anne Friedberg's *Window-Shopping: Cinema and the Postmodern*. Friedberg uses the term *flâneuse* to draw attention to the "gendering of power and visuality" (2) marked by a figure "strikingly absent from accounts of modernity" but involved with the "transformation of gender in post-modernity" (9): "the female urban subject." In *My Paris*, the female post-modern urban subject (the narrator) focuses on the changing displays in the window of an expensive men's shop across the road from her apartment. In some nineteen or twenty progressive entries that cover the narrator's time in Paris, these ever-changing displays demonstrate Scott's montage method. In the initial entry the narrator vaguely notes people bending over to look at the suited mannequins in the window opposite, but a week later, she herself carefully observes the "exquisitely stitched collars" (22), the reflection of the meridian strip in the window, and the "green-clad worker[s] from [the] 'south'" who are cleaning up the dog shit outside the shop. Through association, the "shock" of conflicting images focuses attention on class and race. Two weeks later, as her involvement with Paris grows, she introduces suspense, noting, as she looks at the window, "something strange going on there!" (33). Having just observed a young man whose back is scored with "large deep scars," the narrator sees one of the expensively suited mannequins, his arms in a "knife-sharp cuff," gesturing "magnanimously" to the other and imagines a coded male narrative. In

Spaces Like Stairs, Scott comments on her need to subvert narrative form in order to write stories "shaped" like herself (*Spaces* 67), a female engendered narrative; she mentions spheres ("a nice feminine shape to take off from"), and the need to avoid "linear time, that cause-and-effect time of patriarchal logic" (*Spaces* 70). Added to other observations, then, is this entry's attention to the gendering of narrative.

The entries become more pressing. The narrator observes one of the faceless mannequins on his feet, his hand resting on the dark-wood bench on which he had formerly been sitting. An employee comes out to wash the display windows, a woman in black sits at a bus stop, an ad features an "Indian" in a headdress (39); class, gender and race thus extend and comment on the display. Increasingly graphic (it's now day forty-one), the window features a masculine arithmetic, a "geometric green chair shaped like a Z" (53), standing on edge and surrounded by "neat diagonal rows of shiny shoes" (44). In the adjoining window lies a clown-like patchwork jacket, emphasizing fashionable poverty, expensive materials aping poorer cloth (linen burlap, brute silk). The narrator is reminded of the magic glow, commented on by Marx and Benjamin, the aura of the surrealists' found objects with their diminished exchange value. The day is beautiful, though the narrator is mindful of pollution, an environmental theme that runs throughout *My Paris*. Elsewhere she remarks about being always conscious of the "huge Western I [a possible allusion to Joseph Conrad's novel, *Under Western Eyes*] casting unecological shadow over the earth" (123). Here, the *nous* (*chez nous*) becomes the ego, the "I," refusing Westerners' escape from individual responsibility by joining with the implied collective *nous*.

The window continues to be transformed. By day forty-nine, the chair in the middle window is turned around and tipped up, while in the window at the right, a stuffed brown suit cut wide in the legs and jacket leans on the chair's back. Now, in the left window, a tiny house on a bed of straw appears, reminding readers of the children's classic story, "The Three Little Pigs," in which the house made of straw collapses when blown at by the big bad wolf. The narrator reflects: "House, shoes, stuffed suit. Do they add up to a narrative" (65). This allusion is to the controlling patriarchal narrative that Scott has set herself against. At a later point, she mentions her "tedium vitae" that, as suggested in Benjamin's "Boredom, Eternal Return," is perhaps encouraged by the weather; it allows her to daydream, jumping from thoughts of Sherlock Holmes by his fire, a cosy, nineteenth-century male subject, to the architect, le Corbusier, from whose "contemporary city," Benjamin tells us, we must "secure a foothold ... from which to cast a productive glance, a-form-and-distance-creating glance, on the nineteenth century" (Benjamin 407). Yet this twentieth-century female narrator has a hard time getting back to a cozy, nineteenth-century masculine subject and her contemporary ponderings are juxtaposed with television images of poor families from the south being expelled from their squats.

And so this odd window narrative continues, the male figures watched by the female narrator. In another entry, a standing brown-suited mannequin appears, respectable and ordinary, except that, emerging from the cuffs, are "2 red paper hands," perhaps, thinks the narrator, "bloody from strangling" (79). As in the repeated references to her pursuit of a publisher for a little book on wandering murdered women, the window display is a reminder of the violence threatening the contemporary *flâneuse* and harks back to the idealized patriarchal family in which violence is often disguised by the ordinary. A list of prominently displayed prices emphasizes contemporary consumption. On day seventy-five, just after the narrator sees her own reflection "mirrored in passing" in succeeding boutique windows (a doubling that picks up on Benjamin's broken pronoun "I"), she interprets the rubber heads in the men's store as "decadently eyeballing each other" (97), suggesting some kind of sexual performance. Another day, one of the suits is wrapped like a mummy in a brightly striped scarf that connects the narrator with a recent movie she has seen of women pigeon-holed in Paris's best female prison. In these various displays, the narrator focuses on sexuality, violence, power, and imprisonment, themes that cohere in the word "Sarajevo," jolting the reader out of Paris to the wider stage of world politics and war.

There follows a series on the dog portraits that appear in the display, introduced by the narrator's paranoia and, as always, thematically developed in her surroundings. On the street, a mad blind woman sits on a bench, the whites of her eyes appearing to watch, just as the dog portraits seemed to be watching the narrator. Later, waiting to hear whether she has won a literary award for which she was nominated, she looks at the window again, this time seeing two "black wide-lapelled suits" (136) with white shirts under the jackets, sitting in a civilized fashion, perhaps looking forward to a celebration. Gulls and the snow reflect the window's black and white theme; as so often, the visual image also branches out to include a mental image of snow falling in Sarajevo, as if the whole northern part of the world were connected by the exigencies of weather.

The final movements – perhaps it is possible to think of the window narrative as a sort of musical symphony – first present the two mannequins dressed in black leather jackets worn over well-cut suits. Now that it is late fall, the display shows a field of "sparsely sown apples" and, on the window itself, there's a poem. The narrator comments on the spaces between the otherwise dead words, reminding readers of the importance Scott places on spaces. The window seems "vacuous" (144), like the day, until the world around her bursts into a rapid series of exchanges – with drunks, homosexuals, sexist cops – the poor sharply contrasted with the exquisite opera house where tickets, the narrator thinks, cost "more than food for a week" (144).

The last entry in the body of *My Paris* focuses on time. On the right, a perfectly sleeved male hand rises out of a pile of colored papers, holding a tiny clock. On the left, a standing headless mannequin, in dark pants and "shirred purple vest," points toward it. The narrator's time in Paris is up and she leaves the same day, arriving at its end in Montreal. Nonetheless, the final word of this part of *My Paris* is Bosnia (152), a country still heavily weighing on the narrator's mind and conscience.

But there is an addendum, "Le Sexe de l'art," six and a half pages written on the New Year's Eve just before the narrator leaves Paris. Sexually intense, imbued with emotions that seem absent from the earlier text, these pages are totally woman-centered. The reiteration of images of mist and fog, and the sense of drifting, waiting, of malaise, create a liminal effect – the in-between-ness that evokes the sense of the uncanny – mentioned but not dramatized earlier. Here, the narrator makes a startling discovery: a black, lacy, calf-length dress has replaced the men's suits that have dominated the window throughout the narrator's time in Paris. What does this shift suggest? In this short section, with all her senses "feasting" (*Books in Canada* 10), the narrator dramatizes the unconscious control of sexuality, the objects, spaces and themes that have appeared throughout, now pulsating with her own female desire. The masculine window narrative, translated into the feminine, demonstrates such unconscious control. The two texts come together as New Year's Day begins. In a taxi on her way to the airport, she passes through the Luxembourg Garden, where she sees actors fasting about the war in Sarajevo, observes the "dissatisfied" suburbs, and watches a woman handing out pamphlets about the plight of Bosnian women who are living in a chaotic state of war.

It is through an accumulating conjunction of associations that Scott's work develops its power. She creates evocative disjunctions among conventionally opposed categories: present and past; rich and poor; male and female; writer and layperson; stasis and change; black and white; nineteenth and twentieth centuries; old world and new world, and so on. Her late twentieth-century *flâneuse* understands Benjamin's threshold, that "ideal site for projecting past (dream). Into present (real). And reverse. Producing. Through shock of encounter. Spark of illumination. Which dialectic movement. Actually deep kernel. Of montage history method" (59). The narrator/author transgresses the boundaries between self and other; she experiments with confusing actor and spectator, situating herself, as one critic points out, "at the intersection of the real and textual worlds" (Sojka 158). An English writer, profoundly influenced by the French both in Paris and Quebec, Scott writes: "longing, often, when I read the women novelists of my culture, for a more sensual rapport between writer and her female subjects: for more soft cheeks, for the gracious curves of arms. Longing perhaps for writing that shows its love for women, hence for self as female. Or maybe longing to close the gap between mind and (female) body: in that sense, that space between narrator and story in the English novel as we know it. Longing to 'write with the body'" (*Spaces* 21). This merging she has evocatively accomplished in *My Paris*.

Works Cited

Benjamin, Walter. *The Arcades Project.* Trans. Howard Eiland and Kevin McLaughlin. Cambridge and London: The Belknap Press, 1999.

Borges, Jorge Luis. *Labyrinths: Selected Stories and Other Writings.* USA: New Directions Publishing, 1962.

Friedberg, Anne. *Window Shopping: Cinema and the Postmodern.* Berkeley: University of California Press, 1993.

Scott, Gail. *My Paris.* Toronto: The Mercury Press, 1999.

– *Spaces Like Stairs.* Toronto: The Women's Press, 1989.

– "There's No Such Thing as Repetition." *Books in Canada* 22.5. Summer 1994. 8–11.

Sojka, Eugenia. "Carnivalization in the Post-Colonial Texts of Lola Lemire Tostevin and Gail Scott: Questions of Language and Identity." In *Cultural Identities in Canadian Literature.* Ed. Bénédicte Mauguière. New York: Peter Lang Publishers, 1998. 153–61.

My Paris (excerpt)

GAIL SCOTT

———————————

108. Yesterday visiting *three* of those old commercial passages or arcades.
B calling Ur-forms of 20th. Presaging shopping malls. As fussily intimate.
As old régime interiors. On entering – getting sense for first time – of 19th
living conditions. Eternal cold and dankness rising up from tiles. Under
grey light. From overhead sooty glass-and-iron roof. Filtering melancholy. That "humour" of 19th. Contemporaneously treated as pathologi-
cal. People sitting in small cosy-looking-but-in-reality-unheated. Boutiques
and offices …

Anyway coming down Haussmann. Windy as chez nous. Shivering.
Despite leather jacket. Over heavy sweater. Under blue short man's rain-
coat. Entering café …

Sipping Pernod. Then out again. Past scaffolded façade. Of PASSAGE
DES PRINCES. Renovated to virtual-reality arcade. Featuring holographs.
Robots. Cyberboats. Neuron nests. Marking end of time as we knowing it.

Right on Montmartre. Into narrow still intact early 19th PASSAGE DES
PANORAMAS. Faded curved corridor. Silver palm branches. Meeting in middle. Disappointed eye. Taking in cemented-over floor mosaics. In front of
boutique entrances. Effacing names of original proprietors. Only GRAVEUR
STERN DEPUIS 1840 still writ in tiny tiles. Before door of Stern family business. Also painted-over wood-carved or metalwork boutique façades. Separated by yellow marble columns. Running up between. Though pretty
Salon du Thé. Maintaining original floral wood-finished front. Where long
skirts or redingotes of early 19th Parisians. Coming to escape mud. Racket.
Of narrow streets outside. Relaxing behind newspapers. Before shopping
for tobacco. Perfumes. Cashmere shawls from imperially exotic Egypt. Or
stepping into panoramas or rotundas. On each side of passage entrance.
Which rotundas. Wrapping spectator round in painted scenes of history.
Womb-like. Secure. Making one feel present. Yet at safe distance. From
some famous battle. Or invention.

Exiting. Crossing boulevard Montmartre. Entering PASSAGE JOUF-
FROY. Mocking faces of MUSÉE GRÉVIN, wax museum, window. Staring
cheerily as passers. Strolling toward huge clock at end of hall. With HÔTEL
CHOPIN written under. Male couple coming out. Corridor jogging left. Past
poster shops. Gay postcards. Stamps. Engravings. Kept by idealists left over
from '70s. Smoking. Freezing. Beyond Jouffroy. More obscure PASSAGE
VERDEAU. Surreal mannequin head on awning. Same outdated objects.
Stamps. Presses. Secondhand cameras. Same restaurant cold and dampness.
These labyrinths. Jogging to left. To right. In muddling 19th-century way.
Like train. Like English way of thinking. Gertrude Stein saying. (118–19)

Transatlantic Reading in the Works of France Théoret

KAREN L. GOULD

Fictional readers are literary subjects who engage in the act of reading in novels we read. Like all readers, they read and interpret words, images, and narrative elements that may or may not seem familiar, that may align closely or not at all with their own personal and cultural experience. Their motivations for reading vary and may play an important role in how they understand and interpret what they read. They read to discover and evaluate human experience, and sometimes they are transformed by the texts they encounter. Reading may spur creativity in fictional characters, inspire self-reflection, or lead them to incorporate what they read in myriad ways.

When we read novels in which protagonists engage in the act of reading, we discover literary intersections and intertexts that add new layers of meaning to the primary text. Through the mirrored act of reading, the text we read leads us to another (inter)text, which we consider through the interpretation of another (fictional) reader. If the act of reading in a work of literature is sufficiently developed, we may also analyze the impact of reading on both character and narrative development. As Lucie Hotte notes, "in the act of reading, the reader creates connections between the text being read by the fictional character and the text the reader is considering. The text read by the fictional character thus becomes the reference through which the novel will be experienced in the construction of meaning" (Hotte 69).[1]

Among the major themes spanning Quebec writer France Théoret's extensive literary corpus, *the act of reading* can be traced from her earliest texts to more recent novels, essays, and journal writing. As Théoret emphasizes in *Journal pour mémoire* (1993), reading the works of others has played a significant role in her intellectual development and creative growth as a writer: "I would be completely incapable of living without reading. I need new reading experiences to orient myself. Reading allows me to be modern. For me, books are essential" ["Je serais bien incapable de vivre sans la lecture. Il me faut de nouvelles lectures pour m'orienter. La lecture me permet d'être contemporaine. Les livres me sont essentiels"] (224).

This essay considers the role of reading subjects, the significance of the act of reading, and the impact of transatlantic intertexts in France Théoret's historical novel, *Laurence* (1996), and in her semi-autobiographical novel, *Huis clos entre jeunes filles* (2000). In both *Laurence* and *Huis clos entre jeunes filles*, the protagonist-as-reader constitutes a major literary theme that propels the narrative forward and establishes specific contexts for interpreting meaning in each novel. For Laurence and for the unnamed narrator-protagonist in *Huis clos entre jeunes filles*, the act of reading is in fact closely tied to each protagonist's psychological, intellectual, and moral development as well as to additional thematic tensions that undergird the novels. What the protagonists read, how and why they read, the fictional worlds they explore, and the narrator's perspective on the protagonist-as-reader are essential narrative elements for the construction of meaning in Théoret's texts.

The fictionalized reading experiences in *Laurence* and *Huis clos entre jeunes filles* also introduce important transatlantic intertexts that familiarize Théoret's protagonists with historical, political, and cultural realities previously unknown to them. The literary encounter with Victor Hugo's *Les misérables* in *Laurence* and with Virgil Gheorghiu's *La vingt-cinquième heure* in *Huis clos entre jeunes filles* position the act of reading in each novel as a crucial site of psychological refuge, cultural discovery, and female self-affirmation. These embedded literary encounters establish important links to European history and transatlantic culture, extending the reach of Théoret's novels well beyond the provincial and cultural borders of modern Quebec.

As outlined by Lucie Hotte (2001) and further underscored by André Lamontagne (2004), the appearance of characters who are fictional readers can be found throughout modern and contemporary Quebec fiction, in the works of writers as diverse as Roger Lemelin, Antoine Gérin-Lajoie, Réjean Ducharme, Gérard Bessette, Hubert Aquin, Jacques Poulin, Régine Robin, Nicole Brossard, Dany Laferrière, and others. However, unlike Laferrière's worldly protagonist in *Comment faire l'amour avec un Nègre sans se fatiguer,* who enjoys boasting about the numerous authors he has read,[2] the young female protagonists in *Laurence* and *Huis clos entre jeunes filles* are insecure, impressionable readers who seek in books what their strict religious training and conservative family upbringing have failed to provide. For them, reading becomes a daring, transformative act of moral identification, cultural discovery, and personal defiance. Both protagonists connect what they read to their own lived experience and to the broader world beyond their local circumstance. In addition, *Huis clos entre jeunes filles* places heightened emphasis on the act of reading as *the* site of cultural critique, disorientation, and personal transformation: "I was reading a story that confused my points of reference and exposed their limited scope ... Events similar to those in the novel had occurred and I was discovering them" ["Je lisais un récit qui déroutait mes points de repère et qui dévoilait leur dimension étriquée ... Des événements semblables à ceux du roman avaient eu lieu et je les découvrais"] (HC 100).

Laurence: Reading Hugo in Montreal

Théoret's historical novel, *Laurence* (1996), focuses on women's education and their struggle for independence in Quebec against the backdrop of a culturally dominant Catholic Church, agrarian values of family, faith, and tradition, increasing urban migration, unemployment and poverty, and the changing gender roles of francophone women and men in Montreal from the late 1920s to the mid-1940s. As I have remarked elsewhere, *Laurence* "explores the impact of Quebec's urban migration on the traditional (i.e. patriarchal, catholic, and rural) francophone family as well as on the social construction of gender roles in the city" (Gould 2001, 96).

Having left Catholic schooling at age eleven in order to help with farm work and family responsibilities, Laurence Naud receives support from a local physician and eventually enters a Catholic nursing school in pre-World War II Quebec. Over the course of Laurence's nursing training in Quebec City, the narrator highlights the ignorance and outmoded pedagogies of the nuns who seek to protect young women from knowledge about the outside world. Laurence's real education occurs once she leaves the repressive space of the convent school and convent hospital and begins to aid those who suffer and to engage with the real world.

In *Laurence*, the act of reading and reflecting on Victor Hugo's epic novel, *Les misérables*, functions as a pivotal narrative moment, underscoring the protagonist's psychological need for moral validation and emotional support once she moves to Montreal. A naive reader whose prior training was limited primarily to nursing and religious instruction, Laurence struggles to comprehend the significance of *Les misérables*, oversimplifying the novel's thematic complexities, and mentally rewriting Hugo's ending in order to face her own demons and create a more positive outlook for her future.

Laurence's interest in reading Hugo's novel stems from her desire to become more worldly, to consider what her friend Dr Renoir recommends, and to be inspired by a fictional hero whose circumstance appears to resonate with her own. Although she tackles the reading of Hugo's urban masterpiece with surprising determination, Laurence's lack of literary background or critical training leave her ill-equipped to interpret the historical complexities of Hugo's artistic vision. A keen identification with Jean Valjean as an urban "outsider" leads Laurence to misread and rewrite Hugo's dénouement in order to align it more closely with her own sense of justice.

The psychological and emotional contexts for Laurence's decision to read *Les misérables* are significant. At the doctor's encouragement, she begins Hugo's novel as part of a healing process, reading through the prism of a painful experience that will remain private to all but her physician. Shortly after arriving in Montreal to work as a nurse and live independently, Laurence is raped. Disoriented and ashamed, she seeks help on the street from a passerby who, as it happens, is a French doctor who has relocated to Montreal. Dr Renoir sympathizes with the young woman's plight and takes Laurence to his home for treatment and counseling. There, he introduces her to the story of Jean Valjean, the celebrated hero of *Les misérables*. Laurence identifies with the physician's summary of Jean Valjean's story and especially with the undeserved misery he suffers from stealing bread; she accepts a copy of *Les misérables* as a gift and begins to read it.

An inexperienced and empathetic reader, Laurence shares Jean Valjean's pain. Like him, she has suffered an injustice and conceals a terrible secret. Théoret's narrator observes: "She recognized her kind among *Les misérables*, people who had to rely on themselves, were at the mercy of random violence" (Scott 108) ["Elle se reconnut parmi les misérables qui doivent compter sur eux-mêmes, à la merci de la violence fortuite" (166)]. Knowing only of Hugo's reputation as a great writer, Laurence struggles over several months to read his enormous novel out of a sense of pride, "Victor Hugo seemed to her a giant, a genius. When reading, she felt like the world was new, a world she had never imagined" (Scott 108) ["Victor Hugo lui apparut un géant et un génie. À la lecture, elle naissait à nouveau comme elle n'avait jamais imaginé que cela fût possible" (167)]. Laurence is emotionally moved by Hugo's humanism and captivated by the grand scope of his narrative and by the novel's juxtaposing of the themes of justice and injustice, love and hatred, pleasure and cruelty. Despite her admiration for Hugo, however, she resists the novel's concluding themes of solitude and death and mentally rewrites the last scenes of *Les misérables* to save Jean Valjean from the final poetic death scene. In her alternative ending, the aging Jean Valjean lives a long life, consoles Cosette and Marius, and restores justice. This revision allows Laurence to cling to an enduring notion of happiness: "The idea of enduring happiness, conquered through phenomenal struggle, seemed so legitimate that she corrected the author's error" (Scott 108) ["L'idée d'un bonheur durable, conquis de haute lutte, lui paraissait si légitime qu'elle rétablit l'erreur de l'auteur" (168)].

Reflecting on *Les misérables* thus becomes an empowering act during which Laurence begins to assert her inner voice (and subjecthood) in dialogue with the French literary master: "The end of the novel offered a fresh opportunity for a heart-to-heart with herself. It was no longer Victor Hugo who decided the outcome, but she herself who extended it beyond the end of the novel" (Scott 108–9) ["La fin du roman fut l'occasion d'un nouveau dialogue avec elle-même. Ce n'était plus Victor Hugo qui orientait les enjeux, mais elle qui les prolongeait" (168)]. As a result, Laurence becomes more contemplative about the silence surrounding human suffering. She remembers, for example, the scare of May 1918, the Spanish flu that took so many lives, and the famine that ensued: "The word poverty was taboo, never uttered" (Scott 110) ["Le mot pauvreté restait tabou, le mot ne se prononçait pas" (169)]. As the narrator indicates, reading *Les misérables* enables Laurence to interweave Hugo's epic with reflections on her own family troubles, her longing for paternal love, and her desire for a better future for all those who struggle to live with dignity.

Sociologically speaking, Laurence uses Hugo's "oeuvre-culte" to establish analogies with the world around her and resist the misery and injustice she witnesses. Among other things, reading *Les misérables* awakens Laurence to the realization that the empowered class receives its authority from the masses and that, like Hugo's sinister Javert, authority becomes abusive when the application of justice is confused or unwarranted: "Reading Victor Hugo awakened in her the notion that it was the masses who invested authority with power" (Scott 113) ["La lecture du roman de Victor Hugo l'éveilla à l'idée que les autorités tiraient leur pouvoir de la foule" (174)]. Entering Hugo's fictional world expands the domain of Laurence's experience and deepens her personal convictions: "Her reading of *Les misérables* broadened her mind, made her more principled" (Scott 123) ["La lecture des *Misérables* multiplia ses convictions, augumenta l'angle de ses réflexions" (188)].

In *Laurence*, Hugo's novel functions as a powerful *meta-text*. As the narrator observes, "*Les misérables* was the book of books" (Scott 116)

["*Les misérables* fut le livre qui contenait tous les livres" (179)]. Despite her scant knowledge of the Bible as text, Laurence's Catholic upbringing remains a guiding influence, and the idea of a meta-book is curiously compelling: "For a Catholic, unfamiliar with fairy tales, romance novels, a book had something of the biblical, though she had never read the Bible either. The idea of the Book as something containing the sum total of human experience was always in the back of her mind" (Scott 125) ["Pour une catholique qui n'avait connu ni les contes de fées ni les romans d'amour, il y avait l'enseignement biblique derrière le livre, même si elle n'avait pas lu la Bible. L'idée du Livre qui résume l'ensemble des réalités humaines demeurait une pensée aussi présente que diffuse" (191)]. Once *Les misérables* is completed, Laurence has no desire to read additional works of fiction. Instead, Hugo's famous novel appears to fulfill her need for a narrative capable of providing comfort and hope – including her rewritten ending. Théoret's narrator ironically summarizes: "Laurence had satisfied her curiosity as far as books were concerned. She intuited that no other book would teach her what *Les misérables* had. She had read the Book that contained all other books" (Scott 125–6). ["Laurence avait satisfait sa curiosité quant aux livres. Elle eut l'intuition qu'aucun livre ne lui enseignerait autant que *Les misérables*. Elle avait lu le Livre qui englobait tous les autres" (192)].

As already noted, the protagonist's identification in *Laurence* with Hugo's *Les misérables* produces multiple narrative effects. Most important, the fictionalized act of reading becomes a vehicle for identifying a number of essential human values: love, tolerance, justice, and, when necessary, revolt, which transcend the time and place of Hugo's novel. The cultural and social values Laurence encounters in *Les misérables* challenge the dogmatic "truths" of her religious training and her domineering father. In this sense, Hugo's lengthy narrative helps Laurence confront the conformist dictums of the Catholic school nuns, the blindness of patriarchal thinking, and the inequalities of modern urban life. As in *Les misérables* and the re-envisioned ending that Laurence imagines for it, the concluding scenes of *Laurence* reflect both the continuing conflict between human subjugation and independence and the protagonist's enduring hope for a better future.

Huis clos entre jeunes filles: Reading as Transformation

Published in 2000, France Théoret's semi-autobiographical novel, *Huis clos entre jeunes filles*, shares many of the characteristics of cross-genre "autofiction" (Havercroft 2001). As the book's title and explicit *hommage* to Sartre suggest, *Huis clos entre jeunes filles* depicts the claustrophobic, judgment-driven world of a Catholic convent school outside Montreal where adolescent girls prepare to be teachers during the 1950s. Referencing Sartre's famous existentialist play, *Huis clos* (1944), Théoret's refashioned title calls attention to the gender-marked adaptation of Sartrian concepts, which the narrator pursues thematically when remembering the confining environment of the Catholic girls' school she attended. As in *Laurence*, *Huis clos entre jeunes filles* represents the psychological and intellectual impact of traditional Catholic instruction and boarding school life on generations of Quebec women whose education was dominated by the Catholic Church, prior to the reforms of the Quiet Revolution in the early 1960s.[3]

Constructed as a triptych, *Huis clos entre jeunes filles* begins with a brief section on the narrator's present-tense solitude and awkward encounter with a former acquaintance; in a longer second section, the narrator revisits her adolescent life at a Catholic girls' school; a concluding section includes the narrator's reflections on her present state of mind and emotional outlook. Entering Catholic boarding school at age fifteen, the narrator remembers her resigned silence and passivity in the classroom, "I knew full well my tendency to interrupt listening in order to escape into vague passivity" ["Je connaissais bien ma propension à interrompre mon écoute pour me réfugier dans une vague passivité"] (24). Like Laurence, she recognizes that the religious education she and sixty other school companions received failed to prepare them for the modern world: "My education led me to flee reality" ["Mon éducation m'amenait à fuir la réalité"] (26).

Through serious memory work, the unnamed first-person narrator in *Huis clos entre jeunes filles* considers her lifelong struggle with solitude in search of female independence. As recollections of the Catholic boarding school resurface, she remembers her longing for companionship to ease the loneliness, even as the nuns disapproved of female friendships, discouraging personal alliances that might compete with the authority of God, the Church, and the nuns themselves. In secret defiance of convent authority, the narrator-protagonist hid personal reading material to alleviate boredom in the classroom and escape to other worlds. She remembers as well how Yolande, the *pensionnaire* she most admired, ignored boarding school rules by spending most of her evenings in local jazz clubs. For the most part, however, the narrator recounts how personal desires and non-conformist behavior were continually kept in check, making her struggle to assert independence markedly painful: "The right to my uniqueness, I exerted it despite humiliation and reprimand" ["Le droit à ma singularité, je l'ai exercé en dépit des humiliations et des remontrances"] (14). Here as elsewhere, memory work in Théoret's writing is intimately tied to "the painful search for subjecthood" (Havercroft 39).

In *Huis-clos entre jeunes filles*, readers of modern Quebec fiction will recognize parallels with subject matter developed in Claire Martin's autobiographies, *Dans un gant de fer* (1965) and *La joue droite* (1966), which influenced a generation of Quebec women writers, including France Théoret, as she notes in *Journal pour mémoire* (104). Marie-Claire Blais also explored the somber realities of convent education, albeit more satirically, in *Une saison dans la vie d'Emmanuel* (1965) and *Manuscrits de Pauline Archange* (1968).[4]

Acknowledging the transformative power of the literary experience, the narrator of *Huis clos entre jeunes filles* reflects on the importance of reading and the influence of writers who challenge dominant ideas of family, religion, and cultural milieu. The recurring image of spatial confinement is thus contrasted with the expansive ideas of authors she has read: "The sense of being under protection, confined in advance to pre-determined spaces, is a condition. This feeling horrified me, I shook the walls in violent resistance to my confinement. Many authors needed to be examined. From them I borrowed ideas I couldn't find in my surroundings" ["Le sentiment d'être sous tutelle, restreinte à des dimensions choisies à l'avance, est une prescription. Ce sentiment m'a fait horreur, j'ai secoué mes murs dans un violent combat contre mes limites. Ce sont de nombreux auteurs lus qu'il faut interroger. Je leur ai emprunté des idées que je n'ai pas trouvées dans mon milieu"] (10–11).

The narrator's reflections on her isolation as a student and the importance of reading prompt a series of memories of Yolande, an older classmate from a poor family whose solitary nature and independent spirit revealed her quiet, detached nature. Conversely, the narrator's adolescent self-portrait highlights her intellectual timidity and fear of family censure. Tentative in her observations, the narrator-protagonist engages Yolande in conversations about books not found in the curriculum. These conjured moments of halting dialogue contrast the narrator's inarticulate manner with Yolande's ability to speak for herself and establish her own distinct space: "Her deep voice swallowed syllables, Yolande spoke for herself. No one had to tell her: open your mouth when you speak, like they'd often said to me" ["Sa voix grave escamotait des syllabes, Yolande parlait pour elle-même. Personne n'avait dû lui dire: ouvre la bouche quand tu parles, comme on me l'avait si souvent répété"] (35).

Years later, Yolande continues to embody what the narrator still seeks – autonomy of thought and action despite the prevailing culture of conformism: "I had sensed Yolande's solitude. My intuition hadn't fooled me. Solitude that is more than boredom and isolation did exist" ["J'avais deviné la solitude de Yolande. Mon intuition ne m'avait pas trompée. Cette solitude qui ne confine pas à l'ennui et à l'isolement existait"] (13). This positive portrait of Yolande's solitary strength underscores one of the central themes in Théoret's writing.

In *Huis clos entre jeunes filles* initiation into the world of books represents a formative step in the narrator's early efforts to overcome ignorance and her own silence. Despite the nuns' repeated admonitions about the danger of reading inappropriate material (HC 40), Théoret's young protagonist frequented the under-utilized library in search of forgotten books that would become resources for exploration and insight: "It was in books that I sought encounters with worlds I didn't know. With each reading, I expected the author to tell me about something previously unknown" ["C'était dans les livres que je recherchais l'expression de mondes que je connaissais pas. À chaque lecture, j'attendais qu'une part d'inconnu me soit racontée par son auteur"] (51). These clandestine library visits also prompted her to start writing – first a journal, later poems of spirited revolt which she would eventually shred.

Huis clos entre jeunes filles foregrounds the act of reading as a key narrative event by juxtaposing the nuns' transmission of authorized texts and conservative pedagogy with the protagonist's secular impulse to read and question as a form of knowledge testing and self-discovery. Reading and teaching are thus seriously interconnected activities. Moreover, the harsh critique of religious education in this and other novels by France Théoret is grounded in the view that Catholic canonical study and related pedagogy repeat pre-determined truths that foster social conformity to the exclusion of independent thought: "Our instructors took religious teachings literally, rarely alluding to enemies of the faith. We were made up of homogeneous groups of young girls from modest means, believers called upon to transmit an established tradition" ["Nos enseignantes prenaient à la lettre les enseignements religieux, osant de rares allusions aux ennemis de la foi. Nous formions des groupes homogènes de jeunes filles de milieu modeste, des croyantes appelées à transmettre une tradition établie"] (61).

As a teacher in training, quietly defiant of the nuns' narrow instructional agenda, Théoret's protagonist aspires to a form of teaching that would expand student horizons, encourage individual creativity, and foster a more reflective pedagogical approach based upon reading, writing, and critical thinking. Intellectually anesthetized in the convent classroom, the narrator recalls how she became disconnected from her desire to teach: "I had learned nothing during my training... My passive revolt continued in directions with no way out" ["Je n'avais rien appris au cours de mon stage ... Ma révolte passive se maintenait dans des voies sans issue"] (93).

In *Huis clos entre jeunes filles*, the transformative power of reading is integrated into the thematic substance of Théoret's text through the discovery of Virgil Gheorghiu's disturbing World War II novel, *La vingt-cinquième heure*. While confined to the convent school, the gift of this book altered the narrator's reading practice and changed the boundaries of her world:

On my return, the following Sunday, I found on the writing pad I used as a desk Virgil Gheorghiu's *La vingt-cinquième heure*. I don't know why I thought that Yolande was loaning me a book. Impressive because of the number of pages, the book gave me a secret joy. I touched it, held it in my hands and stroked it. The book illuminated my cubicle. The enigmatic title indicated something urgent. The title presented a menace. An event was occuring after the day had concluded. My imagination ran wild.

[À mon retour, le dimanche suivant, je trouvai sur la tablette qui me servait de pupitre *La vingt-cinquième heure* de Virgil Gheorghiu. Je ne sais pourquoi je pensais que Yolande me prêtait un livre. Le livre, imposant par le nombre de ses pages, me causa une joie secrète. Je le touchai, le prit dans mes mains, le palpai. Le livre illumina ma cellule. Le titre énigmatique pointait l'urgence. Le titre présentait une menace. Un évènement survenait après que le jour fût consommé. Mon imagination s'emballa.] (63)

Théoret's narrator recalls how reading *La vingt-cinquième heure* prompted her to analyze her own limited views: "I was beginning to realize that I had assimilated ideas from another era, and I was ashamed" ["Je commençai à comprendre que j'avais assimilé des idées venues d'un autre âge, et j'en eus honte"] (76). Despondent about her failure to develop a closer bond with Yolande through this book, she escapes into Gheorghiu's text as an antidote to the moralizing lectures of her religious instructors: "In a reversal of discourse, our teacher reduced her vocabulary and delivered a moralizing sermon. I read a few passages of *La vingt-cinquième heure,* raised my head at the slightest change of intonation from our religious instructor" ["Par un usage inversé du discours, notre enseignante appauvrissait son langage et livrait un message moralisateur. Je lus quelques passages de *La vingt-cinquième heure*, levai la tête au moindre changement d'intonation de notre titulaire"] (95).

Published by the little-known Romanian author Virgil Gheorghiu, *La vingt-cinquième heure* was initially translated into French by Monique Saint-Come for political reasons and first published in France, rather than Romania, in 1976. According to French philosopher Gabriel Marcel, who introduces Gheorghiu's book, *La vingt-cinquième heure* addresses transnational issues of human dignity and "authentic life" during one of the darkest moments of modern history (Gheorghiu 12). The scope of *La vingt-cinquième heure* is both historical and autobiographical, examining acts of prejudice and barbarism that permanently scarred the lives of the innocent during and after World War II: "… the emergence of technical society destroyed what we had gained and created over centuries of human culture. Technical society reintroduced contempt for the human being" (Gheorghiu 164). Full of intrigue for Théoret's young protagonist, the novel's mysterious title is explained within the pages of Gheorghiu's novel by a priest who refers to the "25th hour" as Europe's ultimate hour of post-war failure – an hour of bearing witness to the de-humanizing death and destruction suffered at the hands of "modern" Western culture:

–My watch has stopped, he said. Can you give me the time, father?
–It's the twenty-fifth hour!
–I don't understand, Lucian replied.
–I do believe you. No one wants to understand. It is the twenty-fifth hour. The hour of European civilization.

[–Ma montre est arrêtée, dit-il. Tu veux me dire l'heure, père ?
–C'est la vingt-cinquième heure !
–Je n'ai pas compris, dit Lucian.
–Je te crois sans peine. Personne ne veut comprendre. C'est la vingt-cinquième heure. L'heure de la civilisation européenne.] (Gheorghiu 165)

Historically speaking, *La vingt-cinquième heure* portrays the cruel realities of German and Soviet atrocities and American injustice at the end of World War II, when serious ideological disputes over national borders and political regimes provoked acts of intolerance that characterize the world in which Gheorghiu's principal protagonist, Iohann, wanders and is judged. Imprisoned many times over a thirteen-year period, Iohann Moritz is declared Jewish, then Aryan, welcomed and then mistreated by the Germans, identified by the Allies as an ally and then as an enemy, until he succeeds in petitioning for his freedom. Imprisoned, tortured, sold-out to the Germans, co-opted by them, and subsequently imprisoned by the Americans, Iohann is finally set free in the novel's concluding scenes. Although he has committed no crime, Iohann is never confronted as an individual but rather as an ethnic or national identity with presumed political, cultural, and religious affiliations that elicit suspicion and mistrust. In the confused and amoral world of *La vingt-cinquième heure* in which personal identity is de-stabilized and de-valued, basic notions of respect and trust no longer motivate human interactions and the innocent are often perceived as the enemy. Gabriel Marcel remarks in his preface that "mankind seemed to have forgotten how to be human" (Gheorghiu 7).

La vingt-cinquième heure offers a harsh indictment of the modern technological state in which individuals and individual human rights no longer have protection or significance. A forceful transatlantic intertext, Gheorghiu's novel directs narrative attention in *Huis clos entre jeunes filles* well beyond the realm of the local (provincial) and beyond gender as well, to transnational concerns about censorship and injustice across the continents and across historical periods. Théoret's narrator remembers reading about Iohann Moritz's condition in mythopoetic terms: Iohann is the truth sayer, and he is tortured for it. Years later, she provides a vivid, painful description of Moritz's torture:

I had opened the novel to a passage that started with the ultimate
  confrontation with the guard.
Everything had been said and repeated by Moritz who didn't change his
  first deposition one iota. In response to the guard's: what do you say?
  Moritz doesn't answer. Moritz is beaten. He urinates, he vomits,
  blood flows from his torn flesh. His body exudes all of its liquids,
  mixing them up until blood flows from his nose and ears and until
  he is nothing more than one large wound.

I was reading a page that put me in front of extreme evil. I was certain
that I would never forget reading this page. My head ached.

[J'avais ouvert le roman au passage qui débutait par l'ultime confrontation avec le gardien.
Tout a été dit et répété par Moritz qui n'a pas changé d'un iota sa première Déposition. À la question du gardien : tu dis ? Moritz ne
répond pas. Moritz est battu. Il urine, il vomit, son sang s'écoule de
sa chair déchirée. Son corps exsude tous ses liquides, les mêle jusqu'à
ce que le sang s'écoule aussi de son nez et de ses oreilles et qu'il se
réduise à une seule grande plaie.
Je lisais une page qui me situait face au mal extrême. J'eus la certitude
que je n'allais pas oublier la lecture de cette page. J'eus mal à la tête.]
(98)

For the protagonist of *Huis clos entre jeunes filles*, the impact of reading
La vingt-cinquième heure was at times profoundly visceral. As the narrator reveals, Gheorghiu's novel led her on a disturbing journey of discovery
– the discovery of torture, torturers and political victims, and concentra-
tion camps about which she was entirely ignorant. Through her reading
experience, the narrator also learned that historical truths about the human
condition speak across national borders and across the generations, expos-
ing "hatred and the tragic dimension of contemporary history" ["la haine
et la dimension tragique de l'histoire contemporaine"] (100).

Huis clos entre jeunes filles concludes with the observations of a mature
narrator reflecting on her strained friendship with another teacher,
Danielle. Both women wish to eliminate self-censure, and both continue to
struggle against the weight of their conservative training and acquired sense
of inferiority. Théoret's narrator still wonders about missed opportunities
for establishing friendships over the years: "Will I ever find a refuge? The
question is uninterrupted. Waiting for a place of rest, ground that doesn't
move still continues" ["Vais-je jamais trouver un refuge? L'interrogation
est ininterrompue. L'attente d'un espace de repos, d'un sol qui n'est pas
mouvant dure encore"] (135). At the end of the novel, as the narrator's
memories of her sequestered school years give way to present-tense reflections, the fear of solitude is replaced with an affirmation of friendship, "I
am Danielle's friend, I don't know more than that" ["Je suis l'amie de
Danielle, je n'en sais pas davantage"] (136). On the subject of solitude,
reading, and friendship, *Huis clos entre jeunes filles* has come full circle.

In an entry from *Journal pour mémoire* dated February 26, 1991, France Théoret reflects on the significance of reading for her own intellectual and social development: "For a long time I loved reading because it disturbed me and I liked having the extreme certainties of my education dislodged. I took pleasure in this troubling experience. I awakened to my era through reading" ["Longtemps j'ai aimé la lecture parce qu'elle me troublait et que j'aimais être déstablisée dans les certitudes sévères de mon éducation. J'élisais le plaisir dans sa part troublante. Je naissais à mon époque par la lecture"] (JM 205). For Théoret, the acquisition of knowledge, the questioning of "Truth," and the path to critical thinking emerge out of the de-stabilizing process of reading works that challenge her to think and evaluate in new ways. In both *Laurence* and *Huis clos entre jeunes filles*, the drama and denouement of the female subject take place through and around the act of reading transatlantic texts.

Notes

1 All translations are the author's, unless otherwise indicated.

2 André Lamontagne notes in *Le roman québécois contemporain* that "the largest portion of intertexual content in *Comment faire l'amour ...* is connected to reading" (162).

3 For an overview of the history of education and the status of instruction for women, see Jean-Pierre Charland, *Histoire de l'éducation au Québec* (2005) and Andrée Dufour and Micheline Dumont, *Brève histoire des institutrices au Québec de la Nouvelle-France à nos jours* (2004).

4 See Mary Jean Green's seminal study, *Marie-Claire Blais* (1995).

Works Cited

Blais, Marie-Claire. *Manuscrits de Pauline Archange*. Montreal: Stanké, 1968.

– *Une saison dans la vie d'Emmanuel.* [1965] Montreal: Quinze, 1978.

Charland, Jean-Pierre. *Histoire de l'éducation au Québec: De l'ombre du clocher à l'économie du savoir*. Saint-Laurent: ERPI, 2005.

Dufour, Andrée and Micheline Dumont. *Brève histoire des institutrices au Québec de la Nouvelle-France à nos jours*. Montreal: Boréal, 2004.

Dupré, Louise. "Mémoire et écriture : L'inscription du féminin dans l'histoire." *Québec Studies* 31 (2001): 24–35.

Gheorghiu, Virgil. *La vingt-cinquième heure*. Trans. Monique Saint-Come. Paris: Plon, 1976.

Gould, Karen. "Femmes/ville/histoire: Transformations urbaines dans *Laurence* de France Théoret." In *Sexuation, espace, écriture. La littérature québécoise en transformation*. Eds. Louise Dupré, Jaap Lintvelt, and Janet M. Paterson. Montreal: Nota Bene, 2002. 275–89.

– "Gendered Migrations: History, Women, Class, and Urbanity in France Théoret's *Laurence*." In *Doing Gender: Franco-Canadian Women Writers of the 1990s*. Eds. Paula Ruth Gilbert and Roseanna Lewis Dufault. Cranbury, NJ: Fairleigh Dickinson University Press, 2001. 95–107.

Green, Mary Jean. *Marie-Claire Blais.* New
York: Twayne, 1995.

Havercroft, Barbara. "Fragments d'un par-
cours remémoré : *Journal pour mémoire
de France Théoret.*" *Québec Studies* 31
(2001): 36–49.

Hotte, Lucie. *Romans de la lecture, lecture
du roman.* Montreal: Nota bene, 2001.

Hugo, Victor. *Les misérables.* Vols. 1–3.
Paris: Pocket, 1998.

Laferrière, Dany. *Comment faire l'amour
avec un Nègre sans se fatiguer.* Montreal: VLB, 1985.

Lamontagne, André. *Le roman québécois
contemporain : Les voix sous les mots.*
Montreal: Fides, 2004.

Martin, Claire. *Dans un gant de fer*. Montreal: Pierre Tisseyre, 1965.

– *La joue droite*. Montreal: Pierre Tisseyre,
1966.

Sartre, Jean-Paul. *Huis-clos* suivi de *Les
mouches.* Paris: Gallimard, 1969.

Théoret, France. *Huis clos entre jeunes
filles*. Montreal: Les herbes rouges,
2000.

– *Journal pour mémoire.* Montreal: L'hexagone, 1993.

– *Laurence*. Montreal: Les herbes rouges,
1996.

– *Laurence.* Trans. Gail Scott. Toronto:
Mercury, 1998.

Literary Border Crossings: Reconceptualizing Montesquieu's *Lettres persanes* in Lise Gauvin's *Lettres d'une autre* and Chahdortt Djavann's *Comment peut-on être français?*

PATRICE J. PROULX

Culture can only really be understood from the outside, in the friction of different languages, in the weaving and the twisting of languages, through the fact that an "other" language allows for the defamiliarization of one's own language.

[La culture ne se laisse vraiment saisir que de l'étranger, dans le frottement d'une langue à l'autre, dans le tissage et le tressage des langues, dans le fait que la langue autre permet de rendre étrangère sa propre langue.]

Régine Robin, "Speak Watt"[1]

By means of pastiche, of parody, of unrestricted imitation, it is a question of altering models, of transforming them, of rewriting them from a woman's perspective. It seems to me that a number of renowned masterpieces would benefit from being revised in this way.

[Par le biais du pastiche, de la parodie, de l'imitation libre, il s'agit de faire dévier les modèles, de les transformer, de les réécrire au féminin. Il me semble que plusieurs chefs-d'oeuvre réputés auraient intérêt à être revus de cette façon.]

Lise Gauvin, *Lettres d'une autre*

The trope of the outsider's gaze on other cultures has frequently served as a point of departure in literary works which trace out migrant trajectories in relation to shifting configurations of national identity. The introduction of the foreigner's perspective into a new socio-political landscape provides the grounding for a potential reconceptualization of cultural codes and a fruitful exploration of important questions related to individual and collective identity. Eloise Brière, for example, highlights the critical nature of the textualization of difference across national boundaries in contemporary francophone literature, focusing on the transatlantic spaces of Paris and Montreal: "The outsiders' gaze on French and Québécois culture is becoming part of the literary landscape. Theirs is not the bemused, detached view of the tourist soon to depart for other climes, but the critical and ironic gaze of those who assert their right to belong and to be allowed to create differently" (157).

In this essay, I will focus on two authors whose works explicitly engage the trope of the female outsider's perspective through the textual recreation of the marginalized, mostly silenced figure of Roxane in Charles-Louis Montesquieu's *Lettres persanes* (1721).[2] Both Lise Gauvin[3] and Chahdortt Djavann[4] have written fictional or semi-fictional works in which "it is a question of altering models, of transforming them, of rewriting them from a woman's perspective" ["il s'agit de faire dévier les modèles, de les transformer, de les réécrire au féminin"] (Gauvin, *Lettres d'une autre* 134–5), using structural and thematic elements from Montesquieu's eighteenth-century epistolary novel to create narratives in which female protagonists attempt to situate themselves in relation to a new urban space and a new national discourse. In Gauvin's *Lettres d'une autre* (1984), which raises the question "how can one be Québécois" ["comment peut-on être Québécois(e)"], an Iranian narrator named Roxane describes her experiences in Quebec to a friend back home – the text contains insightful commentary on post-referendum Québécois society.[5] Similarly, Djavann's novel, *Comment peut-on être français?* (2006), recounts the story of Roxane, a young Iranian woman who has just arrived in Paris and must adapt to a challenging life there. The protagonist eventually chooses to write to M. Montesquieu, someone she feels an intimate connection with due to her name and her circumstances as a newcomer to Paris who becomes an astute observer of French society. I plan to examine the reconceptualizing of the *Lettres persanes* in these two thought-provoking texts, focusing in particular on the rich implications of the intertextual strategies encoded in the works of Gauvin and Djavann.

The use of the *Lettres persanes* as a framing device in each text opens up a unique discursive space which privileges those narrative elements particular to the epistolary form, effectively foregrounding the idea of literal and literary border crossings. In her illuminating study of Gauvin's text, Monique Moser-Verrey elaborates on the potential of the letter to engage in transcultural dialogue: "The epistolary genre is open to all sorts of correspondences and has always defied time, space, and proprieties … To inscribe one's words in such a space is to give them an established place in this vast network of dialogues that crosses cultures and centuries" (517). In the same vein, Keith Walker asserts that the epistolary genre is an especially appropriate form for examining issues related to the construction of identity in new contexts, speaking to the issue of geographical borders by underscoring the strategic nature of epistolary writing for those who have been displaced, especially women: "[T]he letter should not be a surprising form of literary expression for a francophone woman writer. As an artifact the letter is *in transit*, crisscrossing borders and barriers, negotiating the national and international *in-between* places where, in francophone literature, difference, displacement, differ*ance*, change, and conflict are signified" (247). In addition, this genre, by its very nature, lends itself to an intimate exploration of a wide variety of leitmotifs, as letter writers conjure up and rethink experiences that emblematize their quest for personal redefinition. In Gauvin and Djavann's textual creations, the immigrant protagonists reflect in particular on issues related to physical and cultural dislocation, individual and communal identity, the French language and alterity, socio-political concerns, their trajectories in the new urban space, and the creative act itself.

Lettres d'une autre, published under the heading "fiction/essai," consists of a series of thirteen letters written between 1982–84 by an Iranian student in Quebec to Sarah, a friend who has remained in Iran. With the creation of a letter-writing protagonist named Roxane, Gauvin inscribes her character in a narrative chain reaching back to one of the most famous epistolary novels of the eighteenth century, the *Lettres persanes*. Gauvin, however, privileges the female voice in her work, the textual reproduction of a single letter writer's correspondence serving to reframe Montesquieu's polyphonic, male-dominated narrative in which women authored only ten of the 161 letters, with Roxane signing her name to two of these. Moser-Verrey rightly highlights the fact that the allusion to the *Lettres persanes* in Gauvin's text is important and complex, permeating the text rather than simply serving as a facile point of departure: "As a stylistic device, literary allusion is completely polymorphous. It can range from explicit citation to brief evocation to the most subtle pastiche" (514).

The title of Gauvin's text, with its emphasis on the outsider's perspective, contains a thought-provoking ambiguity: is the protagonist posited as an Other in Québécois society or is she "becoming" an Other while in that society? As Roxane asks herself upon her arrival in Quebec, taking up and transforming a well-known query from the *Lettres persanes*:[6] "How can one be Québécois?" ["Comment peut-on être Québécois(e)?"] (25).[7] The protagonist herself acknowledges her awareness of the potential implications of her intertextual affiliation with an "illustrious predecessor" ["illustre prédécesseur"] (143). While Roxane feels this to be almost a coincidence, she nonetheless eloquently expresses the ultimate importance of this creative connection as it relates to her own textual production: "If I think, in fact, that there is a certain modesty involved in joining in the infinite variation of literary genres and forms, I am convinced that one can't make reference to an idea without profoundly modifying it, without acknowledging the gap that exists" ["Si je pense, en effet, qu'il y a une certaine modestie à s'inscrire dans l'infinie variation des genres et des formes littéraires, je suis convaincue qu'on ne peut jouer de la référence sans modifier profondément la perspective, sans accuser la distance"] (143). Concomitantly, the protagonist understands that the outsider's gaze afforded her by her Iranian origins encourages her to "privilege that which, in the texts that I read, leads to the constitution of a new referent, of a new image" ["privilégier ce qui, dans les textes que je lis, va vers la constitution d'un nouveau référent, d'une nouvelle image"] (134).

Already fluent in French, Roxane immerses herself in her new milieu, making a large circle of friends as she attends the university on a scholarship, participates in academic circles, and undertakes research on her chosen topic of the nineteenth-century Québécois traditional tale. While her alterity is recognized, the protagonist's experiences in Quebec are ultimately very positive, and she remarks that the Québécois are a very welcoming people, having a long-standing tradition of accepting foreigners into their midst.[8] Over the course of the two years encompassing her epistolary venture, Roxane will explore a diversity of concerns in contemporary Québécois society, ranging from unemployment and the economic crisis, to women's liberation, to the literature and language of the francophone province. She shares her thoughts with Sarah, evoking their "tacit complicity" ["complicité tacite"] (27) and articulating the hope that her friend will be interested in accompanying her on her journey to understanding "this corner of America that escapes me and escapes definition" ["ce coin d'Amérique qui m'échappe et échappe à toute définition"] (33). While Sarah herself has no voice in the text, and references to the relationship between the two women are extremely limited, Roxane testifies to her friend's vital role in the existence of this creative and communicative act: "If, in the beginning, art emerges from the ability to enter into communication with oneself, one can't conceive of any art that isn't, at least to some slight degree, received by another. For better or for worse, you must share the responsibility of these texts with me!" ["Si l'art procède au départ d'une capacité d'entrer en communication avec soi-même, on ne saurait imaginer aucun art qui ne soit pas, au moins à un dégré infime, reçu. Pour le meilleur et pour le pire, tu devras donc partager avec moi la responsabilité de ces textes!"] (111). In addition, we discover that Sarah is the one who is encouraging Roxane to publish her letters, her words – paraphrased by the protagonist – affirming the strategic implications of the outsider's gaze: "because, as you say, an outside viewpoint sometimes helps lead to self-awareness" ["parce que, dis-tu, un regard lointain est parfois utile pour ramener à la conscience de soi"] (143).

Thus, in her capacity as foreign observer of Québécois society, Gauvin's protagonist reflects on the complex construction of individual and communal identity in both a provincial and a national context. In her first letter, for example, Roxane presents a thoughtful discussion of the Québécois quest for self-definition and a way of defining a certain "specificity" ["spécificité"] (41) that would not be linked to the values of faith, language, and tradition often associated with "an era of opposition to progress" ["une ère d'immobilisme"] (18) in which "any change was taboo, any incursion from the exterior a threat of perdition" ["tout changement était tabou, toute incursion de l'extérieur menace de perdition"] (18). One of her most revelatory discoveries is her theorization that the Québécois, in their conception of themselves, have already enacted a "doubling" that embodies the viewpoint of the Other in a more critical fashion: "It seems to me there is in all Québécois people an unacknowledged non-Québécois. As if they had long practiced the gymnastics of the other's look on themselves and had succeeded in integrating in their personality a sly, multiform double, ready to break up at the slightest alarm, to disapprove the overly Québécois part of themselves at the slightest sign" ["Il me paraît y avoir dans tout Québécois un non-Québécois qui s'ignore. Comme si chacun s'était longuement exercé à la gymnastique du regard de l'autre sur lui-même et en était arrivé à intégrer à sa personnalité un double sournois, multiforme, prêt à se dissocier à la moindre alerte, à désapprouver au moindre signe la partie trop québécoise de son moi"] (46–7).

Roxane's letters, for the most part, constitute an important series of reflections on her physical and psychological integration into a different society, as she purposefully negotiates the new cultural codes that allow her to situate herself as "Québécois" ["Québécoise"] in both a geographic and a discursive sense, a move encoded in the signature affixed to her final letter: "Your ever faithful, Iranian by birth and Québécois by adoption, Roxane" ["Ta toujours fidèle, Persane d'origine et Québécoise d'adoption, Roxane"] (143). This ending, in which an independent, fulfilled Roxane has definitively and successfully woven her story into the very fabric of another society, radically challenges the denouement of Montesquieu's text, in which an oppressed but defiant Roxane commits suicide in order to symbolically proclaim her freedom. Gauvin's protagonist, then, while characterizing her affiliation to the *Lettres persanes* as "virtually a coincidence" ["une presque coïncidence"] (143), nonetheless succeeds in providing a compelling revisioning of this story in which the emblematic figure of Roxane assumes a new voice and place in contemporary Québécois society.[9]

In *Comment peut-on être français?*, a connection with Montesquieu's epistolary text is inscribed in the title, an explicit reformulation of the question "How can one be Persian?" ["Comment peut-on être persan?"] and a transatlantic echo of Gauvin's "How can one be Québécois?" ["Comment peut-on être québécois(e)?"] (*Lettres d'une autre* 25). As Cristina Alvares makes manifest in her reading of Djavann's novel, the grounding of this reconceptualization lies in Roxane Khân's desire not to affirm her own Iranian identity, but rather to profoundly modify it: "faced with a foreigner, the eighteenth-century Parisian finds himself incapable of being anything other than French, whereas the title of Djavann's novel conveys the sense of how to accede to the other's culture, how to become French, and it postulates an opening that conflicts with the hidden meaning of the first question" ("La réécriture"). Djavann's protagonist, who has fled an oppressive life in Iran for the freedom of France, will nevertheless be confronted with a number of daunting challenges in her attempt to become French, as she neither speaks nor understands the language and needs to find a job to support herself. In the first weeks of her stay, however, the Paris she knows only through books and legends, "her fantasy" ["son fantasme à elle"] (11), slowly reveals itself to her as she happily wanders the city streets unaccosted, becoming a sort of modern-day *flâneuse*.[10] In fact, she revels in her growing knowledge of the cartography of the city, very much aware of the transgressiveness of this appropriation of public space, especially given her Iranian origins: "A girl walking through the streets, that doesn't exist in Iran" ["Qu'une fille arpente les rues, ça n'existe pas en Iran"] (34). As in the case of Gauvin's Roxane, the reader recognizes the transformative potential of the outsider's vision of an "Other" society, as we see Paris through the eyes of Djavann's protagonist. In her incisive analysis of migration and the *flâneur*, Pavlina Radia broadens the traditional conception of this term to include a more diverse group of wanderers who move easily across multiple cultural landscapes: "In the age of postmodern globalization and intense migration, the fixity of geographic borders and cultural boundaries no longer holds ... While in the past, *flânerie* has been primarily associated with bourgeois leisure and detachment, in the wake of postmodernity, it has taken on a more fluid, itinerant form of 'a variety of "wanderings," in terms of ambulation, nationality, gender, race, class, and sexuality'" (171).

After this initial, mostly blissful encounter with the city of her dreams, however, Roxane pragmatically sets out to fulfill her goal of learning the French language, a vital element in assuming a francophone identity. This section of the text – written in the third-person point of view – centers in large part around issues of language and national identity, as the protagonist struggles with the rules of French grammar and pronunciation while trying in vain to remember necessary vocabulary. She equates her failure to master French with her inability to cast off troubling vestiges of her Iranian past, given that, in her mind, the Persian language connects her irrevocably to "the memories of a country in which barbaric dogmas serve as laws" ["les souvenirs d'un pays où des dogmes barbares faisaient office de lois"] (113), and this makes her experience her exile much more keenly: "the strangeness of a foreign language that rejects her made her feel what exile was, what it meant to be exiled" ["l'étrangeté d'une langue étrangère qui se refusait à elle et qui la refusait lui firent sentir ce qu'était l'exil, ce que c'était qu'être exilée"] (73). In addition, her noticeably foreign accent impels others to ask where she comes from, and this serves as a constant reminder of her ineluctable ties to her Iranian origins. Alvares points to the troubling consequences of this situation for the protagonist: "For Roxane, this incessant return to an identity, a memory, a culture, and a language that she wants to get rid of constitutes a failure. It is the mark of exclusion and solitude" ("Comment peut-on").

Nonetheless, Roxane doesn't lose her desire to "become an other in French" ["devenir une autre en français"] (116), and she pursues her study of the language even when working in the mostly menial jobs she undertakes which allow her to continue living in France.[11] The protagonist experiences a sort of epiphany when she encounters Montesquieu's *Lettres persanes* in a civilization class, reading and rereading the text on her own, curious as to how an eighteenth-century French author could have so deftly captured the lives of his Persian protagonists. The next section of the narrative alternates between the third-person and the first-person point of view, as Roxane begins composing letters to Montesquieu as a way of ameliorating her language skills and assuaging her loneliness. She addresses the author as her "dear parent" ["cher géniteur"] (149), the one who created her, in a sense, and who would thus understand her better than anyone else. Alvares illustrates the critical nature of this literary affiliation for the protagonist, as it provides a vital link in her effort to resituate herself: "Roxane needs to choose a purely literary parent in order to recreate herself apart from the laws of her family and her native language, to reinvent herself in the French language, to *be* again [ren*être*] in the Other" ("La réécriture"). Unlike the protagonist in Gauvin's text, then, Djavann's Roxane experiences a true connection with Montesquieu's character of the same name, encouraging rather than rejecting comparisons, and even imagining herself to be a sort of spiritual reincarnation of the fictional figure, whose courageous spirit she admires: "Maybe she wouldn't even have truly existed today if Montesquieu hadn't imagined her. And if she had existed three centuries ago, she would have been Montesquieu's Roxane, the rebellious Roxane, the reasoning Roxane tells herself" ["Peut-être même qu'elle n'aurait jamais existé réellement aujourd'hui si Montesquieu ne l'avait pas imaginée. Et si elle avait existé, il y avait trois siècles, elle n'aurait été autre que la Roxane de Montesquieu, la Roxane insoumise, se dit la Roxane raisonneuse"] (144).

The protagonist thus sets out on her epistolary enterprise, writing a series of eighteen letters to Montesquieu and sending them to different literary-based addresses contingent on her readings of the moment, choosing destinations on the avenue Montaigne, boulevard Voltaire, and rue Corneille, for example. Roxane, through her role as observer of French society, also elaborates on certain intersections between the *Lettres persanes* and her current life in Paris, comparing conditions in France and Iran as Montesquieu's Persian protagonists had done three centuries earlier, and coming to the disillusioning conclusion that "moral standards in Iran have not advanced much" ["les moeurs en Iran ont peu évolué"] (150).[12] Her reading of the *Lettres persanes* thus serves as a springboard for her own critique of contemporary religious hypocrisy and political injustice. In one of her letters examining the question of civil liberties, for example, Roxane evokes the space of the harem as it relates to oppressive conditions for both men and women in present-day Iran: "There are no more eunuchs in Iran. … but Iran has been completely transformed into a harem, women are watched over and men are castrated by the laws of the mullahs" ["Il n'y a plus d'eunuques en Iran … mais l'Iran s'est transformé entièrement en harem, les femmes sont surveillées et les hommes castrés par la loi des mollahs"] (221). While, like Roxane in *Lettres d'une autre*, Djavann's protagonist engages topics such as language, literature, government, and religion, she conveys much more about her own past and her reasons for leaving her homeland, locating the desire to distance herself from her ethnic origins in her formative years: "when I grow up, I'll go abroad, too, far away, and I'll learn another language. That way, no one in my family will understand me" ["quand je serai grande, j'irai moi aussi à l'étranger, loin, et apprendrai une autre langue. Comme ça, personne, dans ma famille, me comprendra"] (191). Even then, she dreamed of becoming a writer, seeing storytelling as a way to enact a counterdiscourse which would question prevailing mores. To underscore the imperative nature of creating a con-testatory voice, the protagonist reveals her admiration for a legendary Muslim theologian named Nasr Eddin Hodja who "denounces, through naïve tales, sometimes the bigotry and sometimes the hypocrisy of the religious" ["dénonce, à travers des contes naïfs, tantôt la bigoterie des religieux, tantôt leur hypocrisie"] (194).

Roxane also uses her writing to express the fundamental alienation she has felt throughout her life, both in Iran and in France. She has thus far been unable to escape from the damage done to her during the years spent in her homeland, expressing a sense of irretrievable loss: "I feel mutilated, severed from more than 20 years" ["Je me sens mutilée, amputée de plus de vingt années"] (261). This vision of a corporeal disjunction resonates with and further illuminates an earlier passage in which the protagonist had evoked the French language as a sort of imperfect prosthetic, forcefully illustrating the origins of her desire to integrate the language into her very being. Ultimately, however, she recognizes the unattainability of this imag-inary state of physical and psychological plentitude: "Her being would never take root in the French language; French would serve as a prosthe-sis, always exterior to her flesh" ["Son être ne prendrait jamais racine dans la langue française; le français lui servirait de prothèse, toujours en dehors de la chair"] (117). In fact, Roxane finds the past increasingly, disturbingly present, rendering futile her attempts to more successfully become a part of French society. While the protagonist desperately desires to start afresh in Paris, she finds herself confronted with and burdened by unsettling mem-ories: "Without warning, images of the past transformed Paris. The past became the present. Memories became physically real" ["Sans préavis, les images du passé transformaient Paris. Le passé devenait le présent. Les souvenirs devenaient réels physiquement"] (73). Dayna Oscherwitz char-acterizes this sort of experience as an example of anamnesis, "a memorial process in which the past resurges upon the present and a person feels as though they are in both places at the same time" (194). Towards the end of the novel, an especially chilling example of this resurgence of the past into the present occurs when Roxane is arrested for riding her bicycle the wrong way down a one-way street and is taken to the police station, having forgotten her identity papers in her apartment. This episode recalls – and forces her to viscerally relive – a traumatic event from her past. Forced into

a prison cell, she protests vehemently, and begins ranting and hallucinat-
ing, finding herself back in Ispahan; tellingly, this is the same city in which
the "original" Roxane had been confined to Usbek's harem. The next
chapter recounts through flashback what had happened on this trip to the
unfamiliar city of Ispahan she had taken with two female friends, Nahid
and Zahra – they had been arrested by an "Islamic committee" ["comité
islamique"] (282) for having removed their socks and shoes in public in
order to massage their aching feet after a day of sightseeing. Confined to
prison cells, Roxane and Nahid were interrogated and then raped by several
men. While Nahid will later commit suicide, a pregnant Roxane finds the
strength to leave the country, seeking an abortion in Turkey, and then
spending two years in Istanbul before moving on to France. A psychiatrist
called to the police station in Paris "diagnosed her as suffering from remi-
niscence" ["diagnostiqua qu'elle souffrait de réminiscence"] (307), and she
is then taken to the psychiatric service unit at Sainte-Anne where she is
further diagnosed with a neurotic depression stemming from having
"grown up under oppressive state control" ["grandi sous l'oppression éta-
tique"] (311).

In her final letter to Montesquieu, Roxane shares with him the fact that
her psychiatrist believes her correspondence with a long-dead author constitutes a manifestation of her abnormality, whereas she feels that if the
author had actually been able to fulfill the function of narratee by "receiv-
ing" her letters, she never would have had the courage to write to him. The
protagonist then situates her own creative act in relation to that of the eighteenth-century author, arguing that while his characters and their letters
were completely fictional, she is at least "imagining" someone who actually
existed: "Didn't you yourself create imaginary Persians? Your Usbek, your
Rica, and your Roxane, they never existed, and I'm sure that when you wrote
your *Persian Letters*, you nevertheless felt their presence at your side. You,
though, you actually existed – so is it that crazy to imagine you?" ["Vous-
même, n'avez-vous pas créé des Persans imaginaires? Votre Usbek, votre
Rica et votre Roxane, ils n'ont jamais existé, et je suis sûre que quand vous
écriviez vos *Lettres persanes*, vous ressentiez pourtant leur présence à vos
côtés. Tandis que vous, vous avez existé réellement; serait-il donc si fou de
vous imaginer?"] (311). She then reveals being haunted by thoughts of
suicide, referring to a prominent Iranian novelist who killed himself in Paris
in 1951,[13] an act which she had never before understood, but which she has
now begun to comprehend: "Living in Paris isn't enough, no matter how
great the magic of Paris" ["Vivre à Paris ne suffit pas, si grande que soit la

magie de Paris"] (311). Her final signature bears witness to her profound alienation from herself and others: "This land is foreign to me, and I am foreign to others and to myself – to you, too, no doubt. I see only a vision of despair. Roxane" ["Cette terre m'est étrangère, je suis étrangère aux autres et à moi-même, à vous aussi sans doute. Je ne vois qu'un champ de désespoir. Roxane"] (312). Unlike the overtly optimistic denouement of Gauvin's text, then, in which a spirited Roxane successfully situates herself in relation to both Iran and Quebec, the ending of Djavann's text initially seems to align itself with the *Lettres persanes*, as Roxane – unable to extricate herself from the past – attempts suicide after leaving the hospital. After another month in Sainte Anne, she returns to her apartment and sits on her bed, staring out the window. The last lines of the novel do provide some hope that Roxane will find the fortitude to survive; it is spring, so a renascence is taking place around her, reflected in the color and clarity of the sky: "The cut-out sky in the frame of the skylight was blue and clear" ["Le ciel découpé dans l'encadrement de la lucarne était bleu et clair"] (314).

The re-envisioning of the *Lettres persanes* resonates on many different levels in *Lettres d'une autre* and *Comment peut-on être français?*, as Gauvin and Djavann give voice to new stories for the paradigmatic figure of Roxane. As we have seen, this intertextual strategy serves as the basis for a critical exploration of myriad socio-political and cultural topics that cross national boundaries. Indeed, Gauvin's and Djavann's texts present the creative act itself as inherently political, with the protagonist of *Lettres d'une autre* explicitly observing: "To what extent, however, isn't the act of creation the most political act one can imagine?" ["Jusqu'à quel point, cependant, l'acte de créer n'est-il pas le plus politique que l'on puisse concevoir?"] (98). In both cases, the female protagonists turn to writing as a way to inscribe their experiences within a new metropolitan discursive space, while at the same time articulating important connections between Iran and Quebec or France. Despite the presence of a number of significant differences in their structural and thematic reconceptualization of the *Lettres persanes*, both Gauvin and Djavann have succeeded in creating innovative texts which privilege the female outsider's gaze as an enriching way of rethinking fundamental concepts of national identity within the framework of a new cultural landscape.

Notes

1 Cited in Gauvin, *Langagement*, 181.
All translations are the author's, unless
otherwise indicated.

2 In the *Lettres persanes*, two Persians
– Usbek and Rica – take an extended
trip to Paris, describing their cultural
encounters and reflections on life in
letters to a variety of different narra-
tees, including Roxane, Usbek's favorite wife who is being confined to his
harem in Ispahan.

3 Born in Quebec, Lise Gauvin is a professor of literature at the University of
Montreal and recently elected President of the Academy of Letters of
Quebec. She has long participated in
debates surrounding language and national identity, often in relation to the
creative act. *L'écrivain francophone à
la croisée des langues* and *Langagement: L'écrivain et la langue au
Québec*, for example, explore this thematic in the texts of authors such as
Ying Chen, Marco Micone, Emile Ollivi-
er, Régine Robin, and Michel Tremblay.

4 Chahdortt Djavann, born in Iran in
1967, arrived in Paris in 1993, determined to learn French and become a
writer. She has written several semi-
autobiographical novels, as well as
pamphlets and essays which testify
to her interest in issues related to the
defense of civil rights, such as *Bas les
voiles!* and *Que pense Allah de l'Europe?* Djavann herself forges an explicit link between her "adoption" of
the French language and her construction of a new identity: "For years, this
language has welcomed my story, my
childhood, my memories, and my
wounds … I reinscribed my past, my
story, replanted my roots in this language. It adopted me, and I adopted
it" ["Cette langue a accueilli, pendant
des années, mon histoire, mon enfance, mes souvenirs et mes blessures
… J'ai réinscrit mon passé, mon his-

toire, replanté mes racines dans cette
langue. Elle m'a adoptée et je l'ai
adoptée"] (*Pour une littérature-monde*
302).

5 The Parti-Québécois held a province-
wide referendum on whether Quebec
should pursue sovereignty. The referendum was defeated by a percentage
of 59.56 to 40.44.

6 In letter XXX, written from Rica to his
friend Ibben, he describes how he is
perceived as an exotic Other when
wearing traditional Persian clothing,
but ignored when wearing a more European outfit. However, when mention
is made of Rica's ethnic origins, someone is certain to say, "Ah! The gentleman is Persian? That's something truly
extraordinary! How can one be Persian?" ["Ah! Ah! Monsieur est persan?
C'est une chose bien extraordinaire!
Comment peut-on être Persan?"]
(*Lettres persanes* 66).

7 For Paul Chamberland, who wrote the
preface to Gauvin's text, this question
refers explicitly to "the 'cultural fatigue' that became associated in post-
referendum years with the question
of the nation. For what could one have
to say about *the* question that's new
and original?" (8).

8 At this point, she mentions how the
notion of hospitality is ingrained in
Québécois society, referring to the
"beggar's bench," a piece of furniture
designed to provide a place to sleep
for unexpected guests or passersby.
The narrator writes: "That shows the
extent to which they respected the
other, the unknown" ["C'est dire à quel
point on respectait l'autre, l'inconnu"]
(49).

9 Moser-Verrey reinforces this idea,
positing that Gauvin "knows how to
invest the new language heralded by
Montesquieu with an interior reflection
in which otherness, femininity, and
Quebecness come together" (517).

10 An iconic nineteenth-century figure, the male *flâneur* figure was associated with public spaces and the observation of the changing nature of the modern city.

11 A humorous example of this occurs in the evocation of her thought processes while working at McDonald's: "While frying French fries, she conjugated this noble action in all tenses and in all its meanings" ["Tout en faisant frire les frites, elle conjuguait cette noble action à tous les temps et dans tous les sens"] (63).

12 As Alvares contends, further highlighting the essential role of the *Lettres persanes* as the text of choice for Djavann's Roxane, "He (Montesquieu) provides her with a model of writing: epistolary novel, travel narrative, a thematic of cultural diversity. But he also provides her with an ideological, political, and axiological model established during the Enlightenment, as the *Persian Letters* served as one of the inaugural texts of this period" ("Comment peut-on").

13 The author she mentions here is Sadegh Hedayat, one of the foremost twentieth-century Iranian writers of prose fiction.

Works Cited

Alvares, Cristina. "Comment peut-on être français? Les nouvelles *Lettres Persanes* de Chahdortt Djavann." *MondesFrancophones.com, Revue mondiale des francophonies*. 7 March 2009. http://www.mondesfrancophones.com/espaces/Frances/comptes-rendus/comment-peut-on-etre-francais/.

– "La réécriture des 'Lettres persanes' de Montesquieu par Chahdortt Djavann et l'émergence d'un nouveau discours féministe." *MondesFrancophones.com, Revue mondiale des francophonies*. 7 March 2009. http://mondesfrancophones.com/espaces/Psyches/articles/djavann.

Brière, Eloise A. "Quebec and France: La Francophonie in a Comparative Postcolonial Frame." *Postcolonial Theory and Francophone Literary Studies*. Eds. H. Adlai Murdoch and Anne Donadey. Gainesville: University Press of Florida, 2005. 151–74.

Chamberland, Paul. "Préface: Lettre à un(e) autre." *Lettres d'une autre*. 1984. Montreal: L'hexagone, 1994.

Djavann, Chahdortt. *Bas les voiles!* Paris: Gallimard, 2003.

– *Comment peut-on être français?* Paris: Flammarion, 2006.

– "De l'apprentissage du français à l'écriture." *Pour une littérature-monde*. Ed. Michel Le Bris et Jean Rouaud. Paris: Gallimard, 2007. 287–303.

– *Que pense Allah de l'Europe?* Paris: Gallimard, 2004.

Gauvin, Lise. *À la croisée des langues: Entretiens*. Paris: Karthala, 1997.

– *Langagement: L'écrivain et la langue au Québec*. Montreal: Boréal, 2000.

– *Lettres d'une autre*. 1984. Montreal: L'hexagone, 1994.

Montesquieu, Charles-Louis. *Lettres persanes*. 1721. Paris: Garnier-Flammarion, 1964.

Moser-Verrey, Monique. "Deux échos québécois de grands romans épistolaires du dix-huitième siècle français." *Voix et images* 12.3 (36) 1987: 512–22.

Oscherwitz, Dayna. "Decolonizing the Past: Re-visions of History and Memory and the Evolution of a (Post)Colonial Heritage." In *Memory, Empire, and Postcolonialism: Legacies of French Colonialism*. Ed. Alec G. Hargreaves. Lanham, MD: Lexington Books, 2005. 189–202.

Radia, Pavlina. "The Hyphenated *Flâneuse*: Privatizing Migration in Hiromi Goto's *The Kappa Child*." *Migrance comparée/Comparing Migration: Les littératures du Canada et du Québec/The Lite-

ratures of Canada and Québec. Ed.
Marie Carrière and Catherine Khordoc.
Bern: Peter Lang, 2008. 171–85.

Walker, Keith. "Mariama Bâ, Epistolarity,
Menopause, and Postcoloniality." *Post-
colonial Subjects: Francophone Women
Writers*. Eds. Mary Jean Green, Karen
Gould, Micheline Rice-Maximin, Keith L.
Walker, and Jack A. Yeager. Minneapolis:
University of Minnesota Press, 1996:
246–64.

France in the Heart of the Eastern Townships

LOUISE DUPRÉ

As a child, I loved school. The blackboard, the smell of chalk, the big maps hung on the walls, the plays we put on for the holidays, everything enchanted me. It must be said that in Sherbrooke, thirty kilometres from the US border, where I grew up, we used to live in a very puritanical society, based on traditional values: God, family, a nostalgic attachment to the motherland. We were still marked by the loyalist origins of the town, by the immigrants who had refused the independence of the United States and who had come to settle in the Eastern Townships, nowadays known as l'Estrie, in order to remain faithful to the king of England.

Fortunately, my mother came from a very open family, very avant-garde. And then there were the Sisters of Charity of Sacré-Coeur de Jésus – the French sisters, as our parents called them – a community that had established itself first in the US in 1905, and then in Quebec in 1907, and who ran the elementary school of the parish, the girls' normal school[1] and the classical college[2] that permitted adolescent girls from well-off families the chance to train to attend university. If the majority of our teachers were Québécois, some were nonetheless from France, like Sister Mary of Sacré-Coeur, my sixth grade teacher, whose photo I keep carefully in my old album. I was eleven, she seemed old to me at the time, even if she must have been less than forty. In the picture, she has no wrinkles, no crows' feet, a lovely smile, clear, frank and direct. She knew how to make us curious about everything: about French, foreign countries, and even math. She loved us and we loved her, we who asked only to learn, to discover the secrets of the wide world.

Did Sister Mary of Sacré-Coeur tell us of her homeland, of the city where she came from, of her social background, of her studies, of her dreams? I cannot recall. With time, I have realized that my memories of that period are pretty vague. But I remember very clearly one event that changed my life. It was in 1961, at the beginning of the Quiet Revolution. Jean Lesage had been elected Premier of Quebec, and he initiated a loan program so workers' children could have a better chance of attending classical college. Sister Mary of Sacré-Coeur asked my mother to come see her at school, and she had little trouble convincing her that I too should complete classical college, and then go on to university. She arranged everything: I sat the admission exams for the Collège du Sacré-Coeur, I obtained a study loan, and, the following year, I began classical studies in my gray skirt and navy blazer. I would study Latin, ancient Greek, French literature, English literature, and later I would go for an undergraduate degree in literature at the University of Sherbrooke.

I never knew what happened to Sister Mary of Sacré-Coeur. Did she stay with the order or did she leave the community in the wave of secularization that swept the Quebec of that time? Did she go back to France? Strangely, I had forgotten her. Or, rather, life snatched me up in its whirlwind and it was only recently, leafing through my photo album, that her face came back to me. It is only recently that I understood her importance in my life, I am almost ashamed to admit. For, if I was able to make it to university, I owe it to her, the first in a series of mentors without whom I would not be who I am today. Thanks to her, I always have enjoyed a special relationship with France. I had very good relationships with the instructors from the Hexagon who taught our classes at the college, and developed wonderful bonds at the university level with French coopérants[3] who, instead of doing their military service, came to teach in Quebec universities. Personally, I did not have the impression that the French had a colonialist mentality towards us.

By helping me to discover French culture, these professors opened me up to an *elsewhere*. I remember my pleasure at reading classical theatre, romantic and symbolist poets; I recognize in myself the influence of Flaubert, of de Beauvoir and of Duras. Other cultures were added to this one, other literatures, including Quebec literature, to which I would devote my Masters and doctoral studies. If that was my choice, it was not a choice against French literature, but rather because of a commitment to Quebec literature, to the necessity of creating a greater appreciation for it at a time when few researchers were doing so. I have always been very uncomfortable when Quebec literature was opposed to French literature, as if one had to choose sides.

The bonds that took root in childhood last a lifetime, it is common knowledge. Hence the fact that I have always had very close ties to France. My heart pounded when I first walked the streets of Paris: I had the impression of being in a new wave movie. I have always had wonderful French friends: collaborators, university colleagues or writers. Lately, I had the joy of working with Brigitte Haentjens, dramatist who had left her native France in 1977 to come first to Ontario, and then to Montreal. The play *Tout comme elle*, that deals with the mother-daughter relationship, gave us the chance to realize that, in France as in Quebec, the women of our generation have a similar connection to their mothers ...

There are enormous differences between Quebec's culture and French culture: this is not about denying them. But there are also more similarities than one might think. At a time when national identities are challenged, where the individual recognizes myriad and diverse forms of belonging, there is a heightened awareness of the fact that the barriers between us as individuals are porous. And it makes one stop and rethink the conventional wisdom about the bonds between Quebec and France.

Translation and notes by Miléna Santoro

Notes

1 *The Canadian Encyclopedia* gives an explanation of this system established in the nineteenth century to train teachers. http://www.thecanadianencyclopedia.com/index.cfm?PgNm=TCE&Params=A1ARTA0005781.

2 Classical colleges only existed in French-speaking Canada, and were the means by which students could gain access to university. They were private institutions, and their programs generally covered the last four years of secondary school and the first four years of university, the equivalent to an undergraduate degree program. See *The Canadian Encyclopedia*: http://www.thecanadianencyclopedia.com/ index.cfm?PgNm=TCE&Params=A1ARTA0001757.

3 This word has no equivalent in English. According to one source, some five thousand Frenchmen wishing to avoid national military service came to teach in Quebec from 1964 to 1984. See http://www.cegepat.qc.ca/quaran teans/cegep_67-69/coopérants.htm. This unique form of transatlantic exchange is chronicled by Jacques Portes in *Les coopérants militaires français au Québec, entre coopération et immigration* (Montreal, PUM, vol. 37, 2005).

54. Supper at C's. Oddly conjuring similar era. Of scarcity chez nous. It being creamed salmon. Like both our mothers making. In '50s. From tin. And powdered milk. Identical. In French or in English. In little houses. Beyond outskirts. Of Montréal. Québec. Sauce made of butter (margarine)/flour/onions. Or their juice. Two cups "milk" (C naturellement substituting crème fraîche). Cooked on double boiler. Also sometimes peas. Poured over toast. Snow likely falling. Or – nighthawks. Diving into heartbreaking pink Paris skyline ...

I telling how Madame X laughing. When I asking where to put what we calling *vidange*, garbage. They calling *poubelle*. Chez nous we also saying *oké*. Where they saying *d'accord*. *Bonjour* where they saying *au revoir*. Further leaving diphthongs slightly open. Inviting. They closing theirs up suavely. So we nasalizing pain, bread. Causing mockery in bakeries. Which rigour in personal presentation – C further speculating – possibly linked to French love of ritual. Citing habit of hailing butcher. Baker. Etc. In predetermined manner. Politesse oblige. Bonjour Madame. Oui Madame. Non Madame. Merci Madame. Au revoir Madame. I opining (grant it – miming Baudelaire) so-called rituals. Possibly only empty expressions of equality. Left over from early post-Revolutionary period. C segueing on romantically. To French formula for greeting. When encountering neighbour on street. Precise order for asking after health. Dog. Weather. Saying such rituals unthinkable chez nous. Given extremes of climate. Making us always in hurry. Ils ont le temps doux, they having clement weather. Flowers everywhere. She adding. Dreamily.

Instead of rituals. Would have said gestures. But this possibly Protestant way of thinking. Ritual requiring precise repetition. Whereas Protestantism preferring notion of proceeding forward. Rite of repetition considered waste of time. Or boring.

Gail Scott, *My Paris* 62–3

Marie Cardinal, Translator of Myths and Theatre: The Words to Say Difference

LOUISE FORSYTH

myths serve as monstrances or as monstrosities [les mythes servent d'ostensoirs ou de dépotoirs]

> Marie Cardinal, "Entrevue," *La Médée d'Euripide* 122[1]

From Algeria to France to Québec: Telling Stories and Thinking Otherwise

Marie Cardinal (1929–2001), a writer of fiction and non-fiction and translator of plays from ancient Greek and English into French, produced a rich body of work, striking for its simple beauty and its unflinching insight into the human condition as lived and viewed from a woman's perspective. Her life was lived in three more or less equal phases on three different continents: Algeria, France, and Quebec. This itinerancy, which produced a sense of never being quite at home, proved to be a remarkable source of vision and energy. Her status as outsider allowed her to engage in her writing with her own desires and demons in the tense context of today's global village.

A sixth generation member on her mother's side in a family of *pieds-noirs*, she and her family were forced to leave Algeria permanently at the end of the Algerian War of Independence. Although she was already an adult, having completed a Licence and Diplôme d'études supérieures at the Université d'Alger, taught philosophy and French literature in several European cities in the early 1950s, and married a French citizen with whom she had three children, the definitive break with the beloved land of her childhood was painful (See *Au pays de mes racines*). She made a first brief visit to Quebec in 1961. In 1962 she moved to Paris, published her first novel and began an extended period of psychoanalysis. The fictionalized account of this pivotal talking cure provides the subject and structure of her best-selling, influential novel *Les mots pour le dire*. Over the next four decades she divided her time between France and Quebec, never losing the heartbeat of the Mediterranean she had been forced to abandon.

The loss of a beloved homeland, playing itself out in counterpoint with memories of a troubled childhood in a violently dysfunctional family, had a profound influence on her personal life, awakening her mordant criticism of the ubiquitous violence and injustice pervading all societies, and her passion as a writer to find *the words to say it*. All her works show that she identified with those who were – singly or collectively – homeless, silenced, oppressed, or impoverished. The concept of being an outsider and the subject of *difference* run throughout her oeuvre, where identities are always hybrid and places to stand or to rest are unsure. Her exploration of the many sides of *difference* is a celebration of the uniqueness of individuals, places and moments and a savoring of dialectical processes whereby human existence reveals ever new and exciting folds. Concurrently with this celebration of *difference* in everyone as a fellow outsider, Cardinal shows the nasty underside of human nature that *difference* too often produces. The perception of *difference* lends itself too easily to attitudes of fear and distrust and to the dangerous temptation of creating labels and stereotypes that put Others in controllable places, and so justifies oppression of those who are perceived as *not fitting in*.

Cardinal's particular attention to women's condition and to pressures for conformity to dominant norms of femininity was a central, but not exclusive, part of her preoccupation to speak the truth about systemic injustices and abuses of power. Insofar as countries and cultures are concerned, Cardinal's loathing for colonizing powers – whether cultural, political, economic, or military – was absolute. The lies and hypocrisy that characterize the dominant rhetoric of such powers and that are used to justify the extreme violence they do stand in stark contrast to Cardinal's simple words that demonstrate her courage *to say difference* and to expose to full and unadorned view the dark side of human nature and its affairs. Her powerful commitment to end misogyny everywhere as a necessary initiative in attaining openness and justice for all oppressed persons was affirmed in her "Avant-propos" to *La Médée d'Euripide*:

[R]e-establishing the facts seems to be necessary. Re-establishing the facts means opening facts up, taking into account all the elements they are made of. Restoring to women their proper place in the adventures of the human species would not only repair an injustice. Above all, it would denounce a racist lie that hurts everyone and now warps the progression of peoples of the West, and probably elsewhere as well … Thinking otherwise! Nothing seems more important to me!

[[I]l paraît nécessaire de rétablir les faits. Rétablir les faits, cela veut dire ouvrir les faits, tenir compte de tous les éléments qui les composent. Rendre aux femmes la place qui est la leur dans l'aventure des êtres humains ne serait pas seulement réparer une injustice, ce serait surtout dénoncer un mensonge raciste qui blesse tout le monde et fausse, maintenant, la progression des gens en Occident, et probablement ailleurs aussi … Penser autrement! Rien ne me paraît plus important!] (37)

The attention of scholars who have written about Cardinal has been addressed almost exclusively to her novels and non-fiction, the extended period of her psychoanalysis, and her place as an Algerian expatriate writer and important voice during the 1970s in the French feminist movement. If these scholars cast a glance at all on her theatre translations, it is solely on *La Médée d'Euripide*, and briefly, in passing. Only Durham studies at length the major re-visioning of myth achieved by Cardinal and the vast historical and geographical context in which her ideas play. In failing to note the work Cardinal did in theatre translation in the 1980s and 1990s, most academics who have been interested in Cardinal as writer and activist have overlooked both a major dimension of her creative work and her important Quebec connection.

A powerful storyteller, Cardinal gave a unique autobiographical dimension to her narratives. Voices arising out of personal experiences and journeys are heard throughout her works. These voices, compelling in their authenticity, are foundational in her strategies for constructing characters. The representations of personal identity produced by her narrative approach create the impression of psychic porosity or fusion. Individuals pass through the barriers usually presumed to define and isolate the self from others, thereby coming to share intimate and frequently unacknowledged emotions, desires and motivations, often with painful results because of the conflicts within or between them. No sympathetic character in Cardinal's universe is allowed to have a comfortable sense of place, nor of coherent and unproblematic identity. The narrative voices in her fiction and non-fiction create the impression of being simultaneously "I" and "not-I," the self and an alter ego. The position of the enunciating voice in her works quite often slips from one character to another, even crossing from one sex to the other, breaking the logic of historical time, or stepping through the barrier between fiction and reality. This powerful ability to create the multiple voices of fictional characters sharing traits with herself or others led Cardinal to give their lives multi-layered kaleidoscopic shadows and reflections. This process of richly creative fragmentation of self and identity was extended during the 1980s and 1990s when she turned her attention to some of the great myths of the world's literature, finding in them the representation of her own peripatetic experiences, those of many others, and scenes of a world endlessly troubled by greed and ambition, colonialism, and war.

The only mythological character with a major role in Cardinal's fiction is Clytemnestra. The material incarnation of legendary Clytemnestra moves in for an extended period of time with the narrator of *Le passé empiété*, giving her own version of her gruesome story in great detail, simultaneously shedding new light on the narrator's own life, her troubled relations with her children, and the mysteries surrounding her father's life. After *Le passé empiété*, all renewals and re-visions of the classics occur in Cardinal's translations. Between 1986 and 2001, she published four theatre translations: *La Médée d'Euripide;* Ibsen's *Peer Gynt;* Euripides' *Les Troyennes;* and *Oedipe à Colone de Sophocle*. All were commissioned in Quebec and created on two of Montreal's main stages. She also collaborated with her daughter Alice Ronfard in the translation of Shakespeare's *The Tempest*.

Cardinal produced works of dramatic literature that are remarkable for the beauty of their language as written and for their orality and theatricality on stage. They resonate with central themes in her fiction and non-fiction and take them to new levels, places, and conceptual spheres. As well, her reflective translation practice made an original and significant contribution to the then relatively unexamined field of theatre translation theory.

Journeys on the Dark Side

Cardinal did not translate plays in which the characters are one-sided or unproblematically innocent, admirable, heroic or victimized. Instead, they are complexly human, capable of overvaulting ambition and faced with the consequences of their own tragic flaws. Her female characters step powerfully outside the narrow box of stereotypical femininity. They reflect moments in Cardinal's life journey and the sense of alienation that never left her as a woman and outsider. It is sometimes even male characters who embody her thematics and intimate experiences, particularly as wanderers, seekers, parents and individuals confronting their own disquieting impulses and mortality.

The circumstances of Cardinal's life were decisive in determining the subjects that preoccupied her: impossible love, troubled parent-child relationships, exile, dispossession, violence, war, madness, guilt, hatred, death, powerlessness, and outrage in the face of injustice. Characters are not always pretty, but their lives ring true.

Cardinal spoke about the first part of her life, writing, and translation practice in her conversations with Annie Leclerc and Hélène Pedneaulte, as published in *Autrement dit* and *La Médée d'Euripide*. However, much about her life and ideas must be inferred from the first-person narratives in her autobiographical novels and essays. All have a similar underlying pattern or plot in which a woman's life and her place in the world are inescapably ripped apart by the human conflicts that surround her. Finding the right words to explore this compelling story from many sides in all its layers and hidden corners was the way she chose to transcend the impasses it presented to her, particularly for her as a woman: "Speech is an act. Words are objects. Invisible, impalpable, cars swaying on the train track of sentences. They have been hermetically sealed by men, who have imprisoned women in them. Women must open them if they wish to exist" ["La parole est un acte. Les mots sont des objets. Invisibles, impalpables, wagons divaguant dans le train des phrases. Les hommes les ont fermés hermétiquement, ils y ont empri- sonné la femme. Il faut que les femmes les ouvrent si elles veulent exister"] (*Autrement dit* 53). From the foundational story of the life of a woman and a land ravaged by human conflicts, she constructed an entire universe showing the tragedy of families divided by death, vengeance, bitterness, silence and loss, yet carrying on with honesty and quiet human dignity.

The young Cardinal seems to have been unaware of France's feudal exploitation and oppression of Algeria's indigenous population and of the extreme animosity against the colonizers which was festering and then broke out in the 1950s. As a child, she savored the care given to her and her family by servants, and she basked in the richly luscious fragrances, flavours, colours, faces, music, and rhythms the Mediterranean landscape offered her: "My real mother was Algeria" ["l'Algérie c'était ma vraie mère"] (*Les mots pour le dire* 112). The Mediterranean awakened her to dialectics in cultural *difference* producing ways of knowing that intoxicated mind, body and spirit:

The Mediterranean is overpopulated and active. Intermingling of cultures has been happening there since the beginning of time. A complex sense of dialectics has been developed there, juggling with reasonable arguments, paradoxes and more or less specious conjectures. This game has caused a certain form of intelligence to be formed, and it expresses itself in a particular way.

[La Méditerranée est surpeuplée et active. Les cultures s'y entrecroisent depuis la nuit des temps. Le sens de la dialectique s'y est développé considérablement, jonglant avec les raisonnements, les paradoxes, les spéculations plus ou moins captieuses. Une certaine forme d'intelligence s'est formée à ce jeu et elle s'exprime d'une façon particulière.] ("Avant-propos," *La Médée d'Euripide* 14)

The freedom, diversity, and intense sensations that nurtured Cardinal's childhood and adolescence remained as a sort of lost paradise throughout her life. They determined the lyricism and sensuality of her writing. However, she was also living with hatred and violent control from her mother, a single parent, dogmatic Catholic, cruel disciplinarian, class snob and islamophobe (in spite of her hypocritically motivated daily charity work): "[M]y mother who, more than any other person, dwells in my bones – not only because she is my mother but because she was terrible: in turn Clytemnestra, Electra and Iphigenia" ["[M]a mère, qui participe plus que toute autre personne à mon squelette – non seulement parce qu'elle est ma mère mais parce qu'elle était terrible, tour à tour Clytemnestre, Électre et Iphigénie"] (*Autrement dit* 22). The narrator's long course of psycho-analysis (1962–68) in *Les mots pour le dire* reflects Cardinal's own struggle with her mother's devastating psychological legacy. The emotions she felt during the psychoanalysis and the truths she discovered about herself and her family were often unattractive, incomprehensible, violent and mad. Nevertheless, she was determined to draw out of the shadows, without respect for personal fears, verbal, or ideological taboos, truths unspoken even to herself – and to find "words to say it."

A particularly traumatic moment that left an indelible wound occurred when the narrator of *Les mots pour le dire* was a young adolescent. Her mother picked a moment in the streets to speak of her hatred for the husband she divorced the year the narrator was born and her determined but fruitless efforts to abort the foetus she was horrified to discover she was carrying: "There, in the street, in a few sentences, she poked out my eyes, she burst my eardrums, she ripped off my scalp, she cut off my hands, she smashed my knees, she ravished my belly, she mutilated my genitals" ["Là, dans la rue, en quelques phrases, elle a crevé mes yeux, elle a percé mes tympans, elle a arraché mon scalp, elle a coupé mes mains, elle a cassé mes genoux, elle a torturé mon ventre, elle a mutilé mon sexe"] (*Les mots* 164). It was not simply learning she had always been an aggressively unwanted child. Much more serious for the narrator and causing her to dwell on her mother's *saloperie* [trashy behaviour] was the recognition of the mother's inability to move beyond the hatred she felt for the man she accused of her first child's death. Passionately fuelling her hatred though seldom acknowledging it, the mother incessantly poured out a relentless flow of venom on the narrator, surrogate in her eyes for the despised father: "What I have called my mother's trashy behavior was not her having wished to abort ... her trashy behaviour was, on the contrary, her not having gone to the bitter end of her profound desire, not having aborted when she should have, and then continuing to project her hatred onto me" ["Ce que j'ai appelé la saloperie de ma mère ce n'était pas d'avoir voulu avorter ... sa saloperie c'était au contraire de n'avoir pas été au bout de son désir profond, de n'avoir pas avorté quand il le fallait; puis d'avoir continué à projeter sa haine sur moi"] (*Les mots* 170). It was the suppression of the mother's negative emotion, the fear and inability to bring it out to the light of day and deal with it that made the emotion so dangerously destructive. Cardinal's writing, which respects no criteria of taste and no culturally imposed taboos, particularly as they limit women's choices and produce troubling issues that are suppressed in silence rather than resolved, derives from the years' long suffering at her mother's hands. A salient quality of her writing is the refusal to use words to conceal. The characters in her theatre translations who, like sophists, use words to deceive or distort truths are always responsible for catastrophe. Cardinal's texts suggest that she believed discourse deriving from widespread practices of using words to deny or gloss over powerful negative emotions such as hatred, guilt and vengeance represent an unspoken evil that wreaks havoc on peoples.

Yet Cardinal's narrative alter ego discovered that she herself was not without violent impulses. The final phase of the psychoanalysis was the painful coming to the surface of what she termed both her greatest fault and her greatest strength: her capacity for violence, violence that was integral to who she was. Looking back on her childhood, the narrator realized that, without consciously knowing what she was doing, she had been able to protect her innermost sense of self, independence, pride and integrity by drawing on powerful sources of instinctive violence that allowed her to draw a sort of line in the sand and so resist her mother's violent aggressions: violence in answer to violence. Although frightened at learning this about herself, she saw at the same time that knowing oneself capable of violence is a sure sign of one's vitality and a powerful source of strength:

Today violence was coming to me like a dangerous and splendid present, a formidable weapon, incrusted with gold and nacre, that I was going to have to handle with the greatest care … I knew that I wanted to make use of it only to construct and not to destruct. Awareness of my violence brought with it, at the same time, awareness of my vitality, my gaiety and my generosity.

[Aujourd'hui la violence me venait comme un présent splendide et dangereux, une arme redoutable, incrustée d'or et de nacre, que j'allais devoir manipuler avec la plus grande précaution … Je savais que je ne voulais m'en servir que pour construire et non pour détruire. Avec la concience de ma violence est venue, en même temps, la conscience de ma vitalité, de ma gaieté et de ma générosité.] (*Les mots* 251)

Although she was a French citizen through her father, Cardinal could not comfortably find her place in France. The conflicts were deep, and she remained an outsider. On the one hand, French was her mother tongue and she was educated entirely through the rigorous, traditional French system. On the other hand, she had come to detest France during family visits with her mother for its moral complacency, its myriad and arbitrary codes of conduct, and its history as unscrupulous colonizer:

I detested France, the propriety of my family, the kings, the castles, the victories, the glories, the monuments, the smart stores, the boulevards, the temperate climate, the delicate, distinguished summer rains. It was hell for me to always have to pay attention to standing correctly, to eating correctly, to being dressed correctly. Shit!

[Je détestais la France, ma famille bien élévée, les rois, les châteaux, les victoires, les gloires, les monuments, les grands magasins, les boulevards, le climat tempéré, la fine pluie distinguée d'été. Pour moi c'était l'enfer: toujours faire attention à se tenir correctement, à manger correctement, à être habillée correctement. Merde!] (*Autrement dit* 15)

She could not, however, fail to recognize her privileged position as a well-educated person belonging to a land-owning family. Writer, translator, teacher and public intellectual, Cardinal knew she drew incalculable benefit from her excellent education:

I was unaware of my privileges. I didn't know at that time that the culture acquired in the course of all those years of study was going to provide me with a treasure such that, later, when I moved on in life, a woman's life, I would be rich beside the women who were my neighbors, because of the words, the books, the images, a whole pile of conventional or natural signs, justified or arbitrary, coded or uncoded, which I had become familiar with and which made my life easier, gave me the impression that I was not excluded, helped me understand my condition and thus rendered it less fatal, easier to overcome.

[Je n'étais pas consciente de mes privilèges. Je ne savais pas, à cette époque, que la culture accumulée au cours de toutes ces années d'études allait me pourvoir d'un trésor tel que, plus tard, lorsque je progresserais dans ma vie, qui est une vie de femme, je serais riche à côté de mes voisines, à cause des mots, des livres, des images, de tout un tas de signes naturels ou conventionnels, motivés ou arbitraires, codés ou non codés que j'avais appris à connaître et qui me rendaient la vie plus facile, me donnaient l'impression que je n'étais pas exclue, m'aidaient à comprendre ma condition et la rendaient, donc, moins fatale, plus aisée à combattre.] ("Avant-propos," *La Médée* 31–2)

The contradictions between memories of joyous sensuality in communion with the Mediterranean landscape and its people and both her mother's harsh, unloving discipline and the lies of French ideologies produced in her a severely divided sense of self.

In 1961 Cardinal's husband, Jean-Pierre Ronfard, who was to become one of Quebec's most influential men of theatre, moved across the Atlantic to Quebec. Cardinal visited him annually and spent much of her time there in the 1980s and 1990s, always maintaining a place in France, however. Cardinal came to feel great affinity for Quebec, finding that it was, despite the differences in climate, a second Mediterranean by virtue of its diversity, openness, cultural effervescence, vitality, and unresolved condition as outsider in North America, torn as its people are among the Americans, the French, the English:

It is a people I love, and I love their language. They have great difficulty situating themselves in the world. They are torn among the Americans, the French, the English. They are fierce and proud. They wish to live a life that is theirs, but what life, where is it?

[C'est un peuple que j'aime et j'aime leur langue. Ils ont une grand diffi-
culté à se situer dans le monde. Ils sont tiraillés par les Américains, par
les Français, par les Anglais. Ils sont farouches et fiers. Ils veulent vivre
une vie qui leur soit propre, mais quelle vie, où est-elle?] (*Autrement
dit* 94)

Marie Cardinal's own situation as outsider led her to feel most at home
among those who were unsure of where they belonged, to respect and cher-
ish *difference* and to challenge all manifestations of arbitrary authority. It
provided her with distance to hone her particularly acute vision on human
behavior and her exquisitely sharpened pen to find *the words to say it*.

Of Myths and Theatre Translations in Quebec

The choice by the narrator of *Le passé empiété* to spend her days with the
phantom of Clytemnestra reflects Cardinal's own choices when it came to
radically re-visioning dominant myths, narratives, discourse and meta-
narratives, to moving beyond simplistic binaries of good and bad, saint
and monster. She felt no complicity with the unproblematically beautiful,
admirable or merely victimized, only for those with a bad reputation: "The
only woman with whom I have relations that are slightly less oppressive is
Clytemnestra. Perhaps because of her bad reputation" ["La seule avec
laquelle j'ai des rapports un peu moins oppressants est Clytemnestre.
Peut-être à cause de sa mauvaise réputation"] (*Le passé empiété* 258).
Clytemnestra, like other real and imagined personages in the narrator's life
and like Cardinal's many characters of myth and legend, proves to be a
complexly troubling mirror of herself: "When you get right down to it, these
women are mirrors where I am reflected. What a drag that is! It's always
the same old story! What a tedious sight! Me as mother, me as daughter, me
as wife, me as woman, as woman, as woman, as woman!" ["Au fond, elles
sont des miroirs dans lesquels je me reflète. L'ennui que cela représente!
Quelle rengaine! Quel fastidieux spectacle! Moi en mère, moi en fille, moi
en épouse, moi en femme, en femme, en femme, en femme!"] (*Le passé
empiété* 258). They were also a reflection of those who peopled her disturbed childhood:

[I]n the Hellenic theatre, when I studied those texts at the University
of Algiers, it seemed to me that I was studying the annals of my family.
I recognized the characters; certain ones lived with me, in my house,

others had lived before in that same house or elsewhere, in regions where I knew every acre.

[[A]u théâtre hellénique, quand j'étudiais ces textes, à l'Université d'Alger, il me semblait que j'étudiais les annales de ma famille. Je reconnaissais les personnages, certains vivaient chez moi, dans ma maison, d'autres avaient vécu avant, dans cette même maison ou ailleurs, dans des contrées dont je connaissais chaque arpent.] ("Avant-propos," *La Médée* 10)

The first play translated by Cardinal was Euripides' *Medea*. She and Jean-Pierre Ronfard, who directed the play at the Théâtre du Nouveau Monde, both felt strongly that existing translations would not play satisfactorily in Quebec. Either the translations were done by academic translators paying little attention to the play's theatrical playability, or else or by contemporary writers having in mind the horizon of expectations and the languages of audiences and theatre people in France. She termed such translations: "a set of turgid, poetico-literary, profoundly boring texts, and in which, what is more, the public in general understands nothing, because they pervert our language to the point of stripping it of all life" ["un ensemble de textes ampoulés, poético-littéraires, profondément ennuyeux, et auxquels, de surcroît, le public en général ne comprend rien, parce que notre langue y est torturée au point de lui enlever toute vie"] ("Avant-propos," *La Médée* 26). What was needed was a good translation that would speak the language of contemporary francophone audiences in Quebec, without adopting *joual*, a widely used language in Quebec theatre but unsuitable for a play from another period and another place. In reading and re-reading Euripides' original text, to the point of feeling she was falling in love with the author, Cardinal succeeded magnificently in finding the words that allowed actors to perform the story while speaking the expressions, rhythms, intonations and images of Quebec.

Cardinal's lifetime resistance to France's affectations of linguistic and cultural superiority over all its former colonies is evident in her ironic determination to create a script that rang true in Québec in giving voice to specific social positions, sexual differences, and personality traits:

I no longer wanted Medea to express herself like a dowager from the city of Tours or like an erudite woman of the Paris court. I wanted her to speak like a woman from my parts. I was finally going to get even with

French translations and adaptations of the great Greek poets that make their texts boring. Boring as, in my childhood, I found the French boring. The French, those persons who spoke properly, who acted properly, who thought properly, who did everything properly.

[Je ne voulais plus que [Médée] s'exprime comme une douairière touran-gelle ou comme une érudite de la cour parisienne, je voulais qu'elle parle comme une femme de mes parages. J'allais enfin régler mes comptes avec les traductions et les adaptations françaises des grands poètes grecs qui rendent leurs textes ennuyeux. Ennuyeux comme, dans mon enfance, je trouvais ennuyeux les Français. Les Français, ces personnes qui parlaient bien, qui agissaient bien, qui pensaient bien, qui faisaient tout bien.] ("Avant-propos," *La Médée* 2)

Cardinal's original intention to tell Medea's story was soon joined by her desire to make the play speak passionately to real audiences, as it did millennia ago on stages in Euripides' time, and to restore the sensual and sensuous power she associated with the Mediterranean. She was dazzled by Euripides' feminism and his superb artistry as poet and playwright:

[F]inding myself face to face with him. The perfect construction of his work, the admirable balance of the text, the rhythm of the sequences, the choice of words, the ways they echo in the dialogue, all that was an indi-cation of such mastery in writing, such a sharp will to write exactly what is written.

[[M]e trouver face à face avec lui. La construction parfaite de son oeuvre, l'équilibre admirable du texte, le rythme des séquences, le choix des mots, la façon dont ils sont repris dans les répliques, tout cela indiquait une telle maîtrise de l'écriture, une volonté si nette d'écrire exactement ce qui est écrit.] ("Avant-propos," *La Médée* 18–19).

She was also convinced that Euripides had created in Medea a complex human being, much more multi-faceted than the female monster usually portrayed by the sexist accounts of the discourses of History, wherein women are usually marginalized into stereotypical roles with attention paid almost always exclusively to their places in patriarchal structures. Not only is Euripides' Medea a vengeful jealous woman and a monstrous mother who killed her children. She is also a tragic hero, a woman capable of great love, awesome feats of strength, and sacrifice. She possesses great knowledge and magic powers. The dangerous journey she chose for herself makes her responsible for her impossible situation in the play. Jason's craven and opportunistic abandonment of her has precipitated the crisis, leaving her in a situation that was perhaps of the greatest interest to Cardinal: the situation of having no place, no city, no country to call home: "I discovered, as I rummaged through the words, that Medea is first and foremost the tragedy of a foreigner, of someone who is not the same" ["je découvrais, en fouillant les mots, que Médée c'est d'abord la tragédie d'une étrangère, de quelqu'un qui n'est pas pareil"] ("Avant-propos," *La Médée* 16).

Cardinal did not alter significantly the plot line of *Medea*. Yet in finding the *words to say it* in the French of Quebec she restored the play's complexity and beauty. While never deviating from her conviction that the author of the play was Euripides, she played an equally creative role as translator. In choosing her words, she worked intensively and reflected profoundly in order to get in touch with the spirit of Euripides' play, despite differences in metre, cadence, rhythm, sounds, meanings, connotation, religious belief, historical and socio-cultural context:

I believe that a real translation is a creation. It is a creation inside another creation. It's becoming saturated with a text and reconstituting it differently *All the while remaining very close* [interviewer's interjection] … to the spirit! Yes! Never departing from the spirit! … That's what I did with Medea. I read, reread, reread, rereread, until every detail of every speech was in my head, until I had the impression of understanding the necessity of every word.

[Je crois qu'une véritable traduction, c'est une création. C'est une création à l'intérieur d'une autre création. C'est s'imprégner d'un texte et le restituer différemment *Tout en restant très proche* […] … de l'esprit! Oui. Ne jamais s'éloigner de l'esprit! … J'ai fait pareil avec Médée. J'ai lu, relu, rerelu, rererelu, jusqu'à ce que chaque détail de chaque réplique soit dans ma tête, jusqu'à ce que j'aie l'impression de comprendre la nécessité de chaque mot.] ("Entrevue" 116–17)

To which Cardinal adds, "A translation is a work of art" ["Une traduction est une oeuvre"] ("Entrevue" 125).

Cardinal continued in subsequent translations to develop working theories that respond to real performance needs, while respecting the creative spirit of original texts, as implemented in the "Préface" to *Peer Gynt*. Peer Gynt was a figure of Norse legend whose quest and itinerance ensure him an obvious place in Cardinal's panoply of characters:

The thing is that translation is, for me, an act of love. To translate is to fall in love with a text and with the person who wrote it ... What I want is, with my words – those of my language and those of my head – to be as close as possible to the author, his spirit, his desire ... Besides, I was doing a translation for Quebec. Indeed, numerous passages in *Peer Gynt* are written in a popular language: it's not a matter of slang or patois, but of everyday speech.

[C'est que la traduction, pour moi, est un acte amoureux. Traduire, c'est tomber en amour avec un texte et avec la personne qui l'a écrit ... Ce que je veux, c'est, avec mes mots, ceux de ma langue et ceux de ma tête, être le plus près possible de l'auteur, de son esprit, de son désir ... D'ailleurs, je faisais une traduction pour le Québec. En effet, de nombreux passages de *Peer Gynt* sont écrits dans un langage populaire: il ne s'agit pas d'argot ou de patois, mais d'une langue de tous les jours.] (*Peer Gynt* ii–iii)

Next, Cardinal translated with daughter Alice Ronfard Shakespeare's *The Tempest*, a play that picks up many of Cardinal's major thematic interests. Ronfard has discussed and illustrated the processes they developed together (See Works Cited). In her *mise en scène*, which received *Le Grand Prix de la Communauté urbaine de Montréal*, Ronfard made extraordinary use of multi-media technologies and cast Prospero, Caliban, Trinculo and the Master of the ship with women actors, not as males in disguise or drag, but as fully functioning performers transcending, without concealing, gender.

The production of Cardinal's translation of *Les Troyennes* elicited enthusiastic critical praise. In the history of the world's theatre, there has probably never been a play that depicts more intensely the agony of war, with the complete demolition of the city of Troy and the impact of the Greek invasion on women, all of whom are either killed or driven into exile: inescapable suffering, devastation, separation, rape, sexual slavery, dispossession and death. As Massoutre has discussed, Alice Ronfard's production of *Les Troyennes* formed the centre-piece of an extended discussion in Quebec theatre circles on the tragic, the genre of tragedy, and the inescapability of war in today's world. Wajdi Mouawad's reprise of Cardinal's *Les Troyennes* at the Trident Theatre in Quebec City opened on September 21, 1999.

The osmosis among the life story of Cardinal and her family, her fictitious characters and narrators, and the classical figures of myth and legend into whose voices she breathed new life, is particularly poignant in the case of her final translation: *Oedipe à Colone de Sophocle*. Cardinal died in 2001 in Aix-en-Provence, a city that radiates the aura of her beloved Mediterranean and where she discovered her love of theatre in the early 1950s. After decades of passage among three continents, she must have felt there, at least to some extent, she had come home. In Sophocles' play, Oedipus, the blind old traveler, archetype of all the ills humanity's flesh and spirit are heir to, has found reconciliation with all that befell him and has come to die in a place which he now knows is home, accompanied by daughters Antigone and Ismene. The parallel with Marie Cardinal's life and spirit journey is deeply moving. Jean-Pierre Ronfard directed the first performance of Cardinal's *Oedipe à Colone de Sophocle* at Espace GO two years after her death.

An indication of the enduring love and respect Marie Cardinal enjoyed in Quebec is seen in the program organized in her honor three years after her death by the Festival de Trois: *Les mots pour dire Marie* (August 9, 2004).

Notes

1 All translations are the author's, unless otherwise indicated.

Works Cited

Cardinal, Marie. *Au pays de mes racines*, suivi de *Au pays de Moussia*. Paris: Bernard Grasset, 1980.

– *Autrement dit*. Paris: Éditions Grasset et Fasquelle, 1977. *In Other Words*. Tr. Amy Cooper. Bloomington: Indiana University Press, 1996.

– "Entrevue de Marie Cardinal avec Hélène Pedneaulte." *La Médée d'Euripide*. Trans. Marie Cardinal. Montréal: VLB Éditeur, 1986. 109–28.

– *Les mots pour le dire*. Paris: Éditions Grasset et Fasquelle, 1975. *The Words to Say It: an Autobiographical Novel*. Tr. Patricia Goodheart. Cambridge, Mass.: VanVector and Goodheart, 1983.

– *Le passé empiété*. Paris: Bernard Grasset, 1983.

– Trans. *La Médée d'Euripide*. Montréal: VLB Éditeur, 1986. First performed at the Théâtre du Nouveau Monde in Montréal, directed by Jean-Pierre Ronfard, 18 November 1986.

– Trans. *Oedipe à Colone de Sophocle*. Montréal: Dramaturges Éditeurs, 2003. First performed at the Théâtre du Nouveau Monde in Montréal, directed by Jean-Pierre Ronfard, 16 September 2003.

– Trans. *Peer Gynt*. Montréal: Leméac/Actes Sud, 1991. First performed at the Théâtre du Nouveau Monde in Montréal, directed by Jean-Pierre Ronfard, 22 January 1991.

– Trans. *Les Troyennes*. Montréal: Leméac, 1993. First performed at the Théâtre du Nouveau Monde in Montréal, directed by Alice Ronfard, 27 April 1993.

Cardinal, Marie and Alice Ronfard, trans. *La tempête*. 1988. ADELinc., 2006. http://www.adelinc.qc.ca (accessed 13 February 2009). First performed by the Théâtre Expérimental des Femmes at Espace GO, directed by Alice Ronfard, 15 March 1988.

Durham, Carolyn A. *The Contexture of Feminism. Marie Cardinal & Multicultural Literacy*. Urbana and Chicago: University of Illinois Press, 1992.

Massoutre, Guylaine. "Pas à pas, mais pas mot à mot. La ferveur de la traduction chez Marie Cardinal ("la Médée" et "les Troyennes" d'Euripide)." *Cahiers de théâtre. Jeu* 68 (sept. 1993): 78–85.

Ronfard, Alice. "Traduire: un travail sur l'irrespect." *Cahiers de théâtre. Jeu* 56 (Sept. 1990): 85–91.

Webb, Emma, ed. *Marie Cardinal. New Perspectives*. New York: Peter Lang, 2006.

(Post)Colonial Performances: Nationalist and Post-nationalist Quebec Theatre in Europe

JANE MOSS

This collection of essays on literary and cultural relations between Quebec and francophone Europe must be read in the context of the on-going debate about the status of Francophone Studies and minor literatures in major languages. Since the manifesto "Pour une littérature-monde en français" ["For a World Literature in French"[1]] declared the death of *la Francophonie* in the spring of 2007, many writers and scholars have felt compelled to voice opinions on the complex issues involved. As an American who works on French North America, I, too, want to join in the discussion. While the notion of *littérature-monde en français* has special appeal to French intellectuals yearning to reclaim their dominance of the French-speaking world, to francophone writers residing outside their countries of origins, and to those seeking recognition beyond their own borders, it seems to me that it threatens postcolonial national literatures by reaffirming the universalist model and Paris as the capital – the Greenwich meridian – of the *république mondiale des lettres* [the world republic of letters].[2] Even if I set aside my skepticism and try to see this all as an idealistic attempt to unite French-speakers in the age of globalization rather than as a new form of cultural imperialism, I still think the concept of world literature in French has dangerous implications for North American francophone literature, especially for theatre.

Over the last forty years, theatre has been an important site for the performance of collective historical memories, the creation of distinct francophone identities, and the affirmation of unique linguistic communities. What happens to the performance of these identitary and linguistic differences when francophone North American theatre is subsumed under the label of world literature in French? What happens to minority francophone communities when literature frees itself from history and breaks the link between literature and nation? Are these goals that Québécois (or

Acadian, Franco-Ontarian, Cajun, and Franco-American) playwrights want to pursue? Depoliticized, denationalized, dehistoricized theatre may be possible, but I would argue that the *américanité* ["Americanness"] of francophone North American theatre cannot and should not be effaced. North American drama in French should preserve its New World origins, connection to geographic space, critical relationship to the anglophone majority, and linguistic particularities. In this essay, I will make my argument by looking briefly at the role that theatre has played in creating a Quebec national literature and then at the reception of Québécois playwrights in Europe.

Before describing specific Quebec theatrical practices and how they play in Europe, I would like to take note of the different terms that literary theorists have invented to classify the growing body of literature in major European languages written by nonnative Europeans or nonnative speakers: *littératures mineures en langue majeures* [minor literatures in major languages]; *petites littératures* [small literatures]; *littératures régionales, de l'exiguïté, de l'intranquillité* [regional literatures, literatures of smallness, of restlessness] (see Gauvin, "Autour d'un concept" 19–40). I suppose that one advantage of embracing the *littérature-monde* manifesto and liberating immigrant, diasporic, or postcolonial writers from the ghetto of Francophone Studies is that there would be no further need to debate terminology. If only it were that simple! Erasing the national or regional identities of writers does not erase what Lise Gauvin identifies as their "surconscience linguistique" ["linguistic hyperconsciousness"] (Gauvin, "Autour d'un concept" 19–40 and *Langagement*). Gauvin defines this as "a special consciousness of language which thus becomes a site of privileged reflection and a desire to examine the nature of language and to go deeper than the simple ethnographic discourse" ("Autour d'un concept" 19). Writing, she tells us, becomes a language act. More than just the inscription of orality into the written text or the mimetic representation of sociolects, the linguistic choices made by francophone writers reveal the status of a literature – how it integrates and defines its own codes, how it conceives of the nature and function of the literary ("Autour d'un concept"). Gauvin reminds us that the francophone North American writer is forced to think about the relationship to other languages (primarily English, but also normative French) because of his or her diglossic and heterolingual situation. The *surconscience linguistique* manifests itself variously as a metadiscourse on language carried on in essays, prefaces, manifestos, and interviews; as the thematization of language; or by the use of strategies such as hypercorrection, code-switching, and neologisms ("Autour d'un concept" 20–1).³ Assimilation in the pursuit of universality is rarely an option: most francophone North American authors would not betray their identity or *appartenance* [sense of belonging] and the French and Belgian literary institutions will not ignore their linguistic difference and their national origins.

The importance of language to the creation of a national literature cannot be over-emphasized, especially in the case of Quebec literature, which François Paré has characterized as a "petite littérature nationale" ["a small national literature"] (31). As early as 1974 Jacques Godbout, the only Québécois *pure laine* [pure-blooded] to sign the *littérature-monde* manifesto, stated emphatically: "[W]hat Québécois writers are trying to say to European French writers, with more or less success, is that French literary language is too polished, too cultivated, too stale, too colorless, too bookish, too codified, too proprietary, too correct for the use we want to make of it. In order to enter into History and violate American time/space, we need a French language that is more flexible and more wild and more useful than theirs, we need an uncivilized French, Québécois French, to civilize us" (As quoted in Gauvin, *Langagement* 39).

Thirty years after Godbout argued for a distinctive literature in Quebec French, Louise Ladouceur went one step further and affirmed the need for linguistically specific francophone theatres that reinforce multiple regional identities: "To make the oral specificity of one's language resonate on the stage is an act of affirmation and resistance for an anxious linguistic community whose identity is largely based on its way of speaking. The distinctive signs of this specificity being most clearly marked in vernacular language, it is in popular local speech that a dramaturgy intent on distinguishing itself from the norm, on building and naming its own repertory, must be written. Thus, parallel to Québécois literature, Acadian, Franco-Ontarian, Franco-Manitoban, Franco-Saskatchewan, Franco-Albertan and Franco-Colombian literatures have been created." (98) As Ladouceur argues, the case for maintaining the connection between language and identity is strong for Canadian francophones both in and outside of Quebec.

As we know, a key strategy for the collective project of constructing a Quebec national literature in the 1960s was the rejection of French literary models and linguistic norms. Since the project depended on legitimizing the use of oral Quebec French as a literary language – as Michèle Lalonde contends in her manifesto *Défense et illustration de la langue québécoise* (1979), it is not surprising that theatre was a privileged site for promoting vernacular French. Michel Tremblay, Jean Barbeau, Jean-Claude Germain, and other playwrights of what is called "le nouveau théâtre québécois" ["the new Québécois theatre"] wrote their plays in language that was a literary transcription of *joual*, the spoken language of the urban working class. Transgressing rules of grammar and syntax, introducing canadianisms, québécisms, and anglicisms, daring to be blasphemous and vulgar, playwrights and theatre collectives liberated the stage from language correctness that stifled creativity. In addition to using popular speech, they employed Brechtian and other counter-culture theatrical strategies to build a national and nationalist dramaturgy that revised and affirmed collective identity at the same time that it reflected more authentic images of social reality and expressed sovereigntist aspirations. This theatrical revolution was part of a process of cultural decolonization that also included the creation of national literary institutions – publishing houses, scholarly journals, a corps of critics, literary prizes, North American French dictionaries, etc.

While new forms of theatrical discourse were enormously successful in Quebec, early efforts to introduce European critics and audiences to francophone Canadian drama met with resistance.[4] Rather than comment on the specific sociopolitical message of new Quebec theatre, critics wanted to view theatre through universalizing lenses.[5] Critical reception often fell back on stereotypes related to language, primitivism, and violence. Quebec French was described as colorful, popular, folkloric, and old-fashioned – in other words, that of an uncultivated people. In his discussion of the 1973 reception of Michel Tremblay's *Les belles-sœurs*, Jean-Pierre Ryngaert says: "This question of linguistic comprehension will be at the heart of exporting Québécois theatrical texts to France for a long time, culminating in commissions for translations, as if vocabulary was the essence of theatre and of all the dramatic texts in the world *joual* had a monopoly on linguistic difficulty" (150). Ryngaert quotes one critic who saw Tremblay's "belles-sœurs" ["sisters-in-law"] as "paysannes déracinées" ["uprooted peasant women"] (as quoted in Ryngaert 152) and others who invoked "la mythologie bûcheronne" ["the woodsmen mythology"] of *Maria Chapdelaine* when describing the playwright himself (151). Fifteen years later, after viewing a 1987 Parisian production of Michel Tremblay's *Albertine, en cinq temps* in which French actresses were directed by André Brassard, the director of the original Montreal production, playwright Louise Lahaye wished that "some day Québécois texts may be exported to France alone, by themselves, without needing the support of a Québécois theatre company, a Québécois director, a local adaptation" (62).

Unfortunately, the perception of Quebec theatre remained much the same in the late 1980s and early 1990s when Michel Marc Bouchard's *Les feluettes* and *Les muses orphelines* and Marie Laberge's *L'homme gris* and *Oublier* were staged in Europe.[6] Because European audiences had difficulty understanding Quebec actors, productions with original casts posed problems and theatre directors felt often compelled to include glossaries and definitions of *joual* in the programs. Because European actors had difficulty pronouncing the transcribed vernacular of the plays, the texts were sometimes adapted or translated from the original into international French. In addition to commenting on the language of the plays, critics emphasized the violence and dark view of human relations of Quebec plays, which they connected to the harsh geography and climate of Quebec, as well as to the legacy of conservative Catholicism.[7] Despite Bouchard's popularity with French and Belgian directors,[8] critics continue to comment on his "langue charnue et voyou" ["fleshy, gutter language"] and on how his plays present "a dark analysis of this francophone American land, seen as oppressed by familial strictness and Catholic morality" (Costaz 105–6).

One aspect of a larger cultural phenomenon in Quebec after the defeat of the 1980 referendum on sovereignty-association was the turn away from politicized nationalist theatre that dramatized historical grievances, linguistic inferiority, and social ills. But if playwrights tired of sociopolitical drama, they continued to explore the literary potential of Quebec French and to invent new dramatic forms. The "nouvelle dramaturgie québécoise" that appears in the 1980s stages more intimate dramas, normalizes the use of Quebec French, and rejects psychological and stage realism. The most innovative strategies of this new dramaturgy are the ludic experimentations with language to create original poetic forms of theatrical discourse and the postmodern experimentation with hybrid forms, fragmented dialogue, dramatic illusion, and character.[9] Often referred to as a theatre of language because of its self-conscious use of highly literary language, this contemporary theatre also marks the return of the text after a period in which improvisational and imagistic forms dominated avant-garde Quebec theatre. Normand Chaurette and René-Daniel Dubois led the way in creating what has been called post-nationalist or post-Québécois theatre in the 1980s.

They were soon joined by Carole Fréchette, Larry Tremblay, and Daniel Danis – three Quebec playwrights whose plays are published, staged, and critically acclaimed in Europe as well as in North America.

Although the subject matter, tone, and theatrical imagination of these Quebec playwrights differ greatly, they do share some key strategies: the desire to create a new theatrical language freed from the restraints of sociological realism imposed by the *nouveau théâtre québécois* use of *joual*, a penchant for narrativization that liberates the stage from mimetic realism and allows for explorations of character subjectivity and reflections on universal questions through monologue, and the use of other anti-realistic stage elements. The experimentation with language and monologue infuses drama with an emotional charge and leads to cathartic transcendence of the tragic events that often constitute the subject matter of their works. The language of these playwrights is self-consciously literary and used for a variety of effects: sometimes it is lushly and verbosely lyrical, sometimes sexually graphic and vulgar, sometimes an expression of existential anguish. This new theatre of language and narrativity, which could be called postdramatic theatre for the expression of the postmodern condition, raises serious questions about human nature, spiritual and emotional emptiness, the relationship between language and identity. These playwrights often dramatize the struggle against meaningless and loneliness, alienation and death. Moving beyond specifically Québécois subject matter, they denounce all forms of criminal and political violence. While Quebec directors have sometimes been put off by the technical difficulty of staging nonrealistic plays and by the sophisticated literary language and intellectuality of many of these works (Vaïs 149–50), European directors have embraced Quebec playwrights who privilege universal questions over regionally specific subject matter and who experiment with theatrical forms. When asked to explain the enthusiastic reception of their work in Europe, Larry Tremblay, Carole Fréchette, and Daniel Danis all mention language and theatricality as the keys.[10] Since language was frequently seen as an obstacle to overcome in earlier attempts to stage Quebec drama in France and Belgium, it is clearly key to the inclusion of Quebec (and North-American French-language) plays in any future repertoire of world theatre in French. If North American francophone writers were now to accept the idea of *littérature-monde en français*, would it require them to turn their backs on decades of work to establish their legitimacy and to look again to Paris for models of modernity? Examining the work of Quebec playwrights who have successfully made transatlantic passages suggests that they are not trying to pass for French.[11]

It should be said that these transatlantic passages have been facilitated by a number of cultural organizations subsidized at various levels of government. Theatre festivals such as the Festival international des Francophonies in Limoges and Avignon-Off have been very important in the process of importing Quebec plays. Proponents of francophone drama in Paris have also been instrumental: Lucien Attoun showcased Quebec plays on France-Culture's program Nouvelle Répertoire Dramatique and at the Théâtre Ouvert, while Gabriel Garran staged Quebec plays at the Théâtre International de Langue Française. Theatres in Brussels and Liège have also welcomed Quebec playwrights. Since the 1990s, a number of Québécois and Néo-Québécois playwrights have been invited as writers-in-residence at French and Belgian theatres, found European publishers, seen their plays staged,[12] and been honored.[13] All of this can be interpreted as signs of the new French openness to francophone writing that underlies the *littérature-monde* manifesto. Optimism, however, must be tempered by the acknowledgment that the exportability of Quebec theatre sometimes depends on hiding what Louis Patrick Leroux calls its "québécité langagière et sociopolitique" ["linguistic and sociopolitical Quebecness"] ("Le Québec en autoreprésentation" 46). The "dramaturgie internationalisante" ["drama with an international bent"] that finds acceptance on European stages does so, according to Leroux, by minimizing the use of vernacular Quebec French and by stifling nationalist political messages ("Le Québec en autoreprésentation" 46). European directors do seem to show a marked preference for plays with universal themes, written in poeticized language, and employing avant-garde experimental forms, yet some are still looking to stage Quebec's New World difference, its *nordicité* [Northernness] or Amerindian roots. Given the enormous talent of the playwrights who came after the nationalist *théâtre joualisant* and who continue to build the *nouvelle dramaturgie québécoise*, European directors have much to choose from.

Among the contemporary Quebec playwrights who enjoy success in Europe, Carole Fréchette stands out. Although she began her career in the 1970s as part of the Marxist feminist collective, le Théâtre des cuisines, Fréchette turned away from militant political theatre in vernacular language when she began to write her own plays. Poetic in style and nonrealistic in structure, Fréchette's work explores universal humanist themes such as the quest for personal fulfillment in contemporary societies characterized by dehumanizing social alienation, materialism, and disintegrating family structures. She dramatizes the moral and material distress of solitary individuals living in a world filled with social injustice, poverty, and political violence and where love offers the possibility or the illusion of giving meaning to life. Fréchette's humanism *au féminin*, her highly literary language, and avant-garde staging strategies appeal to European theatre directors. Frequently invited as a playwright in residence, she wrote *La peau d'Élisa* (1998) during a stay in Brussels and *Le collier d'Hélène* (2000) while a guest in Beirut. Five other plays were commissions: *Morceaux choisis* for La Compagnie Ariadne in 2000, *Serial Killer* for the Théâtre de l'Est Parisien in 2003, *Route 1* for the festival celebrating the centennial of the French newspaper, *L'humanité* in 2004, and *La pose* for the Comédie Française in 2007. The emotional appeal and universality of her work explains why it is produced not only in France, Belgium, and Switzerland but also in translation in Germany, Belarus, English Canada, and Mexico. In Canada, she was honored with the 1995 Governor General's Award for *Les quatre morts de Marie* and the 2002 Siminovitch Prize for playwriting; in France she received the SACD (Société des Auteurs et Compositeurs Dramatiques) Francophone Prize at Avignon in 2002 and the Sony Labou Tansi Prize for *Le collier d'Hélène* in 2004. She now publishes in Europe, where some of plays have been performed before reaching Quebec audiences (see Moss, "Carole Fréchette et le théâtre au féminin").

With its self-consciously literary language, daring originality, and surrealistic imagination, Larry Tremblay's theatre also attracts international attention. There have been stage and radio productions of seven of his plays and publications in France and Belgium, plus translations in Italy, Scotland, Mexico, India, and English Canada. Leroux suggests that Tremblay's self-referential, language-driven, postdramatic aesthetic is in tune with the artistic sensibilities that currently dominate European theatre (e-mail 13 August 2008). Certainly, his absurdist approach to theatre, his preoccupation with universal questions such as death, mind-body connections, language, and the role of art in society distance Tremblay from the sociopolitical concerns of naturalist Quebec drama. This would explain the popularity of *Le déclic du destin* (1989) and its sequel, *Le problème avec moi* (2007), *Leçon d'anatomie* (1992), *Les mains bleues* (1998), and *Le ventriloque* (2000). Yet Tremblay remains attached to his North American roots as *The Dragonfly of Chicoutimi* (1995) and *Abraham Lincoln va au théâtre* (2008) make clear. Describing his reactions to

Tremblay's plays, French director Michel Cochet speaks of his fascination with the hallucinatory, irrational, fantastical elements of the plays with their jarring mixture of humor, existential anguish, and dark humor. Interestingly enough, Cochet's comments seem to suggest that Tremblay's uniqueness can in part be attributed to his Quebec origins, which free him from the weight of French cultural and theatrical traditions. Tremblay himself believes that what attracts Europeans to his work is

the work on language (musicality, poetry in which contradictory images appear in the same sentence): … the ostentatious theatricality of my texts, which distances them from the more common realist/psychological theatre and to a certain extent brings them closer to a theatre of speech and of the body-as-speech.

I believe, without pretension, that my works depend on a writerly language rather than a referential language (a language of the streets, or different levels of language corresponding to social classes). It is my personal appropriation of the French language that – I imagine – interests French and Belgian directors.

[le travail sur la langue (musicalité, poésie où des images contradictoires se retrouvent dans la même phrase); … la théâtralité affichée de mes textes, qui les éloigne du courant dit réaliste/psychologique et les rapproche en partie d'un théâtre de la parole et du corps-comme-parole.

Je crois, sans prétention, que mes œuvres relèvent d'une langue d'auteur et non d'une langue référentielle (une langue de la rue, ou encore différents niveaux de langue exprimant des couches sociales). C'est mon appropriation personnelle de la langue française qui – j'imagine – intéresse les metteurs en scène français et belges.] (e-mail 14 July 2008)

Tremblay's comments reinforce Lise Gauvin's argument about the francophone writer's special sensitivity to language. The *surconscience linguistique* of Quebec's *dramaturges de la parole* is the product of the minority status of French in North America as well as a reflexion on vernacular Quebec French.[14]

From the beginning of his career, Daniel Danis has been embraced by directors, publishers, and translators in Quebec, English Canada, and Europe. He has also been much honored by critics and institutions. His first play, *Celle-là*, won the Governor General's Award in 2003, as well as the Paris Drama and Music Critics Prize for Best New French-language Production. His second play, *Cendres de cailloux*, won first prize in the International Text Competition at the Maubeuge Festival and Radio-France International's Prize. *Le langue-à-langue des chiens de roche* earned him a second Governor General's Award in 2002, followed by a third in 2007 for *Le chant du dire-dire*, which was also named Best New French-language Production by the Paris Drama and Music Critics. *e (roman-dit)* received the Grand Prize for Dramatic Literature for a francophone work in 2006. His work has been published in Canada by Leméac and Talonbooks and in France by Actes Sud, Théâtre Ouvert, L'Arche, and L'école des loisirs. His plays have been staged in Paris at the Théâtre Ouvert, the Théâtre National de la Colline, L'Espace Prévert, the Théâtre du Vieux-Colombier, at Festivals in Avignon and Limoges, and in numerous cities in Europe, English Canada, and Mexico, both in French and in translation. Danis now divides his time between his home in the Saguenay and France, where he has been writer in residence at the Théâtre National de la Colline and a visiting faculty member at Le Fresnoy, the National Studio for Contemporary Arts.

For all of his success in Europe, theatre directors and critics hardly ever fail to make references to the playwright's provincial roots or to mention the distinctiveness of his North American French.[15] Alain Françon, who has been directing French productions of Danis's plays since 1995, comments "There is something rare, authentic, a curious mixture of modernity and archaism in Daniel's writing … This language makes one think of primitive art" (qtd. by Polle 84). For Françon and other French theatre people, Danis is exotic, somewhat primitive, firmly attached to the imposing natural landscape of Quebec. The pedagogical dossier prepared by Logomotive Théâtre for its production of *Cendres de cailloux* included a *lexique québécois* for audiences on its 1996–99 French tours.[16] The program notes for the 2007 Compagnie Gérard Gérard production of *Le chant du dire-dire* offer further evidence that the French fascination with Quebec's *nouvelle dramaturgie* is related to stereotypes of North American francophones:

Le chant du dire-dire is a Québécois text fashioned by the snow and climate of winter. The landscape of a nowhere beyond the reach of compasses … Others, like Normand Chaurette or Carole Fréchette, constitute with Daniel Danis the new generation of Québécquois playwrights. Appearing after Michel Tremblay, they draw their unusual dramatic language from the oral heritage of "Joual" …

It is in oral tradition that Québécois theatre found its identity. It makes its appearance as a pillar of *la Francophonie* …

It is this language, and its urgent need to be spoken and heard, that was the point of departure for this production.[17]

[*Le chant du dire-dire* est un texte québécois façonné par la neige et le climat des grands froids. Le paysage d'un nulle part hors de portée des boussoles …

D'autres comme Normand Chaurette ou Carole Fréchette, constituent avec Daniel Danis la nouvelle génération des dramaturges québécois. Apparus après Michel Tremblay, ils puisent leur langage dramatique, insolite dans l'héritage oral du "Joual" …

C'est dans la tradition orale que le théâtre québécois a trouvé son identité. Il apparaît comme un pilier de la Francophonie …

C'est de cette parole, et de sa nécessité à être dite et entendue, que nous sommes partis pour cette création.] (6)

The program's brief biographical note mentions that Danis grew up in the Abitibi-Témiscamingue region, "long the kingdom of woodsmen, trappers and Algonquin Indians" ["longtemps restée le royaume de coureurs des bois, des trappeurs et des amérindiens Algonquins"] (9). It goes on to tell us that Danis now resides in the Saguenay, described as an immense region possessing the Saguenay River, "the only navigable fjord in North America" ["seul fjord navigable en Amérique du Nord"] and Lac Saint-Jean, "a veritable inland sea" ["véritable mer intérieure"] (9). The portrait of Danis as a frontiersman in the Great Northern Wilderness is reinforced by a quotation from the playwright himself in which he makes the connection between his language and his *appartenance*: "I long believed that it was my brain that guided my hand, but now I know that my language is in my foot … because it is my foot that touches the ground and connects me to this mother earth" ["J'ai cru longtemps que c'était mon cerveau qui guidait ma main, je sais maintenant que ma langue est dans mon pied … parce que c'est lui qui touché le sol et me relie à la terre-mère"] (9). The insistence on the primitive exoticism of Danis's language, on his connection to the northern wilderness, ironically recalls the oft-quoted comment by nineteenth-century Quebec poet Octave Crémazie who suggested that the French would be more interested in a Canadian who wrote in the Huron or Iroquois language than in those who wrote in French (as quoted in Gauvin, *Langagement* 24).

Dominique Lafon and others have argued that the invention of a specific Quebec dramatic language, the kind of self-consciously literary version of popular oral speech being created by Daniel Danis, was made possible by the nationalist use of *joual* in the *nouveau théâtre québécois*. Lafon explains: "The maternal language is the language of the mother, first *joual*, but then the say-say, the tongue-talk, a reinvented poetic language, freed from hexagonal French" (190). Like Gauvin, Lafon points to "l'effet joual" ["the *joual* effect"], by which she means the stylistic modernization of theatrical language that emancipates speech from its submission to borrowed or learned norms of correctness (192–94). In Danis's theatre of language, Lafon sees a strong connection between language and territory, language and the body. She describes his "language in which meaning plays out in anaphore, phoneme, rhythm, in the creation of original sound sequences that express the language of the body more than the language of meaning" (194). Gilbert David speaks of an original "poetics of orality" that creates "a language of strange familiarity" in Danis's theatre (68–70). Analyzing what he calls "la parole performative," David points to monologues and oratorios, elegies and trance-like rituals, vulgar arguments and cosmic celebrations, erotic lyricism (73–8). Amidst the carnivalesque profusion of language, David notes an abundant use of neologisms, poetic repetition, alliteration, parallelism, doubling of descriptive adjectives – all of which gives the impression that Danis is inventing ludic idiolects (73–80).

Danis has now produced an impressive body of work – plays, *romans-récits*, and mixed media performance pieces. Whether written for adults or children, set in Quebec or elsewhere, all of Danis's plays have universal messages expressing his compassion for victims of social injustice, prejudice, poverty, violent crime, war, natural disasters, and other forces that impede the human potential for love and happiness. In order to survive, they need friendship, love, tenderness, and communication. Facing constant threats from natural disaster and human violence, living in societies whose institutions do not guarantee their welfare, deprived of a benevolent deity, his characters suffer physically and morally, yet they continue their personal quests dignity, happiness, and communion with the natural world and their collective quests for equality and peace. Danis transcends regionalism and creates a universal body of work distinguished by the invention of an original language and hybrid theatrical forms that create possibilities for his characters to re-tell and re-enact their stories. It is a body of work that richly deserves recognition by the world republic of letters.

As this brief look at the reception of Quebec plays in francophone European countries has shown, linguistic and cultural differences – once considered obstacles to importing Quebec theatre – are now seen as adding value. What had been interpreted as markers of cultural inferiority are now praised as signs of literary virtuosity and refreshing originality. Explaining Quebec drama's appeal to European audiences in terms that stress its *américanité*, Daniel Danis says:

These are writings that take root in Québécois French, but which transcend it to become a poetry considered distinct from that which the French are accustomed to hearing. The vocabulary and syntax have a vitality different from theirs ... The French themselves seem close to our language in its reality, but since we use a different syntax and are marked by our Americanness, that strikes the imagination.

[Ce sont des écritures qui prennent racine dans un français québécois, mais qui le transcendent pour en faire une poésie considérée comme distincte de celle que les Français ont l'habitude de fréquenter. Le vocabulaire et la syntaxe ont une vitalité différente des leurs ... Les Français, eux, semblent proches de notre langue dans sa réalité, mais, comme nous utilisons une autre syntaxe et que nous sommes empreints d'américanité, cela frappe l'imaginaire.] (qtd. in Vaïs 151)

Since the transatlantic passages of post-nationalist Quebec plays depend on their distinctiveness and alterity, to efface those differences would be to undermine the appeal of these wonderful postcolonial performances.[18]

Notes

1 All translations are the author's, unless otherwise indicated. Portions of this article, reprinted by permission of the publisher, first appeared in my article "Daniel Danis, New Québec Dramaturgy and World Literature in French," *Contemporary French and Francophone Studies* 13.1 (January 2009): 25–33 (Taylor and Francis Ltd, http://www.informaworld.com).

2 Cf. Le Bris on "littérature-monde en français" and Casanova on "la république mondiale des lettres." See Guy Spielmann's chapter in this volume for additional discussion of the "Littérature-monde" manifesto.

3 In a series of articles since the mid-1990s, I have analyzed the thematization of language in the work of Larry Tremblay and Daniel Danis, and the use of vulgarity in contemporary Quebec theatre.

4 *L'annuaire théâtral* 27, on the theme

of "Circulations du théâtre québécois" and edited by Gilbert David and Dominique Lafon, is devoted to documenting and analyzing the reception of Quebec theatre abroad. In his article, "D'une enterprise nationale au rayonnement planétaire," Claude Des Landes describes some of the earliest productions of Quebec plays in France as fiascos, but says that the 1970–90 period laid the groundwork for the success that came in the 1980s. Diane Pavlovic's article, "Les mouvances d'une dramaturgie: au-delà du statut de curiosité" analyzes the institutional links that facilitated exchanges and the evolution in Quebec drama that made it more acceptable to European audiences. She believes that the success of the last twenty years is due to the fact that Quebec dramaturgy is now "more diverse, and often more complex, in terms of form, more literary and more 'planetary' in its preoccupations, more detached from the politically motivated speech and kind of realism that prevailed for a long time ..." (47). Michel Tanner's article, "Le théâtre québécois et la communauté française de Wallonie: rencontres et conflits" claims that the language of some Quebec plays is incomprehensible to Belgian audiences. He recounts how *joual* and English passages, Quebec accents, and local references were eliminated in productions of plays by René-Daniel Dubois, Daniel Danis, and Jean-François Caron (80).

5 In his analysis of the 1973 French critical response to *Les belles-sœurs* for *L'annuaire théâtral* 20, Jean-Pierre Ryngaert says: "The sociopolitical context is never named. The battle over language is never taken into account, or perhaps it is totally misunderstood. Turning to the universal is convenient, because it allows one to ignore what was really going on locally. The tactful diplomatic reception eliminates all reference to nationalism" (152).

6 *L'homme gris* was adapted for productions in Paris and Brussels by Jacques De Decker and published in *Avant-scène théâtre* 785 (1 March 1991). Ironically, Québécois Michel Biron who saw the Théâtre National de Bruxelles production of Laberge's 1987 play, *Oublier*, remarks that the text, which had been "remanié" ("touched up") by De Decker and Laberge, hit a number of false notes. Biron mentions the problem that the Belgian actresses had articulating certain vernacular expressions and that the costumes were inappropriate for the play's winter setting (123-6). *Études théâtrales* published a volume containing Noëlle Renaud's version of *Les muses orphelines* and Eugène Durif's version of *Le chien* in 1988. The practice of "adapting" Quebec texts for European stages has not disappeared completely: a European French version of Bouchard's light comedy, *Les grandes chaleurs*, was done by Christian Bordeleau for L'Espace La Comédia in Paris in June 2000.

7 Belgian publisher Emile Lansman, who has published many Quebec playwrights, tempers his enthusiasm for Quebec drama by expressing some exasperation with its obsession with impossible love, unhappy homosexuality, tortured family relations, absent mothers, missed opportunities, guilt and remorse, lapsed morality, etc. (87–8).

8 Bouchard's "Théâtrographie" viewable on the web, shows that he has been enormously successful in Europe since the early 1990s. *Les feluettes*, *L'histoire de l'oie*, *Les muses orphelines*, and *Le chemin des passes dangereuses* have been staged many times by many different theatre companies. More recently, his light come-

dies *Les grandes chaleurs* and *Papil-lons de nuit* have been staged. The practice of "adapting" his texts has, unfortunately, not disappeared: Christian Bordeleau did a European French version of *Les grandes chaleurs*, for L'Espace La Comédia in Paris in June 2000.

9 See Riendeau 13–18; Moss "Franco-phone Drama" and "Théâtre de la langue, théâtre narrativisé, théâtre post-dramatique … et Daniel Daniel."

10 In addition to comments made by Danis and Fréchette and cited by Vaïs, I am relying on comments made by L. Tremblay in a personal e-mail to me on 14 July 2008.

11 Happily, European audiences and critics have evolved along with Quebec dramaturgy over the last three decades. Explaining the enthusiasm of European francophones for certain Quebec playwrights, Diane Pavlovic writes: "A certain quality of emotion, a triumphant vitality, a pretty casual attitude toward tradition and its heavy weight, in a word, a breath of sensuality and freedom, these are the comments that come up often over the years from those who are regularly invited to explain what appeals to them in the theatre written here" (53).

12 In addition to Michel Marc Bouchard, Marie Laberge, Normand Chaurette, Carole Fréchette, Larry Tremblay, and Daniel Danis, other Quebec playwrights who have seen their work produced in France and Belgium include René-Daniel Dubois, Michel Garneau, Jean-François Caron, Geneviève Billette, Dominick Parenteau-Lebeuf, and Sébastien Harrisson. Abla Farhoud and Wajdi Mouawad, two Quebec writers with Lebanese roots, have been particular favorites in France. Both have also lived in France for extensive periods of time. Mouawad now divides his time between France and Canada, so it

comes as no surprise that he would sign the "Littérature-monde" manifesto. Guy Teissier has detailed the French critical reception of Robert Lepage's work, which I do not discuss here since I believe it transcends the category of Quebec drama. Publishers Actes Sud-papiers, Éditions théâtrales, Éditions Lansman, L'arche, L'école des loisirs, and Théâtre ouvert have all edited plays by Quebec writers.

13 Quebec dramatists named Chevaliers de l'Ordre des arts et des lettres of the French Republic include Michel Tremblay, Marie Laberge, Daniel Danis, and Carole Fréchette. In addition to awards received by Fréchette and Danis that are mentioned in the text, Normand Chaurette has won the Tchicaya U Tam'si Prize for *Petit navire*, the CIC Paris theatre prize for *Les reines*, and the Essor Prize from the French Minister of Education and Culture for *Stabat mater I*.

14 Describing his experience with French productions of his plays *Saganash, Aux hommes de bonne volonté*, and *La nature même du continent,* Jean-François Caron claims that the French actors and directors appreciate the difference and uniqueness of his dramatic language, which often makes deliberate errors of syntax, orthography, and grammar (160). He suggests that the foreignness of his language makes French actors work harder to understand the texts, to bridge the distance between European French and his original use of language (161). I would suggest that the *surconscience linguistique* described by Gauvin accounts for the French fascination with Caron, as with Danis and other Québécois *dramaturges de la parole*.

15 Discussing the critical reception of Normand Chaurette's *Le petit Köchel*, Sylvano Santini cites an article by Robert Lévesque ("Les douceurs colo-

niales d'Avignon," *Ici*, 20–27 July 2000) that argues that the positive reviews by French critics were tainted by a tone of condescension and by constant references to Chaurette's Quebec origins (Santini 162–4). This is particularly ironic since, as Yves Jubinville notes (109), Chaurette rejected the stage use of *parlure québécoise* in favor of a *dramaturgie de l'écriture*.

16 The original production of *Cendres de cailloux* by Logomotive Théâtre in 1996 was followed by three years of touring, 1996–97, 1997–98, 1998–99.

17 I reproduce the Program's inconsistent spelling of the adjective *québécois*. The same program page includes a definition of the term *joual* for its French audience.

Works Cited

Biron, Michel. "Lettres de Belgique." *Jeu* 46 (1988): 123-6.

Caron, Jean-François. "La langue unique de l'auteur." *Jeu* 120 (2006): 155-61.

Casanova, Pascale. *The World Republic of Letters*. Trans. M.B. DeBevoise. Cambridge: Harvard University Press, 2004.

Cochet, Michel. "Michel Cochet on Larry Tremblay: An Auto-Interview." In *Transatlantic Passages: Literary and Cultural Relations between Quebec and Francophone Europe*. Eds. Paula Ruth Gilbert and Miléna Santoro. Montreal: McGill-Queen's University Press, 2010. 175-7.

Compagnie Gérard Gérard. Program, *Le chant du dire-dire*. http://www.ciegerardgerard.fr/doc/DDP-LeChant duDireDire.pdf. Accessed 30 July 2008.

Costaz, Gilles. "Un auteur québécois à l'affiche. Bouchard et ses bouteilles à la mer." *Avant-scène théâtre* 1211 (15 October 2006): 105-6.

David, Gilbert. "Le langue-à-langue de Daniel Danis: une parole au corps à corps." *Études françaises* 43.1 (2007): 63–81.

Des Landes, Claude. "D'une enterprise nationale au rayonnement planétaire." *L'annuaire théâtral* 27 (2000): 30–43.

Gauvin, Lise. "Autour du concept de littérature mineure – variations sur un thème majeur." *Littéraures mineures en langues majeure. Québec/Wallonie-Bruxelles*. Brussels/Montreal: Peter Lang/Presses de l'Université de Montréal, Coll. Documents pour l'Histoire des Francophonies / Théorie, 2003, 19–40.

– *Écrire pour qui?* Paris: Karthala, 2007.

– *Langagement. L'écrivain et la langue au Québec*. Montreal: Boréal, 2000.

– "Le théâtre de la langue." *Le monde de Michel Tremblay*. Gilbert David et Pierre Lavoie, dirs. Montreal: Cahiers de théâtre Jeu/Editions Lansman, 1993. 335-57.

Godbout, Jacques. "La question préalable." *Pour une littérature-monde*. Michel Le Bris et Jean Rouaud, dirs. Paris: Gallimard, 2007. 103–11.

Jacques, Hélène. "Le secret des choses. Larry Tremblay en quatre temps." *Jeu* 120 (2006): 8–14.

Jubinville, Yves. "Le partage des voix: Approache génétique de la langue dans les dramaturgies québécoises contemporaines." *Études françaises* 43.1 (2007): 101–19.

Ladouceur, Louise. "Parler, écrire et traduire dans la langue de Dalpé." *Jean Marc Dalpé: Ouvrier d'un dire*. François Paré et Stéphanie Nutting. Ottawa: Prise de parole, 2007. 97–112.

Lafon, Dominique. "La langue-à-dire du théâtre québécois." *Théâtres québécois et canadiens-français au XXe siècle. Trajectoires et territories*. Eds. Hélène Beauchamp and Gilbert David. Montreal: Presses universitaires du Québec, 2003. 181–96.

Lahaye, Louise. "Du théâtre québécois à Paris." *Jeu* 51 (1989): 61–3.

Lalonde, Michèle. *Défense et illustration de la langue québécoise*. Paris: Seghers, 1979.

Lansman, Émile. "Éditer des dramaturges de la francophonie: Le 'cas' du Québec." *L'annuaire théâtral* 27 (2000): 82–9.

Le Bris, Michel. "Pour une littérature-monde en français." In *Pour une littérature-monde.* Michel Le Bris et Jean Rouaud, dirs. Paris: Gallimard, 2007. 23–53.

Leroux, Louis Patrick. "Le Québec en auto-représentation: Le passage d'une dramaturgie de l'identitaire à celle de l'individu (théâtres biographiques, rhapsodiques, autogynographiques, autoréflexifs, autofictionnels et autobiographiques)." Diss. Université de Paris III, 2008.

– E-mail to author, 13 August 2008.

Logomotive Théâtre. Program for *Cendres de cailloux.* Cendres_dossier_pedagogique.pdf. Downloaded 8 July 2008.

Moss, Jane. "Carole Fréchette et le théâtre au féminin." *French Review* 78.6 (May 2005): 1117–26.

– "Daniel Danis, New Quebec Dramaturgy, and World Theatrical Literature in French," *SITES* (January 2009): 23–31.

– "Larry Tremblay and the Drama of Language." *American Review of Canadian Studies* 25.2–3 (Summer-Autumn 1995): 251–67. Trans. by Jean-Guy Laurin, "Larry Tremblay et la dramaturgie de la parole." *L'annuaire théâtral* 21 (Spring 1997): 62–83.

– "Théâtre de la langue, théâtre narrativisé, théâtre post-dramatique … et Daniel Daniel." Keynote address at Conference "Dire-Dire les voix. Affabulations, mythologies et 'corps parlants' dans le théâtre de Daniel Danis." Université de Montréal, March 2008.

Paré, François. *Les littératures de l'exiguïté.* Hearst: Éditions du Nordir, "Essai," 1992.

Pavlovic, Diane. "Les mouvances d'une dramaturgie: Au-delà du statut de curiosité," *L'annuaire théâtral* 27 (2000): 44–54.

Polle, Emmanuel. "Daniel Danis, de l'art brut avec des mots." *Avant-scène théâtre* 1179 (1 March 2005): 84–5.

Riendeau, Pascal. *La cohérence fautive. L'hybridité textuelle dans l'œuvre de Normand Chaurette.* Québec: Nuit blanche éditeur, 1997.

Ryngaert, Jean-Pierre. "Le Québec comme reserve d'émotion et territoire de l'âme pour les Français: Michel Tremblay et Daniel Danis à Paris." *L'annuaire théâtral* 27 (2000): 147–59.

Santini, Sylvano. "La double étrangeté du *Petit Köchel* – De la 'petite littérature' à la 'littérature mineure.'" *Littératures mineures en langue majeure.* Eds. JeannePierre Bertrand and Lise Gauvin. Brussels/ Montreal: Peter Lang/Presses de l'Université de Montréal, Coll. Documents pour l'Histoire des Francophonies /Théorie, 2003. 159–77.

Tanner, Michel. "Le théâtre québécois et la communauté française de Wallonie: Rencontres et conflits." *L'annuaire théâtral* 27 (2000): 76–81.

Teissier, Guy. "French Critical Response to the New Theater of Robert Lepage." *Theater sans frontières: Essays on the Dramatic Universe of Robert Lepage.* Ed. Joseph I. Donohoe and Jane M. Koustas. East Lansing: Michigan State University Press, 2000. 231–54.

– "'De la dithyrambe pure à la critique acide.'" La France accueille Robert Lepage …" *L'annuaire théâtral* 27 (2000): 160–77.

Michel Cochet on Larry Tremblay: An Auto-Interview

How did you learn about the texts of Larry Tremblay?
It was Michel Fournier, who was working at that time at the Centre National du Théâtre, who helped me discover the plays of Larry Tremblay.

Along with my work as a director, I run an arts collective (l'Association à mots découverts) whose mission is to work with playwrights during the writing process, allowing them to see their work acted out on stage. The association usually works with writers who live in France, but we had decided to make an effort to learn about Québécois theatre. Among all the texts that we read, Larry's had the most striking effect on the actors present at the readings – an effect between amazement, fascination, and rejection. It was, for me in any case, the intuition of an important artistic encounter... several months later, I decided to take the plunge and I proposed to Larry that we stage *Le déclic du destin* and *Les mains bleues*. The production was mounted at the Théâtre de l'Atalante in Paris in 1999 and *Le déclic du destin* was staged again at the Avignon Theatre Festival the next year.

What aspects of Larry's work motivated your choice?
I consider Larry Tremblay an atypical writer, even within the context of Quebec dramaturgy. His writing is so unique that it is immediately identifiable. There's a vision, a way of representing the world and humanity, of putting them on stage, that belongs to him alone and which touches me profoundly. He is irreducible, in the sense that his work does not belong to any theatrical tradition, from here or anywhere else ... part mystery or madness, which provokes astonishing reactions from the audience.

For example?
I can only speak of my own experience with French audiences, and I think that in Montreal it is different since Quebec audiences have undoubtedly more direct and less referential access to theatre, at least they are less influ-

enced by the great texts of the French dramatic repertory, by the tradition of rationality, and by a pre-conceived notion of so-called "culture" or so-called "artistic excellence" … Here, Larry's plays, those which I have staged and seen staged, have the effect of meteorites, as if the spectators all of a sudden found themselves without any benchmarks, embarking without preparation on a journey through troubled waters from which they cannot escape. *Le déclic du destin* and *Les mains bleues* are cruel stories that offer little resolution, or at least do not reassure the audience; in effect Larry has the ability to play on the unconscious and the emotion that can disturb us here in France. I am thinking in particular of *Les mains bleues* which deals with the transfer of affection from man to animal and with the murderous vengeance of a supposed mother aimed at her son. I saw the Paris production of *Le ventriloque* directed by Gabriel Garran: it was the same thing. There is a moment when reason gives way, when the spectator is invited to let himself go and lose himself without putting aside his head or his intelligence, on the contrary… it is not about a sensory object, or a formal quest for a purely esthetic unknown. It is about immersion in a hallucinatory universe at the centre of which our truth remains to be found … hence the spectator's fascination or rejection, but in any case there is no lukewarm response, which is exciting.

In bringing the texts to the stage, what do you think you did successfully?
The key to Larry's work which one must never forget is humor. It is a fundamental, almost philosophical, characteristic. When he plumbs the depths to explore questions of loss of identity, sexuality, emotional unbalance, he always re-surfaces with a burst of laughter. A laughter that feeds the imaginary, the oneiric, and which smashes barriers … a kind of invitation to a mocking madness which can seem grating or violent, but which is also tender.

That was striking with *Le déclic du destin*. We started to work with Christophe Dellocque, the actor, on the first level of the text. I was asking him to give in to the anguish of the character, without holding back in his reading. The result was deadly boring. It was after taking a radically different approach from that of the first reading, in flipping it like a pancake, asking him to play a man who tells us his nightmare in a normal way, with conviction and a smile on his lips, that everything began to make sense. Laughter and dissonance opened up access to terror. The same thing happened with *Les mains bleues,* the character of Jérémie at first seemed to me to be playing a game, able to laugh at his own distress, a painful but healthy laugh. All of a sudden, this character had the lightness needed for audiences to accept him, behind the playing and the fantasy appeared the tragedy of being unloved and abandoned.

What gave you the most difficulty?
Nothing in particular. Nothing was easy, but it was all done with pleasure. We needed to find the middle ground. Larry Tremblay is a poet and a man of the theatre. Unlike authors who define themselves as poet playwrights in order to be considered literary – all the problems of theatricality notwithstanding – Larry is concerned with the stage above all else, at least in his texts for the theatre. The language is intended to produce the performance. It carries the weight, like the walls of a house. One only has to understand how language functions for him. Resolve the equations. The poetry and the uniqueness of his writing then fall into place ...

The only thing that I would re-work ... if I had to do it all over again ... has to do with *Les mains bleues*. I let myself be affected by the darkness of the play. The space in which the play was staged was very confined, with the public very close to the stage. Certain fantasies, notably the appearance of the Princess hanging by a rope, provoked an almost physical uneasiness. Why not? But I wasn't able to re-establish the forward movement of the play, I realize that now. The text deserved more tenderness and distance. Even if it concludes with the impossibility of forgiveness.

Translated with notes by Jane Moss

Biographical Note

Larry Tremblay is a prolific Québécois playwright, actor, and director who also taught at the Université du Québec à Montréal. Since 1992, he has created a unique body of work that has been critically acclaimed, translated, and performed in Canada, the United Kingdom, India, France, Belgium, Italy, Mexico, Argentina, and Brazil.

---

8. ... Anyway – returning to divan. And lifting heavy volume of B's *Paris, Capitale du XIXe*. From turquoise roxy-painted bedside table. Subtitle *Le Livre des passages*. *Passagenwerk* in German. Not yet available in English. Therefore weighing the more delightfully on wrists. Not a real history. Rather – vast collection of 19th-century quotes and anecdotes. Initially seeming huge pile of detritus. But – on looking closer. More like montage. Possibly assembled using old surrealist trick. Of free association. I opening at contents' list. "A" – *Passages* – glass-roofed arcades, malls. Hawking 19th century's new imperial luxury. Juxtaposed on "B" – *Mode*. Each new season. Ironizing time. Next to "C" – *Antique Paris, catacombes, démolitions* – Paris's underpinnings. Pointing to "D" – *L'ennui* – Eternal return. Present tense of dandy. Hovering over "E" – *Haussmannisation, combats des barricades* – Haussmann's wide boulevards. Versus the people. Progress's double coin. Segueing into "J" – Poet *Baudelaire*. First modern. Peer of "M" – *Flâneur* – whose initial post-French-Revolutionary languor not ultimately resisting rising capitalist market. "X/Y" – *Marx* – realism. Next of *Photography ... Social movements. Dolls. Automatons.*

A person could wander here for months.

Gail Scott, *My Paris* 13

From *Flâneuse* to Cybernomad: Roaming the World with Régine Robin

MARY JEAN GREEN

Since much of Régine Robin's work is autofiction, a genre she has helped to define, she can best be described in her own words. My favorite such description appears (twice) in her short fictional piece entitled "Journal de déglingue entre le Select et Compuserve" (the speaker here is, in fact, located at the Paris bistro on the Boulevard du Montparnasse known simply as "le Select"):

Yes, I've seen Regine Robin. She was still here half an hour ago. She must have gone to buy cigarettes at the shop next to the Dôme, or maybe you'll find her at Tschann's Bookstore unless she's walked up the Rue Montparnasse toward the Place Edgar-Quinet … Or else at this time of year she may be in Montreal, in Outremont, at the sidewalk café of La Moulerie or at the Cafe Souvenir on Rue Bernard. Ah! I don't know. She might have taken a plane to visit her daughter.[1]

[Mais oui, j'ai vu Régine Robin. Elle était ici il y a encore une demi-heure. Elle a dû aller acheter des cigarettes au tabac du Dôme ou bien vous la trouverez chez Tschann, à moins qu'elle n'ait remonté la rue du Montparnasse vers la place Edgar-Quinet; … Ou alors, à cette époque de l'année elle est peut-être à Montréal, à Outremont, à la terrasse de La Moulerie, ou au café Souvenir, rue Bernard. Ah! Je ne sais pas. Elle a pu prendre l'avion pour aller voir sa fille]. (*L'immense fatigue des pierres*, 129–30, 140).

Robin is, as we say, a citizen of the world, and I have on occasion described her as a *cosmopolitan*.[2] But she is, above all, a denizen of Paris, where she is "at home" in the bistros where she reads her newspapers and is known by the waiters. She is equally a denizen of Montreal, where, as she represents herself on the homepage of her website, she is "at home" in her Outremont study. In the homepage photograph and its accompanying description, repeated in the version of the website published under the title *Cybermigrances,* Robin appears surrounded by her favorite books, of which she singles out Franz Kafka and Walter Benjamin. Both these writers are, in a sense, immigrants, grounding their work in a city that is and is not their own – the German-speaking Kafka in Prague, the German Jewish refugee Benjamin in Paris. Like Robin herself, her intellectual mentors are constantly crossing between two worlds.

Robin's transatlantic crossings are most apparent in the three slim volumes that I am going to call her fiction: first, her iconic novel of Quebec immigration, *La Québécoite*, published in 1983; her less-known but even more fascinating collection of short fiction published in 1996, *L'immense fatigue des pierres*; and her 2004 text, *Cybermigrances*, which is a transcription and transformation of her experimental autobiographical website. Of course, Robin's fiction is not entirely fiction: it is more properly defined as autofiction, to use the term Robin has herself analyzed at length in her work, *Le golem de l'écriture* (if you use any critical term to describe her work, you can be sure she has already written an essay on it). In her autofiction Robin concocts plots from the stuff of her own life experience, imagining herself in new situations much as the narrator in one of her short stories puts together plausible but imagined biographies from the real-life experience of clients in a Montreal boutique that bears the name *Biographie sur mesure.*

Transatlantic crossings are at the center of each of these texts: in all three, characters shuttle back and forth between Paris and Montreal (and, on occasion, New York and Jerusalem), bringing the perspective of one world to bear on the other. In fact, the same personal wanderings often enter the universe of Robin's writings on what I have chosen to call "cultural theory": her vision of history is forever shaped by the experience of Eastern European relatives who perished in the Holocaust, her analysis of urban geography grounded in her own deambulations in cities all over the world. If I attempt to limit myself here to the three volumes of autofiction, I do so with the knowledge that I am, in a sense, tearing them out of the closely woven fabric of Robin's work.

Régine Robin, the writer/scholar and source of her autofiction, cannot be considered a single person, nor a simple one. In her novel *La Québécoite* Robin's persona, like her a Parisian, lives three lives, with three different men, in three different neighborhoods in Montreal. To separate fiction from non-fiction, only one of the men, the first, corresponds to her real-life Montreal husband. In *L'immense fatigue des pierres,* her personae wander about the world, exploring lives she has or might have lived, a Jewish childhood in Occupied Paris (this one is autobiographical), or a dreamed-of life as a successful writer of popular fiction living on New York's Upper East Side (this one is not). In these texts, she often fully and lovingly furnishes houses and apartments that her persona may momentarily inhabit.

On her website, as in *Cybermigrances,* Robin divides herself into two persons: in one section of the website, under the name of Régine Robin, she displays her professional cv and bibliography. On the other half, under the name of Rivka A., she engages in what she calls autofictional experimentation. Rivka Ajzersztejn (spelled with two j's and two z's) is, of course, the real childhood name of the writer we now know as Régine Robin, a name legally acquired through francization of her first name plus the last name of her first husband. On her website, as in *Cybermigrances,* these two aspects of her persona engage in transatlantic e-mail correspondence, in which Rivka A., in Paris and writing from a .fr address, describes her busy social schedule to Regine Robin.ca, who takes refuge from the wind and snow of winter in Montreal in her Outremont study.

As is true of her peripatetic mentors, Kafka and Benjamin, Robin's identitary schizophrenia has, I would argue, been essential in the transformation of the urban spaces in which she chooses to place herself (or perhaps I should say her/selves), a transformation which, as in the work of Kafka, allows her reader to see familiar urban landmarks in a strange new way. Even in *real life*, a term Robin likes to use in English in her theoretical texts, her writing has contributed to the understanding of immigrant experience, imprinting on the cultural discourse of Quebec the experience of a resident who is yet *not at home.* Considered a pioneering work of immigrant literature in Quebec, *La Québécoite* is structured by a triple movement of transatlantic crossing – and re-crossing. In each of the novel's three parts, the protagonist, whose habits of ensconcing herself in cafes with cigarettes and *Le monde* immediately identify her as a Parisian, makes herself a home in a particular neighborhood in Montreal. And at the end of each section she takes a plane back to Paris.

If Robin's persona makes herself a home – in fact, three homes – in Montreal, she does not make herself *at home.* Wandering around Montreal – noting the shop signs on the Rue St-Denis, taking the bus from west to east along Sherbrooke – she is called back in memory to Paris, where similar *flâneries* follow metro lines and arrive – or, strangely, fail to arrive – at different destinations, evoking the deportation of Jews in Occupied France. It is through these transatlantic crossings of memory, reiterated in the characters of the old Jewish refugee, Professor Himmelfarb, and the narrator's aunt, Mimi Yente, that Robin is able to bring into focus what was, when the book was published in 1983, a different vision of Montreal, a Montreal whose reality resided not only in the stately homes of Outremont (or on the Plateau Mont Royal as brought to life by playwright Michel Tremblay) but in neighborhoods shaped by the presence of immigrants.

The Côte-des-Neiges neighborhood where Mimi Yente resides with her cat is filled with shops selling bagels, cheesecake, and stuffed carp, food that evokes the tastes and smells of the Jewish shtetls of Eastern Europe. For the protagonist herself, memories of a Jewish childhood in Paris converge on an unexplained but clearly traumatic scene, as all the Paris metro lines she evokes seem to end at Grenelle, site of the old sports stadium, the Vel d'hiv, where thousands of French Jews were interned prior to their deportation to Auschwitz. This group presumably included the narrator's mother, although not Robin's, who managed to hide herself and her children throughout the Occupation. The experience of the narrator's loss is evoked in the lines repeated throughout the text: "After Grenelle – I don't know any more. The line gets lost in my memory"(*The Wanderer* 56) ["APRÈS GRENELLE – JE NE SAIS PLUS. LA LIGNE SE PERD DANS MA MÉMOIRE" (*La Québécoite* 73)]. Through these instantaneous transatlantic passages of memory, Robin evokes the ethnic and political persecution that have led her immigrant characters to seek refuge in Montreal, an experience put into parallel with that of the third man with whom she makes a home, a refugee fleeing an unnamed Latin American dictatorship. Through the interplay of perspectives, the Montreal of *La Québécoite* becomes a multicultural space, whose urban life is enriched by bagel shops, Greek restaurants, and the produce sold at the Italian market on Jean-Talon.

It is this transcultural perspective that casts new light on the wave of *pure laine* nationalist sentiment, implicitly anti-immigrant, that was sweeping Quebec in the 1970s and early 1980s, when Robin was writing *La Québécoite*. Especially since the resistance of some Italian-immigrant neighborhoods to the imposition of obligatory schooling in French rather than English, immigrants had come to represent an implicit threat to the Québécois identity being constructed at the moment, an atmosphere recalled in Robin's text by frequent references. In her later reflections in *Cybermigrances*, Robin makes clear the point made, forcefully if implicitly, in *La Québécoite* that the Quebec nationalism of the 1970s recalls earlier persecution of immigrants in France: "It's hard to say what Montreal represents for me: being sheltered, totally sheltered, a refuge. And that's where nationalism interferes. It tarnishes the image of refuge, sets off a paranoid mechanism by reawakening a persecution complex that was very real when I was a child" ["Il est difficile de dire ce que représente Montréal pour moi: être à l'abri, totalement à l'abri, le refuge. Et c'est là que le nationalisme interfère. Il vient ternir l'image du refuge, relance une machinerie paranoïaque en réveillant un imaginaire de la persécution qui, elle, fut bien réelle au temps de mon enfance"] (54). As she admits in the same place, she had never felt truly at ease in Paris either, after spending her early childhood moving from apartment to apartment in flight from the Germans, as she had recounted in her short story, "Gratok." In fact, it is to this sense of unease that she belatedly attributes the assertively Parisian identity she shares with her fictional personae, summed up in the words with which she humorously characterizes herself in *Cybermigrances*: "No one could be more Parisian than I am" ["Plus Parisien que moi, tu meurs!"] (53).

Perhaps because of the relative lack of discussion *La Québécoite* has evoked in France, little attention has been paid to the clear critique it levels at *French* xenophobia in the same period, when anxiety about the presence of immigrants had reached a crescendo in France. The year of the book's publication, 1983, is, after all, the date of the famous *Marche des beurs*, when the French immigrant community was moved to a mass protest against a series of violent assaults on individual immigrants by the police. Although the protagonist's (and Robin's own) memories of Occupied Paris in the 1940s precede the more recent influx of immigrants from the Maghreb, Robin's protagonist is conscious of the relevance of their experience. Castigating herself for not being familiar with their lives, the narrator writes in *La Québécoite*:

And the Immigrants in your homeland, do you know them?
In the Goutte d'or, Aubervilliers, Nanterre
at the time of the Algerian war and the shanty towns
   Dirty nigger
   Dirty Arab. France for the French. (*The Wanderer* 169)
[Et les immigrants de chez toi, les connais-tu?
À la Goutte d'or, à Aubervilliers, à Nanterre
du temps de la guerre d'Algérie et du bidonville
   Sale nègre
   Sale bicot. La France aux Français. (87)]

She is able to recognize as familiar the xenophobic responses these new immigrants have evoked: "And the law on immigrants passed last summer practically fascist. Yes, these countries are all alike!" (*The Wanderer* 69) ["Et les lois sur les immigrés quasi-fascistes, votées l'été dernier. Oui, tous ces pays se ressemblent" (87)]. Although, at the moment of its appearance, *La Québécoite* seemed, in the eyes of some Quebec critics, to pit a sophisticated Parisian cosmopolitanism against a provincial Quebec, Robin's critique is clearly double-edged, her vision shaped by the back and forth motion of her protagonist's cultural crossings.

To the very real credit of Quebec, Robin is now considered a major Quebec writer, and her voice has often been raised and heard in contemporary debates. It is perhaps typical of the French approach to the same issues that her perspective as a native-born Parisian, excluded and marginalized by her cultural heritage as the daughter of Polish Jews, does not seem to have been taken as seriously in France. In my own experience, Robin's fictional texts, published in Montreal, are not readily available in France, even at her beloved Librairie Tschann in her own Montparnasse neighborhood, which was prominently mentioned in my opening quotation. In Paris, these books are more likely to be found on the other side of the Jardin du Luxembourg in the Librairie du Québec.

Again to the credit of Québec, the concluding image of *La Québécoite* in 1983 now seems to have predicted much current thinking about the creation of a new transcultural Quebec identity, at least as expressed in the 2008 report of Quebec's Consultation Commission on Accommodation Practices Related to Cultural Differences, headed by Gérard Bouchard and Charles Taylor. In *La Québécoite* the aptly named Morning Star [Etoile du matin], the second-hand furniture shop owned by the protagonist and her Latin American lover, is clearly a hopeful vision of the future. The shop sells *antiquités* from various lands and provides a space where the various cultural memories they embody can speak to each other, a conversation echoed in the owners' immigrant and non-immigrant friends who frequent the shop: "Inside it would be dark, crammed with an amazing array of furniture that needed to be stripped, kerosene lamps, samovars of every kind, and brass pieces straight from the market in Athens or Heraklion" (*The Wanderer* 166) ["L'intérieur serait ... encombré d'un bric à brac impressionnant de meubles encore peints qu'il faudrait décaper, de lampes à pétrole, de samovars de toutes provenances et de cuivres tout droit venus sans doute du marché d'Athènes ou d'Héraklion" (199)]. The protagonist's dream of this vision becoming a reality of Quebec identity seems to be echoed in the words of the Bouchard-Taylor report, especially in the section concerning "the edification of a common identity," of which point four urges "[t]he edification of a genuine national memory that takes into account ethnocultural diversity and makes Québec's past accessible to citizens of all origins" (88).

The concluding passage of *La Québécoite* repeats the anti-*melting pot* images of a transcultural Montreal that have shaped the text, the city seen as a lumpy immigrant stew and, particularly, the dominant image of Montreal as a patchwork, made up of juxtaposed neighborhoods. Of course, for Robin, these juxtaposed realities have little meaning if no connection is made between them, and this is the role of the *flâneur*. As I have long argued, Benjamin's *flâneur* in Robin's work is more appropriately termed, in the feminine, *la flâneuse*,[3] a term she has finally adopted for herself in the introduction to her recent book *Mégapolis* (2009). The *flâneuse* is the character, both narrator and protagonist, who travels incessantly around the city, providing the link between its disparate realities. Implicitly, in the second-hand shop this connecting role is played by the customers and friends of the owners, revealing this display of second-hand furniture to be an early appearance in Robin's work of the installation. This is an art form to which she refers explicitly in her short story, "Journal de déglingue entre le Select et Compuserve," where her chatroom correspondents imagine an installation that would, literally, turn back the pages of history, representing an idealized East Germany that had never come into existence. In *Cybermigrances*, Robin imagines turning her real-life website into a sort of installation, the visitor wandering between areas and making new and original connections. The installation also repeats the form of the collage or assemblage that remains a model for all three of Robin's texts under discussion, as many of us have commented – including Robin herself, some of whose characters actually become collage artists.

In *L'immense fatigue des pierres,* the collection of short fiction that appeared in the 1990s, over a decade after *La Québécoite,* Robin opens new forms of interconnectedness that complicate the repeated back and forth crossings and re-crossings that constitute the simpler structure of *La Québécoite*. As introduced by the airline routes of the mother and daughter in the title story, the circular movement of departure and return is transformed into a network, with stopping points in Paris, Jerusalem, New York and Montreal (or rather at "La Guardia, Kennedy, O'Hare, Roissy, Orly, Ben Gurion" [14]). Here, no location is a point of origin but any may become a home.

This form of movement on a multi-nodal airline network is an approximation of Robin's own current existence, as represented in *Cybermigrances*, a constant circulation between her homes in Montreal, Paris, and Berlin, with frequent sojourns in New York. These multiple transatlantic crossings complicate the pattern James Clifford[4] finds more typical, the back-and-forth movement of the bipolar immigrant diaspora that dominates *La Québécoite*. And it is the pattern I saw reflected in Robin's conversation when I (literally) ran into her in front of the Select on the Boulevard du Montparnasse a year or so ago. She was, as always, about to take a plane, this one taking her to her apartment in Berlin. But she nevertheless took the time to tell me about her most recent publication project, which has now appeared in January 2009 with her Paris publisher, Stock. Entitled *Megapolis: Les derniers pas du flâneur*, it undertakes a series of *flâneries* in modern urban agglomerations around the world as Robin's *flâneuse* follows routes suggested by writers, filmmakers, and photographers who have blazed new trails in the unstructured space of the modern urban metropolis. In the introduction Robin proudly claims the description of her work offered by her former students, who, in their published essay collection in her honor, called it "une oeuvre *in*disciplinaire" ["an un-disciplinary work"]. In our conversation at the Select, Robin, like her own narrators, regaled me with intriguing anecdotes gathered in the course of her travels to places like Buenos Aires, Los Angeles, New York, London, and Tokyo, passing from the Americas to cross the Atlantic and the Pacific, an itinerary far surpassing the airline routes mapped in *L'immense fatigue des pierres*.

But in *L'immense fatigue des pierres* and, especially, in *Cybermigrances* Robin moves beyond the network of physical travel mapped by metros and airlines to explore the wonders of the World Wide Web. The web first appears in Robin's fictional work in the story, "Journal de déglingue entre le Select et Compuserve," which features a chatroom inhabited by participants from Paris, Berlin, Rome, New York, and Los Angeles. As suggested by the story's title, this virtual conversation, which the narrator accesses from her apartment, alternates with her real-life encounters with an alternate identity in New York, with which she is confronted as she sits at a table in a nearby bistro, the Select, where identities are taken on and cast off with much greater confusion than on the internet. When the French writer/narrator who here calls herself Nancy Nibor (obviously an anagram of Robin) is taken for the American Pamela Wilkinson, she discovers that this New York artist has mysteriously created collages from her own lost photos: is this a mere case of mistaken identity or an imagined existence of herself in

New York? The name of the mysterious Pamela Wilkinson turns up again in an anecdote related in *Cybermigrances*, where she becomes a character or characters contacted by e-mail in Buenos Aires and Vancouver, who eventually blends with the (fictional?) character of Parisian writer Régine Robin.

In *Cybermigrances* the form is wholly dominated by the instantaneous and multimodal communication made possible on the internet. Although Robin seems to aspire to a world of multiple crossings unimpeded by space or time, it is the problem of time that seems to preoccupy her in her most recent autofiction. The perspective offered by individual memories of various immigrants is essential to the creation of the multiple perspectives on history in *La Québécoite*. Although moments in time can be conflated in human memory and imagination, historical time in Robin's world retains its impenetrability and stubborn irreversibility. This becomes an issue in the stories in *L'immense fatigue des pierres*. Although the installation imagined by the chatroom participants in "Journal de déglingue" could allow a visitor to imagine the experience of an idealized East Germany that might have been, the experience can never be perceived as real. In "Manhattan Transfer" the narrator imagines the life her East European relatives might have enjoyed had they immigrated to the United States before the Holocaust. In the end, however, even Robin's creative imagination cannot fill in the space left blank by the historical reality of their deaths.

In *Cybermigrances* the once-divided city of Berlin becomes a central "place of memory," in the sense given this term by Pierre Nora. In Robin's fictional universe as it has in her own life, Berlin becomes a living palimpsest that contains the reality of the Holocaust and traces of a lost European Jewish world. At the same time, it is a living memorial to the death of the socialist dream and the repression symbolized by the Berlin wall. As the narrator wanders through the streets, her imagination transforms an elderly passer-by into a retired SS man; she follows him until, in an unexpected turn of events, he reveals himself to be a Holocaust survivor. An old postcard found by the narrator in a flea market leads her to retrace the paths of star-crossed lovers in East Berlin, where one eventually becomes the Stasi minder of the other. Remnants of disparate historical periods turn up at unexpected moments, like the incompletely effaced traces of the Berlin Wall. More than the contemporary museums Robin describes in her essay *Berlin chantiers*, the city itself becomes, in the eyes of the unrelenting *flâneuse,* an installation that brings the major tragedies of the twentieth century together in a single place.

As the narrator reflects in *Cybermigrances*, her preferred forms of collage and installation are essential to her representation of the disjointed nature of modern history: "I use the forms of collage, of montage, of assemblage, everything that can represent the times out of joint that we have lived through" ["J'ai recours aux formes de collage, de montage, d'assemblage, de tout ce qui peut faire trace des temps désajointés que nous avons vécus"] (53). Yet, in the case of history, even the determined efforts of the *flâneuse* cannot provide an explanatory link, and she must finally admit the failure of her attempts to make sense of history. As she explains, she uses these disjointed forms not to make impossible connections but "to testify to the impossibility of making connections" ["de façon à témoigner de l'impossibilité de faire lien"] (53).

By the time she writes *Cybermigrances* the narrator is, symbolically, no longer in a café but a cybercafé: Robin's two worlds, the Select and Compuserve, have been conflated, and the narrator looks forward to enjoying instant e-mail, fax, and phone contact with friends and colleagues around the world from her favorite Paris café – although, I might add that, as of my last visit, the Select had not yet offered wireless internet services to its clients, unlike the local MacDonald's. Yet this is the model to which Robin aspires in her new definition of the writer of multiple migrations, a cybernomad of a new cybermigrance: "The writers of migration in Quebec or elsewhere, of which I am one, would be the new nomads of our fragmented world burst apart ... writers of the era of the cell phone, the Internet, *cybernomads* of a new *cybermigrancy*" ["Les écrivains de la migration au Québec ou ailleurs, écrivains dont je suis, seraient alors les nouveaux nomades de notre monde fragmenté et éclaté ... des écrivains de l'ère du téléphone portable, de l'Internet, des cybernomades, d'une nouvelle cybermigrance"] (55).

Notes

1 All translations are the author's, unless otherwise indicated.

2 See my article, "Why Montreal: Régine Robin's Rewriting of the City in *L'immense fatigue des pierres.*"

3 See my article, "Cartographies de la mémoire."

4 See Clifford's chapter on "Diasporas" in *Routes.*

Works Cited

Bouchard, Gérard, and Charles Taylor. *Building the Future: A Time for Reconciliation (Abridged Report).* Quebec: Commission de consultation sur les pratiques d'accommodement reliées aux différences culturelles, 2008.

Clifford, James. "Diasporas." In *Routes: Travel and Translation in the Late Twentieth Century.* Cambridge, MA: Harvard University Press, 1997. 244–77.

Désy, Caroline, Véronique Fauvelle, Viviana Fridman and Pascale Maltais. *Une oeuvre indisciplinaire*. Ste-Foy: Presses de l'Université Laval, 2007. 207–11.

Green, Mary Jean. "Cartographies de la mémoire, réinscription du feminin: L'autofiction chez Régine Robin." In *Sexuation, espace, écriture: La littérature québécoise en transformation*. Eds. Louise Dupré, Jaap Lintvelt, Janet M. Paterson. Montreal: Éditions Note Bene, 2002. 93–113.

– "Why Montreal: Régine Robin's Rewriting of the City in *L'immense fatigue des pierres*." *Québec Studies* 38 (2005): 5–16.

Nora, Pierre. "General Introduction: Between Memory and History." In *Realms of Memory: Rethinking the French Past I*. Trans. Arthur Goldhammer. New York: Columbia University Press, 1996.

Robin, Régine. *Cybermigrances: Traversées fugitives*. Montreal: VLB éditeur, 2004.

– *Le golem de l'écriture: De l'autofiction au cybersoi*. Montreal: XYZ, 1997.

– *L'immense fatigue des pierres*. Montreal: XYZ, 1996.

– *Mégapolis: Les derniers pas du flâneur*. Paris: Stock, 2009.

– *La Québécoite*. Montreal: XYZ, Éditions Typo, 1993. *The Wanderer*. Tr. Phyllis Aronoff. Montreal: Alter Ego Editions, 1997.

Transatlantic Crossings in the Work of Alice Parizeau and Naïm Kattan

SUSAN IRELAND

Today, when I stay in Paris, I need to feel my bond with Montreal in order to experience the richness and beauty of the French city.

[[A]ujourd'hui, quand je séjourne à Paris, j'ai besoin de ressentir mon lien avec Montréal pour éprouver la richesse et la beauté de la métropole française.]
Kattan, Villes de naissance 27[1]

In *Dangerous Pilgrimages: Transatlantic Mythologies and the Novel*, Malcolm Bradbury remarks that in the relationship between North America and Europe, "[b]eyond all matters of conquest and world politics, power and economics, there has always been a mythic surplus: of tales and fantasies, dreams and mythologies" (3), a surplus often expressed through literature and art. The links between Quebec and France constitute a good example of the North America-Europe relationship and, as in the anglophone context discussed by Bradbury, these interactions are reflected in a corpus of literary works that can be described as "transatlantic novels" (9). Indeed, a substantial number of Québécois novels feature protagonists who cross the Atlantic as immigrants coming to Montreal, as travelers visiting France, as soldiers going to fight in wars in Europe, or as other kinds of exiles and wanderers. This essay will examine two such narratives, Naïm Kattan's trilogy *Adieu Babylone*, *Les fruits arrachés*, and *La fiancée promise* and Alice Parizeau's *Côte-des-Neiges*, both of which are situated in the mid-twentieth century. It will focus in particular on the ways in which the characters' transatlantic crossings shape their identities and inform their vision of Québécois society during a key period in the history of Europe and Quebec.

Although neither Parizeau nor Kattan is originally from France or Quebec, both spent an important part of their formative years in Paris before moving to Canada. Born in Kracow in 1930, Parizeau lived in Poland until 1945, studied in Paris from 1945 to 1953, and moved to Canada in 1955. Similarly, Kattan was born in Bagdad in 1928, spent four years studying in

Paris (1947–51), and emigrated to Canada in 1954. Indeed, Kattan himself points to the parallels between Parizeau's trajectory and his own, noting that "we had in common our foreign origins, our adoption of French as our language, and our desire, our wish to work in our new society" ["nous avions, en commun, notre origine étrangère, notre adoption du français comme langue d'expression et notre désir, notre volonté d'oeuvrer dans notre nouvelle société"] (*Portraits d'un pays* 77). It is perhaps not surprising, then, that Paris and Montreal figure prominently in both authors' fictional works and that journeys between the two cities play a key role in their protagonists' lives. Similarly, Kattan uses terms such as *passeur* and *écrivain du passage* to characterize his role as a writer (in Barreiro 17), and Jacques Allard has described him as "a transcultural traveler" ("Naïm Kattan" 7), an expression that applies equally well to Parizeau. These epithets, which suggest movement, exchange, and transculturation, also reflect the central thematics of Kattan's trilogy and *Côte-des-Neiges*, both of which are structured around a transatlantic journey and a voyage which is at once geographical and psychological in nature.

Côte-des-Neiges

Although she is an immigrant herself, Parizeau chooses two French Canadians *de souche* as her main characters in *Côte-des-Neiges*. Set primarily in the 1930s and 1940s, the novel recounts the lives of Madeleine (Mado) and Thomas de Boucherville, who are both from humble backgrounds, but who establish a flourishing biscuit factory in Montreal and eventually move into a large house situated in a predominantly anglophone neighborhood on Côte-des-Neiges. Throughout the novel, their story is intertwined with major historical events such as the Spanish Civil War and World War II, thus reflecting Parizeau's belief that "the destiny of the peoples of the American continent is closely linked to that of Europe" (Berthelot and Dunn 120). In particular, the many forms of transatlantic crossing evoked in the text highlight the ways in which Thomas and Mado's destinies as French Canadians are shaped by events taking place in Europe, especially in France.

In a discussion of voyages between France and Canada, Pierre Guillaume remarks that in the early twentieth century, "Few men, no doubt, left France for Canada, but a good many ideas crossed the Atlantic" (17). Many episodes in *Côte-des-Neiges* allude to the movement of ideas between the two continents and serve to illustrate "the extent to which Quebec society was changed by the influence of countries on the other side of the

Atlantic" (Berthelot and Dunn 119). Frequent reference is made to the fact that French Canadians seem uninterested in world affairs, and the humanist doctor Norman Leroy, a key symbol of intellectual exchange in the novel, stresses the importance of being knowledgeable about developments occurring in Europe. When he takes an interest in Mado and Thomas and resolves to teach them about politics, he introduces them to concepts such as communism and fascism, and as he and Thomas look at an atlas together, Norman gives voice to one of the central messages presented in the novel: "Europe seems a long way away to you, but that isn't the case. Today, it isn't only ideas that travel great distances and spread everywhere, but people too ... The continents are moving closer to each other. You no longer have the right to ignore the fact that the rest of the world exists" ["Cela te semble loin l'Europe, mais ce n'est pas vrai. Ce ne sont plus seulement les idées qui traversent les espaces et se répandent partout, mais aussi les gens ... Les continents se rapprochent. Tu n'as plus le droit d'ignorer que le monde existe"] (114). Three sets of events in particular illustrate the effects of the flow of ideas across the Atlantic. First, the espionage subplot in which some of Montreal's anglophone elite provide the Russians with information on the country's nuclear program constitutes a negative form of exchange and underscores the dangers of being politically unaware. The episodes related to the Spanish Civil War, on the other hand, which include a scene in which André Malraux speaks to a group of McGill and University of Montreal medical students, depict the sharing of information in a more positive sense, and when Norman and Thomas's brother Joseph go to Spain to support the Republican cause, they are both profoundly marked by the experience. In Joseph's case, the transformative effects of the voyage are both physical (he loses an arm) and psychological and are encapsulated in his comment, "I'm not the same person as I was before" ["Je ne suis plus comme avant"] (158). Most importantly, perhaps, the journey strengthens his sense of himself as a French Canadian, and the theme of nascent Québécois nationalism is foregrounded by Norman too, who compares it favorably to ideologies such as communism and fascism in that it is not aggressive, but is rather, as he tells Mado, "a kind of love-song celebrating your own world and your own community" ["une sorte de chant d'amour à la gloire de votre propre univers et de votre propre collectivité"] (144).

Finally, the long section of the novel devoted to Mado and Thomas's journey to France and to their experiences during World War II demonstrates how their greater political and cultural awareness enables them to grow on the personal and professional levels. Although they at first feel disoriented in France and encounter the inevitable stereotypical reaction to their French – "You speak a strange kind of French" ["Vous parlez un drôle de français"] (244) – this initial sense of foreignness is soon replaced by their appreciation of the Frenchness of Paris, which contrasts with their experience of the economic and linguistic dominance of English in Montreal: "It's wonderful ... everything's in French. It's as if we were at home, but just in our neighborhood ... there isn't a single newspaper in English, not a single book, nothing! I can tell I'm going to love this country with all my heart" ["C'est merveilleux ... tout est en français. C'est comme si on était chez nous, mais juste dans notre quartier ... pas un journal en anglais, pas un livre, rien! Je sens que je vais aimer ce pays de tout mon coeur"] (243). These positive reactions are reinforced by the couple's creation of a Parisian "family" composed primarily of the hotel owner Monsieur Louis and the Polish student Olek Kowalski, who teaches them how to feel at home in the city. Determined to conquer the French market, Thomas also learns how to adjust to a culturally different set of business practices. When he obtains his first French contract, his symbolic move to the best room in the hotel prefigures his change in social status in Quebec at the end of the novel, and his sound business strategies refute the commonly held view that French Canadians "are not born businessmen" ["n'ont pas la bosse des affaires"] (58). Following the advice of an American contact in Paris (Jack Carol) who predicts that French wholesalers will buy up stocks because of the likelihood of rationing, Thomas is able to secure new contracts and works with his brother and father in Montreal to guarantee that orders are filled. Subsequently, he uses his knowledge of the situation in France to ensure that he will have enough supplies of sugar and flour in Montreal should there be shortages there too. His personal "victory" – his success as a French Canadian businessman – is thus made possible to a large extent by his journey to Paris.

The effects of the journey to France are most evident when Mado and Thomas return to Quebec. Although they travel to Paris together, they go back separately, each in dramatic circumstances, after France enters the war. Mado and her new-born son leave France first when Jack is able to get them onto a British military plane bound for London; from England, Mado makes the dangerous crossing to Halifax by boat, and when she finally reaches Montreal, she remains without any news of Thomas for over two years. Her life during this period, which is recounted in a chapter entitled "Victoire de femme" ["A Woman's Victory"], underscores the diverse ways in which the time she has spent in Paris influences her view of herself and of Québécois society. As her contribution to the war effort, Mado campaigns on Radio-Canada to encourage people to buy "Obligations de la Victoire" ["Victory Bonds"] (311), her credibility as a spokesperson deriving from her account of her "epic journey" ["épique voyage"] across the Atlantic (314). A public figure, she now plays an active role in the transmission of ideas and engages in discussions of many aspects of the war. The majority of French Canadians are opposed to conscription, for example, but Mado's experiences in France lead her to support it; like Norman Leroy, who previously argued for Canada's intervention in the Spanish Civil War, she bases her argument on the interconnectedness of the two continents: "It's not a question of defending Great Britain as Dad maintains, thinks Mado, but of avoiding the worst here, at home. They think we're safe, but they're wrong" ["Il ne s'agit pas de défendre la Grande-Bretagne, comme le prétend papa, pense Mado, mais d'éviter le pire ici, chez nous. Ils s'imaginent que nous sommes à l'abri, mais ils ont tort"] (329). Her ability to hold her own in discussions of the war also contests the notion that French Canadians are uneducated. In particular, in the episode in which she dines on a yacht with a group of English-speaking businessmen, the latter are astonished at her knowledge of the situation and conclude that she cannot possibly be French Canadian, a supposition that provokes a strong affirmation of origins on her part and suggests a strengthening of her perception of herself as French Canadian: "I'm French Canadian and my family, like my husband's, has lived here since the early days of the colony" ["Je suis canadienne-française et ma famille, comme celle de mon mari, sont établies ici depuis les débuts de la colonie"] (334).

Mado's actual "crossing" ["traversée"] (331) – the dangerous voyage back from France – is mirrored in a series of more figurative border crossings. When she becomes the "real boss" ["vrai patron"] (314) of the biscuit factory in Thomas's absence, for example, she breaks through the gender barriers that were still very much in place in the 1940s – an idea underscored in the chapter title ("A Women's Victory"). Described as "a consummate businesswoman" ["Femme d'affaires jusqu'aux bouts des ongles"] (336), she is involved in every aspect of running the business and obtains new contracts with the Canadian army thanks to her war experiences. The portrayal of Mado as a successful businesswoman thus suggests the need to dismantle the patriarchal structure of society. Indeed, Mado sees herself as "autonomous and free" ["autonome et libre"] (314), considers herself her husband's intellectual equal – "I've read more than Thomas and I'm capable of thinking for myself" ["j'ai lu plus que Thomas et je suis capable de penser par moi-même"] (145) – and vehemently rejects Joseph's contention that a mother's place is at home with her child: "Neither you nor anyone else will be able to shut me away in the house anymore. I'm capable of doing something else and I won't give up my place" ["Ni toi, ni personne, ne pourra plus m'enfermer à la maison. Je suis capable de faire autre chose et je ne cèderai pas ma place"] (321). The image of the house, which recalls Patricia Smart's notion of "the Father's House" (6), suggests a further dimension of Mado's "victory." Mado purchases the house on Côte-des-Neiges while Thomas is still in Europe, her move across the city symbolizing the transgression of linguistic and cultural boundaries as well as of traditional gender roles. Chosen and owned by Mado, the house represents her triumph over the anglophone owners who do not wish to sell it to her because she is French Canadian, and the fact that her crossing the boundary between anglophone West and francophone East is presented as a parallel to her epic *traversée* highlights the need to redress the unequal relationship between the two communities.

As in Mado's case, the account of Thomas's return to Quebec demonstrates how he has come to better understand himself and society. After Mado leaves Paris, Thomas is unable to reach Saint Nazaire to take a boat to Canada and (along with Olek) is captured by the Germans while attempting to reach England disguised as a French soldier. Subsequently classified as a French prisoner-of-war, he spends two years in a German prison camp before making a daring escape with Olek and finally getting back to Quebec via Holland and England. Upon his return, he finds himself cast in the role of "great French-Canadian hero" ["grand héros canadien-français"] (343), a role that contrasts with his own view of himself as "neither a hero, nor a combatant" ["ni un héros, ni un combattant"] (347). Indeed, the many references to the telling of Thomas's story highlight the way in which it is recuperated by public officials and becomes part of the national narrative of the war. In particular, the fact that Thomas is often "displayed in public" ["exhibé en public"] (343) as an "exceptional person who has had adventures beyond the imagination" ["être exceptionnel ayant vécu des aventures qui dépassent l'imagination"] (344) evokes the myth-making tendencies of those who would like to give Quebec a glorious war story. As one character ironically remarks, Thomas is exhibited for reasons of political expediency: "It's a way for them to get people to forget for a little while that they refused to go and fight for the common cause" ["C'est un moyen pour eux de faire oublier un peu leur refus d'aller se battre pour la cause commune"] (344). Thomas, for his part, wants above all to return to a normal life but, as he worries about the influence communism will have after the war, acknowledges that his world-view has been permanently colored by the experiences he and his family have had in Europe: "As an individual, I would like to turn my back on all of that, but because of what I've been through on the other side of the Atlantic, I'm ashamed of my powerlessness" ["En tant qu'individu, je voudrais être détaché de tout cela, mais en raison de ce que j'ai vécu de l'autre côté de l'Atlantique, j'ai honte de mon impuissance"] (353).[2]

The final pages of the novel reinforce the emblematic nature of Mado and Thomas's trajectories. Here, as Thomas drives home in the snow, the juxtaposition of his present concerns and of his memories of Europe emphasizes his desire to use his new insights to improve the lot of French Canadians. In this context, the house on Côte-des-Neiges again serves to underscore the theme of social mobility, and the sign in English at the entrance to the property (*"Private property no trespassing"* [366]), which stands in contrast to the Frenchness of Paris, highlights the work that remains to be done with respect to linguistic rights.[3] In this sense, the image of Thomas driving slowly but surely up the hill to the house represents French Canadians' uphill struggle for equality: "Slowly, patiently, Thomas goes up Côte-des-Neiges ... [he] doesn't give up and carries on until he gets to the top" ["Lentement, patiemment, Thomas monte la Côte-des-Neiges ... [il] ne se décourage pas et insiste jusqu'à ce qu'il parvienne en haut"] (366). Likewise, the utopian vision of changing Quebec for the better, which appears in the very last paragraphs, provides the answer to the question Thomas poses when he reflects on the selflessness and commitment he witnessed in Europe during the war: "What have I done for my own people?" ["Qu'est-ce que j'ai accompli pour les miens?"] (348). The changes he envisages for the future, which include providing better opportunities for French Canadians in areas such as education, housing, and working conditions, suggest the emergence of a strong social conscience on his part and reinforce the idea that his journey to France has enabled him to see the situation of his compatriots more clearly. Ultimately, then, the transatlantic encounters portrayed in *Côte-des-Neiges* raise questions about French-Canadian identity and point to "the decisive role played by the post-war period in the process of redefining French-Canadian identity, an identity that was soon to be known as Québécois" (Nepveu 75).

For Kattan's characters, as for the author himself, the France-Quebec relationship is complicated by the fact that the two countries form part of a tri-polar mapping of identity which also includes Iraq. Indeed, Kattan frequently remarks that, for him, three cities are inextricably linked: "Montreal is my city. In my mind, Montreal includes and incorporates Baghdad and Paris in such a way that, during my frequent stays in Paris, the latter comprises part of my life in Montreal" ["Montréal est ma ville. Elle comprend et intègre dans mon esprit Bagdad et Paris, de sorte qu'au cours de mes fréquents séjours à Paris, cette ville comprend une part de ma vie montréalaise"] (*L'écrivain migrant* 22). For this reason, perhaps, the question of identity lies at the heart of his semi-autobiographical trilogy. Taken together, the three volumes recount the life of a young Jew from Bagdad who goes to study in Paris soon after World War II and who later emigrates to Quebec. For the protagonist, the transatlantic crossing to North America thus constitutes the final stage of a physical voyage that also takes him from adolescence to adulthood, and the portrayal of his journey in the trilogy highlights the complex relationships between migration, identity, and place.

In a 2001 essay, Kattan remarks that an immigrant writer must choose one of two paths, "exile or a second birth" ["l'exil ou une deuxième naissance"] (*L'écrivain migrant* 21), and that if one opts for the latter, as he himself has done, writing about the native land is an important first step: "in this case, the writer begins by naming his place of origin, by giving expression to it and asserting its existence so that it does not just become part of the background, a factor doomed to be forgotten or wiped out" ["[l]'écrivain commence alors par nommer le lieu premier, le dire, l'affirmer afin qu'il ne devienne pas un arrière-plan, un élément voué à l'oubli ou à l'oblitération"] (*L'écrivain migrant* 22). *Adieu Babylone*, Kattan's first novel, constitutes such an affirmation of origins. Devoted to the unnamed narrator's memories of growing up in Bagdad, the text provides a poignant portrait of Iraq's Jewish community, which would soon be forced into exile. At the same time, however, certain passages recount the first stage of the protagonist's transcontinental journey, the voyage of the imagination that leads to an enduring love of France. His information comes primarily from literary works, and the idealized picture he creates is shaped by his reading a wide range of authors including the Comtesse de Ségur, Daudet, Anatole France, Péguy, Gide, Malraux, Aragon, and the Romantics. In these sections of the novel, the frequent use of self-irony and humor and recurrent images of intoxication and enchantment highlight the naiveté of the narrator's vision of France as the "chosen land which would fulfill all his desires and quench even the most insatiable thirst" ["[t]erre d'élection qui comblerait tous [s]es désirs, qui assouvirait les soifs les plus insatiables"] (161). When discussing crosstown excursions in Montreal which involve using a different language, Sherry Simon remarks that, "the very act of passage, willingly undertaken, carries with it the desire for knowledge and self-transformation" (6). In *Adieu Babylone*, the narrator's determination to master French in order to gain access to the West (symbolized by France) suggests a similar type of passage. Indeed, the narrator has already crossed the East-West border through his imagination – "I was already living in an imaginary Paris" ["Je vivais déjà dans un Paris imaginaire"] (237) – and the novel closes with further images of departure as he sets off for France after obtaining a much desired scholarship to study in Paris.

The second volume in the trilogy (*Les fruits arrachés*), which relates the protagonist Méir's encounter with France, focuses on the theme of personal identity and illustrates how being an Iraqi Jew in France just after World War II informs the image of France Méir will take with him to Quebec. The positive side of his experience, his "love affair" with France, is symbolized by his relationships with a series of women, only one of whom is actually French. As Michael Greenstein observes of Kattan's work in general, "a female figure acts as counterpart to the immigrant, frequently representing cultural, religious, or national entry into the new country for a male protagonist caught between two different civilizations" (118). In *Les fruits arrachés*, Halina, a Polish scholarship recipient who is already familiar with the city, provides Méir with warmth and understanding when he first arrives in Paris, while Maxie, whom he meets in Holland, embodies the West's fascination with the Orient. These two women eventually disappear from Méir's life, however, and it is Anne, a young French woman from a bourgeois family, who represents the promise of integration and of a potential "marriage" with France.

Although Kattan has affirmed that Paris is "the only place which is better than the dream it inspires" (Allard, "Entrevue" 18), the passage from dream to reality is portrayed as problematic for his protagonist since the city also becomes "the place where his identity is dislocated" (Simard 41). This destabilization, which is conveyed through images of solitude and emptiness, creates a sense of dispossession and not-belonging: "a deserted city, in an inanimate and indifferent setting, which seemed hostile to me" (*Paris Interlude* 102) ["Ville déserte, au décor inanimé et indifférent, qui m'apparaît hostile" (*Les fruits arrachés* 114)]. Most importantly, Méir – who perceives himself as both Jewish and Arab – has to confront stereotypes and simple classifications that amputate part of his identity. Ironically, he is in his turn viewed through the prism of literature and seen as the exotic Other: "You're from Baghdad … You're Ali Baba, the thief. Sindbad, Aladdin. Our whole childhood" (*Paris Interlude* 42–3) ["Tu viens de Bagdad … Tu es Ali Baba, le voleur, Sindbad, Aladdin. Toute notre enfance" (*Les fruits arrachés* 47)]. This tendency to associate him with a fantasy world is compounded by a general lack of knowledge about the Middle East: "People ask me where Iraq is and they confuse it with Iran. They talk to me about the *Thousand and One Nights*. They're amazed to learn that there are Jews in Baghdad. They ask if they're black" (*Paris Interlude* 105) ["On me demande où se trouve l'Irak et l'on confond avec l'Iran. On me parle des *Mille et une nuits*. On est étonné d'apprendre qu'il y a des Juifs à Bagdad. Sont-ils Noirs?" (*Les fruits arrachés* 116)]. Although Méir desires to adapt to French culture, he does not want to be reduced to a single dimension of his identity (Arab *or* Jew) and thus finds himself in "the difficult position of one who carries many traditions within himself" (Simon 65). At the end of the novel, he still dreams of spending his life with Anne, but not in France, which he now views as a country too weighed down by tradition for him to be able to find a livable space there: "We couldn't withstand Paris … we can't be happy here" (*Paris Interlude* 207) ["Nous ne résisterons pas à Paris … Ici, nous ne pourrons pas être heureux" (*Les fruits arrachés* 228)]. For this reason, the novel ends as it began, with images of a new departure, and the short final section evoking the protagonist's journey to America suggests the quintessential immigrant experience, as a euphoric but apprehensive Méir looks out at the New York cityscape from the harbor. At this point, Anne, whom Méir describes as "an extension of my own being" (*Paris Interlude* 208) ["le prolongement de mon être" (*Les fruits arrachés* 229)], continues to represent France and the French part of his identity he does not want to give up, and the image of his "impassible carapace" underscores the multi-dimensional nature of the identity he is taking with him to America: "I already had a double skin. Soon it would be triple, an impassible carapace … I was carrying Europe with me" (*Paris Interlude* 208) ["J'avais déjà une double peau. Elle sera triple, infranchissable carapace … J'emporte l'Europe" (*Les fruits arrachés* 229–30)].

La fiancée promise, which features the same protagonist as *Les fruits arrachés*, portrays Canada as a country open to immigrants. The depiction of Méir's experiences in Duplessis-era Montreal contains many of the standard ingredients of the immigrant novel (the difficult process of looking for work and accommodation, worries about money), and his voyage is mirrored in other crossings from the old world to the new, particularly those of Jews from Eastern Europe whose trajectory is similar to Méir's – "After the war, when they were children, they had spent a few years in France or Belgium before coming to Canada" ["Après la guerre, enfants, ils avaient passé quelques années en France, en Belgique, avant de venir au Canada"] (42) – and also those of the small community of Iraqi Jews, all of whom present Canada as a welcoming country. The title of the novel, which suggests the important role played by women in the narrative, evokes a potential "marriage" with Quebec and thus raises the question of Meir's place in Canada. The first reference to the fiancée, who symbolizes the promise of belonging, appears in the very first pages when a fellow traveler (a Holocaust survivor) on the train from Halifax to Montreal tells Méir that a Jewish girl he knows would make "a good fiancée for you" ["[u]ne bonne fiancée pour vous"] (5). Subsequently, the theme of marriage recurs frequently in the novel, and Méir has, or envisages, a relationship with a series of potential fiancées including the Hungarian Magda, the Iraqi Rose, a Polish Jew (Evelyne), the English Canadian Helen, a French Canadian from Trois-Rivières (Diane), and a Belgian immigrant (Claudia). These women, who stand for diverse aspects of Québécois culture, represent the different forms Méir's metaphorical marriage with Canada might take.

The interrelated themes of identity and belonging, which are again at the heart of the text, center on Méir's position as a French-speaking Jew in Quebec, a position which makes him "a rare species at the time" ["une espèce rare à l'époque"] (37) since the Jewish community in Montreal in the 1950s was almost entirely composed of Yiddish- and English-speaking Ashkenaze Jews. Indeed, Méir's fellow traveler on the Halifax-Montreal train links language with belonging at the very beginning of the novel when he asks Méir, "How are you going to manage? All the Jews speak Yiddish" ["Comment allez-vous faire? Tous les juifs parlent yiddish"] (3). Subsequently, Méir has to deal with constant attempts to fit him into traditional religious-based categories. French-Canadians, for example, suggest that he seek help from "his own people" ["les siens"], the anglophone Jewish community, but he does not feel part of this group. Likewise, he resists the desire on the part of some Jews to automatically classify him as "one of them" – "This idea of a community based on destiny bothered me" ["Cette communauté de destin m'embarrassait"] (2) – and recurrent images of imprisonment underscore his rejection of identities projected onto him by others: "I don't want to be forced to be Jewish, to be a certain kind of Jew" ["Je ne veux pas qu'on me force à être juif, à être un certain genre de juif"] (193).

In response, Méir turns to his "French" identity to help him forge his own place in Montreal. In particular, he uses his knowledge of French to open up avenues of communication and exchange at a time when there was "little significant contact between Jews and French Canadians" (Simon 96). Despite the fact that some potential employers discourage him at first, perceiving his Frenchness as too European – "We don't need intellectuals in this country ... You should have stayed in Paris" ["On n'a pas besoin d'intellectuels dans ce pays ... Vous auriez dû rester à Paris"] (15, 20)[4] – he successfully establishes a French-language bulletin designed to create connections between the Jewish and francophone communities.[5] In addition, his French identity serves as a means of escaping the "community based on destiny" (2). In the very first scene on the train, when he is asked where he is from, he responds, "I'm from Paris" ["Je viens de Paris"] (2). Variants of this initial conversation recur repeatedly throughout the novel: "So, you're from Baghdad, he said. / Yes, from Paris, I mean" ["Ainsi, vous venez de Bagdad, affirma-t-il. / Oui, c'est-à-dire de Paris"] (44); "Are you the person who's come over from the Orient? ... After a long spell in Paris" ["C'est vous qui venez d'Orient? ... Après un long passage à Paris"] (73). This French identity is also foregrounded in many of his relationships with women: Rose looks to him for a Parisian model of courtship; Helen introduces him to her mother as "My Parisian friend" (123); and for Diane, he is "the European, the one who took her to the Old World without ever leaving Montreal" ["l'européen [sic], celui qui conduisait Diane au vieux monde tout en restant sur place"] (179). These recurrent references to the Parisian Méir underscore the idea that the French dimension of his identity constitutes an integral part of his relationship to Quebec, an impression reinforced in his response to the question of why he chose to come to Canada: "Because of French. / I had chosen French culture. A long time ago" ["À cause du français. / J'avais opté pour la culture française. Depuis longtemps"] (55). Towards the end of the novel, however, when attending a conference in the Laurentians, Méir on three separate occasions answers the inevitable where-are-you-from question with the words "From Montreal" (197, 198, 199); the substitution of "from Montreal" for "from Paris" suggests a corresponding shift in his sense of belonging and points to the possible incorporation of Quebec into his identity.

The key images of the *traversier* and the tightrope highlight Méir's trajectory. During a trip to Quebec City, Méir spends a night on the ferry shuttling back and forth between the two sides of the river, an image that evokes his geographical and identitarian voyages between France and Quebec, and East and West. Indeed, while his initial reaction when he finds himself in the middle of the river – "I had come from nowhere and I had no destination, no destiny" ["Je n'arrivais de nulle part et n'avais pas de direction, de destinée"] (157) – suggests the dislocation of identity and is described as a "nightmare" ["cauchemar"] (157), the to-and-fro movement is subsequently associated with positive images of rebirth and self-creation: "I recognized the colors of my body, which was coming back to life in the darkness, was gaining strength from the continuous movement of the water and was creating itself, inventing itself, autonomously" ["je reconnaissais les couleurs de mon corps qui renaissait dans l'ombre, vivait du mouvement continu qui s'inventait, se créait, autonome"] (158). The image of the tightrope in the last paragraph of the novel, like that of the ferry, highlights the themes of passage and destiny. Here, Méir describes a recurrent dream in which he and Claudia walk fearlessly towards each other on a tightrope. Although the novel is open-ended and no marriage has taken place, the positive depiction of Méir's relationship with Claudia who, like him, has lived in Paris but is not from there, suggests the creation of a different kind of "community of destiny,"[6] one born of migration and willingly chosen rather than one prescribed by others. Méir had earlier remarked of his relationship with Claudia, "We were both shipwrecked. We were going to drown or be saved together" ["Nous étions deux naufragés. Nous allions nous noyer ou nous sauver ensemble"] (226). Just as the symbol of the ferry intimates that, as immigrants in Quebec, they will not drown, the tightrope dream reinforces the idea that they will not fall into the "void" (231) of not-belonging and leaves the reader with the impression that Méir is on the way to answering the question of how to be a French-speaking Jew in Montreal.

When discussing fictional portrayals of the Paris-Montreal relationship, Gilles Marcotte observes that, "In Quebec literature, the encounter between Paris and Montreal on the diegetic level … has not taken place. The fictional Parisian who turns up in Montreal is generally disappointed … as for the opposite scenario, that of the Montrealer arriving in Paris, it is an understatement to say that the outcome is usually disastrous" (39). Perhaps because they are immigrants who bring new perspectives with them to Quebec, Kattan and Parizeau provide a more nuanced depiction of the Paris-Montreal encounter. In particular, Parizeau's Canadian couple who appreciate the Frenchness of Paris and Kattan's would-be Parisian who emigrates to Montreal both illustrate the changing face of Montreal, which is being reshaped by Québécois nationalism, immigration, and the evolving role of women in society. At the same time, Parizeau and Kattan form part of the growing community of authors who have made the transatlantic journey themselves and have used it as the focus of their literary works. In this sense, their novels form part of the "huge fictional story of the transatlantic world as it move[s] through history" (Bradbury 9).

Notes

1 All translations are the author's, unless otherwise indicated.

2 Thomas also recognizes the effect of distance on the impact of ideas that cross the Atlantic: "Fascism, Soviet totalitarianism, right-wing dictatorships, these things exist elsewhere, but here, at home, it's above all a question of the survival of a minority culture; words don't have the same meaning" ["Le fascisme, le totalitarisme soviétique, les dictatures de droite, cela existe ailleurs, mais ici, chez nous, il s'agit de survivance en premier lieu d'une culture minoritaire, les mots n'ont pas le même sens!"] (348).

3 Thomas comments at length on the sign: "'I wonder why I haven't had a sign in French put up yet,' Thomas asks himself. 'Why is it that I have to have this notice in English in front of my house when I live, earn my living, and raise my child in French, just as I was raised myself, and all my ancestors before me?'" ["'Je me demande bien pourquoi je n'ai pas encore fait installer une affiche en français,' se dit Thomas. 'Comment se fait-il que je doive avoir devant chez moi ce pan-

neau en anglais, quand je vis, je gagne mon argent et j'élève mon enfant en français, comme je l'ai été moi-même et avant moi la lignée de mes ancêtres?'"] (366).

4 His writing style is also described as "too European. Literary" ["trop européen. Littéraire"] (17).

5 Kattan himself set up the *Bulletin du Cercle juif* in order to "build a bridge between Jews and French Canadians" ["jeter un pont entre les Juifs et les Canadiens français"] (*Portraits* 7).

6 Claudia is introduced to Méir as "a Parisian" (200), and he immediately comments on the similarities between their trajectories: "I'm from Paris, too, I said. Like you, I've lived there, but I wasn't born there" ["Moi aussi je viens de Paris, dis-je. Comme vous j'y ai vécu et je n'y suis pas né"] (200).

Works Cited

Allard, Jacques. "Naïm Kattan ou la fortune du migrant." *Voix et images* 11.1 (1985): 7–9.

– "Entrevue avec Naïm Kattan." *Voix et images* 11.1 (1985): 10–32.

Barreiro, Carmen Mata. "Etranger et terri-

torialité: D'une approche pluridiscipli-
naire à une approche transdisciplinaire."
Globe 10.1 (2007): 15–29.

Berthelot, Ann and Mary Dunn Haymann.
Alice Parizeau: L'épopée d'une oeuvre.
Montreal: Éditions Pierre Tisseyre, 2001.

Bradbury, Malcolm. *Dangerous Pilgrimages: Transatlantic Mythologies and the
Novel.* New York: Viking, 1996.

Greenstein, Michael. "Iraquébec: Naïm
Kattan's Trans-Mimetic Diaspora." *Textualizing the Immigrant Experience in Contemporary Quebec.* Ed. Susan Ireland
and Patrice J. Proulx. Westport, CT:
Praeger, 2004. 117–26.

Guillaume, Pierre and Laurier Turgeon,
eds. *Regards croisés sur le Canada et
la France: Voyages et relations du XVIe
au XXe siècle.* Quebec/Paris: Éditions
du CTHS/Presses de l'Université Laval,
2007.

Kattan, Naïm. *Adieu Babylone.* [1975]
Montreal: Bibliothèque québécoise,
2005.

– *L'écrivain migrant: Essais sur des cités
et des hommes.* Montreal: Hurtubise
HMH, 2001.

– *La fiancée promise.* Montreal: Hurtubise
HMH, 1983.

– *Les fruits arrachés.* Montreal: Hurtubise
HMH, 1977. Translated as *Paris
Interlude.* Trans. Sheila Fischman.
Toronto: McClelland and Stewart, 1979.

– *Portraits d'un pays.* Montreal: L'hexagone, 1994.

– *Les villes de naissance.* Montreal:
Leméac, 2001.

Marcotte, Gilles. *Écrire à Montréal.*
Montreal: Boréal, 1997.

Nepveu, Pierre. "Désordre et vacuité:
Figures de la judéité québécoise-
française." *Etudes françaises* 37.3
(2001): 69–84.

Parizeau, Alice. *Côte-des-Neiges.* Montreal: Pierre Tisseyre, 1983.

Simard, Sylvain. "Naïm Kattan romancier:
la promesse du temps retrouvé." *Voix
et images* 11.1 (1985): 33–44.

Simon, Sherry. *Translating Montreal:
Episodes in the Life of a Divided City.*
Montreal: McGill-Queen's University
Press, 2006.

Smart, Patricia. *Writing in the Father's
House.* Toronto: University of Toronto
Press, 1991.

From Europe to Quebec Cinematic History

WERNER NOLD

I was born in Switzerland, in the canton of Grisons. My mother tongue is Romansh, a language I forgot while learning German when my parents moved to Brugg, in the Swiss German region. After that, we lived in Montreux, in the French-speaking part of the country, and French became the third language I learned at the age of twelve. French was thus an important consideration for me, when I decided to emigrate.

Why emigrate? After my studies in photography, I had an overwhelming desire to get into filmmaking. In 1955, there was practically no filmmaking in Switzerland, and, without a university diploma or sufficiently elevated social status, I had no hope of making it in France.

My godmother, Nora, my father's sister, was a nurse at the Boisvert hospital in Baie-Comeau. We had corresponded for several years. For that reason, Quebec was not completely unknown to me. Unfortunately, she passed away before I got here. But in terms of my interest in Quebec, my godmother certainly was an influential factor. In 1951, I saw Félix Leclerc sing in Lausanne. It was a revelation! Moreover, at the photography school I attended, we all swore by Yousouf Karsh, the famous Canadian photographer, who had captured that fabulous portrait of Churchill. A French-speaking and cultivated America? That was exactly what I needed.

On 21 September 1955, I made that unforgettable trip up the majestic St. Lawrence river, discovering the flamboyant fall colors. Unlike in Switzerland, there are no mountains here to obstruct the sunset. That infinite horizon ... Suddenly, to my mind, everything was possible!

Of course, the first days in Montreal were tough: at that time, there was no infrastructure in place to help immigrants integrate, and I was penniless. Where to sleep? My young wife and I had no relatives to help us out. We had to start from scratch. But it did not matter! Naïve, unworried, optimistic, I quickly had to find work. I cannot recall how many jobs I was turned down for, because I had no *Canadian work experience*. But how was I to obtain this experience if I did not work? In short, I had to accept any work, and for a pittance, but that was how one got that precious experience. So, starting out fresh is hard, and one becomes nostalgic: how I longed for a bit of salami and a piece of Gruyere! But there was never any question of returning to Switzerland, as that would be admitting defeat.

Finally, I found a job in photography and filmmaking, with the Quebec government. Life was good! I was sent to Quebec's North shore to take pictures and shoot a few reels of film. The trip was aboard the *Marie-Stella*, a boat from the Ministry of Health, equipped to diagnose tuberculosis in the indigenous population. In order to lure them to have their x-rays taken, we showed movies on the dock of each village, using the boat's generator. *Un homme et son péché* [*A Man and His Sin*] was very popular – the character of the Indian, Bill Wâbo, made them all laugh. The latest Canadiens hockey game, shot on film in those days (there was no electricity in these communities), was also very much in demand. Traveling this river and tying up at all these docks, from Quebec to Blanc Sablon, was a powerful integrating force for this Swiss expatriate. During one trip to Schefferville, I was even expulsed from the Church by the priest, *manu militari*, because I was a Protestant. I took pictures in Abitibi of the process of rural electrification. For the series *Mon pays, mes amours*, I filmed all the churches of the Richelieu valley, from Lake Champlain to Sorel. I also filmed a series on commercial careers for the Minister of Public Instruction. In sum, I was *canadianized*! I had forgotten the salami and the Gruyere and I was no longer wondering about perhaps having to return to Switzerland.

Since I found that my photos were too lifeless, I became a cinematographer. Moving images were perhaps the solution to my problem. But even then, I was not quite satisfied. In fact, life is not in the movement, but in the gaze. Indeed, since I found my shots were massacred in the editing room, I began to edit them myself. That was when I finally found *the* way to truly express myself. Apparently successfully, I guess, since my colleagues quickly started asking me to edit their films.

By five years after my arrival, I was completely stateless. Neither Swiss nor Canadian, so who was I?

In 1961, I started at the National Film Board of Canada, the Mecca of cinema in this country. And that at the precise time when the NFB was starting up a "French unit." These filmmakers accepted me right away as one of their own. They never made me feel like I was an immigrant. This group of university graduates – writers, doctors (!), lawyers, geologists ... – had left their own fields to conduct their own kind of Quiet Revolution. It was perfect timing for me, because I had criss-crossed the country, more than most of the fellows at work. We all roamed Quebec, camera in hand, in search of an identity. I did too. And so it was that this passionate group, from all walks of life, invented what would later be called *cinéma direct*. They set the entire world of documentary filmmaking on its ear. In 1962, I was offered the editing job for *Pour la suite du monde* [*For Those Who Will Follow*], by Pierre Perrault and Michel Brault, which garnered me international recognition.

This quest for an identity and professional recognition did not leave me with much time for my family, which I thus lost. It was quite a shock. Finally, I became so well integrated that I married a Québécoise a few years later. It must be said that she was from the same field. She was "born" at the NFB, as she puts it ... Lucette and I have been together for some forty years now, and it is complete *cinematographic* harmony.

In 1972, I already had the impression of being a pillar of the NFB. I was awarded a fellowship by the Canada Council for the Arts that allowed me to take stock. Lucette and I left for a year, traveling in the US and Europe. After having taken this opportunity to steep in such a cultural bath, I was thirsty to get back home and start editing again. My mid-life crisis was over, and I was once again happy in my work.

Documentary filmmaking has its limits, and if one wants to go further, one must opt for drama. This form of storytelling permits one to say just about anything. But the fiction I like best is still deeply marked by the documentary tradition. One has only to think of the features *À tout prendre* [*Take it all*] by Claude Jutra, *La vie heureuse de Léopold Z* [*The Merry World of Leopold Z*] by Gilles Carle, *Entre la mer et l'eau douce* [*Drifting Upstream*] and *Les ordres* [*Orderers*] by Michel Brault, *La gammick* by Jacques Godbout, *Le déclin de l'empire américain* [*The Decline of the American Empire*] by Denys Arcand, *Les garçons de Saint-Vincent* [*The Boys of St. Vincent*] by John Smith, to mention but a few.

In 1976, we made the documentary *The Games of the 21st Olympiad* by Jean-Claude Labrecque. This was the first and undoubtedly the only Olympic film shot entirely in sync sound – we are as close as possible to the athletes, their dreams, their disappointments, their victories. For me, this film is the apotheosis of all our *cinéma direct* techniques.

In 1985, I was awarded the Order of Canada in acknowledgment of my contribution to Canadian cinema. I was very proud to obtain the highest distinction of my adopted country. It was a wonderful recognition. I have dual citizenship, Swiss and Canadian. You can imagine my astonishment when I learned from the Swiss consul himself that I did not have the right to accept such a distinction from another country! ... Finally, since it was in no way a military decoration, Switzerland accepted the idea. That is the fundamental difference between my two countries. From Switzerland, I inherited a *good* education. I was taught to be dependable, hardworking, rigorous. A real Swiss watch! Which is in fact what allowed me to become what I am. Indisputably, however, coming to live in Quebec was the wisest and most important decision of my life.

Werner Nold, November 2008.
Translation by Miléna Santoro

Three *Demoiselles sauvages* in Search of Other Worlds: Corinna Bille and Gabrielle Roy in the Films of Léa Pool

RACHEL KILLICK

La demoiselle sauvage: An Enigma of Identity

In Swiss author Corinna Bille's 1975 short story "La demoiselle sauvage" (the eponymous lead story of a collection of twelve), the protagonist is discovered wandering and distressed in the mountain woods, presenting an enigma of identity highlighted by the conflicting indications of the title collocation. While expressions such as *la femme fatale* or *la femme sauvage* have widely discussed stereotypical currency, *la demoiselle sauvage* ambiguously combines two unstable designations depending on very different, yet closely intertwined categories of belonging and exclusion, one concerned with social hierarchies of status and age, the other with socialization itself, contradictorily conceived as both a desirable regulation of animal instinct and an alienation of the embodied self.

Demoiselle, in the later twentieth century, seems a largely out-moded, if not downright archaic label. The old use of the term, "young girl of noble birth or married woman of the petty aristocracy" (*Le Robert*),[1] recalls a vanished past of lords, ladies, and aristocratic privilege, whose barbarities, hidden behind the constrictive protocols of courtly etiquette, still resonate in the disturbing world of folk- and fairy-tale. Meanwhile its lingering sense of "unmarried female, young or old" seems increasingly redundant in modern Western society where changing circumstances and attitudes have undermined the centrality of marriage as a social institution and all but abolished the very notion of spinsterhood.

The term, *sauvage* ("shy" or "wild"), referring etymologically to woodland space (Latin *silva*) outside the bounds of civilization, is similarly problematic, with creatures dwelling therein perceived neutrally, as shy and fearful of outside contact; positively, as resistant to contamination by it;

or negatively, as barbaric, cruel, and lacking in the social and moral values of "civilized" human society. *Sauvage* thus announces the title figure as "other" and potentially both timid and dangerous, adding further layers of ambiguity to her portrayal. The glancing play of these different meanings is then itself highlighted by one final resonance of the title, for the word, *demoiselle*, skimming the divide between the social and the natural, is also the damsel fly, a fleeting glint over water. Above all then, the collocation, *demoiselle sauvage,* holds in unresolved suspension an elusiveness of identity, which persistently defies attempts to immobilize it within a single frame of reference.

Three *demoiselles sauvages*

Bille's Prix Goncourt de la nouvelle (Goncourt prize for the short story) for her 1975 short story collection completed a hat-trick of awards to Swiss authors, decisively raising the profile of francophone Swiss literature in the literary world of France.[2] It also coincided with Léa Pool's 1975 departure from Switzerland to Montreal, and ultimately to a career as film-maker in Quebec. Reflecting the anxieties provoking and provoked by this transatlantic passage, her first two feature films, *La femme de l'hôtel* (1984) and *Anne Trister* (1986), focus on the uncertainties of the displaced self adrift in the impersonal world of the modern city, the tenuous and transitory links with other companions in distress, and the cyclical processes of collapse, remaking, and un-making of an elusive and labile identity. The intimate significance of these experiences for Pool is overlaid in both cases by a primary emphasis on creative transformation, represented in *La femme de l'hôtel* by the fictional figures of film-maker and actress and in *Anne Trister* by Anne, the painter. Pool's 1991 adaptation of "La demoiselle sauvage" adopts an alternative strategy of self-protection, using the literary work of Bille, her fellow Swiss, as means of indirectly exploring anxieties of displacement and estrangement.[3] This joint exploration of the *demoiselle sauvage* figure is reprised by Pool in a broadly similar protective perspective in her 1997 documentary on the French-Canadian author Gabrielle Roy, whose restless preoccupation in both her life and her work with the quest for as an yet un-realized identity set her firmly for Pool within the same paradigm of personal and creative behavior as herself and her predecessor Bille.

Corinna Bille (1912–1979): "La demoiselle sauvage," the short story (1974)

Bille's "La demoiselle sauvage" both reflects and transposes the author's cultural and personal experience of her twentieth-century Switzerland. Geographically and politically fragmented by its challenging terrain into twenty-six different cantons, linguistically divided into four language groups,[4] and culturally split within the divergent ambits of its three main linguistic neighbours, Bille's homeland is a casebook site for the interrogation of identity as pre-eminently realized in individual autonomy or in collective common cause, with their attendant ambiguities of eccentric but isolated freedom or secure but claustrophobic conformism. Bille's father, the painter Edmond Bille, was above all concerned that his children's view of the world should not be confined to "the constricted universe of Romandy" ["un univers romand étriqué"][5] and that they should benefit from every possible stimulus, cultural or natural. They were not, however, entirely spared the discrepancies between their father's avant-garde lifestyle and the conservative disapproval of the Valaisan peasantry. A further difficulty, encountered by Bille from the young age of eight, and subsequently throughout her convent education, was the censorious attitude of the Catholic Church towards the body, an attitude at total variance with her passionate response to the physical stimuli of the natural world. The alienating damage inflicted on the natural development of the self by religious dogma and its institutional embodiment in the moral and legal constraints of a confined, inward-looking society thus became a constant thematic thread in her writing, not least in "La demoiselle sauvage."

At one level, this is a tale of murder and suicide in a contemporary setting, where engineers build dams, aircraft fly overhead, tourists flock to "Son et Lumière" spectaculars, and drugs are traded in bus-station bars. But this cursory summary of plot and setting is entirely misleading as an account of the ambiance and thematic focus privileged by Bille, who presents this everyday reality as if at the wrong end of a telescope, shuttered off, "othered," vanishingly small, and curiously distorted in its miniaturization. Foregrounded instead is wilderness as the site of an older order of instinctual natural identity, hauntingly symbolized at the beginning of the story by the figure of the motionless girl in the forest clearing.

Bille's version of Pan and Syrinx is considerably more problematic, however, than this opening image might suggest. The girl is indeed linked throughout to the seasonal rhythms of the natural world. One striking description shows her covered in leaves; elsewhere metaphors depict her as fragrant grassy field; with bees and honey filling her outstretched hands; fading to the skeleton veining of a dead leaf; assimilated to the strange metallic pallor of moonlit snow. But alongside such symbiosis, the rejected values of a repressive social identity increasingly intrude in slippages between sensation and consciousness, skillfully realized by Bille in a complex, off-key interplay of voice between dialogue, third person description, interior monologue, indirect and free indirect speech. The particular preoccupation driving these reflections is the irrelevance of the notion of God and of a divinely sanctioned moral order to the natural functioning of the world. Hence the indifference of *la demoiselle sauvage* to society's protective frameworks of legal and moral constraint, manifest in her rejection of her civil and social identity as the former Mlle L ... or Mme D ...,[6] her disregard of the marital status of the male protagonist, and her absence of emotion as she describes her murder of her husband.

In contrast, her male counterpart, Elysée d'A ..., likes to view himself as a rational being in control of his social and natural environments as confirmed by his network of social connection (old aristocratic roots, family, and social circle) and his profession as engineer, responsible for the safe harnessing for his community of the natural resources of water. His equivalents are the police and the law with their analogous responsibility for surveillance and control of the potentially volatile world of human relations. However, though all these attachments are present throughout and indeed renew their dominance of his life at the end of the tale, they are overtaken from the very first sentence by the elemental, never totally silenced force of sexual attraction.

Background characters reinforce the ambiguities of identity of the two socially opposed but sexually akin protagonists. *La demoiselle sauvage* has, as her pale negative double, the coldly austere aunt in charge of her failed socialization, but, as more forceful and challenging equivalents, the women of Elysée's hunting party. These women, to the discomfort of their male companions, introduce an Amazonian element, openly contesting the physical and social subordination long imposed upon them, and demonstrating their excellent natural abilities with the gun. They thus reprise the penchant for physical self-affirmation, violently displayed by *la demoiselle sauvage* in the murder of her husband, and disturbingly echoed in her fetichistic fashioning of "the silver Spectre" ["le Spectre d'argent"], the tiny, silver-paper replica of her lover Elysée.

The main doubles of the engineer are the unseen representatives of public order, but more ambiguously, the murdered husband. Elysée's virility, explicitly celebrated by *la demoiselle sauvage*,[7] is set in strong apparent opposition to the husband's sadistic impotence, but the reifying impulse of the husband's literal tattooing of his wife is unsettlingly linked by the author to sexual penetration, capable likewise of marking in blood female subjection and reification. The story opens in fact on penetration by the male gaze as the as-yet unnamed *l'homme* slides serpent-like towards his female quarry through the undergrowth; Elysée's kisses are masochistically enjoyed by *la demoiselle sauvage* as pebbles blocking her mouth or scars burnt into her skin; and love-making always has for her, "despite the pleasure, a taste of suffering and blood" ["malgré le plaisir ... un goût de souffrance et de sang"] (36). But conversely, in a further revealing echo of the impotent husband, predatory impulse in Elysée soon lapses into castratory fear which he attempts to relieve by the classic move of projection onto the other of the responsibility of his own submission, his gift of a black cat preemptively casting *la demoiselle sauvage* in the role of (guilty) witch.

The short story form is of major benefit to Bille's portrayal of a fantasmic world of sensation and emotion released from the repressive anchoring of moral and social convention. The concision of the genre allows a convenient evacuation of the story-line so that the narrative of murder, flight, and suicide is reduced from potential thriller to symbolic device for entry into a natural world beyond morality and law. The setting, similarly, with the exception of a few fleeting allusions,[8] is freed from detailed reference to Switzerland, to consist almost entirely of an oneiric world of rampant vegetation and threatened or crumbling habitation, where fairy-tale merges with nightmarish hallucination to evoke the disturbing "otherness" of the unfettered human psyche. The protagonists, meanwhile, stripped of the extraneous detail of everyday existence but with functional support from the secondary characters, represent in extreme and intense form the complex conflictual pulls of natural instinct and social constraint, each seeking in the other for the duration of their liaison, not a real person, but an absolute of physical self-realization, that transcends the contingencies of individual and social being. You love me, says Elysée: "Because you are not you but another. And I too am not myself but another" ["Parce que tu n'es pas toi mais une autre. Et moi, je ne suis pas moi mais un autre"] (41).

For the *demoiselle sauvage* that is Bille herself, the role of writing is crucial, enabling the creation of an "other" world, where, as she puts it, "the young lady of my father's castle" ["la demoiselle du château de mon père"] and "an Eve too wild for society" ["une Eve trop sauvage"] can at last come together in pursuit of an impossible experience of unrestricted passion: "From this life I could not live, I made short stories, novels. The act of writing is the equivalent of the act of love. Murder too sometimes. There are assassins, drunkards, arsonists in my stories. And curiously, they are part of my construction of myself" ["De cette vie que je ne pouvais vivre, je fis des nouvelles, des romans. L'acte d'écrire est l'équivalent de l'acte d'amour. Le meurtre parfois aussi. Il y a des assassins, des ivrognes, des incendiaires dans mes histoires. Et chose étrange, ils participent à la construction de moi-même"] (quoted in Favre 33).

Léa Pool: *La demoiselle sauvage* as film

The other worlds of nature and dream and the a-social, a-moral fantasmic personage of *la demoiselle sauvage*, as imagined by Bille, provide the starting point for Pool's own reflection, through the very different medium of film, on paradoxes of identity and otherness. Superficially many of the same elements are present: the same two protagonists of girl and engineer; a similarly conceived setting, based on an opposition between natural and man-made environments; the same plot-line of murder, flight, and suicide; the same main incidents (discovery of the injured girl in an isolated place, her transferral to the engineer's summer abode, the visit of the hunting party, the girl's solitary existence after the engineer's departure at the end of the summer, her disappearance as winter sets in, and the final discovery of her body in the Rhone). However, the generic proclivities of film as a linear narrative within a pre-eminently visual medium produce a different shaping of the story from Bille's written text, and a reworking of the *demoiselle sauvage* theme that echoes the specificities of Pool's own desire to escape the constrictions and discontents of the Swiss communities of her youth.

Organized in strict chronological sequence, the film starts, typically for Pool, in darkness, to sound-off of argument and attack, before opening into a sequence where the camera focuses first on a grey wall with closed shutters, next on the girl running towards her car, then on the car's tumble into grey river. The enigmatic quality of Bille's *demoiselle sauvage*, "miraculously" present and unexplained in the wilderness of the forest clearing, though intradiegetically maintained for Pool's engineer, is thus absent for Pool's cinema audience, apprised, from the start, of the violence of the marital relationship. The confusion of real world and its re-presentation, encouraged by the visuality of film, also produces a very different conception and perception of the protagonists from those of the Bille text. From Bille's very first sentence, the protagonists are defamiliarized, their proportions bizarrely changed, their actions, thoughts and sensations disconcertingly collapsed the one into the other. The film however must work with visual images, dialogue, and sound; and image and dialogue, where a modern scenario at least is concerned, more easily emphasize the familiar, the conventional, and the everyday. Thus the vaguely medieval mysteriousness of knight and damsel, and the faery of woodland nymph, tend largely to disappear in the precise and perfect delineation of the film's photogenic stars, the designer-chic casual wear provided for the rescued girl, and the modern comforts of the engineer's summer chalet. Similarly verbal communication between the protagonists loses the subtle off-key shading of unspoken thoughts and mental reservation characteristic of Bille's protagonists, and allusiveness shifts instead to the purely emotional melancholy of the musical score.

But handling of landscape is perhaps *the* major element in Pool's reorientating of Bille's discourse on identity and otherness. The dappled light or deepening gloom of trees and undergrowth in which Bille's *demoiselle sauvage*, as forest creature, slips in and out of sight, survives in one shot only of Pool's film, the brief glimpse of the girl, half-hidden in the leafy bushes of the engineer's family garden, just before her final disappearance. Otherwise Pool's chosen setting throughout is the harsh barrenness of the Swiss mountains, and her privileged focus, the startling opposition between the inhuman beauty of soaring slopes and blue, coldly shimmering lake, and the enormous block of the man-made dam. This masculine harnessing of natural forces forms a background thread in Bille's story, but minimal reference ensures that primary emphasis is firmly kept on the world of instinct in which the rational world only feebly and intermittently intervenes. In Pool's film by contrast, the confrontation of the natural and the made-by-man assumes a dominant place. Both girl and engineer appear dwarfed by the stark immensity of the natural landscape, so that any "one-ness" they might have with it is irretrievably compromised. Containment becomes a matter of overriding importance, and the subterranean noises echoing through the tunnels of the dam relay the menace of hidden forces restrained with difficulty by the mass of concrete. But long shots of the protagonists as tiny figures on top of the dam or at its foot, and contrasting close-ups of their enclosure within the tunnels and grilles of its inner structures, underline also the opposite idea of mechanisms of oppressive constriction that dwarf and overwhelm those they purport to protect. In parallel, the prominence of the dam is complemented (in contrast to occasional passing mention by Bille) by high visibility of the police as they and their dogs, responding to society's fear of violent disruption, attempt to track down the small, physically frail figure of the fugitive girl.

It could therefore be argued that Pool's rendering of Bille's tale, privileging the visual possibilities of awe-inspiring landscape, has reneged on Bille's portrayal of *la demoiselle sauvage* as an a-social being whose identity is most fully constituted in the elusive "otherness" of its physical response, offering instead a more conventional picture of a woman crushed out of existence by the control mechanisms of a patriarchal society.[9] Another reading might however situate the film within a different understanding of the *demoiselle sauvage* figure, corresponding to the particular difficulties of Pool's own youthful experience of her Swiss "home." This she has described as primarily one of alienation and exile, arising from her Polish-Jewish roots, her father's refugee "statelessness," and her unconventional (for 1950s Switzerland) family circumstances of unmarried parents and an upbringing mainly carried out by her father.[10] In that perspective, Pool's re-shaping of Bille's original into a portrait of a forbidding, if astoundingly beautiful, natural landscape, and an equally forbidding portrait of the bleakness of Swiss society – grey concrete dam, dark villages, grey town, aggressive police, and the unbending faces of its citizenry – constituted in some sense a cathartic closing off of a chapter. As Pool commented in interview, the film ambiguously combines the best and the worst of her memories, but above all therapeutically transforms them in the joyful release of their cinematographic reworking:

I was very keen to make a film in Switzerland. It was a period when I had thought several times of going back. Curiously, "the scene of the crime" ... was in fact a happy place of my childhood. It was the place of my holidays. It would have been "logical" for me to make *Emporte-moi* [*Set Me Free*] in Switzerland for example, but I did not want to do that. Which is after all a way once again of keeping a distance. In choosing a subject like *La demoiselle sauvage* which was not mine but which I was transposing, I took the happiest part of me to make into something that is basically extremely tragic. But shooting the film was a very happy experience for me. Is it the closure of something? Perhaps.

[J'avais très envie de faire un film en Suisse. À cette époque-là, j'avais pensé rentrer à plusieurs reprises. Étrangement, "le lieu du crime" ... est plutôt un lieu heureux de mon enfance. C'était le lieu des vacances. Ç'aurait été "logique" que je fasse *Emporte-moi* en Suisse par exemple, mais je n'ai pas eu ce désir-là. Ce qui est quand même encore une fois une façon de rester à distance. En choisissant un sujet comme *La demoiselle sauvage*, qui n'était pas de moi mais que je transposais, j'ai pris la partie la plus heureuse de moi pour en faire un sujet extrêmement tragique au fond. Mais le tournage pour moi a été un grand bonheur. Est-ce la clôture de quelque chose ? Peut-être.] (Grugeau 19)[11]

Léa Pool's *Gabrielle Roy* (1997): A Canadian *demoiselle sauvage*

Six years after *La demoiselle sauvage*, Pool continued her filmic reflection on the distinctive othernesses of the *demoiselle sauvage* figure with a documentary on the life and work of another literary creator, the French Canadian author Gabrielle Roy. Just as Pool's family history of Jewish displacement culminates for her in her father's arrival in Switzerland from Poland, and her own departure from Switzerland to Quebec, so the wanderings of Roy's forbears from the *le vieux pays* ["the old country"] to New World destinations, first in Acadia, then in Quebec, and finally in Manitoba, culminate in Roy's own travels from Manitoba to Europe, and then back from France and England to ultimate settlement in Quebec.

Such transcontinental and transatlantic passages reflect in both cases the particular difficulties of multiple marginalization. Thus, for Pool, the unyielding constrictions of Switzerland, compounding the smallness of its Jewish and francophone communities, precipitate a desire for other, unrestricted spaces of self-realization, just as for Roy in Manitoba, escape from the beleaguered mentality of the small francophone community of Saint Boniface became an imperative need. There are resemblances too of familial environment, the general absence of Pool's mother echoing the remoteness of Roy's elderly father towards his last-born child, Pool's affectionate relationship with her father reminiscent of the strong mutual attachment of Roy and her mother. But if parental absence is experienced as a loss, parental presence too may be felt as a restrictive disempowerment. So Roy's departure from Manitoba, leaving behind her mother and the safe, socially acceptable profession of primary school teacher, is superficially justified by the daughter as a vicarious victory for the mother who also longed for her freedom, but at a deeper, more guilty, level is experienced as the desperate desire to escape a parent's emotional hold. As Pool explains to Grugeau:

I found a great deal of myself in Gabrielle Roy. She was a primary school teacher like me. We travelled in opposite directions to each other, since I left Switzerland to come and construct myself here ... in short my experience resonated very much with hers. All that guilt with regard to her mother ... not the fact of having left her mother, but of not being able to treat it as a matter of course, not to be capable of moving beyond it.

[Je me suis beaucoup retrouvée en [Gabrielle Roy]. Elle était institutrice comme moi. On a fait un trajet inverse, puisque je suis partie de la Suisse pour venir me construire ici... bref j'ai trouvé chez elle plein de résonances. Toute cette culpabilité par rapport à la mère ... pas le fait d'avoir quitté la mère, mais de ne pas pouvoir aller au plus simple, de ne pas être capable de dépasser cela.] (Grugeau 20)

Pool's empathy with Roy's thematic preoccupations, in particular "her sensitivity with regard to her childhood and her mother" ["sa sensibilité dans son rapport à l'enfance et à la mère"] and with "[the] simplicity, [the] efficiency and effectiveness – carefully controlled, of course" ["[la] simplicité, [l']efficacité, extrêmement travaillée par ailleurs"] of her writing, further promotes the sense of a shared identity: "I read certain passages and I burst into tears. Moments like that are very rare ... Gabrielle Roy has a way of telling her stories that touches me deeply" ["Je lis certains passages et j'éclate en sanglots. C'est rare, ces moments-là ... Chez Gabrielle Roy, il y a une façon de raconter qui me rejoint vraiment"] (Grugeau 20). A careful selection of excerpts from Roy's autobiographical and fictional writings thus underpins the documentary, emphasizing key aspects of identity and otherness, as experienced by Roy socially and culturally as a member of a discriminated group (the French Canadians in Winnipeg), individually in terms of the pressures of family and personal relations, and, more viscerally and more generally, in the existential dis/continuities of the self in time, and also in space. Focusing on Roy's preoccupation with childhood and age, Pool shows Roy's high-school photograph, accompanied by voice-over text from *La détresse et l'enchantement*, stressing the strangeness to the self of its different temporal phases.[12] Roy's concomitant, spatial outreach to all who feel themselves exiles and strangers is similarly highlighted by Pool's inclusion of a passage from Roy's first success, *Bonheur d'occa-*

sion,[13] the novel of a dispossessed rural underclass, adrift in the deprived 1930s slums of Montreal's working-class Saint-Henri, and further passages from two immigrant stories, "Où iras-tu Sam Lee Wong?" ["Where will you go, Sam Lee Wong?"] and "Un jardin au bout du monde" ["Garden in the Wind"], the tales respectively of a Chinese man and a Ukrainian woman, each exiled from their homeland and their past on the vast spaces of the Prairies.[14]

For Roy herself, however, the westward swell of endless plain under the immensities of an overarching sky has an emotive spatial attraction far outweighing the harshness of the challenges it poses to the immigrant settlers. Filled with the "humble immortality of air, wind, and grass" ["l'humble immortalité de l'air, du vent, des herbes"] (*Un jardin au bout du monde* 217), it symbolizes for her the eternal quest for self-transcendence and a return, albeit temporary, to the infinite dreams of childhood. A fragment of text testifying to the intense attachment of Roy to the windswept horizons of her Manitoban birthplace (*La détresse* 132–3), is therefore incorporated by Pool into the film, as an important aspect of Roy's self-definition.

The sound-track of the film confirms the closeness of Pool's identification with Roy as a fellow *demoiselle sauvage*. A black opening frame, accompanied by sounds-off first of birdsong, evocative of early morning, and of childhood, then of the rhythmic movement of a train, introduces a sound-track in which music from Chopin, Schumann, Rachmaninov, and others, mingles with a variety of human voices to recreate aurally the emotive atmosphere of Roy's personal and literary universes. But the central focus is Roy's own voice in the excerpts from her writing and, equally and simultaneously, Pool's voice reading those texts with a lyricism and clarity that movingly matches those of the original.

The depth of Pool's identification with Roy is protectively balanced by the many other voices presenting their views on Roy both as individual and author. But, as with her adaptation of Bille, it is the refraction of Roy's literary work in the visual medium of Pool's film, which both confirms the kinship and affirms the specificities of their respective creative visions. Pool's biopic necessarily follows a basically chronological progression from childhood to old age, but the filmmaker captures Roy's insistence on the erosions of identity and the ambiguous linkages and disconnections between our present and former selves, through montage techniques intermingling black and white photographs and early black and white movie footage with color footage of Roy's beloved landscapes of Manitoba and Quebec's Petite

Rivière Saint-François and actress recreations of Roy as child, adult, and elderly woman. Above all, Pool constantly plays with juxtapositions, overlappings or soft fades between photographs of Roy at different stages of her life, ending the film with a sequence in which running water is superimposed on a photograph of Roy in old age, as Pool in voice-over reads the death-bed reflections of Marthe, the old Ukrainian creator of the garden "au bout du monde."[15] Close-up and then pull-back shots follow, of dead sunflowers in snow, a withered echo of their summer glory in an earlier image in the film, and this final sequence then concludes in a move of simultaneous return and closure, with a juxtaposed photograph of Gabrielle Roy, the young woman.

A second feature of Roy's writing, highlighted in the film, is her constant insistence on the importance of movement in the creation of her imaginative universe. Pool responds to the challenge of static documents with shifting camera shots, with montage techniques suggesting change and passage, and with alternating close-ups of different witnesses and their testimonies. The acted sequences also bring dynamism to the documentary account, while the passages from Roy's fiction similarly elicit shots of the protagonists in motion. A range of camera shots highlights the railroad as a defining symbol of Roy's physical and fictional universes, and further visual symbolization of movement grows out of Pool's imaginative response to Roy's writing: white horses galloping and rearing in a misty background of snow; children running joyfully in the sunshine down a grassy slope.

Roy's lyrical attachment to landscape provides an opportunity for Pool to display the virtuoso visual possibilities of film, with respect this time to the vast infinities of Canadian space, in contrast, geographically and symbolically, to the vertical impenetrabilities of the mountains of *La demoiselle sauvage*. The plains of Roy's Manitoba are re-created in stunning images of the heart-stopping beauty of yellow prairie curving away under a cobalt heaven; of immense horizons traversed in long and diminishing perspective by "the small back roads" ["les petites routes de section"], of a single tree, caught, as in an impressionist painting, against a cotton-wool sky, while elsewhere a close-up of melting snow or resistant river ice symbolically suggests the promise of springtime, or a flagging of hope. In her visual handling of narrative sequence, the personal and artistic spaces of Roy's life and work, and the landscapes of Manitoba and Quebec, Pool thus successfully maintains her own independent identity as an original creative artist, whilst simultaneously honoring a North American kindred spirit whose reflections, in a different medium, on nature and society, identity and otherness, resonate with many of her own.

Conclusion

Across the Atlantic Ocean, Bille, Pool, and Roy join hands as *demoiselles sauvages*, who from their different but parallel starting points escape confinement to explore the unrealized othernesses of their personal and creative selves. For Bille in her short story, refusal of social and moral conformism and the embracing of physical being are paramount; for Pool, in her film adaptation of Bille, refusal of Switzerland emblematized as a place of exile and of imprisonment of the soul; for Roy, in her writing, refusal of a narrow French-Canadian Catholic survivalism and the search for the wider values of a self that embraces otherness (of people, of the natural world, of its own different ages) as the essential core of its self-realization. All three illustrate the increasing prominence of the "other voice" of women in the never-ending search for a place in which to become fully "oneself." Roy, moving well beyond her Manitoban origins, was, as Carol Shields suggests in Pool's documentary, the virtual inventor of the female Canadian author and with *Bonheur d'occasion* gained the unique double accolade of recognition in France (Prix Femina, 1947) and success in translation in anglophone North America. Bille, long relegated by her male peers to a small role as a regional writer, finally, at fifty-six, asserted her individual voice with *La fraise noire* [*The Black Strawberry*] (1968) and then with her Prix Goncourt. Pool, in the cultural effervescence of Quebec in the 1970s, identified cinema as her personal medium and subsequently achieved success as a woman director, aligning a whole production team to her female vision of the othernesses of identity. All three *demoiselles sauvages* however, characteristically resist conscription to a political cause. Bille wrote, as she put it, "so as not to die" ["pour ne pas mourir"] (Favre 34). Roy, similarly, experienced writing as an inescapable inner necessity, while Pool, for her part, views the making of her films as part of the endless search for an identity only transiently glimpsed in each individual piece. It is thus within the elastic spaces of their work that each of these *demoiselles sauvages* is most deeply engaged with the vital core of her being, with that untamed, elusive, child-like "otherness" that is the elemental stuff of the artist's creative vision.

Notes

1 All translations are the author's, unless otherwise indicated.

2 The other winners were Jacques Chessex, *L'ogre* [*The Ogre*], Prix Goncourt (1973), and Georges Borgeaud, *Voyage à l'étranger* [*Journey Abroad*], Prix Renaudot (1974).

3 Pool's third feature film, *À corps perdu* [*Straight for the Heart*] (1988), is her first adaptation of a literary text, Yves Navarre's *Kurwenal.* The male voice of the reporter-photographer protagonist provides a further distancing mechanism.

4 In 1980, the year following Bille's death, the different language percentages of the Swiss population were 73.5 percent German, 20.1 percent French, 4.5 percent Italian, and 0.9 percent Romanche (see Iso Camartin, in *Modern Swiss Literature and Diversity*, ed. John L. Flood, 72).

5 Romandy is the collective name of the French-speaking cantons of Switzerland. The biographical details of this paragraph are all derived from Gilberte Favre, *Corinna Bille*, 28, and in many cases, though not this one, from the cited remarks of Bille.

6 The girl's maiden name is not revealed until a few pages into the story; her married name only appears on the final page in the newspaper cutting announcing the discovery of her body in the Rhone. Bille's text (26) also stresses the social alienation of the girl's orphaned childhood.

7 "[S]he saw that he had arms the colour of ripe apricots ... Yes, he had an admirably balanced body, toughened by many sports, combining strength and sinewy grace ... Now she knew a man and he was life itself" ["elle vit qu'il avait les bras de la teinte des abricots mûrs ... Oui, il avait un corps d'un admirable équilibre, rompu à beaucoup de sports, tout ensemble solide et d'une grande finesse ... Maintenant, elle connaissait un homme et il était la lumière même"] (Bille 19).

8 For example, to goiter, to Swiss agriculture ("mayen" being the intermediate spring and autumn grazing ground for Alpine lifestock), to the late enfranchisement of women. Swiss female enfranchisement, undertaken first in the individual cantons from 1959 on, was only achieved on the federal level in 1971. Cantonal enfranchisement for women was only finally completed at the beginning of the 1990s.

9 See Chantal Nadeau's article.

10 See Tony Simons 23.

11 Pool's 1998 film *Emporte-moi* offers a more direct examination of the difficulties of her childhood roots and family history but with Montreal as the distancing location for the fictional Hanna, the film's adolescent protagonist.

12 "The child that I was is as strange to me as I would have been in her eyes, if only that evening, on the threshold of life, she had been able to see me as I am today. From birth to death, from death to birth, we never cease, through memory, through dream, to move, as it were one towards the other, towards a meeting with ourselves, even as the distance grows between us" ["Cet enfant que je fus m'est aussi étrangère que j'aurais pu l'être à ses yeux, si seulement ce soir, à l'orée de la vie ..., elle avait pu m'apercevoir comme je suis aujourd'hui. De la naissance à la mort, de la mort à la naissance, nous ne cessons, par le souvenir, par le rêve, d'aller comme l'un vers l'autre, à notre propre rencontre, alors que croît entre nous la distance"] (*La détresse* 80). Patricia Claxton translated this in *Enchantment and Sorrow*.

13 Literally *Second-hand happiness*, but translated by Hannah Josephson as *The Tin Flute.*

14 In the collection of short stories, *Un jardin au bout du monde* 59–130, 151–217. This collection has been translated into English by Alan Brown under the title *Garden in the Wind.*

15 "[O]ld, broken, in truth almost dead, Marthe found herself returning, as if in search of herself, to the distant regions of her own youth. And she saw then that the health and strength she had lost, her vital energy, her love and her ardent attachment to life were in her eyes the true part of herself. She told herself à propos of that young being, now almost totally vanished: 'That was truly the real me. It's now that I am no longer myself.' And she experienced a feeling of surprise and pain, as if she had found herself confronted by the essential injustice laid on human life" ["vieille, brisée, presque morte en vérité, voici que Marthe retournait, comme pour se chercher elle-même, dans les lointaines régions de sa propre jeunesse. Elle s'apercevait alors que sa robuste santé perdue, son énergie vitale, son amour et son ardeur à vivre étaient à ses yeux la part vraie d'elle-même. Elle se disait à propos de cet être jeune, presque totalement disparu : 'Pourtant c'était bien moi. C'est maintenant que je ne suis plus moi.' Et elle en éprouvait de l'étonnement et de la peine comme si elle se fût trouvée devant l'essentielle injustice faite à la vie humaine"] (*Un jardin au bout du monde*, 211–12).

Works Cited

Bille, S. Corinna. *La demoiselle sauvage.* Lausanne: Bertil Galland, 1974.

Camartin, Iso. "Romanche, a Minor Literature: Limitations and Perspectives." *Modern Swiss Literature and Diversity.* Ed. John L. Flood. London: Oswald Wolf; Institute of Germanic Studies, 1985. 71–8.

Favre, Gilberte. *Corinna Bille. Le vrai conte de ma vie.* Lausanne: Éditions 24 heures, 1981.

Grugeau, Gérard. "L'exil intérieur. Entretien avec Léa Pool." *24 Images* 106 (Spring 2001): 16–21

Nadeau, Chantal. "La représentation de la femme comme autre. L'ambiguïté du cinéma de Léa Pool pour une position féministe." *Québec Studies* 17 (1994): 82–96.

Pool, Léa. *La demoiselle sauvage* (1991). Cinémaginaire, the National Film Board of Canada and Limbo Film.

– *Gabrielle Roy* (1997). Les productions de l'impatiente and Buffalo Gal Pictures.

Roy, Gabrielle. *Bonheur d'occasion.* Montreal: Société des éditions Pascal, 1945. Translated as *The Tin Flute.* Trans. Hannah Josephson. Toronto: McClelland and Stewart, 1947.

– *Ces enfants de ma vie.* Ottawa: Stanké, 1977.

– *La détresse et l'enchantement* (1984). 3rd edition. Montreal: Boréal, 1996. Translated as *Enchantment and Sorrow: The Autobiography of Gabrielle Roy.* Trans. Patricia Claxton. Toronto: Lester and Orpen Dennys, 1987.

– *Fragiles lumières de la terre. Écrits divers. 1942–1970.* Montreal: Éditions quinze, 1978. Translated as *The Fragile Lights of Earth.* Trans. Alan Brown. Toronto: McClelland and Stewart, 1982.

– *Un jardin au bout du monde.* Montreal: Beauchemin, 1975. Translated as *Garden in the Wind.* Trans. Alan Brown. Toronto: McClelland and Stewart, 1977.

Simons, Tony. "Léa Pool, *Anne Trister*." In *Where Are the Voices Coming From? Canadian Culture and the Legacies of History.* Ed. Coral Ann Howells. Amsterdam/New York: Rodopi, 2004. 231–45.

Contemporary Art Forms and Popular Culture

21. I opening *Le Monde*. Young Algerian professor expelled. Just as doctoral defence coming up. But not French wife and kids. Slender woman in white pantsuit. Immaculate straight-cut hair. Crossing street in direction of art-deco hotel opposite. Façade draped in grapes. Songbirds singing in them. Only mouth giving away woman's age. Tight. Slightly turned-down at corners. Mouth of disappointment.

Curve of disappointment on own mouth. Spied recently in café mirror. Making me want to shape up immediately. At the time watching the québécoise C's lovely full lips. Even when distressed. Producing moue of self-mocking humour. Mocking French mocking québécois way of speaking. Nasalizing pain, bread. Mouth half-opened. Instead of lips rounding over aspirated consonant. Like a kiss. Parisians surely owing beauty. To ubiquity of mirror. Barely post-Revolution – most homes having two. While in England – rare. Even in châteaux.

22. ... Crime here upsetting a routine. As in colleagues from chez nous ... She in white blouse and long skirt. Very contained. Basic female requirement. For balanced heterosexual couple. He with brilliant high forehead. Lapsing into English. Walking down du Bac. Complaining about ubiquity of visual image. E.g. Gulf War in real time. On TV. Giving faux-sense of democracy. Because *in reality* "one" passively absorbing. Compared to. Say. Here he looking round meaningfully. Compared to certain less anecdotal more analytic narratives. Requiring participatory i.e. *truly* democratic effort. Maybe. I thinking. Straightening in boutique façade mirror. Then passing cops by café – I whispering speak French so they not asking for visa. Forgetting québécois accents.

Arm 'n arm we strolling. Chatting. Chatting. Passing hotel façade on which vines also gossiping. Climbing familiarly on shoulders of plumtrees. Down Cherche-Midi, Noon-Seeking Street. Old Roman road. Where sun rarely shining. Rarely hitting aging black dresses. Of tired boutique women. Into Roman restaurant. Divine antipasto ...

Sipping grappa. Waiter hearing accents. Gesturing toward terrasse. Your compatriot's out there. Meaning famous québécoise pop singer Diane Dufresne. Chez nous we calling her la Diva. Though once accidentally falling off stage. At Paris Olympia.

Très cher I telling P later. She saying stop fetishizing price tags. Value here measured otherwise.

Gail Scott, *My Paris* 24–6.

Riopelle and Me: *Impression passagère*

BONNIE BAXTER

When you go to sea, you have to know how to lay up provisions for many weeks. After that, you can live anywhere, very simply ... Here, on the Île aux Oies, it's like being on my boat; I can withstand long sieges, spend the winter if necessary. An island is a sailboat without a mast. In any case my sailboat is my painting.

Jean Paul Riopelle[1]

Introduction

We seldom speak of "booking passage" anymore – that is something lost to Romantic period films and historical documents – now, we take trips, vacations, tours, junkets, or simply travel. It's a telling linguistic transition. As artists, we travel to find our success, to make the right connections, to add lustre to our careers and find other artists whose ideas we can share: to learn how they work, to find new ideas, to see things from a different point of view that will break into our daily process and inform our work. But "passage" refers to the journey itself: the passing-of-time so significant a part of any kind of travel before the jet age. In the art market, art is a product, but for an artist, it is a process, a passage that seldom takes a direct route or arrives at the expected destination, but is always worth the journey. For most artists, the process of art becomes the process of life itself and for no one was this truer than Canada's most celebrated painter, Jean Paul Riopelle.

Passages are journeys of transformation; "rites of passage" transcend a mere shift in time and allow for transition into another phase of existence. As a printmaker I also carry the alternate or complementary meaning of passages as the application of layers that result in a richly textured present rather than a past that grows increasingly distant with time. Looking back at my *impressions passagères* [my passing impressions], the journey that represents my life as an artist breaks down into a series of chapters consisting of a long series of passages from one place to another, from one set of friends and lovers and colleagues and associates, to another. One of the most significant passages was my time working with Jean Paul Riopelle and the extraordinary people who surrounded him.

Background

In some ways, the itinerant life is typical of successful artists even today, a necessity created by the art markets' seasonal shifting and the necessity for the artist to appear at openings, to be seen by their public, their collectors, and their gallery owners. But for Riopelle and many of the artists who flourished in the post–World War Two era, it was much more than this. The need for physical contact, to be in the same space with others, was an expression of freedom and to some extent a habitual pattern of existence created by the exigencies of Europe's exile artists[2] of the 1930s and 1940s and the curious transatlantic network that they created.

Repulsed and excluded by increasingly obscurantist strains of nationalism that arose in the early twentieth century, artists, philosophers, and scientists, of all means and media, flooded into the few culturally significant cities of Europe – Paris, Prague, and London – where artists were still free to express themselves. Escaping from ever advancing conformism of new-born nationalist regimes and their expanding borders, some even took the step of moving to the United States, establishing and reinforcing new cultural strongholds that became focal points for the radical exchange of ideas and techniques.[3]

Printmaking was considered a particularly apt and appropriate form of artistic expression during the war and in the post-war era when artists searched for a way to separate themselves from the elitism of church and state – the inflexible hierarchies of power they felt had contributed to the development of rampant nationalism and fascism. They joined forces with a more egalitarian outlook – art for everyone. The print, readily mass-produced, could be purchased by anyone, and new ideas, new symbols and icons, could be spread easily. Many galleries employed printers to make prints of work their artists had originally created in other mediums. Called "interpretation prints" they were often signed by both artist and printer; although not original prints, they were a respected and common art form in Europe. However, in Quebec, interpretation prints were viewed with suspicion and questioned as to their authenticity. In Paris, artists such as Miró, Picasso, and Kandinsky collaborated on fund-raising print editions to support the Republicans of the Spanish Civil War and to fund the Communist cause. For this reason, among visual artists one of the most significant of these new focal points (certainly the most significant for printmakers) was William Stanley Hayter's print shop and school, Atelier 17, first established in Paris in the late 1920s and then moved in the 1940s to New York, then back to Paris in the 1950s. When Hayter moved his Atelier to New York at the outbreak of the war, many artists followed him or found him there; Riopelle was among them.

Riopelle was born to the democratic freedom of peace-loving Canada, but his self-imposed exile to Europe was real, a product of the suffocating regime that existed in the province of Quebec until the 1960s – a period of time referred to as *La grande noirceur* [the great darkness]. He was among those artists who created and signed the then infamous and now famous *Le refus global* in 1948 – a manifesto initiated by a group of artists calling themselves Les automatistes, led by the great painter and teacher Paul-Émile Borduas. In it they state the right of artists to "break permanently with the customs of society and Church."

Quebec society of the 1940s and 50s was dominated by the leadership of politicians whose policies were tied to dictates of the powerful fathers of the Catholic Church. Despite, or because of this, under the long red skirts of this authoritarian society, the cities' pavements were pulsing with the sounds of jazz, the rattle of illicit dice, queer clubs, and the radical

Françoise Sullivan and Claude Gauvreau, "Exposition Mousseau-Riopelle chez Murielle Guilbault." Nov. 1947. Gelatin silver print, 22.5 x 22.5 cm; Musée national des beaux-arts du Québec, 1999.228 Photo: Maurice Perron

thinking of near neighbour New York. The mayor of Montreal infamously clamped down on "sin city," conducting raids on night clubs and even going so far as to clear all the undergrowth on Mont-Royal simply because this famous Montreal landmark could harbour the illicit sexual encounters it was becoming known for. The mood was generally stultifying, but the voices of modernism and the rising tide of *la Révolution tranquille* [the Quiet Revolution] could not be completely shut down. In effect, the atmosphere was a microcosm of the radical nationalism of Europe. *Les automatistes* were inflamed by the ideals of Surrealism and abstract expressionism that had crossed the ocean with European artists escaping the oppression of fascist governments and the neo-classical aesthetic they were enforcing.

Riopelle had travelled to France in 1946, forming close ties to Paris and the surrealist movement. He was a participant in two seminal exhibitions: Exposition Automatisme and Exposition internationale: Le surréalisme in Paris in 1947. In the same year, he would be the only Canadian to sign the surrealist's manifesto: the *Rupture inaugurale* [Inaugural Break] that severed the Surrealist's ties with the Communist movement. Riopelle may well have made his permanent home in France at this time had his wife, Françoise, not become pregnant. Wanting to be amongst family, they returned home for the birth of their daughter, Yseult.

As it turned out, the atmosphere of social protest would follow Riopelle to Montreal. Riopelle convinced his fellow Automatistes, Fernand Leduc and Paul-Émile Borduas, to write their own manifesto rather than signing that of the surrealists.[4] While Borduas wrote the principal text for the *Refus global* manifesto and would lose his job at the École du meuble because of it, Riopelle, who was relatively young at the time and beyond the influence of any École, received little overt censure. Nonetheless, his participation in this anti-establishment publication followed him even to his death in 2002 at the age of seventy-eight when his funeral at Montreal's Église Immaculée-Conception caused consternation and scandal.[5] While two fellow signatories of *Le refus global* boycotted the funeral on the basis that it was not in keeping with Riopelle's feelings about the church, a Catholic commentary wrote: "Why did the Archdiocese of Montreal lend one of its beautiful churches for the funeral of a trashy blasphemer? What is it that makes some clergy so terribly afraid to say no to the secular world?"[6]

Riopelle's move to Paris in 1946 and then, more permanently, in 1949 would be one of a long series of moves in his life. His trips across the Atlantic were frequent, his homes many. While most Canadian and almost all significant Quebec artists have spent time in France, few went as well prepared or succeeded so completely. His reputation flourished in France, not only because of his talent, but his ability to find connections and especially to forge friendships with great artistic personages working in every medium. He surrounded himself with people who worked at the very top of their profession, whether furniture makers, art dealers, restaurateurs, writers, or other artists – he liked the best of everything and the best of everyone. Even before leaving for Paris his work had caught the attention of the great leader of Surrealism in France, André Breton, who invited Riopelle to participate in an international exhibition of surrealist art in 1947. In his travels he crossed the paths of many significant figures, including Samuel Beckett, Joan Miró, Alberto Giacometti, Alexander Calder, Franz Kline, and Georges Braque. He joined the circle of expatriate artists in Paris that included Marc Chagall and Natalia Goncharova. His bohemian lifestyle gave him his 'bad boy' reputation. In Paris he and his gallerists fostered his image as a wild Canadian or "the peerless trapper,"[7] as André Breton dubbed him. He had his first solo show in Paris the same year he arrived, and by 1954 he worked under the wing of the highly influential and successful dealer Pierre Matisse, son of the famous painter Henri Matisse. It was not until 1966 that Riopelle joined the illustrious stable of Galerie Maeght and began a period of intense involvement in the medium of print that would lead, eventually, to our meeting in 1985.

Riopelle's Experience with Print before We Worked Together

To this day, Riopelle is primarily recognized as a great painter. Retrospectives invariably ignore his involvement in the print medium, but for Jean Paul Riopelle his printmaking was an essential part of his artistic practice. It represented a particularly malleable and opportune medium in which to record the quick shifting ideas of his intensely creative periods. They certainly helped to extend his career as an art-maker when his physical limitations made it increasingly difficult to paint.

Riopelle came to printmaking under the best possible auspices when he visited the legendary Atelier 17 in New York in 1946 for a month and learned some basic print techniques. A haven for Europe's "exile artists," Atelier 17 boasted a who's who of visiting artists who studied print under William Stanley Hayter's innovative tutelage like acolytes before a high priest. When Riopelle visited there he met Miro, Kline, Willem de Kooning, and Jackson Pollock as well – Miró and Kline would become lifelong friends. Nonetheless, it wasn't until 1954 that his prints first appeared in exhibition

1968, Riopelle at the ARTE press. Photo: Catalogue raisonné, Jean Paul Riopelle archives.

and even after that print was not a significant part of his output. Despite the legendary draw of Hayter's Atelier, truly widespread acceptance of print came later. By the 1960s the innovations initiated in Hayter's Atelier 17 had spawned a verdant new body of experimental art movements in North America. In Quebec, the Quiet Revolution, with its secular outlook and social democratic inclinations, brought the seemingly egalitarian and almost inherently political art form of printmaking to new heights of popularity. All considered, perhaps it was no surprise that Riopelle did not completely embrace print until he joined Galerie Maeght. Aimé Maeght, the gallery's owner, was himself was a professed lithographer, and in 1966 his dealers Jacques Dupin and Daniel Lelong dragged Riopelle to the ARTE print work-shop on Rue Daguerre in Paris and introduced him to René Le Moigne, a master lithographer who would serve as Riopelle's lithographer for the next thirty years.[8]

By the time I met him, Riopelle had an almost uncanny understanding of the print process and an intuitive feel for its potential. At that time, Euro-pean printers refused to stray beyond the boundaries of print processes set by decades, even centuries, of precedence. Even something as basic to con-temporary print practice as combining more than one printing method, such as lithography and intaglio on a single print, was considered disreputable. This was a point of frustration for Riopelle. Just as in his painting, Riopelle was daring and experimental; he liked to mix it up and was allergic to abiding formulas. I had been trained in Quebec according to the European print tradition, but I hailed from cowgirl stock and had worked in print shops in New York where any method was accepted as long as it worked – I was "game" to try anything. Riopelle appreciated that, and I became one of a very small group lucky enough to work with him. Together, he and I would push the boundaries of traditional print, creating entirely new processes and techniques.

My Background

I was born in Texarkana, Texas, just across the border from Mexico. It was a place that held tightly to a "Dick and Jane"[9] version of America, a picket-fence world where a little girl should aspire to follow the guidance of her father and older brother until she got married and followed her husband – not the most liberal place to grow up in the 1950s. Despite my parents and my gender I studied painting at Monticello College in Illinois. I spent my summers working in New York City. I took my first printmaking courses under Laurence Barker at Cranbrook Academy of Art in Michigan while studying painting and sculpture. In the summer after I left Cranbrook, I worked as a taxi driver outside of Detroit to earn money to go to Europe.

In the early 1970s I became, in my own way, an exile artist, I moved to Quebec with my boyfriend Pierre – gaining distance from my stifling upbringing. We divided our time between Quebec and Italy, but it was in Italy I felt I had found my spiritual home. I bought a stone farmhouse in the Sabine hills surrounded by acres of olive trees where I could paint. I drove a motorcycle with a sidecar for my dog, Diablo, exhibited in Rome, painted a mural for a tomb, taught art and English lessons in the medieval village of Forano Sabino, worked for a psychiatrist in Rome, and was even judged Miss Forano at a beauty pageant.

I gave up my home in Italy in 1975 to settle permanently in Quebec. I printed at the *Atelier de l'île* in Val-David and at GRAFF in Montreal. By 1982, I was more than ready to establish something solid and permanent and all my own. I bought the house that I am still living in now in the secluded mountain village of Val-David, Quebec and, with impeccable timing, founded my own custom print studio, the Atelier du Scarabée, just as the art of print began waning as a popular and reputable art form in North America.[10]

The Atelier grew into a dynamic and experimental custom print studio responsible for collaboration and production of etchings, lithography, relief prints, screen-prints, and handmade paper. Serendipitously, Riopelle had also established a studio only twenty minutes away in another mountain hideaway called Estérel. My being on the board of the Conseil de la culture des Laurentides (The Cultural Council of the Laurentians) meant knowing Lucette Lupien, the general director there, and because of the friendship we developed, I also came to know her husband, Werner Nold, a fellow contributor to this collection. At the time, he worked as a film editor for the National Film Board of Canada and had just finished editing a wonderful film on Riopelle[11] directed by Pierre Letarte and Marianne Feaver.

Riopelle hated cameras. He avoided interviews, but Pierre Letarte, along with his crew of three, practically moved into Jean Paul's house. Over the course of almost two years they were with Riopelle constantly, either in Estérel or in France. The result was a warm and personal film. It was during that editing process that Jean Paul, returning from France, said he wanted a printer who would etch his plates for him. In Quebec, while some artists paid printers to edition their work, most artists still etched their own plates. Riopelle was looking for someone who would prepare a plate for him to draw on and then etch the plate to be printed. Lucette recommended me, saying that I printed for important artists, such as Betty Goodwin. Riopelle asked that I meet him and his companion of that time, Hollis Jeffcoat, an American, and a painter in her own right.

When I arrived at their home I walked into a big living room where Jean Paul was with a lot of people sitting in a circle of chairs – talking and drinking. In later years I would get to know him and expect the polar bear skin he always had draped over his chair and the wide black belt he wore to support his spine, but at this point it was rather unexpected. In fact, the entire collection of visitors seemed a bit like some eccentric after-hours party of circus folk. They asked about my printing for Betty Goodwin and I said I didn't print for Betty Goodwin, I printed for Kitty Bruneau. It didn't seem to make a difference. The other guests left, some to homes in Montreal, others to catch a plane to France. I stayed behind and Jean Paul asked me to invite my chum, my partner Michel Beaudry whom I'd met in 1983, to come over for dinner. He came on the motorcycle and we ate and drank, and drank and ate, for the longest and most wonderful time. When we left,

Jean Paul said, "à demain" ["see you tomorrow"] which is how he ended
our meetings for the next eight years from 1985 to 1993.

It was a run-on relationship. Jean Paul came to us in Val-David the next
day and we stayed with him and Hollis the next weekend with our Irish
Setter, Café, who lived with them all week and ate paté every day while I
taught at Concordia University and Michel worked in Montreal. Hollis
called the dog Rose and made paintings from their moonlight walks together
in the snow. We came directly to Estérel from Montreal, not even bother-
ing to go back to Val-David. We slept there, we worked there, we ate, drank,
and traveled – everything flowed into everything else – it was a way of life
more than a job. In retrospect, it was an amazing balancing act: working
with Jean Paul, teaching, and continuing my personal practice as an artist.

Working/Living with Riopelle

And so, I spent the last half of the 1980s and the first half of the 1990s
working with artist Jean Paul Riopelle: overseeing the production of his
complete corpus of etchings during that period. I etched the plates and in
the beginning I did the printing as well, later on, as the volume increased,
I oversaw the printing, which was done by various different printers over
the years. Together we would develop his print ideas at Atelier du Scarabée,
discussing how things could and would be done, what colors to use, and
the order in which the plates would be printed. We worked together often
and because his homes and studios were divided by the Atlantic, we also

Jean Paul Riopelle and
Bonnie, Estérel, 1990.
Photo: Lucette Lupien

traveled, together or apart, in order to work on his prints. As long as
we were able to keep on working, we didn't worry too much about money.
I worked under the commission of Galerie Maeght-Lelong in Paris (now
simply Galerie Lelong), Philippe Briet Gallery in New York City, The
Moos Gallery in Toronto, and Galerie Esperanza in Montreal. While he
had worked on his etchings with printers in France before working with
me, he would have no others after we began working together. Once
Riopelle had made a commitment to a particular printer, be it for intaglio,
lithography, or serigraphy, he was totally faithful despite the fact that many
printers wanted to print for him and often made very interesting offers.
Faux Riopelle prints would sometimes appear on the market and when
Riopelle had stopped creating prints altogether, interpretation prints also
began to turn up.

Printmaking is an art of layers; life with Riopelle was also an art of layers.
Life never happened on a single plane. Riopelle's approach to the print was
highly unorthodox: he seemed to see the print as only a first layer. I would
sometimes have to hide/reserve initial prints from him or risk his taking them
prematurely to his studio where he would rework – *rehausser* – their raw
surfaces, each one a variation on an original theme which, if I wasn't quick
enough, would itself disappear under layers of inspiration. The print allowed
Riopelle to experiment freely – the original idea for the print would evolve
into many new expressions with the print forming a base or even, at times
being taken apart and reassembled as a collage. I sometimes wonder if his
love of print was another aspect of his love of evasion, each layer obscur-
ing the next, giving it intrigue and complexity.

Riopelle, Atelier de Vanves, 1967.
Photo: Claude Gaspari, Catalogue raisonné, Jean Paul Riopelle archives

We developed a wonderful work method that allowed us to keep working no matter where Jean Paul, who was chronically nomadic, happened to be. It was a combination of screen-print procedures coupled with misunderstandings and serendipitous mistakes. Usually I would give him a printing-plate I had covered in hard ground varnish. Jean Paul would scratch a drawing onto it (his tool of choice for this was often a screwdriver), and I would etch the plate where the metal was exposed and make a print in black and white. He'd put this black and white proof (an early print that would serve as a reference) on his wall and with different acetates (transparent films) and different colored markers, he would build up his color print layers (one color per plate represented by each separately colored film of acetate). In the first series I printed for him, the *Anticosti Series*, I would transfer the positive images of his drawings onto each plate using a highly toxic method known as the KPR method.[12] After a while I complained about the toxicity and Jean Paul suggested we adapt the "sugar lift" technique[13] used for etching in France that involved using condensed milk. I went ahead and tried to figure this out at my Atelier, not knowing that in France condensed milk came in a tube. I developed a method where I would transfer his drawing onto a silkscreen covered with light sensitive emulsion which, when exposed, would create a positive stencil of his drawing through which I would then print canned condensed milk onto the plate. As with the traditional sugar lift method, I covered the condensed milk with a thin layer of varnish after which I dissolved the milk to expose the metal on the plate with his drawing, and then I would aquatint the plate and let the acid bite where the plate exposed the remaining image. It turns out condensed milk from a can is the ideal viscosity and it worked perfectly. I did all future editions for Jean Paul using this method, a completely non-toxic way of working.

Around the same time I came to know Riopelle he also became associated with Philippe Briet, who was working for Karl Flinker at the time. Flinker had charged Briet with bringing examples of North American painting to France by its Ministry of the Foreign Relations in the 1980s. Briet idolized Riopelle and arranged an exhibition of his work at Caen in 1984. A few years later in 1989 Briet would open a gallery in New York,[14] the Philippe Briet Gallery, Inc.

Briet wanted to open his gallery featuring a print that Riopelle made for the opening called *Honni soit qui mal y pense*.[15] Jean Paul wanted to call it *Bonnie soit qui mal y pense*, but everyone thought the reference would

Top:
Riopelle and Philippe Briet, Caen Musée des beaux-arts Exhibition, 1984.
Photo: P. Victor, Catalogue raisonné, Jean Paul Riopelle archives

Bottom:
Hollis Jeffcoat and Philippe Briet, Caen, 1984.
Photo: P. Victor, Catalogue raisonné, Jean Paul Riopelle archives

Bonnie Baxter and Philippe Briet, Atelier du Scarabée, 1987. Photo: Michel Beaudry

Bonnie Baxter and Riopelle, Atelier du Scarabée, 1987 Photo: Michel Beaudry

be lost. We did the print: it was wonderful and no one understood the reference in the title or cared.

Jean Paul often had the look of a scared animal, vulnerable and sensitive. With his anxious coal-black eyes and nervous little laugh – he seldom looked anyone in the eyes, but despite all appearances, he never missed anything. Still, he didn't make it easy. He enjoyed being evasive, in his work, in his life, and in his words. He would make appointments with journalists and then not turn up for them. He rarely went to his own openings. He only granted a handful of interviews in his entire lifetime, most of which were disasters. He preferred to talk about fishing, or hockey, or food. He was never on time.

Honni soit qui mal y pense, 1987, Riopelle, color etching. Original print, image size: 44.6 x 60cm on Arches paper 56.2 x 75.5 cm. Atelier du Scarabée, Galerie Lelong Éditeur, Paris. Catalogue raisonné, Hibou Éditeurs archives.

I knew Jean Paul in his later years but even for a man in his sixties, his health was not good and he did very little to improve the situation. He would never consider an operation, not even to remove his cataracts, a simple procedure that would have helped him a great deal. He would cite the tragic death of his great friend Diego Giacometti who went into the hospital to have his cataracts removed and died there. Michel took him to the doctor to see about his back when it was really hurting him. He was certainly in terrible pain. At this point in his life not only did he have osteo-porosis but two of his vertebrae were missing and the others were crushing each other. Michel had difficulty getting him into the car. He trusted only Michel or Riopelle's general handyman and driver to drive, as a bad jolt could have meant a broken bone.

It's hard to imagine, now, how he endured all the travel. But there was the other side of Riopelle, the part that deserved the nickname "peerless hunter" that he had been given in Paris as a young man. In this regard, Hollis was his perfect match. She had learned to hunt at an early age, could gut a fish and skin a rabbit. She and Riopelle loved to be in the bush. The two of them would paint all day and then drink and entertain all night and still wake up sparkling with energy and crystal clear when the rest of us were hung-over. It was understandable for Hollis – she was thirty years younger than Riopelle – but Riopelle's generation seemed to have entirely different constitutions.

Jean Paul liked to please people, to entertain them and make them laugh. He was a wonderful storyteller when he got started, unwinding his stories in his gravelly voice, a glass of Ricard always at hand and a Gitane sending up an unhealthy atmosphere of smoke – another layer of evasion. He was without reverence, an iconoclast for whom nothing was sacred, not even his own dignity. I remember him crawling through a dog door into our house just to make Walter Moos the gallery owner laugh and throwing his dentures in the bushes when he wanted to be contrary. But inevitably he needed his space and he would retreat, particularly from confrontation. I suspect this is one of the reasons he traveled so often. "What is a friend? A milestone in life at a particular time. The little bit of "shared existence" we were talking about earlier. Giacometti gave me, that sleepless night, a bit of his life; and I did the same. My friends, Maître Garson for example, are those who have continued to see me, wherever I am, never mind the distance or whether I'm sick. After long separation, sometimes. But sooner or later, the faithful *rendez-vous*, a little life shared again" (Riopelle).[16]

Riopelle, 1989.
Photo: Bonnie Baxter

He maintained three homes: his studio/home in Sainte-Marguerite-Estérel where I first met him, his home on Isle-aux-Grues (also in Quebec), and his home in Saint-Cyr-en-Arthies, ready for him should he decide to switch to one or the other. In 1989 Jean Paul had gone back to his studio in Saint-Cyr, France, just outside of Paris. He called one day and wanted Michel and me to come to work on a project given to him by Madeleine Arbour for Via Rail.

I got the impression that the project was a pretext. He just missed us. So we came to him.

The studio was actually a huge converted garage with tiny living quarters. Jean Paul loved cars, loved speed, he loved to be at the helm (he also flew planes and owned a sailboat called the Serica-junior). He had two Bugatti, a Jaguar, and a few others I can't remember the names of. He even had a master auto mechanic who would come regularly to ensure the engines were in good order. By this time in his life he no longer drove frequently. His back was bad and in Quebec he actually preferred what he called his Hearse, the only car that would supply a smooth enough ride for him.

It was one of those special times when I was reminded of what a truly great artist Jean Paul was. He had already been there a while without us and had obviously gone through what I like to think of as a *tempête de production* [work storm].[17] The walls were encrusted and jewel-like with massive numbers of prints he had reworked. Whenever I'd walk in on his work like that I'd say to myself – "Oh My! this boy DOES have talent."

Not having grown up under the sway of the Riopelle mystique I was used to relating to Jean Paul the man, whom I ate and drank and worked with, over the practical details of executing his extraordinary work. At times like these it took my breath away to be before the magnitude of his talent and his sheer capacity for creative output.

The four of us, myself, Michel, Riopelle, and his companion at the time, Huguette Vachon,[18] did spend some time working on the Via Rail project, but for the most part we enjoyed being in France and celebrating Huguette's fortieth birthday. The project was to be an homage to the homeless "outsider artist" Scotty Wilson.[19] We also went to Paris to meet Jean Paul's lithograph printer Le Moigne and went to eat at the restaurant La coupole. Two years earlier, on the occasion of my own fortieth birthday in 1986, Michel and I had eaten at La coupole with Hollis and Jean Paul.[20]

But after all, it was spring and we drove around the countryside in Jean Paul's Bugatti, stopping at *châteaux* and other special little places. There was a restaurant in a village that had his paintings on the wall. A place was

Top:
Bonnie Baxter and Riopelle, Via Rail discussion, 1989.
Photo: Michel Beaudry

Bottom:
Huguette Vachon, Bonnie Baxter, and Riopelle, Via Rail layout, 1989.
Photo: Michel Beaudry

Riopelle with his machinist and
Robert Didier, the caretaker,
Saint-Cyr, 1989.
Photo: Bonnie Baxter

Riopelle's studio/garage in Saint-Cyr, Michel Beaudry in the Bugatti, 1989.
Photo: Bonnie Baxter

always set for him, much the same as at the Bistro à Champlain in Estérel. Once, when Michel was driving the Jaguar home from a restaurant *après un repas bien arrosé* [after a meal where the wine flowed freely] and the police stopped the car, Jean Paul got out of the car and the police said something like, "Oh, bonsoir Mr Riopelle, please don't let us keep you." It was obvious that Riopelle had a great deal of local respect. Paris and its countryside were glorious and we had a wonderful time.

Bonnie Baxter, Riopelle, and
Huguette Vachon *au Château*, 1989.
Photo: Michel Beaudry

Riopelle and Bonnie Baxter,
Saint-Cyr, France, 1989.
Photo: Michel Beaudry

Bonnie Baxter, Huguette Vachon, road trip through fields of *colza* (rapeseed), France, 1989. Photo: Michel Beaudry

My work with Riopelle did not end until 1993. Although we still saw each other occasionally until 1995, I now realize was that his creative time had really come to a close in 1992 with the death of Joan Mitchell, Riopelle's most constant companion throughout the sixties and seventies.[21] She had been his second rib, despite all those who surrounded him and loved him and protected him, she, with all her temperament and stubbornness, was the foundation that gave him strength. In retrospect, he was never productive after the news of her death except in his final painting: a forty-five-metre-long triptych painted in Joan Mitchell's memory called *Hommage à Rosa Luxemburg*. It seems, in trying to make sense of this passage of Riopelle and me, that, for Riopelle, each of his homes was an echo of the other, a micro-infrastructure built around his loves and his requirements – friends and companions, gallerists, a gorgeous natural setting, a village filled with locals who knew and respected him, a friendly and admiring restaurateur, a studio space, a printer, a caretaker ... Yet each place offered the richness of its own particular flavors that would draw him to move again and again, making the travel worthwhile, and with each passage would come the force of discontinuity to act as a catalyst for creativity. This was an inheritance of the lifestyle of the Exile Artists of the mid twentieth century. Still, at the heart of it all, perhaps, was Joan Mitchell, a phenomenal painter, intimate companion, a friend, a truly thorny critic and caustic catalyst against whom he could measure his own wit and achievement, maintaining a sort of external perspective and a desire to achieve: a polar star in Riopelle's passage through life.

At the time I didn't grasp this. I had never met Joan Mitchell. Although I sensed that her life touched his profoundly, I didn't realize how closely his productivity was tied to her existence in his life. These are things I deduce now from what was left out of our conversations and that is saying a great deal, as we tended to work together on a visceral level, favoring gestures and looks to words.

Jean Paul and my final years working together were, in some ways, disastrous. We worked on a project called *Mouchetache*, a titled that played with the combination of the sound of the word mustache and *mouche* [fly] *tache* [stain] which referenced the process of making the images and the idea of a *coffret de mouches* [captain's chest of fishing flies]: a project idea of Jean Paul's that we had been talking about for years. We couldn't get funding from Galerie Lelong in Paris. We did finally find support from Galerie Michel Tétrault and his business partner who thought a series of prints would make a wonderful addition to the exhibition Tétrault was planning as a celebration of Jean Paul's seventieth birthday. We should have known better, but artists tend to think more about a project than the consequences of whom they're showing with so, despite Tétrault's already having a questionable reputation, we moved forward with the assurance of his backing.

The idea behind *Mouchtache* was fun, each of the *mouches* [fishing flies], made by Jean Paul's great friend and celebrated fisherman Paul Marier, represented one of Jean Paul's friends or a famous figure like the "whore of Babylon" or "Jackrabbit Johanssen."

The process itself was both playful and ingenious. We rolled out long sheets of clear acetates on the lawn at either my home or at Jean Paul's. Paul Marier would take one of the *mouches* he had made, attach it to his fly cast fishing rod, dip it in India ink, and then cast the "fly" onto the acetate. It would land with this expressive black splat, which he repeated a number of times. All of these covered strips of acetate were to be cut to plate size and each one of them would be used to make a plate of a different color of the overlapping *mouche taches* [fly stains]. These plates were to serve as the background plates for each five-plate image. Jean Paul loved to sit and watch and see the whole thing orchestrated. There were many wonderful shared meals and everyone involved worked enthusiastically to

Top:
Paul Marier, Riopelle, Huguette Vachon, Nicolas Vachon, and friend
at Estérel, 1993. Photo: Bonnie Baxter

Bottom:
Paul Marier, Bonnie Baxter, 1993. Photo: Michel Beaudry

The *mouche* team. From left to right: Michel Tétrault, Paul Marier, Huguette Vachon, Maurice Perron, Jean Paul Riopelle, Bonnie Baxter, Michel Beaudry, Carmen Perron, 1993. Photo Maurice Brière

make this project happen. I was in charge of the prints. Paul made the *mouches*. Lise Gauvin[22] was to write accompanying texts. The wonderful Maurice Perron[23] crafted the captain's chest of drawers to house the *mouches*, the prints, and a set of texts (including writings by the conservationist Archie "Grey Owl" Belaney, *Le hibou gris*,[24] Jean Paul's hero), and an essay on fly-fishing by an eighteenth-century nun.

My entire house and studio in Val-David was turned into a print shop for the project. I was also preparing for my first solo exhibition at a museum that was set to open just a month after Riopelle's exhibition. It was very lucky that my work was sculptural at this time and I was able to free my house and print studio for the production of *Mouchetache*. My two printers camped on the land, the garage was an acid-bath room, the dining room table was used to dry the printing-plates, the bathtub was used to dissolve the sugar lift, and the studio accommodated the proofing of the plates.

Finally all the preliminary work was completed. Then it was time for Jean Paul to do his part and he could not, it was no longer in him. I had known from the beginning it was risky business to give him a deadline. Jean Paul never worked under a deadline. He always said, "When I paint I never

Bonnie Baxter, acid-bath, 1993.
Photo: Michel Beaudry

Bonnie Baxter rinsing the aquatint,
1993. Photo: Michel Beaudry

hesitate and when I hesitate I never paint." All of the preliminary work on the four plates of each image was worth nothing without his intervention, without the plate he was to put on top. Tétrault would not pay me, I could not pay the printers I'd hired. We argued. The rest of the team was angry at Jean Paul, but I could not protect him, and he could not protect me. The work was never finished. In the end, I had to hire a lawyer to retrieve what I was owed. It was a sad end to my relationship with Jean Paul Riopelle.

Printer Gianni Galati with *mouches* on press, Atelier du Scarabée, 1993.
Photo: Bonnie Baxter

Riopelle with *mouche* splats, Atelier du Scarabée, 1993.
Photo: Bonnie Baxter

Riopelle drifted into his final chapter of life living in virtual isolation, cut off almost completely from old friends and family on Île aux Oies, cared for by his companion, Huguette Vachon. It was not until 2005 that I was able to work with these issues of a spectacular relationship that had literally gone "splat." The passage of "Riopelle and I" came to a close and life, as it tends to do, introduced a new chapter. It was time to rethink my own practice, to have my own creative crisis. I went in search of a means of expression that was capable of articulating my changing map of the world, a new, more visceral connection to the cycles of life and death. A new beginning came with a deliberate conflagration, the burning of much of my own work from the past decades. Using some test-proofs from the plates I had created for the project *Mouchetache*, twelve years earlier, I added my own layers, my own *impressions passagères* to create the large format digital prints, *Coming out of sleep* [*Après mouchetache*] and *Reine mouchetache*, finally putting to bed my sense of loss and frustration.

Coming out of sleep (après mouchetache), 2005, Bonnie Baxter. Original digital print on canvas, image size 304.80 x 152.40 cm, Centre Sagamie, Atelier du Scarabée editor, Val-David, Québec

Reine mouchetache, 2005, Bonnie Baxter. Original digital print on canvas, image size 152.40 x 152.40 cm, Centre Sagamie, Atelier du Scarabée editor, Val-David, Québec

In a way, these prints represent portraits of Riopelle and myself: each image containing the fly that Paul had made to represent us. The top image, *Coming out of sleep*, represents Riopelle: a grand natural vista perfect for hunting and fishing and his *mouches* (his heroes, his admirers, lovers, companions, aids, and friends) swarming like insects, complicated by the underlying engraving of the Japanese bill. The image at the bottom, *Reine mouchetache*, represents me: I take the role of queen, after all ... *Bonnie soit qui mal y pense*. My *mouche* "splat'" marks my temple and the "bonnie-fly," with it's sparklingly sharp hook, rests dangerously close to the image of my own watchful eye embedded in the complex engraved curves of the British queen's monetary representation – beauty, craft, and market are all overtaken by the glance of the human soul as it peers beyond the layers of human society and human endeavor. I think Riopelle, the "peerless hunter," would have liked the play on words and appreciated the paradox of the poppies, their sense of majestic carnage and their forgiving remembrance.

This chapter too would pass. I decided to move forward with a new series of artwork, "Jane's Journey." From Val-David I went back across the Atlantic, for another motorcycle ride across Europe, this time on my sixtieth birthday with my best chum, my husband, Michel, just as we had done when we were twenty, although not with each other. I traveled across Europe and the United States to see how they, and I, have changed, and how memory and time have their own way of layering imagery. I posed myself in the guise of a virtual Jane (a self-created archetype of North American womanhood based on a composite of Janes, from Jane Doe, Calamity Jane, Jane Mansfield, and Plain Jane to Jane of the *Dick and Jane* readers) before the grand sites and settings of Paris (as she appears on the cover of this collection), Rome, and the little medieval village of Forano in the Sabine Hills.

So time and distance collapsed upon themselves and I find that the rewards of having shared passage with Riopelle and the other souls, great and small, that I have know have taken me very far away from the layer-less expectations of femininity in the 1950s which I began with. At times, life's passages can seem to create layers that are dense and impenetrable, but for the most part they provide reassuring evidence of the simultaneity, synchronicity, and serendipity that abounds in life. Jean Paul Riopelle was surely one of my greatest rites of passage, a marvelous, transforming experience of learning how to live life as an artist, as a human being, how to revel in the passage, to value the *impressions passagères*, good and bad, and find the extraordinary in the ordinary.

Author's note

My thanks to Christine Unger who researched historical aspects of the text and gave me invaluable editing advice on the text throughout the process. A fabulous person who seems to know what I mean even before I am able to say it.

My thanks also for the insight and the keen eye for detail supplied by Yseult Riopelle, Michel Beaudry, and Hollis Jeffcoat, whose own memories of Riopelle helped to supply some of the gaps in my own. I am particularly grateful for Yseult Riopelle's generosity in supplying six wonderful images, and for her blessing of this essay.

Thank you to Alana Riley and Jocelyne Belanger who have helped refine the text with their thoughts. I am also indebted to the editorial skills of Luc LaRochelle whose "mot juste" has helped me with more than just words.

And finally, thanks to my two much loved fairy godmothers who take me on adventures I would never have imagined.

Notes

1 Gilbert Erouart, Jean Paul Riopelle, Donald Winkler, and Fernand Séguin, *Riopelle in Conversation*, Trans. Donald Winkler (Toronto: House of Anansi, 1995).

2 Stephanie Barron, Sabine Eckmann, and Matthew Affron, *Exiles + Emigrés: The Flight of European Artists from Hitler* (Los Angeles County Museum of Art; Montreal Museum of Fine Arts; Neue Nationalgalerie [Germany], 1997).

3 "The condition of cultural exile ... is, in part, a heightened instance of the condition of the American artist, for whom transaction with foreign models is a nearly inescapable exercise." Joseph I. Horowitz, *Artists in Exile* (New York: Harper Collins Publishers, 2008), xvii.

4 Roald Nasgaard, *Abstract Painting in Canada* (Douglas & McIntyre, 2008), 71.

5 Françoise Sullivan, Pierre Théberge, Guest. Host, Gloria Macarenko. Reporter, Anna Asimakopulos. "Jean Paul Riopelle's Funeral Causes Controversy" *Canada Now* (CBC Television broadcast, Duration: 02:00. 18 March 2002). http://archives.cbc.ca/arts_ entertainment/visual_arts/clips/749/.

6 "Riopelle: Death of a Giant?" *Catholic Insight,* Gale Group (1 May 2002).

7 André Breton is quoted as saying: "Riopelle's painting is the art of a peerless trapper. Traps for beasts of the earth and of the skies. Traps for the traps. It's when those traps are snared that real freedom has been achieved" (Erouart et al, 13).

8 Yseult Riopelle (Interviewer), "René Le Moigne," *Jean Paul Riopelle: Catalogue raisonné des estampes*, Dir. Gilles Daigneault, Monique Burnet-Weinmann (Montreal: Hibou éditeurs, 2005).

9 *Dick and Jane* was a series of elementary school readers used to teach English throughout North America from the 1930s to the 1970s. Their limited and hypnotically repetitive vocabulary and narrow, sexist, and racist views of what constituted a valid home life helped to shape the prejudices and expectations of far too many young minds.

10 "After the great success prints had enjoyed in the sixties and seventies came the letdown of the eighties." Michèle Grandbois, "The Quebec Experience," *Sightlines: Printmaking and Image Culture*, Ed. Walter Jule (Calgary: University of Alberta Press, 1997), 171.

11 Marianne Feaver, and Pierre Letarte, dir., *Riopelle* (National Film Board of Canada: 1982). http://www3.nfb.ca.

12 KPR was a method used to create a printing plate from an existing photograph or drawing. The process uses a chemical called KPR (Kodak Photo Resist), which is now unobtainable because it is considered harmful.

13 Sugar Lift is an aquatint technique in which the artist paints onto a plate with sugar syrup. An aquatint ground is substituted for the syrup before biting the image into a printer's plate.

14 Sadly Briet was found murdered in his New York apartment in 1997 at the age of thirty-seven. http://fr.wikipedia.org/wiki/Philippe_Br iet_(Galeriste) or http://www.speedy look.com/Philippe_Briet_(Galeriste). html.

15 "Honni soit qui mal y pense," translated as "Evil be to him who evil thinks," is the motto that appears on the Royal coat of arms of the United Kingdom. http://en.wikipedia.org.

16 Erouart et al, 13.

17 After periods of not working at all he would explode into a storm of productivity, even calling me at night to bring him more paper.

18 Huguette Vachon was Riopelle's companion at that time and until the time of his death.

19 Scotty Wilson had been included in the Surrealists' circle and was infamous for his inability to speak French despite the fact that he lived in Paris. The story was that, in order to communicate, he would keep little pieces of paper in his pocket saying *Pain* [bread] or *Vin* [wine] or whatever else he might need, in French and give them to people.

20 In 1986 we stayed with Hollis Jeffcoat in Paris, after delivering the Anticosti prints to Galerie Lelong. She had just left Riopelle, who was devastated by her departure and had followed her to France.

21 Joan Mitchell, Jane Livingston, Linda Nochlin, Yvette Y Lee, *The Paintings of Joan Mitchell*, (Whitney Museum of American Art: University of California Press, 2002).

22 Lise Gauvin's work is also referenced in this collection in the essay "Literary Border Crossings: Reconceptualizing Montesquieu's *Lettres persanes* in Lise Gauvin's *Lettres d'une autre* and Chahdortt Djavann's *Comment peut-on être français?*" by Patrice Proulx.

23 Maurice was one of the fifteen signatories of *Le refus global* in 1948 along with Jean Paul Riopelle as well as being the photographer who documented those who signed the manifesto as seen in the exhibition catalogue produced by the Musée national des beaux-arts du Québec, *Mémoire objective, mémoire collective*. Photographies de Maurice Perron, Québec, du 2 décembre 1998 au 26 septembre 1999.

24 Archie Belany (1888–1938), dubbed "Grey Owl," was a Canadian born in England who portrayed himself as a Native American, writing books, lecturing, and making films on wilderness life and the importance of conservation. http://www.econet.sk.ca.

Crossings: *In Situ* Art in Transit

FRANÇOIS MORELLI

My first travels to France date back to 1976. As I was finishing art school, I was in search of monuments and works of art that had left their mark and fueled my studies, dreams, and aspirations. Being an awkward cousin and speaking *joual*, the trips have flowed over the years, always associated with fleeting artistic projects: installations and performances. I practice a performance-based art that is compatible with my present and daily life. I seek to erase the distance between here and my studio; to turn my everyday activities into a living artwork. I make sure that I am able to move about freely while adapting my tools and my methods according to contextual changes. Through an economy of means, I facilitate mobility and cut down on compromise. I use art in order to negotiate the distance between myself and others. I make sure that my encounters are fed by my projects and vice versa. By de-hierarchizing techniques, I act as iconoclast and artisan of applied images. Adept at the forms of the decorative arts, I shape pictographic friezes. I tell, without words, stories that interweave and interlace. Hybrid and relational, my works slip and slide their way into the cornice molding of a soft and fluid architecture. Every doorway opens to a transition between an ordinary world and a beyond in progress. In search of passageways and crossings, of liminal moments and spaces, I reconnect with ancestral traditions and rituals surrounding food, dreams, and walking.

In 1974, with a first piece entitled *Les premiers pas* (*First Steps*), walking becomes a motor and generator of meaning, a form of performance art. I walk to reduce the space between points A and B, here and there, myself and others. I walk until I am exhausted. I walk to carry things, to leave my mark, and to situate myself in the public sphere. With *Migration*[1] in 1984, I leave from the United Nations in New York for Saint-Jean-Port-Joli. I travel with my double (a sculpture made from hay and mud) attached to my back. I go up the Hudson and St. Lawrence Rivers. I follow, in reverse, the path of the first French who left to discover America. I get around on foot, by bus, and by car. I do not drive. I cross the border under the prying eyes of customs agents. *La marche transatlantique (Transatlantic Walk) 1945–1985*[2] begins at the Berlin Wall and ends in Philadelphia, where Thomas Jefferson signed the American Declaration of Independence, on the sixth of August, 1985 (the fortieth anniversary of the bombing of Hiroshima). "What are you doing?" –"I am going home and taking my friend to the United States of America." – "'tis not normal!" –"Yes, 'tis normal. 'tis *kunst* and 'tis normal!" My friend is a human vessel that has been flayed and burned alive. This wreck of a human being I fill with water along the way, in the fountains of Trocadéro in Paris, the canals of Amsterdam, the East River of Manhattan, and finally the empty fountains of Philadelphia.

I push a crate that conceals two oversized sex organs for *Cycle transculturel*[3] in 1986–87. I travel in a loop, with Nice as my point of departure and destination, by passing through Genoa, Rome, Naples, Palermo, Malta, Tunis – skipping Alger – Rabat, Granada, Barcelona, and Marseille. A dervish wrapped in gardening hoses, I have a date with my Mediterranean roots. I show up on the town square, among the stalls of the squid peddlers at the fish market in Marseille, at the flower market in Nice, on the beaches of Antibes, in the Chapelle des Pénitents blancs of Saint-Paul de Vence. I picture these peripatetic maneuvers as an existential gesture in a space-time continuum. Originating as physical marks with symbolic meaning, they are situated between movement and restless wandering. Far from being metaphors, they are instead tangible and compose using the unknown of chance and renewed potential. Between each departure and arrival, there is an infinite number of possibilities and forks in the road.[4] I let myself be tempted by the drift in order to end up elsewhere. Given the choice, I often find myself between two paths … "Between two joints, you could do something, between two joints you could get your ass moving" ["Entre deux joints, tu pourrais faire quelque chose, entre deux joints tu pourrais te grouiller le cul"].[5]

Home Wall Drawing. L'art de manger (2004), my most recent project in France, is first and foremost an excuse to de-compartmentalize artistic disciplines and re-think the process of creation, circulation, and reception of installation art. It is about merging the studio, the place of dissemination, and the place of reception; about revisiting the roles and values of the cultural artifact, about reviewing the political issues of a committed art, and finally about reestablishing ritual, magic, and people at the center of my artistic concerns. Using the principle of barter, I open new pathways to exchange and sharing. From January to June 2004, I spent time in France.

I went from city to city, from one house to another, with my tools (two suitcases filled with rubber stamps, inks, cameras, sketch pads) and a cellular phone. By taking advantage of two residences – one at the studio of the Conseil des arts du Canada at the Cité internationale des arts in Paris and the other at the École nationale supérieure des arts du Limousin in Limoges – I carried out twenty-three encounters.

I drop off invitations at bookshops, at Internet cafes, at art galleries. I send them to friends and the information is passed on by word of mouth: a one-of-a-kind work of art in exchange for a meal. I am in search of domestic places (walls, ceilings, floors ...) in order to produce a work of art using rubber stamps. In exchange for my work, you cook me your favorite meal: the kind you set aside for your friends, your family, or your community. The kind that you put the finishing touches on for holidays, birthdays, and cherished moments. In exchange, I will produce a mural with my rubber stamps. A technique that I have been developing for more than twenty years and that I execute in galleries, arts centers and museums ... on paper, cloth, skin, and walls. This time it is at your home, inside your habitat, that the work of art will take shape. It will be printed in parallel with your cooking, in the intimacy and proximity of your habits, before your eyes, near your body. You will watch the design take shape, sometimes alone, sometimes with others. You will listen attentively to my answers to questions from your children, your lover, your friends. Only one condition, the structure has to be stationary and part of the architecture; no removable support will be permitted ... No tear-away surface.

A guildsman, I weave myself into the French fabric, making more round trips, crisscrossing multiple projections, wandering about and widening my network of acquaintances. In the land of gastronomy and good taste, our exchanges are a testimony to privileged moments often full of risks and expectations. In this arrangement, each party believes that he or she profits. For the hostess, a work of art is worth more than a meal. For me, the meeting is the work of art. And yet these recipes often at the origin of meaningful transformation are the bearers of a cultural inheritance transmitted from one generation to another and show immeasurable morals and values. I have the impression of crossing an agrarian France that is deeply rooted in its soil and, with its ways of doing things well, is faced with the seasonal migration of livestock to summer pastures. We are not first cousins, but rather complicit parties to the intersection of time and space.

I am interested in the decorative and folk arts situated on the periphery of good taste. I am interested in ornamentation and the decoration of the repulsive, excessive, and hybrid object. I like what is vulgar, common, and simple. I like what is far from purity and full of paradoxes and contradictions ... But most of all I like to draw. I draw all the time, before writing and after taking action. Drawing takes the place of my forked tongue, my franglais. I advocate a form of moving pictography in which the signs walk in arabesque. I draw small and large, with my hands, my feet, my mouth, my eyes, my nose, Alouette. "Oh! Alouette, je te plumerai le bec, Alouette, I will stamp you there ..." I print with small, medium, and large rubber stamps. The stamps are commercially fabricated. They are made to specifications and based on found images and my own designs. I stamp the way a ticket puncher at the Porte des Lilas station punches holes: "Little holes, little holes, always little holes" ["Des petits trous, des petits trous, toujours des petits trous"].[6] Obsessive, I juxtapose, I superimpose, I repeat, I space, and I structure my images. I question these images becoming texts and I challenge a singular and dominant reading. I have fun multiplying associations until meaning collapses. Neither logic nor coherence rules these stories. I have fun turning architecture into a book and making reading it a bodily experience. The Gestalt of graphic arts calls out to us at a distance and once seduced, one loses oneself in the density and chaos of detail. A container is outlined and traced on the wall in the shape of a stencil. Between the interior and the exterior, between its content and its surface, between the act of filling and covering, there is the porous quality of bodies. These bodies that flow and from which escapes a plethora of images. There is saturation and an overflow. The drawing often suffers from bulimia. The passage from the tattoo parlor to the beauty and cosmetics salon takes place. I leave my marks ... vase, head, mask, elephant, horse, turtle, fish, and dog ... in red and black, in black and blue, in yellow and black, in red and green ...

We set up a first meeting that serves to reassure and to eliminate doubts. We visit the places and discuss our preferences and our phobias: "I visited your website and I liked what I saw. However, I would like to eliminate the syringes, the scissors, and the insects ... Myself, I like the flowers in red and black, and why not a stag all red coming down the stairs, and what about you, do you have any food allergies?" – "No, I eat everything. I prefer fish and poultry, however. I avoid red meat. I love vegetables and fresh fruits." – "Do you like to cook?" Once the questions have been answered, we set a date for the dinner. Usually I arrive in the afternoon before the guests, in order to get settled and take advantage of the silence before the dinner. I make myself at home and I get the lay of the land. I set up my studio. During

Top:
Home Wall Drawing – Éléphant / Elephant
(Dallet – 26-03-04)
Sylvie Baduel – Jacques Malgorn
Meal/repas: Pâtes au curry de girolles, fromages (Saint Nectaire, Gapron, Salers, Blue d'Auvergne), gâteau & glace.

Bottom:
Home Wall Drawing – Chien / Dog
(Gennevilliers / Ivry sur Seine – 30-03-04)
Madeleine Van Doren – Bernard Point
Meal/repas: Morue sauce blanche salade & fromage.

Home Wall Drawing – Vase / Vase
(Montpellier – 29-04-04)
Emmanuelle Etienne – Alain Lapierre
Meal/repas: Apéritif au saucisson,
soupe de poisson de Sète, poisson
au citron et riz, fromage & salade.

Home Wall Drawing – Cerf / Stag
(Limoges – 19-05-04)
Jean François & Claire Demeure
Meal/repas: Pigeons en croûte
de sel, salade, fromages & Milla
de Claire.

this time, she prepares food. I photograph her cooking and she photographs me working. Someone is at the door. The guests arrive and the introductions are followed by questions: What for? I reply: "For this meeting, for this meal, for this present moment, and for as long as the work of art and the hostess live together."

Yesterday (in 2008), I find out that you must leave your apartment. You do not know what to do with the wall drawing. I reply to you that it is up to you to decide; you could repaint or you could tell those who are moving in the story of this work of art: "I remember this Québécois artist who came to eat at my home and who drew on my walls." You tell him or her everything and above all do not forget the friends, the menu, and the recipes. Then, the new owners will decide what to do.

All this activity takes place *in situ* far from museums, galleries, and arts centers. It is at the intersection of a liminal time and space and records human encounters and privileged moments. I cross the Atlantic and I disembark to the everyday life that calls out to others to come over. An outsider on the move, I take advantage of my ambiguous and improvised status. Ideally, the welcome, like the proposal, is unconditional. I wander about and I place myself in the present in uncharted territory. What happens is spontaneous and occupies an unforeseen universe. In the face of risk, I go for broke. This is made possible by a live – and living – performance art. A form of art that takes things apart and facilitates exchange and passage. This art allows me to create opportunities while opening gaps. Artifacts are presumably only first fruits and serve as a rough reminder. Don't you believe it; doomed to disappear, it is in the memory of places and people, and not in its material form, that the story takes refuge and maintains its integrity. My body, the bearer of images and objects, compromises so as to bring to fruition every piece. I sow seeds throughout my travels. Over the years, a memory has taken hold and a community of actors has grafted itself onto my imagination. It seems to me that with the years, the differences have dissipated and the space between these continents has narrowed. That in alterity, the effort required to cross the room, the street, the city, the country, or the continent, is equal to the desire and the will to create.

Translated by Davina Buivan Kotanchik

Notes

1 In *Migration* (1984) I carried around
on my back a sculpture stuffed with
hay. I was re-thinking the conditions
of migration, emigration, and immigration. I was questioning my identity as
well as the status of the art object that
accompanied me. The sculpture became ambiguous and its movement
was destabilizing and contributed to
creating confusion. Passage through
customs, in particular, called into
question the terms of identification
and of the nomenclature of the object.

2 In *La marche transatlantique* (*Transatlantic Walk) 1945–1985* (1985) I carried around on my back a figure made
from fiberglass. I would stop to bathe
it, fill it with water, and empty it.
When asked, I would answer that I
had been walking for forty years (since
Hiroshima in 1945), traveling towards
the West and reflecting upon the distinction between fusion and fission.

3 In *Cycle transculturel* (1986–87) I
transported two objects. One of these
objects represented a female sexual
organ and the other a male sexual organ, both enlarged and out of proportion. I transported them in a large
black box on wheels. As I was crossing
as many institutionalized controls as
possible (customs checkpoints and air-
ports principally) I would experience
the practical details of resistance to
sculptural objects.

4 With these three projects, I pushed
my physical and psychological limits.
I was rethinking the piece with each
new place and public. I was seeking
to depart from the frameworks prescribed by art and to become part of
a daily life that called out to the other.
I was seeking the liminal space by
radically changing the order and
chaos of the moment.

5 Robert Charlebois, "Entre deux joints,"
Solidaritude (Barclay 80173, 1973).
See another Charlebois song on pages
301–4 of this volume.

6 Serge Gainsbourg ,"Le poinçonneur
des lilas" (Mercury France 1958).

A Quiet Evolution: Artist's Books in Quebec and France (Beausoleil, Dorion, Desautels)

ALISA BELANGER

Since the advent of modernity in Quebec, the artist's book has emerged and thrived in parallel with the mainstream book industry. Many leading Quebec authors have explored this form of publication as an alternate means to develop their poetics. Starting in the 1990s, Claude Beausoleil, Hélène Dorion, and Denise Desautels began to embrace this genre both in France and Quebec. Whereas their predecessors often crossed the Atlantic to escape an oppressive cultural atmosphere at home, these poets belong to one of the first generations after the Quiet Revolution to view travel and publication abroad essentially as a matter of choice. Associated with a diverse cross-section of contemporary poetry that ranges in focus from urban lyricism to ontological philosophy to *l'écriture de l'intime*, all three of these authors remain active figures in Quebec literary institutions. Their contributions to artist's books reflect shifting relationships between the francophone "margins" and the Parisian "center" by demonstrating non-hierarchical exchange between poets from Quebec and artists in France.[1]

Notoriously difficult to characterize as a genre, the artist's book has long been the subject of a rivalry between specialists from France and the United States. This debate seeks to distinguish between two basic types of work: those in which artists, writers, and bookmakers come together to create a coherent project through their collaborative efforts, a tradition that grew out of luxury editions in the late nineteenth and early twentieth centuries, and those in which a single artist controls the use of the book as a medium for artistic expression, a practice closely associated with international art movements in the 1960s and 1970s.[2] Throughout francophone Europe, such a distinction remains relatively clear. The originality of form tends to receive more attention from avant-garde visual artists working alone, whereas collaborative artists' books with texts from established authors generally inherit from the bibliophilic tradition. Yet the Quebec artist's book combines the traits of both traditions and thus draw into question any clear-cut divide between sub-genres. For this reason, Claudette Hould suggests in the *Répertoire des livres d'artistes au Québec, 1981–1990*[3] that book-objects and one-of-a-kind books should also be integrated into the category of artist's books. She frames this suggestion in the context of a larger shift from French to North American influences on Quebec production in the 1980s.

Some attempts have nonetheless been made to recognize the specificity of the Quebec artist's book tradition independent of outside influences. For instance, Silvie Bernier outlines its history based on local developments, such as the founding of Editions Erta by Roland Giguère.[4] Furthermore, Isabelle Jameson suggests in her "Histoire du livre d'artiste" that Quebec artist's books focus on distinct questions of territoriality rather than taking up the rebellion against the fine art establishment prevalent in artist's books made elsewhere. This question of place becomes complicated in works published by Quebec poets in France. While Beausoleil reacts by developing a transatlantic poetics that incorporates national identity at its core, Dorion instead treats her artist's books more like deterritorialized objects. Taking a mediate approach, Desautels draws on her experience in Quebec in order to bridge the gaps between multiple traditions.

Transnational Fusions: Beausoleil Sings America

Among the most prolific Quebec writers of his generation, Claude Beausoleil has published over sixty titles since 1972, the year after his first trip to France. Although critics have expressed reservation about the abundance and readability of his texts, he often serves as an ambassador for Quebec literature and is one of its most well-known authors abroad.[5] Influenced by Hubert Aquin and Gaston Miron, he clearly recognizes opportunities available in the Hexagon, yet refuses to see himself as a North Atlantic subaltern in search of French recognition. As he puts it in *Écrivain cherche lecteur*: "When I leave Montreal for Paris, I don't leave the periphery to go towards the center; I leave a center, my center, to go towards a larger center" (230). In his countless texts for artist's books, Beausoleil multiplies the positions from which the poet speaks to suggest an internalized "center."

Throughout his career, Beausoleil has developed an American baroque characterized by impulse, excess, playfulness, and meta-poetic reflection. He maintains that his popular upbringing in Saint-Henri influences his desire to mix codes in poetry, as well as his editorial practices. In an interview with Mel B. Yoken, Beausoleil affirms that "poetry must assume its place in media" (72). Likewise, he describes his work for artist's books as "spontaneous and random,"[6] a freedom that should be interpreted not as a mere lack of restrictions, but rather its own form of aesthetic commitment. Early in his career, he created facsimiles and book-objects on a shoestring budget at the Éditions *Cul Q*. Among them, *Promenade Modern Style* (1975) is a narrative homage to Marlene Dietrich with "a 1930's dream's end framing that engulfs the literary project" ["un cadrage fin de rêve 1930 qui gruge le projet littéraire"]. More tongue-in-cheek, *Mao bar salon* (1978) is a custom-printed matchbox calling for "texts that move / mountains" ["des textes qui déplacent / les montagnes"].[7] After using such experimentations to poke fun at the literary establishment, he began to focus in earnest on questions of transcultural exchange in the 1980s. Around the time that he published *Grand Hôtel des Etrangers* (1988), he also began to appropriate the artist's book as a serious tool to reflect on language and identity.

A turning point could be marked by *Migrations* (1992) and *Fusions* (1993). The first commemorates an art installation by René Derouin, who has devoted the better part of his career to cultural exchanges between Quebec and Mexico.[8] In dense blocks of text, Beausoleil suggests that a circumscribed origin lies behind any movement or speech. Imitating human cries through the repetition of long "i" vowels, he writes: "the limits of space imagine the infinite of lines" ["[l]es limites des lieux imaginent les infinis du trace"]. He describes hemispheric migrations in terms that perhaps refer to prehistoric movements as well as modern travels. In *Fusions*, created by Jocelyne Aird-Bélanger and a team at Val-David, he would again take up the North and South, this time as overlapping categories. Exalting an "endless cross-mixing" ["[m]étissage insondable"] in authors from Louis Fréchette and Octovio Paz to Émile Nelligan and Ezra Pound, he signs his poem for this work from Paris, a detail that portrays *américanité* as a "internal song to be invented" ["chant intérieur à inventer"], wherever the poet may travel. Finally, in *La mise en songe* (1994), Beausoleil confirms that this American identity can flourish even in Europe. Created in Paris with Canadian artist Pat Bandani, this work invites readers to project French- and Spanish-language poems from circular disks onto a dark surface. It thus returns to the whimsical forms that Beausoleil originally favored, now enriched by an engagement with transnational questions. From *Migrations* to *La mise en songe*, Beausoleil moves from the *poète de service* who writes primarily in honor of an artist to a full-fledged participant in the conception of the collaborative work.

The elegiac tones of Beausoleil's writing take on more solemn qualities in the artist's books that he soon started publishing with Jacques Clauzel, a painter and print-maker based in the South of France. Through the use of minimal forms traced in layers of aged pigments, Clauzel addresses memory and the sacred.[9] In his artist's books, he often aims to challenge authors by asking them to write in dialogue with works atypical of their own aesthetic. His artist's books with Beausoleil tend to highlight a tension that Maurice Benhamou describes as "an art of the minimal confronted with excess" (5). The resulting "third work" combines mediums while continuing to acknowledge the autonomy of the poet and artist (Clauzel 56). In their first joint project, a book of aphorisms, Beausoleil writes: "poetry shares / the love of secrets" ["la poésie partage / l'amour du secret"]. Borrowing its title from this last line, *L'Amour du secret* (1994) underscores the mystery that unites art and poetry. This theme again resurfaces in *Du regard* (1995), an accordion-shaped volume with a series of Clauzel's pre-writing signs, one of which resembles a cross. As a post-Quiet Revolution writer, Beausoleil seems fascinated by the joint re-interpretation of spiritual symbols: "we reinitiate / what follows from figures / in a word / we are riveting / the secret darkness of things" ["[n]ous recommençons / la suite des figures / en un mot / nous rivons / le noir secret des choses"]. The collective subject that emerges from this process nonetheless remains fragile: "Amazed I discover / a surface born / of the singular torment / of our identities" ["Je découvre ébloui / une surface née / du tourment singulier / de nos identities"]. These are decisively *plural* identities that come together through the traditional rhymes of "recommençons" and "rivons," as well as "née" and "identité," infusing the collaborative work with a sense of harmony. In this way, *L'Amour du secret* and *Du regard* suggest affinities between the writer and artist based on difference rather than commonality.

Beausoleil's allusions to Quebec identity become explicit in *Ailleurs ; le poème inachevé* (1995), which he devotes to Alain Grandbois. In a dream-like atmosphere created by the refrain "he muses" ["il songe"], Beausoleil evokes a poet-traveler who seeks new sources of inspiration. Using the ambiguity of references to snow "over there" ["la neige là-bas"] and from the East ["neige d'Orient"], he creates a parallel between Grandbois' voyages to China and his own trips to France. Though some readers might miss allusions to Hankou and "other islands … in a remote night" ["d'autres îles … d'une nuit d'éloignement"], the final poem refers to Grandbois by name in order to situate this work in a history of Quebec cultural production abroad. More than sixty years after Grandbois published *Poëmes* (1934) as

Ailleurs; le poème inachevé. Gallargues-le-Montueux, France: A travers, 1995. Paper, acrylic, linotype, hand-manuscript text. 26.5 x 15.5 cm. 14 copies. Personal collection, Jacques Clauzel.

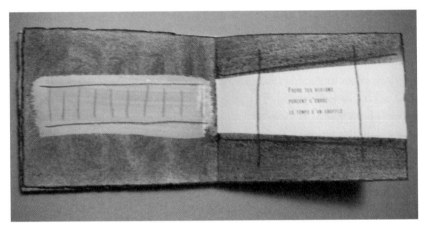

Kérouac Jack. Gallargues-le-Monueux, France: A travers, 1996. Paper, acrylic, lead-type prints. 13 cm x 16.5 cm. 135 copies. Personal collection, Jacques Clauzel.

an artist's book in China, Beausoleil can now speak from a literary history as well as a place of origin. In this way, he draws on memory as the common theme that links his texts to Clauzel's artwork. Similarly, by choosing a famous Franco-American as the central figure for his next collaboration with Clauzel, *Kérouac Jack* (1996), the poet can speak of "over there" ["là-bas"] as a common reference point for France and Quebec. This double position from which he writes will appear increasingly fluid as he grows more at ease with a transatlantic poetics in his artist's books.

By the following decade, Beausoleil seems as at home in France as in Quebec. In *Sous les traces* (2003), for instance, he writes simply: "the movement / of the miscellaneous unites" ["le mouvement / du divers unit"]. More recently, in *L'épreuve du fugace* (2008), Beausoleil goes so far as to claim that the concrete fusion of his poems with lithographs by the French artist Auck "is not ruse / but voice(s)" ["n'est pas ruse / mais voix"]. The ambiguous "x" in "voix," which can mark either the singular or plural form, implies that Beausoleil may now envision migrations across the Atlantic based on the same notion of *métissage* that he seems originally to have considered only American. Thus, he creates another new "fusion" through artistic synthesis and transcultural exchange.

The Book as One: Aesthetic Unity in Works by Dorion

If artist's books are merely one among many genres in Beausoleil's vast literary production, they represent a privileged space for Hélène Dorion, who has published nearly two-thirds of her titles as artist's books. Far from limiting her readership, these works include texts that are generally reprinted in her volumes of poetry, which have been welcomed with both critical acclaim and popular success on both sides of the Atlantic.[10] Much like Emily Dickinson, she approaches language, landscapes, and the Infinite through philosophical introspection. It is all the more surprising that literary criticism tends to neglect her artist's books given that they seem better suited to her poetics than commercial publications. The book conceived as a coherent work that unifies art and language offers Dorion more than just another expressive medium: it becomes an actual incarnation of the thought at work in her poetry.

In describing her writing, critics return systematically to the same terms: concise, spare, unadorned, transparent, and abstract.[11] Dorion nonetheless insisted on the connection between form and content as co-director of Noroît from 1991 to 1999, telling Stéphane Baillargeon from *Le Devoir*: "It's an incarnated word [*parole*], a poetry with meaning and feeling that wants to return to sure values – against the grain in an atmosphere of materialism and productionism" (D1). Since she conceives of poetry as a necessarily marginal social practice, it seems fitting that she would adopt the artist's book to promote what Christian Parisot calls an "exceptional relationship with the reader," by which it slows down the reading process through fascination (n.p.). Time remains embedded in the artist's book, unlike the objects that it crosses through in *L'Intervalle prolongé* (1972),

Dorion's first published volume, where she already demonstrates an interest in the visual arts by including some of her own drawings. If her poetry refers to a "center," it can only reside in the philosophical unity of the whole. *Hors champ* (1985) leaves no uncertainty: "There is no center here … Circumscribe the opening – her, proud and minimal" ["Il n'y a pas de centre ici … Circonscrire la brèche – elle, superbe et minimale"] (70).

Throughout Dorion's early poetry in the 1980s, the world can only be grasped by its ends and edges. Her texts are often constructed around the phrase "there is" ["il y a"] modified by a restrictive clause.[12] Initially, negations abound: nothing, no one, never.[13] Wishes and questions tend to offer the sole bridges between the *je* and *tu*, allusions to a collective noun appearing only rarely. The text circles around the ephemeral and impossible to name except by indefinite terms like *ce qui, ce que,* and *cela*. Yet, this focus on the fissure in existence is offset by an insistence on the immediacy of referents, especially in *Les Retouches de l'intime* (1987): this wind, this tree, these hours, these words, these looks, this face [*ce vent, cet arbre, ces heures, ces mots, ces regards, ce visage*] (30–5). Even while asserting an impossible divide between the Self and the surrounding world, the poem thus strives to eliminate the gap between the word and the thing. In *Un visage appuyé contre le monde* (1990), there begins to emerge the possibility of "our intimate and shared humanity" ["notre humanité intime et commune"] (101). Though words still fail, they carry a greater appeasement than before. Most arresting here is the reduction of the subject that produces a fleeting sense of wholeness: "To be nothing / but another heart / that beats in the immensity" ["N'être rien / qu'un coeur de plus / qui bat dans l'immensité"] (29).

In the course of this evolution towards a new poetic serenity, Dorion wrote her first poems intended for artist's books: *L'Empreinte du bleu*, based on engravings by Marc Garneau and *Carrés de lumière* with paintings from Jean-Luc Herman. Both published in 1994, these works could be read as a mirror pair. In response to very different visual aesthetics, their texts offer contrasting approaches to the same central paradoxes. An oversized work, *L'empreinte du bleu* is impressive in its refinement; the intricate organic shapes on its images seem drawn in black velvet thread. Yet, the color blue evokes here an abundance of melancholic memories that the writer must organize: "the flight, the drifting, the pathway / of the gaze brought back by the poem" ["la fuite, la dérive, le trajet / du regard ramené par le poème"]. Whereas the light that falls on these images is "ceaselessly retained" ["sans cesse retenue"], the six planes of delicate color painted by Jean-Luc Herman in *Carrés de lumière* each become a square of light "tied

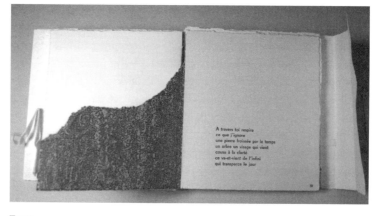

Top:
Carrés de lumière. Paris: Editions Herman, 1994. Paper, fabric, ink.
15 cm. 10 copies. Personal collection, Jean-Luc Herman.

Bottom:
Fragments du jour. Paris : Éditions Lafabrie, 1990. Paper, engravings.
12.5 x 11.5 cm. 101 copies. Personal collection, Bernard-Gabriel Lafabrie.

to infinity" ["amarré à l'infini"]. After comparing these blocks of color to
sand, rocks, stars, and a distant horizon, Dorion concludes: "Nothing is
missing / nothing comes undone / in this blue / a messenger of the purest
love / where everything starts over" ["Rien ne manque / rien ne se défait /
dans ce bleu / messager du plus pur amour / où tout recommence"]. Smaller
than most paperbacks, *Carrés de lumière* was hand-written in the author's
manuscript and, thus, retains artisan qualities. If the first of these works
stirs a reflection on chaos, the second inspires calm.

Though the colophon of *Carrés de lumière* specifies that it was made in Paris and Saint-Hippolyte, where Dorion most often resides, her artist's books seem to defy specificity of place. It could be said that Dorion published the first of these in France, when Bernard-Gabriel Lafabrie made *Fragments du jour* (1990) with a text soon reprinted in *Les États du relief* (1991); however, this work demonstrates the editor's admiration for her writing more than a joint effort. The artist's books that Dorion made with Julius Baltazar during the late 1990s prove still further deterritorialized. *Passages de l'aube* (1996), *Les Murs de la grotte* (1997), and *Voyages de Porphyre* (1997), exist in only two copies, for the author and artist. More like manuscripts than publications, they not only present the book as a utopian space but also mark an essential turning point in Dorion's poetics. In this series, Dorion begins to concentrate on Oneness, or the profound unity of all things. In "Fille d'argile et de souffle," Madeleine Gagnon explains: "Ses frontières géographiques sont en quelque sorte accidentelles – elle est, de toute façon, appuyée contre le monde entier" (11). Choosing to write "la Terre" with a capital "T" in *Voyages de Porphyre* (1997), Dorion expands the universal scope of her writing at the very moment when it proves most intimate in its material form.

In her retrospective collection *Mondes fragiles, choses frêles* (2006), Dorion revises earlier occurrences of "la Terre," thus reinforcing the new cosmic dimension of her poetry developed through her work with Baltazar. The importance of *Voyages de Porphyre* is likewise shown by *Portraits de mer* (1998), an accordion book by Béatrice Quérrec, to whom Dorion gave permission to draw into the text.[14] The nebulous strands of blue and brown traced in and around the text emphasize the sense of a return to origins. Finally, in 1999, Dorion would produce three more works with Baltazar, *Pierres invisibles* (1999), *Chemins du poème* (1999), and *Battements de Terre* (1999), the last of which also includes images by Olivier Debré. In order to forge a coherent work from two engravings by each artist, Dorion draws on the four elements and seasons. Thus writing a story of Creation, she succeeds in guaranteeing the coherence of the masterpiece thanks to her poetics alone.

If the final reworking of *Portraits de mer* marks the close of an era, as Dorion suggests in an interview with Jacques Paquin (7), it is perhaps because the poet achieves a virtually incomparable level of aesthetic unity between text and image. In *Le bruit du passé* (2001), edited by Daniel Leuwers, Dorion would soon write: "Your life disappears / between the pages that unfold" ["Ta vie disparaît / entre les pages qui s'ouvrent"]. This

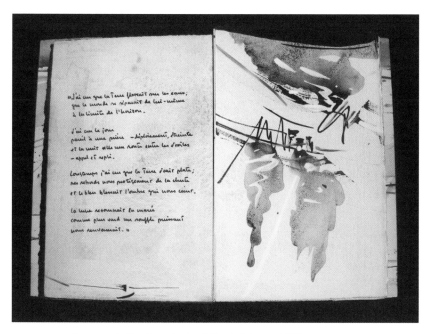

Voyages de Porphyre. Paris: Julius Balthazar, 1997.
Paper, hand-manuscript text, ink drawings. 14 x 20 cm. 2 copies.
Personal collection, Julius Balthazar. © ADAGP

meta-textual reference suggests a stronger interest in the book not only as One but also as a sacred object at the limits of immateriality. In *Et ce n'est que vie* (2002), Anne Berubé captures Dorion's search for harmony through her smooth digital prints accompanying texts from *Pierre invisibles*. Almost three-dimensional in appearance, these images doubtlessly reflect the tranquility and precision that Dorion seeks out in poetry. To quote *Battements de terre*, her published volumes and artist's books indeed reinvent each other like so many "lights / that break up and re-form straightaway" ["lumières / qui se brisent et aussitôt se refont"].

Sublime Embrace: Desautel's Poetic Mediations between Self and Other

Among the poets of her generation, Denise Desautels is perhaps best known for her interest in the visual arts and the coherence of her career, for which she was awarded the 2009 Prix Athanase-David. Frequently calling herself an *archéologue de l'intime*, Desautels addresses childhood, corporality, memory, and, above all, mourning, to which she continuously returns as the central trope of her poetry, leading Paul Chanel Malenfant to propose that her work could be described as a vast literary tomb (247). She uses the visual arts as a means to step away from her writerly obsessions and then return to them from a new perspective ("D'abord l'intime" 228). During the 1990s, she produced more artist's books than any other type of work. They reveal not only the impact that such collaborations have on her poetics but also the extent to which a single writer can enrich production of the genre.

The emphasis that Desautels places on the private sphere never excludes collectivity from her writing; rather, she portrays the sociopolitical as mediated by individual experience. Recognizing her position as a female francophone writer situated in time and place, Desautels cites *Une voix pour Odile* by France Théoret: "I write from where I come from. I speak from where I am" ["J'écris d'où je viens. Je parle d'où je suis"].[15] As she grew up before the Quiet Revolution, this space includes a Quebec isolated from the rest of North America and reverent toward Europe. In "Who's afraid of America ?," Desautels writes: "*I'm afraid of America* [in English in the original] while dreaming my European dreams in great, imported books. Two feet buried in the cement of a little, closed courtyard on the Mont-Royal Plateau" ["I'm afraid of America en rêvant mes rêves européens dans les grands livres importés. Les deux pieds enfouis dans le béton d'une petite cour close du Plateau Mont-Royal"] (74). Although this poetic essay resolves such tensions and recognizes a Quebec identity open to cultural exchange, Desautels remains conscious of the need to transcend minority status as a writer.

Before contributing to artist's books, she was well-experienced in collaborating with artists. This genre became a major part of her work after 1986, when she co-directed with Gilles Daigneault an issue of *La Nouvelle Barre du jour*, "Installations / fictions," a collective book-object pairing up twenty-three writers and artists. The same year, Desautels published three pivotal works: *La répétition*, with photographs of La Salle de classe by Irene F. Whittome; *Nous en parlerons sans doute*, co-written with Anne-Marie Alonzo, based on photographs by Raymonde April; and, *Écritures / ratures* a "workshop notebook" that she created with Francine Simonin, wherein artistic sharing comes to the forefront of her concerns: "one another: the essential" ["l'une et l'autre: l'essentiel"] (126). Desautels would soon thereafter publish *Le signe discret* (1987) in Lausanne with a frontispiece by Francine Simonin. These illustrated editions could all be considered immediate forerunners to her artist's books.

Thus, Desautels began to publish in Europe before she created her first artist's book, *Black Words* (1990), with Betty Goodwin, who is known for her dislocated bodies floating in space. The poet responds to their lack of spatial reference by exploring the omnipresence of death, which "meets every landscape" ["la mort rejoint tous les paysages"], and evoking a sense of emptiness: "the decor spins in place the ground falls apart / elsewhere doesn't exist" ["le décor tourne à vide le sol s'effondre / ailleurs n'existe pas"]. In this context, the body reconnects the subject to the world: "the eye the mouth the shoulder the hand / bond words and things" ["l'œil la bouche l'épaule la main / lient les mots et les choses"]. This portrayal of body as its own landscape proves especially significant since *Black Words* was created for Collectif Génération. The work could easily be deemed "French" by virtue of its publisher, although it was made by an artist and a writer who are both from Montreal. Instead, like *Voyages de Porphyre*, it seems to create its own conceptual space not linked to geography.

Desautels soon began to produce artist's books in both France and Quebec. In *Théâtre pourpre* (1993), which respects the classical codex, she investigates how the body stores memory and projects it onto the landscape as the individual moves. Questioning the "planeness of surfaces" ["planéité des surfaces"] in paintings by Jean-Luc Herman, her texts depict the city (presumably Paris, where she signs the work), where walls, music, windows – even trees and flowers – act as facades that alternately absorb and reflect the subjectivity of the viewer. Conceived by Jacques Fournier in Montreal, *Le Vif de l'étreinte* (1994) takes on a more innovative form with sets of poems and images inside a wooden frame and fabric box. Watercolors by Claire Beaulieu show figures embracing, then the profile of another in the fetal position. The poems depict their colors as forces that act on the viewer: "these greens and these pinks / overlapping / yell softly" ["ces verts et ces roses / superposés / hurlent tout bas"]. Desautels creates a disjoint between violent verbs, like yell, writhe, or hit, and soft nouns, such as silk, organdy, or leaves, to show how material perception is mediated by emotion, in the "back and forth / between soul and flesh" ["va et vient / entre la chair et l'âme"]. Despite their formal differences, *Théâtre pourpre* and *Le Vif de l'étreinte* both express threats to the body that contrast with the serenity of their images.

Since working together on *Le vif de l'étreinte*, Fournier and Desautels have developed close ties leading to some of the finest examples of artist's books from Quebec, including *La passion du sens* (1996). Based on an installation by Sylvia Safdie, this work resembles a *sefer*, or holy book. Its

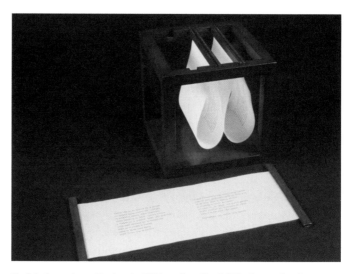

Parfois les astres. Montreal: Editions Roselin, 2000. Paper, Sugikawa tissue and mahogany. 20 x 20 x 20 cm. 14 copies. Photograph courtesy of Michel Dubreuil.

first page, which reads only "And yet black / slate / inexhaustible / meaning" ["Or le noir / l'ardoise / inépuisable / le sens"], suggests a return to earlier collective discourses on art and mourning. Through what Sylvie Alix calls a technique of "addition" (20), words inserted on the following pages create new phrases around this one. They conclude with "the passion of meaning" ["la passion du sens"], a term used by Roland Barthes to describe the reader's search for resolution at the end of a work (124). Desautels denies any such closure through her portrayal of "the sharpness of meaning ... crumbling in the air, just before it reaches the ore of the slate" ["l'aigu du sens ... s'effritant dans l'air, juste avant d'atteindre l'or de l'ardoise"]. Likewise, the book's form encourages open-ended readings. A sheet of glass standing vertically at its center reflects Desautels' texts onto a slate base; a bronze stone can then be moved on the base to make their reflection disappear. This placement of stone, which imitates a Jewish mourning ritual, leads the reader to reflect upon relationships between language, loss, and memory.

In designing such a multifaceted piece, Fournier not only enabled collaboration between the artist and writer but also acted as an artist himself. He likewise designed *Parfois les astres* (2000), in which three texts are suspended inside a square frame. This form seems to inspire the *je-tu-nous* structure chosen by Denise Desautels and Louise Dupré for their three poems[16]: *je* is linked to silence, *tu* is tied to dreaming, and *nous* leads

De la douceur. Montreal: Editions Roselin/Paris : Editions de la Cour Pavée, 1997. Paper, balsa wood, copper etching. 16 cm. 36 copies. Photograph courtesy of Ginette Clément.

towards hope. In its most restrained sense, the plural pronoun "we" can be interpreted as the two poets speaking together; however, it also refers to a larger community of all those who inspect "our palms / striated with lines that we fight to read" ["nos paumes / striées de lignes qu'on s'acharne à lire"]. Although the body of the reader is *incorporated* into the text and literally figures in the words, any sense of peacefulness derived from the sensuality of language is counterbalanced by violence: "I persist in throwing to the winds / an old cry, a call, a war at times" ["je m'entête à lancer au hasard / un vieux cri, un appel, une guerre parfois"]. Integrated in a cowritten text, this "I" exhibits the rare characteristic of being *plural*, not a universalized self but a composite voice created by individuals speaking both together and alone. It reflects Desautels' ongoing commitment to conceive of relationships based on shared underlying desires.

Each of these works contrasts with *De la douceur* (1997), *Novembre* (2001), and *L'enfant mauve* (2004), a trilogy that Desautels and Fournier created during the same period with Jacqueline Ricard, editor of Éditions de la Cour Pavée in Paris. These three works follow an identical format, chosen in advance: they contain three black square panels on which image and text face each other. They prove unusual in the Parisian artists' book milieu, where collaborative works with established authors often deviate less from the standard fine white paper folio. The quality of contributions by

Desautels and Fournier to works edited at La Cour Pavée is likewise evident in *Quinte & sens* (2005), a pentagon-shaped book whose pages, including texts by five different authors, unfold like flower petals. Here, Desautels' poem contemplating symbolic and sensorial *essence*, and Fournier's impeccable binding enhance the French bibliophilic tradition with the aesthetics of the Quebec artist's book. Through her ongoing engagement with art, Desautels forges poems of sublime beauty that evoke collective solidarities to combat the solitude of mourning.[17]

Continuity of Traditions

Beausoleil, Dorion, and Desautels share an insistence that each collaborative project must above all reflect *complicité* between its contributors. Although far from solitary examples of these transatlantic experimentations, they have sustained more systematic exchanges in France than most in their generation. Along with others like Louise Warren and Nancy Huston, they have incorporated artist's books from France into their work as an integral part of their own poetics. As these books tend to remain hidden in private collections, it would be difficult to judge how many poets have made similar trajectories. Offering an alternative outlet to publishing in the Parisian "center," these works deserve additional attention from critics.

Since Beausoleil advocates effectively for the accessibility of literature, it might be tempting to hold up his work as an example what makes Quebec poetry unique in France. In *Librement dit*, he affirms that it tends to outshine (and outsell) French regional poetry thanks to this type of difference (88–90).[18] Beausoleil's voluminous literary production speaks as much about a way of life as a way of conceiving literature. In contrast, Dorion refuses to view art and writing as cultural products; instead, she considers them practices that make traces of time tangible and offer a space of shared humanity (*Sous l'arche du temps* 69–83). Artist's books seem to play an ever more important role in her aesthetic philosophy, an approach closer to that adopted by Desautels, for whom they often represent a *body*. Activating the sense of touch, they create new ways to mediate between individual subjectivity and the universal need to mourn.

Dorion and Desautels both view art and writing in a reciprocal relationship that can create meaning through collaborative effort. In 2007, they worked together on *Sainte Sébastienne II. Hommage à Louise Bourgeois*, edited by Jacques Fournier, with a painting by Françoise Sullivan [Figure 8]. Their texts engraved on metal sheets slide like cards into the "flank" of

Sullivan's red square painting, thereby enacting the martyrdom of the feminized saint. The reading process thus becomes a constantly renewed cycle: "the arrow doesn't falter – pierces life / behind and ahead of the self / one sees its trace ever fresh" ["la fleche ne faillit pas – perce la vie / derrière et devant soi / on en voit la trace toujours fraîche"] (Dorion). Far from easy despair, both authors suggest an on-going commitment to art and life in reaction to such violence: "the terror, its fragments, its rivers / but the fingernails hold fast" ["l'épouvante, ses fragments, ses fleuves / mais les ongles tiennent bon"] (Desautels). Paying tribute to women who explore the body through art, the main section of the work literally stands as a sign of continued strength.

In its dedication to Louise Bourgeois, *Sainte Sébastienne II* again reinforces links between artists from both sides of the Atlantic. Yet it also pays homage to Françoise Sullivan, who signed *Refus global* in 1948, a work that not only marks the advent of modernity in Quebec but also represents the first collective artist's book in its history. Sixty years later, *Sainte Sébastienne II* is a work that defies classification according to prevailing definitions of artist's books outside Quebec. It is perhaps the greatest tribute to pioneers like Sullivan or Grandbois that contemporary poets and artists from Quebec continue to develop independent local traditions for the artist's book while also enriching its production abroad.

Notes

1 I would like to express my deepest gratitude to Julius Balthazar, Claude Beausoleil, Jacques Clauzel, Denise Desautels, Hélène Dorion, Jacques Fournier, Jean-Luc Herman, and Gabriel-Bernard Lafabrie for providing me access to their own libraries and personal collections. I am also indebted to the Société des Professeurs Français et Francophones d'Amérique, whose generous support through the Bourse Marandon facilitated travel to conduct part of the research presented in this article.

2 Within the French tradition, Anne Moeglin-Delcroix argues that the term *livre d'artiste* should be reserved only for works produced by visual artists who seek to use the book as a medium for artistic expression. According to her, they differ from works that evolved near the turn of the 20th century in reaction against the commercial book industry, when visual artists, writers, and engravers began to conceive of collaborative works as coherent aesthetic projects rather than illustrated books or bibliophilic collectors' items. This terminology is more or less reversed in the U.S. tradition, where Johanna Drucker calls works developed by avant-garde artists like Ed Ruscha "artist's books" and refers to collaborative works by artists and writers or fine-printed books as *livre d'artiste*, in French.

3 Hould defines the Quebec artist's book in the following terms: "the artist's book is a published original creative work, a work of art in which the text or the book, as a physical medium, constitutes a focus for material and conceptual exploration" (15). I will borrow this definition for works from Quebec, while maintaining the distinc-

tion established by Moeglin-Delcroix between the "artist's book" and "artists' book" in France. All translations are the author's, unless otherwise indicated.

4 See "À la croisée des champs artistique et littéraire : le livre d'artiste au Québec, 1900–1980," as well as *Du texte à l'image: le livre illustré au Québec.*

5 To mention only France, starting in 1997, Beausoleil served as a correspondent to the Académie Mallarmé, into which he was inducted as a member in 2004, becoming the second Quebec poet since Gaston Miron to receive the honor.

6 Unpublished interview with the author of this article in Montreal on 15 December 2008.

7 Since the artist's books addressed here omit page numbers, and some, like *Mao Bar Salon*, take on unconventional shapes without identifiable pages, this article will reference only entire titles for works belonging to this genre.

8 In search of an "American" identity, Derouin traveled to Mexico several times during the fifties. For more information on his work, see Diane Saint-Armand, *Empreintes et reliefs René Derouin* (Quebec: Ministère des affaires culturelles, 1982), as well as two works edited by the artist: *Pour une culture du territoire* (Montreal: L'hexagone, 2001) and *Ressac: de Migrations au Largage* (Montreal: L'Hexagone, 1996).

9 See *Jacques Clauzel* especially its texts "Temps, espace et trait dans l'oeuvre de Jacques Clauzel" (Torreilles 9–18), as well as "Jacques Clauzel – Tracks and Pathways" (Dhainaut, 61–76).

10 Hélène Dorion was the first Canadian

woman to win the prestigious Prix de l'Académie Mallarmé in 2005, the year before she was inducted into the Académie Mallarmé as well as the Académie des lettres du Québec. Described as one of Quebec's most "accessible" poets in *L'Actualité*, the Montreal *Gazette* classified her among its People of the Year also in 2006.

11 In French, these terms are "dépouil-lée," "nue," "économe," "transparent," "abstrait." For example, see Guay Hervé "La poésie est la limite" (*Le Devoir* 6 April 1996. D1); Bernard Noël, "Une barque remplie de visage" (*L'Autre Sud* 4 (March 1999): 6–8); and François-Michel Durazzo, "Le voyage initiatique dans *Portraits de Mers*." (*Liberté* 251 (February 2001): 137–44). On time in her poetry, see Isabelle Cadoret, "'N'être rien qu'un instant/de l'univers': l'expérience du temps et de l'espace chez Hélène Dorion" (*Études françaises* 39.3 (2003): 103–16).

12 More precisely, Dorion creates a refrain of exclusion by which what exists ["il y a"], is restricted to "all that there may be" ["il n'y aurait que"] and "all that there will be" ["il n'y aura que"], until the poet gradually begins to envision a new type of existence: "there will be" ["il y aura"]. See *Hors Champ* (37, 62, 83), *Les retouches de l'intime* (23, 46) and *Les corridors du temps* (57, 60).

13 See especially "La Ressemblance de la terre" in *Les corridors du temps* (81–96).

14 Interview with the author of this article in Montreal on 15 December 2008.

15 Quoted for example in "Trois questions, trois pièges." *Liberté* 39.4 (August 1997): 49.

16 See as well "France in the Heart of the Eastern Townships" by Louise Dupré in this volume. The two authors so thor-oughly blend their writing in *Parfois les astres* that they could no longer be certain who wrote which words once the project was completed.

17 In 2005, Fournier and Desautels also collaborated with Bonnie Baxter on a work entitled *Apparitions* that draws together the artist's and writer's explorations of the limits of autobiography in an "endless" form that can be read indefinitely by turning the book. Much like the trilogy with Jacqueline Ricard that preceded it, *Apparitions* also plays on themes of mirror-images through the use of reflective materials that engage the reader in the text-image-object relationship.

18 On the recent debate about Quebec poetry between critics on both sides of the Atlantic, see also Yannick Gasquy-Resch's article "Ce vigoureux français venu d'ailleurs" (*Le Monde* 31 March 2006).

Works Cited

Alix, Sylvie. *Intimités poétiques: les livres de Jacques Fournier*. Joliette, Quebec: Musée d'art de Joliette, 2000.

Baillargeon, Stéphane. "Les poètes du bitume." *Le Devoir,* 3 April 1993. D1.

Barthes, Roland. *Image-Music-Text.* Trans. Stephen Heath. New York: Hill and Wang, 1977.

Beausoleil, Claude. "Poésie et co-édition." *Écrivain cherche lecteur: L'écrivain francophone et ses publics.* Ed. Lise Gauvin and Jean-Marie Klinkenberg. Montreal: Bibliothèque nationale du Québec, 1993.

– *Librement dit : carnets parisiens.* Montreal: L'hexagone, 1997.

– *Mao bar salon.* Montreal: Editions Cul Q, 1978.

– *Promenade Modern Style.* Montreal: Editions Cul Q, 1975.

Beausoleil, Claude, and Jocelyne Aird-

Bélanger. *Fusions*. Val-David: Incidit, 1993.

Beausoleil, Claude, and Auck. *L'épreuve du fugace*. Paris: n.p., 2008.

Beausoleil, Claude, and Jacques Clauzel. *Ailleurs; le poème inachevé*. Gallargues-le-Montueux: A Travers, 1995.

– *L'Amour du secret*. Gallargues-le-Montueux: A Travers, 1994.

– *Du regard*. Gallargues-le-Montueux: A Travers, 1995.

– *Sous les traces*. Unpublished, 2003.

Beausoleil, Claude, and René Derouin. *Migrations*. Val-David: Éditions du Versant Nord, 1992.

Benhamou, Maurice. *Jacques Clauzel: La vérité en peinture*. Langlade: Editions Anne Lagier, 2004.

Bernier, Silvie. "À la croisée des champs artistique et littéraire: le livre d'artiste au Québec, 1900–1980." *Voix et Images* 11.3 (1986): 528–36.

– *Du texte à l'image: le livre illustré au Québec*. Sainte-Foy: Presses de l'Université Laval, 1990.

Clauzel, Jacques. "De ma conception du livre d'artiste." *Les livres de Jacques Clauzel: Espace poétique, espace pictural. Catalogue*. Challe: Lunel, 1997. 54–6.

Desautels, Denise. *L'oeil au ralenti*. Montreal: Noroît, 2007.

– "Trois questions, trois pièges." *Liberté* 39.4 (August 1997): 47–53.

– "Who's afraid of America ?" *Cent lignes de notre américanité. Actes du Colloque tenu à Moncton du 14 au 16 juin 1984*. Moncton: Perce-Neige, 1984.

Desautels, Denise, Claire Beaulieu, and Jacques Fournier. *Le vif de l'étreinte*. Montreal: Éditions Roselin, 1994.

Desautels, Denise, Louise Dupré, and Jacques Fournier. *Parfois les astres*. Montreal: Éditions Roselin, 2000.

Desautels, Denise, and Betty Goodwin. *Black Words*. Paris: Collectif Génération, 1990.

Desautels, Denise, and Jean-Luc Herman. *Théâtre pourpre*. Paris: Éditions Herman, 1993.

Desautels, Denise, Sylvia Safdie, and Jacques Fournier. *La passion du sens*. Montréal: Éditions Roselin, 1996.

Dorion, Hélène. *Les Corridors du temps*. Trois-Rivières: Écrits des Forges, 1988.

– *Les États du relief*. Chaillé-sous-les-Ormeaux, Montreal: Le Dé bleu/Le Noroît, 1991.

– *Intervalle prolongé*. St-Lambert: Noroît, 1983.

– *Mondes fragiles, choses frêles*. Montreal: l'Hexagone, 2006.

– *Les Retouches de l'intime*, Saint-Lambert: Noroît, 1987.

– *Sous l'arche du temps*. Montreal: Leméac, 2003.

– *Un Visage appuyé contre le monde*. Saint-Lambert/Chaillé-sous-les-Ormeaux: Noroît / Le Dé Bleu, 1990.

Dorion, Hélène, and Julius Baltazar. *Voyages de Porphyre*, Paris: n.p., 1997.

Dorion, Hélène, Julius Baltazar, and Olivier Debré. *Battements de terre*. Montreal: Éditions Simon Blais, 1999.

Dorion, Hélène, and Marc Garneau. *L'empreinte du bleu*. Montreal: Simon Blais, 1994.

Dorion, Hélène, and Jean-Luc Herman. *Carrés de lumière*, Paris: Éditions Herman, 1994.

Dorion, Hélène, and Béatrice Quérrec. *Portraits de mer*. La Chapelle chaussée: Dana, 1998.

Drucker, Johanna. *The Century of Artists' Books*. New York: Granary Books, 1995.

Gagnon, Madeleine. "Fille d'argile et de souffle." *Nous voyagerons au cœur de l'être, autour d'Hélène Dorion*. Ed. Paul Bélanger. Montreal: Noroît, 2004. 9–20.

Hould, Claudette. *Répertoire des livres d'artistes au Québec, 1981–1990*. Montreal: Bibliothèque nationale du Québec, 1993.

Jameson, Isabelle. "Histoire du livre

d'artiste." *Cursus* 9.1. Fall 2005.
http://www.ebsi.umontreal.ca/cursus/
vol9no1/Jameson.html accessed 12
September 2008.

Malenfant, Paul Chanel. "Écrire comme
mourir: tombeau des mots." *Voix et
images* 26.2 (Winter 2001): 247–63.

Moeglin-Delcroix, Anne. *Esthétique du livre
d'artiste: 1960-1980*. Paris: Bibliothèque
nationale de France, 1997.

Nick, Didier, ed. *Jacques Clauzel*. Aubais:
Nick Editions, 2002.

Dorion, Hélène. Interview with Jacques
Paquin. "Hélène Dorion: pensée du
sensible, ouverture du poème." *Lettres
québécoises* 129 (Spring 2008): 7–10.

Yoken, Mel B. *Entretiens québécois.
Volume II*. Montreal: Editions Pierre
Tisseyre, 1989.

La Chanson Québécoise: Not the Same Old (French) Song

BRIAN THOMPSON

The song connection between Quebec and France goes back some four centuries, but has become a real exchange and cross-fertilization only in the last sixty years or so. France was until then the *Mère patrie*, the obvious source of language and culture in what had been known as *Nouvelle France*. Belgium and Switzerland are relatively recent arrivals on the transatlantic scene.

Initially, songs in Quebec were those brought by the early French sailors and settlers, largely from Anjou, Normandy, Brittany, and Poitou, or other provinces. Literate colonists brought composed songs with written lyrics but the much larger number of illiterate peasants and farmers also brought songs from a rich French oral tradition. These traditional folksongs already existed in multiple regional versions and developed even more numerous home-grown versions among the widely scattered population in Quebec: some 234 for "À la claire fontaine"[1] (according to Gilles Vigneault [1928–], who worked in the archives as a young man [Legras 128]) and 350 for "V'là l'bon vent" (Normand 18) – as they were sung and passed on in various social occasions: weddings, baptisms, funerals, get-togethers of various sorts, or during long winter *veillées*. Original songs were also produced locally, whether by adapting French songs to New France localities ("Sur la route de Louvier" becomes "Sur la route de Berthier") or commemorating local events and the realities of daily life, as in "Les Raftmans" (Normand 19). After the English victory in 1763, the cultural minority clung to its roots and preserved a wealth of traditional French songs often lost in France. This treasure of traditional music remains essential into the late twentieth century, as Gilles Vigneault, another Québécois treasure, notes: "the folksong was at once our operetta, our opera, our theatre, our literature and our poetry. It stood in for all the mirrors which normally provide a people a reflection of itself so that it knows who it is, where it comes from, where it's going" (Vigneault 224).[2]

In the first half of the nineteenth century, patriotic songs appear. "Un Canadien errant" (Antoine Gérin-Lajoie, 1830) is the first Canadian (we would now say Québécois) song to have international success. The second half of the 19th century sees a renewal of attachment to the *Mère patrie* with songs like Louis Fréchette's "Vive la France." Traditional bawdy songs from France were also popular, but were severely expurgated under the influence of French Canadian clergy (Roy, as cited by Normand 25). Although there were other singer-songwriters in the 1930s and 1940s, notably Ovila Légaré in the folk tradition, Willie Lamothe in the country/western vein, and Le Soldat Lebrun during the Second World War, the development of a home-grown written song tradition that is not imitative of French models begins, for all intents and purposes, with Mary Travers, "épouse Bolduc" (1894– 1941), considered the "mother" of Québécois song (Legras 123). "La Bolduc" – as she became known – left her mark on Québécois song, in part by singing of everyday life in Quebec, in part by her style, a syncopation influenced, according to Michel Rivard, by American country music (Troadec, "Exclaim" 122), and by her characteristic *turlute* (a kind of yodel). Vigneault notes her influence on the major French singer-songwriter Charles Trenet (1913–2001), who refers to her in his 1950s song, "Dans les rues de Québec," and even attempts her *turlute*!

Québécois historian Robert Thérien underlines the importance of sound recording and mass communication in the 20th century for the creation of the modern Québécois song tradition: "It's radio that gave birth to Québécois song" – amplified by TV in the 1950s (Thérien, personal emails). But Jacques Normand (1922–1998) also played a crucial role in putting Québécois song on the world map, so to speak. On the one hand, as Gilles Vigneault notes, though influenced by French song, he had the audacity to compose his own songs as well as to sing "I love the nights of Montreal" when, as everyone knew, the nights of Paris were so beautiful, and all you could hear on the radio at the time was Tino Rossi's "Nuits de Chine" (Troadec, "Exclaim" 227), a song popular from the early 1920s to the 1960s. But more importantly, as director of Le faisan doré, the most fashionable cabaret in Montreal since the arrival of the French duo of Pierre Roche (1919–2001) and Charles Aznavour (1924–) in 1948, Normand was instrumental in getting French impresario Jacques Canetti (1909–1997), who was in Montreal briefly in July 1950 to promote his artists and to search for "Canadian" talent for the French label Polydor, to listen to Félix Leclerc (1914–1988), an unknown and unappreciated singer-songwriter. Leclerc had to be tricked into the radio station the next day on the pretext of recording songs for a friend's party – he would never have accepted to sing for a French impresario. After a few songs, Canetti knew he had found "[his] Canadian," offered Leclerc a contract with Polydor (which Leclerc signed later in the day without reading it), and flew back to Paris. In September, an incredulous Leclerc received a contract for a five-week stint at l'A.B.C., a major music-hall in Paris for December – his friends had to push him to actually go. He recorded several songs for Polydor in January and won Le Prix de l'Académie Charles-Cros (the critics' prize of the French recording industry) for "Moi mes souliers," in February! Canetti then programmed him for fourteen weeks at his own theatre, Les Trois Baudets: the Québécois peasant had conquered Paris without changing his look, his texts, or his language.

A number of other Québécois singers had tried to make it in France by imitating the French, to no avail (Thérien, personal emails). On Leclerc's triumphant, if brief, return to Montreal in April 1951, his friend Jacques Normand presented his "famous Canadian *chansonnier*"[3]: "Allow me to thank France and the French critics for having revealed Félix to us!" (Thérien, *Leclerc* 2004). Leclerc would spend three years in France, tour forty cities, and blaze the trail for Québécois song. Upon his return to Montreal he was greeted by enormous crowds, banner headlines ("Our Félix is back"), and a big banquet at the Windsor Hotel, with the usual speeches. When it was his turn, he could not get a word out, but managed to whisper to Canetti: "What an injustice. I'm just the same as before. No one wanted anything to do with me. Why?" (Canetti 77).

As Canetti puts it: "How can a single man open thus the doors of a country? Félix Leclerc made the name of Canada ring in our ears and in our hearts, he made a living blood circulate that was no longer flowing in our veins. Thanks to him, from now on the "patriarch," Québécois song has gained a rightful place here" (Canetti 77). Pascal Normand concludes: "An exile in Europe and the admiration of the French public were necessary for his compatriots to accept him in his full originality: in fact, he was a QUÉBÉCOIS at a time when it was fashionable to be either American or French. But Québécois? ..." (Normand 58).

If La Bolduc is the mother of Québécois song, Leclerc is indeed its father. Since 1979, the ADISQ, the Quebec professional recording association, has been giving annual awards, the equivalent of the Grammy awards in the US and the Victoires de la musique awards in France, that bear his name: the Félix. In a bow to the transatlantic nature of his career, since 1996 La Fondation Félix Leclerc, administered by his daughter, Nathalie, has been giving an annual Félix Leclerc Prize to both a Québécois and a French singer, encouraging the dynamics of this cross-cultural exchange (Prévost-Thomas gives a list of winners, 170–1).

Leclerc was a revelation for the French as well. For Charles Trenet, he is "the first singer-songwriter in years to bring something new, to bring poetry to French song" (Normand 43–5). The patriarch of French singer-songwriters, Georges Brassens (1921–1980), and the Belgian superstar Jacques Brel (1929–1978) – both among Canetti's numerous discoveries, by the way, along with Léo Ferré, Boris Vian, Jacques Higelin, and more recently my own friends Jean-Marie Hummel and Liselotte Hamm – often said that it was Leclerc's success that encouraged them to give it a try (Thérien, *Leclerc* 2004), and in particular to go on stage with a simple guitar (Legras 123).

Such transatlantic inspirations are not uncommon. Though he had studied piano without much enthusiasm, Robert Charlebois (1944–) was inspired upon hearing "Eau vive" sung by Guy Béart (1930–): he found himself "in an enchanted world" (Normand 92), saved up his money and bought a guitar. Luc Plamondon (1942–) was similarly moved by Aznavour: "When I listened to him, his songs transported me ... it's songs like that that I wanted to write. It's no doubt because Aznavour was the first French singer to write in everyday language, love songs in the language spoken day to day" (Normand 131). "Pleure un bon coup ma p'tite Véro" by Francis Lalanne (1958–) was a decisive influence on Lynda Lemay (1966–): "A revelation! I said to myself, Ah, it's possible to be intimate like that in one's lyrics" (Troadec, "Lemay" 104).[4]

Leclerc's success was not immediately followed by a flowering of urban singer-songwriters in Quebec: it was not fashionable and there were few appropriate venues for such artists. Raymond Lévesque (1928–), for example, had to move to France for five years (1953–58) (Thérien, personal emails), and it's there that he wrote the justly famous "Quand les hommes vivront d'amour," inspired by the war in Algeria. It is considered a Québécois hymn alongside Gilles Vigneault's "Mon pays" and "Gens du pays." Lévesque's song has been recorded by over forty French and Québécois singers, from Eddie Constantine in 1954 to a hip-hop version by LMDS in 2000 (Prévost-Thomas 172), but most famously by Félix Leclerc, Gilles Vigneault, and Robert Charlebois (1944–) to end the opening show of the Superfrancofête, the International Festival of Francophone Youth, on 13 August 1974 on the Plains of Abraham in Quebec City before an audience of well over 120,000.[5]

In 1959, Raymond Lévesque, back from France, joined forces with Clémence DesRochers (1933–), Jean-Pierre Ferland, Hervé Brousseau (1937–), and Claude Léveillée – later replaced by Jacques Blanchet (1931–1981) – to form a group baptized "Les Bozos" in homage to Félix Leclerc and his song, "Bozo." They sang in the first *boîte à chansons* in Montreal, "Chez Bozo." Within a few years there were some 250 such song clubs, not only in Montreal and Quebec City but elsewhere in the province. As Adréanne Lafond noted in *Le nouveau journal* in December, 1962, "the time has come for our artists to interpret French-Canadian compositions and to forget foreign composers and lyricists" (Normand 64).

Whereas in France singer-songwriters were often drowned out by the wave of "yé-yé," rock'n'roll, and American song in the 1960s (Johnny Hallyday, Sylvie Vartan, les Chaussettes noires ...), Québécois *chansonniers* soon became the standard-bearers for a whole series of social and political demands of a broad-based movement known as the Quiet Revolution (Thérien 2008–09), and played a major role in the "conscientization" – to borrow Paolo Freire's term – of many Québécois: we Québécois have our own language, our own culture, our own *chanson*, and are not just some second-class cultural backwater of France! Nor should we be second-class citizens of a largely English-speaking Canada!

Why song? Because after 22 June 1960 – the election of a Liberal government after sixteen years of what is referred to as *la grande noirceur* [the long darkness] of the Duplessis regime – there was a cultural and political springtime. "We discovered," Vigneault states, "that song could contribute to something besides entertaining us: to inform, then to convert." And that, with a simple theme: "to name ourselves in the world, to name ourselves on the planet. We didn't have a country, and we decided to name one" (Vigneault 231), not a country turned in upon itself, but open to the world, as he sings: "From my big solitary country/I cry out before falling silent/To all men on Earth/ My home is your home" ["De mon grand pays solitaire/Je crie avant que de me taire/À tous les hommes de la terre/Ma maison c'est votre maison"] ("Mon pays").[6]

The popularity of *chansonniers* like Jean-Pierre Ferland (1934–), Vigneault, Claude Léveillée (1932–), Claude Gauthier (1939–), Raymond Lévesque, as well as of those who covered their songs (including Renée Claude [1939–], Pauline Julien [1929–1988], Monique Leyrac [1928–]) was such that it had a negative impact on the song clubs, which could no longer afford such stars and began to dwindle in number by the late 1960s (Thérien, personal emails).

Robert Charlebois began as a *chansonnier*, opening for Leclerc in 1962 at the ripe old age of seventeen. He grew up, as Robert Thérien puts it, with poetic French song in one ear and American rock'n'roll in the other. He returned from California after the 1967 World's Fair, which had showcased Quebec to the nations assembled in Montreal, convinced that "the only way to advance is to establish a collaboration with the whole world"[7] and eager to try "something different" (Thérien, personal emails). He was working with the Quatuor de jazz libre de Québec when his friend Louise Forestier (1943–) suggested putting a show together. Yvon Deschamps, artistic director at the Théâtre de 4'Sous, needed something to close out his season and tried to get them to do a traditional mix of songs, skits ,and monologues, which did not sit well with Charlebois. The frustrated producer, Paul Buissonneau, at the end of his patience, told him: "Shove it up your ass, your f*ing show!" ["Mettez-vous-le dans le cul, votre hostie de show!"]. As a provocation, Charlebois seized on this as the title for his "anti-show," but since the newspapers would not print *hostie* (literally, "host," as in communion wafer: many Québécois swear words are of such religious origin), it was shortened to "L'Osstidcho." Presented on only three occasions over several months in varying venues ("Osstidcho" in May 1968, "Osstidcho Kingsize" in September, and "Osstidcho meurt" in January 1969), it was nonetheless a musical and scenographic revolution which opened doors for other artists. According to Sylvain Cormier, it was "the most important show in the history of song in Quebec" (Cormier).[8] The song "Lindberg," a duo between Charlebois and Louise Forestier, was the first song by a *chansonnier* to be number 1 on the Québécois charts, in January 1969 (Thérien, personal emails). This song and others, like "California" and "La marche du président," used a specifically Québécois language, *joual*, spoken by working-class Québécois, marginalized by both the French-speaking elite and the anglophone ruling class but able to contribute to defining a Québécois cultural identity. This amounted to a statement of independence from the clergy as well as from forces of cultural colonization, be they from France, the US, or the anglophone majority in Canada. As Cécile Prévost-Thomas puts it, Charlebois breathed into Québécois song what it needed to transcend the boundaries of its own esthetics and become audacious on the world stage (Prévost-Thomas 174).

Both Charlebois and Louise Forestier would go on to have considerable success in Europe. In July 1968, Charlebois represented Canada at the Festival International de la chanson française in Spa, Belgium, where he won first prize for interpretation with "California" (Normand 92). With "Lindberg" number one on the charts in France, Belgium, and Switzerland, director Bruno Coquatrix invited Charlebois to L'Olympia, the top music-hall in Paris, in April 1969, to open for Georgette Plana – a bad idea: her audience was totally inappropriate for the Québécois phenomenon. Things went badly: Charlebois ended up smashing a drum set and throwing it into the audience, much to the dismay of a Québécois critic: "And to say it's *that* that represents us abroad!"[9] – only to return in triumph in 1972 to an Olympia sold out weeks in advance (Normand 96).

If French singers had toured successfully in Quebec since the end of the nineteenth century,[10] it had been an almost entirely one-way street until Felix Leclerc arrived in 1950. The Montreal singer Guylaine Guy was female singer of the year in 1956 and played L'Olympia the next year. Claude Léveillée wrote some songs for Piaf – she had come to see him at "Les Bozos" in 1959 and invited him to Paris – Jean-Pierre Ferland had moderate success (Thérien, personal emails), but Gilles Vigneault showed real staying power, without changing anything about his appearance, music, or language to fit the expectations or fashions in Paris, Brussels, or Geneva. Both Charlebois and Diane Dufresne became stars in France during the 1970s.[11]

One of the engines driving transatlantic recognition in both directions in the ensuing years was the phenomenal success of musical comedies written by the Québécois Luc Plamondon,[12] in collaboration with French composers: *Starmania*, at the request of Michel Berger, and then *Notre-Dame de Paris* with Richard Cocciante. Fabienne Thibault, Diane Dufresne, Isabelle Boulay, Garou, Daniel Lavoie (actually from Manitoba, but now based in Quebec), and Natasha Saint-Pier became household names in France. Isabelle Boulay (1972–), for example, after singing the role of the *serveuse automate* in *Starmania* some 350 times in Europe, brought out her second album, produced in France by Olivier Bloch-Lainé, was signed by French label V2, opened for Serge Lama at L'Olympia in 1999, opened the next year for Francis Cabrel throughout France as well as at L'Olympia, had her own show at L'Olympia and then her consecration at the much larger Zénith, with a new album, *Mieux qu'ici-bas*, produced by Benjamin Biolay. The album sold over two million copies. She has continued from success to success, with multiple Félix and Victoires de la musique awards, on both sides of the Atlantic.

The greatest commercial success, of course, has been that of Céline Dion, in both French and English. After an early French album (covers of songs written by Luc Plamondon) and a very successful *1 fille et 4 types* (number one in Canada, Quebec, and France, where it was certified double platinum),

Dion has turned mostly to French singer-songwriter Jean-Jacques Goldman who wrote and composed the best-selling *D'eux* French album, with extraordinary results. She has won innumerable awards in both English and French, and sold over 200 million albums worldwide. She was even awarded the French Légion d'honneur in May 2008. Although Dion's French releases, thanks to Goldman, are often seen to have more credibility than her English albums, for the French public, Québécois song has sometimes been reduced, as it were, to these outstanding "voices,"[13] such that the wealth of creative talent in Quebec is still barely known in France.

There have been, however, other notable Franco-Québécois collaborations. Pauline Julien (1928–1998), who began her singing career in Paris cabarets, developed a close friendship with French singer-songwriter Anne Sylvestre (1934–) and frequently sang her songs. Anne returned the compliment with a song addressed to Pauline, "Dis-moi, Pauline," including this line: "The only good kisses come from Quebec" ["Il n'est bon bec que de Québec"] (Hidalgo 117). With the help of Québécois poet and director Denise Boucher, they put together a theatrical show, *Gémeaux croisés*, in which they sang their own or one another's songs. Created in Belgium in November 1997, the show toured France and Quebec for two years to rave reviews. [I remember driving from Boston to Montreal to see it!]

Following the 2005 hurricanes, Zachary Richard (1950–) – originally from Louisiana but adopted, like Daniel Lavoie, by Quebec – collaborated with French superstar Francis Cabrel (1953–) on a benefit concert in Paris in November of that year. One of the fruits of the concert was a musical one, "La promesse cassée," co-written by the two artists, with all proceeds going to support New Orleans artists devastated by the storms (http://www.zachary richard.com). Richard's rendition of the traditional tune from Louisiana, "Travailler, c'est trop dur," made it a French standard.[14]

Over the years some well-known French singers like Aznavour and Cabrel have also regularly toured Quebec. They can arrive, do a couple of interviews, give a few concerts, and be quite successful. Sixty years after starting his career in Quebec, Aznavour returned for the 400th anniversary of Quebec City and sang for over 100,000 people on the Plains of Abraham on 6 July 2008. Going in the other direction has been harder, requiring both a local structure of support, an extended stay, and repeated trips to really make an impact. Relatively few Québécois artists have managed, like Leclerc and Vigneault, to pull it off. Over the last fifteen or twenty years, however, there have been a number of Québécois artists with impressive French and, indeed, European careers. Often, they have been helped by French *parrains* [godfathers] who take them under their wing: Charles Aznavour for Linda Lemay; Jean-Jacques Goldman and, earlier, Eddy Marney for Céline Dion (at least for her French-language career!); Francis Cabrel for Isabelle Boulay; Pascal Obispo (1965–) for Natasha Saint-Pier (1981–), from New Brunswick (Troadec, "Exclaim" 142).

There are, in addition, a number of "transatlantic" singers who are worth mentioning; that is, those who started or developed their career on the *other* francophone side of the Atlantic. We've mentioned Aznavour and Pauline Julien. The Belgian diva, Lara Fabian, found her first success in Quebec in 1991 with a platinum record and many awards, before returning to Belgium in 1997 with increasing success. By 1999 she had sold six million records in Europe, and Polydor decided to republish her earlier records from Quebec, as well. Serge Lama, too, had his first success in Quebec. Others move back and forth. Nicolas Peyrac returned to France after fifteen years in Quebec and toured France in spring 2009 with his new album, his seventeenth, *Case de départ*, having returned not only to his country but to the acoustic guitar of his beginnings.[15] Michel Rivard,[16] though based in Quebec, stayed on in Belgium after a European tour with his classic group, Beau Dommage, writing ten songs in a couple of months: "it's as if I discovered a new style there" (Normand 159). After a final tour in France, the group dissolved, Rivard again stayed behind, with material help, including housing, from Maxime LeForestier, with whom he collaborated (including the song "Bille de verre"),[17] but found the row tough to hoe: a month-long show in Paris ended up *costing* him $10,000. Vigneault and Pauline Julien encouraged him, but told him it would take ten years to really penetrate the French market. As Rivard told Pascal Normand: "there it's a sort of jungle and when one doesn't want to give in to facility, you have to expect that ... There are so many people there who want to sing, there are so many shows to see ... I think that if you do not agree to make that kind of investment, you won't find your place ... unless you arrive by chance with a "hit" that is going to be played everywhere and persuade a producer to take the risk of renting a venue, paying for the musicians and all the PR" (Normand 160).[18]

Among the major contributors to exchanges between Quebec and Europe, over the last couple of decades, in particular, have been the numerous festivals on both side of the Atlantic. Some have established specific transatlantic collaborations. Quebec provided the example over forty years ago with the Festival d'été de Québec. The Coup de cœur francophone in

Montreal celebrated its twenty-second edition in 2008. Over the years it has developed a network of, now, thirty-six cities across Canada in addition to the festival proper in Montreal, allowing artists to constitute a tour instead of a being limited to single venue.[19] Jean-Pierre Foulquier was so impressed with the Quebec festivals that he started Les FrancoFolies de La Rochelle in 1985: "If they can do it, we can too!" (http://www.franco-folies.fr/accueil/index.html). Sister festivals in Spa, Belgium (http://www.francofolies.be/) and Montreal (http://www.francofolies.com/Francos2008/accueil_en.aspx) have since developed. The twentieth edition of the Franco-Folies de Montréal in 2008 was specifically centered on *Nouvelles scènes du Québec et de France*, bringing together established and up-and-coming artists from both countries. French artists were paired with Québécois counterparts. Some twenty-five French singers or groups were invited to celebrate and strengthen transatlantic exchanges, which in recent years have rather favored the Québécois.

Les Déferlantes francophones festival (http://www.deferlantes-francophones.com/2008/index2.html) has promoted North American francophone artists – mostly from Quebec, but also New Brunswick, Manitoba, or Louisiana – for the past eleven years in Cap Breton on the French coast. Unfortunately, given the economic situation on both sides of the ocean, the founding director, Maurice Segall, negotiated a one-year hiatus, suspending the festival for summer 2009 while maintaining occasional concerts throughout the year, "Les Quatre Saisons."[20] The July 2008 Festival Chansons de Parole in Barjac (http://www.chansonsdeparole.com/) was a collective homage to Quebec by a varied assortment of French and Québécois artists, notably Anne Sylvestre singing songs by Pauline Julien.

Other festivals have sprung up in many locations in both France and Quebec and have had a major impact on the transatlantic careers of several artists. Two examples will illustrate the process. In 1989, Linda Lemay (1966–) won the song contest at the Festival International de la Chanson de Granby (http://www.ficg.qc.ca/), which held its fortieth edition in 2008. Her award included an opening act for Claude Léveillée at a festival in St. Malo on the French coast, "Québec chante à St. Malo" (now defunct, unfortunately), and a workshop with French singer-songwriter Romain Didier (1949–) in Digne. Totally unknown in France, she wowed the crowd and the press: a lead article in *Ouest France* was entitled "Lynda Lemay triomphe" (Troadec, "Lemay" 87).[21] Her second French success was at the FrancoFolies de la Rochelle in July 1995, where she won the Prix du Sentier des Halles, a five-night engagement in the well-known Paris song club for May 1996. In April 1996 she also won two prizes at yet another festival, Le Tremplin de la Chanson des Hauts-de-Seine, just outside Paris. Invited in July 1996 to the famous Montreux Jazz Festival for a homage to Charles Trenet,[22] she "blew away" Trenet, Aznavour, and Gérard Davoust who sought her out to congratulate her. Davoust became her publisher and Aznavour took her under his wing, advised her on her third album, and gave her support he has given no other artist, praising her in interviews and writing a "blurb" for her new album, recorded in France: "Original ideas, fertile and very personal imagination, writing of rare quality, a special personality, full of freshness. Astonishing, surprising, exceptional! Listen to her." Her French supporters rented L'Européen in Paris for two months in November-December 1998; largely through word of mouth, the final weeks were completely sold out. Invited by twenty-eight promoters for the following fall, all her shows sold out before the posters even went up. Her 2000 album sold over half a million copies, and she did over one hundred concerts in France in 2002-03. "In fact," she says, "my credibility came by way of France" (105). She was back in France in spring 2009 for twenty-five concerts, including four at the legendary Olympia, where she has sung some forty times. Michel Troadec calls her a "transatlantic woman. Québécois in her flesh, her voice, her song. French in her language, her career, her loves" (86).

A more recent arrival, Pierre Lapointe (1981–) also got his start by winning first prize at Granby in 2001. He sang in France each of the next three years, as well as at the Festival Pully Lavaux in Switzerland (Prix du Jury). His Prix Félix Leclerc at the 2004 FrancoFolies de Montréal assured him of a trip back to France in 2005. In May of that year he won the Prix Coup de Cœur de l'Académie Charles-Cros, was a hit at the "Alors chante …" Festival in Montauban, then won the Grand Prix du Disque in November for his self-titled album, and, back in Quebec, no fewer than five Félix awards. In April 2007 he sang at the major Printemps de Bourges festival as well as at La Cigale in Paris, then won the Prix Rapsat-Lelièvre, a specifically transatlantic prize awarded each year to a Belgian singer at the FrancoFolies de Montréal and to a Québécois singer at the sister festival in Spa. It is clear that contests, prizes, and festivals with transatlantic connections are playing a major role in artists becoming known and even garnering major transatlantic success.

There are also some new structures in place, like the Québécois label Exclaim – now known as Archambault Musique – established in Paris in

2005. It is a subsidiary of a major international communications conglomerate, Québécor. The director, Hervé Deplasse, with whom I met at length, sees his role as one of developing Québécois artists in Europe over the long term: distribution, promotion, accompaniment. Among their artists: Florence K, Dumas, Zachary Richard (Québécois by adoption), as well as a few French or even Franco-Swiss artists like Edouard Desyon. One of the groups they represent illustrates another recent phenomenon. When Les Cowboys fringants, a lively group marrying traditional Québécois folk and country music sounds with very up-to-date social and political concerns, first arrived in Paris in April 2004 after several years of growing notoriety back in Quebec, they played – to their astonishment – to a packed house at L'Elysée Montmartre, with the entire (largely French) audience singing along in *québécois*. It seems they were already known both through their web site (http://www.cowboysfringants.com), records brought back to France by tourists, and through email and phone networking among their French/European fans, known as "Cousins fringants," who can pretty much assure a full house anywhere by sharing rides, housing, etc. (Lévesque 31). As I write they have just added a third show in Paris (February 2009). One interesting footnote: one of their members, Jérôme Dupras, stated in an interview about their current record and tour, *L'expédition*: "we have managed to *erase our Canadian side*, without disowning it of course, and to offer something homogeneous and universal, at least in the choice of texts" (Supervielle 17, emphasis mine). This seems to fly in the face of what the sole woman in the group, Marie-Annick Lépine (also a solo artist with Exclaim), has said in another recent interview: "I love shows that make me travel, that show me cultures other than my own" (Lévesque 31). Perhaps they'll be able to do both …

It's true that Céline Dion has erased any trace of a Québécois accent, and her French records (after her early collaboration with Eddy Marney), like many of Isabelle Boulay's, are essentially "made in France" without much Québécois residue. Québécois singer-songwriter Pierre Lapointe, too, is sometimes criticized for not singing in *québécois*, preferring what he calls "normative French" (Legras 125–7). There are still some kinks to be ironed out in the question of cultural "identity" as song, like many other things, becomes more transatlantic and transcultural. Could it be that occasionally Québécois song *is* the same old French song? Stay tuned.

Author's note

My thanks to Robert Thérien, Hélène Hazéra, Cécile Prévost-Thomas, Denis Mouton, Hervé Deplasse, Maurice Segall, and others whose erudition, suggestions, and advice proved invaluable.

Notes

1 In 1845 La Société Saint-Jean-Baptiste chose "À la claire fontaine" as the national hymn; it was not replaced until 1 July 1980 by "O Canada" by Calixte Lavallée and Adolphe-Basile Routhier (Norman 25).

2 All translations are the author's, unless otherwise indicated.

3 In Quebec, a *chansonnier* is a singer-songwriter, whereas in France the term designates, typically, a satirical or humorous monologist, a kind of stand-up comic.

4 According to Serge Lama, who invited Lemay to open for one of his concerts at the festival Chorus des Hauts-de-Seine in April 1996 as she was just beginning her career in France, there's a "before" and an "after" Lemay: "She arrived and smashed the barriers of modesty that certain women have. She took off the locks. Many women recognized themselves in Aznavour's songs. Today, they recognize themselves in what Lynda sings because she expresses exactly what women are thinking" (Troadec, "Lemay" 94).

5 The whole show is captured on the classic double album, *J'ai vu le loup, le renard, le lion*. Years later, they still didn't know which of them was the wolf, which the fox, which the lion! (Vigneault 235)

6 It's worth noting that Vigneault had heard Leclerc sing at the seminary in Rimouski back in 1948 and had said to himself that he hoped one day to write

and sing songs like that (Vigneault 229).

7 *Perspective*, 9 November 1968, by Denise Boucher, cited by Normand 93.

8 My friend, Bruno Roy, poet, novelist, and essayist, has recently published an entire book analyzing the show and its importance: *L'Osstidcho ou le désordre libérateur*. Montreal: XYZ, 2008).

9 Lucien Rioux, *Robert Charlebois*, collection "Poésie et chansons", Seghers, 1973, cited by Norman, 96.

10 Notably, in the first decade of the 20th century, Yvette Guilbert, the libertine, and Théodore Botrel, the ultra-reactionary. Many French stars sang in Montreal, in particular, during the 1950s and 1960s (Hélène Hazéra, in an email notation to the author, 2 February 2009).

11 Richard Desjardins, on the other hand, although successful for a number of years, was unceremoniously dumped by his French record company when his latest record didn't meet sales expectations (Desjardins). He is held in high esteem by critics and fellow songwriters: Cabrel sang "Quand j'aime une fois j'aime pour toujours" on a compilation – something he never did for anybody; Renaud fought for his recognition in France. His original career between song and documentary filmmaking marked him as an outsider (Hélène Hazéra, in an email notation to the author, 2 February 2009).

12 Luc Plamondon on the Quebec-France

connection: "Even in France, they wonder how it is that French song is created in Quebec ... I was asked why the two most important francophone singers (Diane [Dufresne] and Robert Charlebois) were Québécois. In twenty years, Québécois song has gone from the Middle Ages to the 21st century ... I don't think there are authors in France whose father and grandfather didn't even know how to write ... which is my case. We aren't crushed by our culture, but we have the instinct for the beautiful, for the discovery of things which have value, a creative instinct" (Normand 137).

13 Cf. Rudent, Catherine, "La télévision française et les 'voix québécoises' populaires: Le trompe-l'œil d'un étiquetage médiatique," *Intersections. Canadian Journal of Music/Revue canadienne de musique,* 27.1 (2006): 75–99, cited by Prévost-Thomas 167.

14 Hélène Hazéra, in an email notation to the author, 2 February 2009.

15 Interview on the "Cinq dernières minutes" segment of the 1pm *Journal télévisée*, France 2, 30 January 2009.

16 Cf. a hilarious video by Rivard, not without relevance here: http://fr.youtube.com/ watch?v=q3zBPnIYavI.

17 My friend Denis Mouton points out that Rivard plays a similarly supportive role for Pierre Barouh every time he comes to Quebec and often joins him on stage.

18 Fabienne Thibeault had better luck, but recognized it for what it was. Her comparison between Paris and Quebec is worth noting: "Over there, once you're accepted, it's less hard than here where you always have to be absolutely the best. Because of the size of the population, in Europe, there's room for almost everyone who's ready to work. Here they ask you to be different each year, but, at the same time, not to change ... Still, in Paris, it's *Starmania* that opened doors for me. The critics were more favorable to the Québécois than to the French: maybe we're more 'musical' than they are!" (Normand 156).

19 The festival I organized in the Boston area from 1993 through 1998, "L'Air du temps," changed its dates from March to November to collaborate with the Coup de cœur in Montreal and share certain artists.

20 Conversation with the author, 22 January 2009.

21 Article by Michel Troadec, author of the in-depth "Chorusgraphie" of Lemay, which I follow here, indicating pages parenthetically.

22 Denis Mouton notes that it was a Québécois, Gilbert Rozon, who brought Trenet, as it were, out of retirement, persuaded him to sing and record again, and became his last impresario (email to the author).

Works Cited

Blain, François. "Le baromètre du temps qui passe." *Chorus* 64 (Summer 2008): 137–44.

Canetti, Jacques. *Mes 50 ans de chansons françaises*. Paris: Flammarion, 2008.

Cormier, Sylvain. "L'Osstidcho – le mythe retrouvé." *Le devoir* (8-9 February 2003). Web. 29 January 2009. http: www.ledevoir.com/2003/02/08/20096. html.

Desjardins, Richard. "Le livre de ma vie." *Chorus* 64 (Summer 2008): 140–1.

Deplasse, Hervé. Conversation with author. Disques Archambault, Paris. 19 January 2009.

Hazéra, Hélène. Conversation with author. Radio-France. 19 January 2009.

Hidalgo, Fred. "Je me souviens ..." *Chorus* 64 (Summer 2008): 116–17.

Legras, Marc. "Chanter au Québec." *Chorus* 64 (Summer 2008): 118–34.

Normand, Pascal. *La chanson québécoise: Miroir d'un peuple.* Montreal: Éditions France-Amérique, 1981.

Prévost-Thomas, Cécile. "Céline, Isabelle, Lynda, Pierre et les autres?: Les raisons du succès international d'une certaine chanson québécoise." In *À la rencontre d'un Québec qui bouge: Introduction générale au Québec.* Ed. Robert Laliberté. Paris: Les éditions du CTHS, 2009. 167–86.

Roy, Raoul. *Le chant de l'alouette.* Sainte-Foy, Québec: Les presses de l'Université de Laval and Ici Radio-Canada, 1969.

Sylvain, Jean-Paul. *Félix Leclerc.* Montreal: Éditions de l'homme, 1968. As cited in Normand, 43–5.

Supervielle, Thierry. "Les Cowboys fringants: L'expédition verte." *XRoads* (December 2008): 16–17.

Thérien, Robert. *Félix Leclerc: Chansons perdues, chansons retrouvées.* CD booklet. Expériences, 2004.

– Personal emails to author. December 2008-January 2009.

Troadec, Michel. "Exclaim, un label québécois en France." *Chorus* 64 (Summer 2008): 142.

– "Lynda Lemay: La scène est son royaume." *Chorus* 46 (Winter 2003–04): 86–108.

Vigneault, Gilles. "La Chanson québécoise, c'est le miroir de poche qui nous a permis de nous regarder en face." Interview with Jean Sarrazin. In *Dossier Québec.* Ed. Jean Sarrazin. Paris: Stock, 1979. 223–38.

Weber, Albert. "Gaële: Cockpit franco-québécois." *Chorus* 64 (Summer 2008): 156.

Ce soir je chante à l'Olympia
Tonight I'm Singing at the Olympia

ROBERT CHARLEBOIS

Ce soir je chante à l'Olympia

Ce soir je chante à l'Olympia
Je sais qu'le tout Paris est là
J'ai des trémolos dans la voix
Comme si c'était la première fois
Salut Bruno je te revois
Dans la fumée de ton cigare
Je sais qu'tu veilles sur moi ce soir

Comme le fantôme [d]e l'Olympia
Les oiseaux chantent dans les bois
Pavarotti à l'Opéra
Mais si vous préférez ma voix
Ce soir je chante à l'Olympia
Ce soir je chante à l'Olympia
Soir de première soir de gala
Barbara a mis son boa
Et Bécaud sa cravate à pois
Gainsbourg s'est arrêté au bar
Nougaro est toujours en noir
Là bas au bout du corridor
J'entends le rire de Salvador
Et dans cette arche de Noé
Dabadie et Delanoë
Parmi la foule [s]e sont noyés
C'est l'atelier des paroliers
Julien est là avec Miou-Miou
Elle est sa préférence à lui

Tonight I'm Singing at the Olympia

Tonight I'm singing at the Olympia
I know *tout Paris* will be here
I have tremolos in my voice
As if it were the first time
Hey, Bruno,[1] I can still see you
In the smoke of your cigar
I know you're watching over
   me tonight

Like the phantom of the Olympia
The birds are singing in the woods
Pavarotti[2] at the Opera
But if you prefer my voice
Tonight I'm singing at the Olympia
Tonight I'm singing at the Olympia
Premiere evening, gala evening
Barbara's[3] wearing her boa
And Bécaud[4] his polka-dot tie
Gainsbourg[5] stopped off at the bar
Nougaro[6] is always in black
Down at the end of the hall
I hear Salvador's laugh[7]
And in this Noah's ark
Dabadie[8] and Delanoë[9]
Have drowned in the crowd
It's the lyricists' workshop
Julien[10] is here with Miou-Miou[11]
She's the one he prefers

France Gall est-elle avec celui	Is France Gall[12] with the guy
Qui lui joue du piano debout	Who plays piano for her, upright
Diane Dufresne et Polnareff	Diane Dufresne[13] and Polnareff[14]
Sont arrivés en astronef	Arrived in a spaceship
N'essayez pas d'les reconnaître	Don't try to recognize them
Sous leurs frisettes sous leurs lunettes	Beneath their curls, behind their glasses
Fabienne Thibeault et Gilles Vigneault	Fabienne Thibeault[15] and Gilles Vigneault[16]
Préfèrent chanter à Bobino	Prefer singing at Bobino[17]
Moi je l'avoue j'me sens chez moi	Me, I admit, I feel at home
Quand je reviens à l'Olympia	When I come back to the Olympia
Y'en a qui chantent dans des Palais	Some sing in Palaces
Qui n'ont de palais que le nom	Palaces in name only
Palais des Sports ou des Congrès	Palais des Sports or Palais des Congrès
Pour cette année je vous dis non, non, non, non	For this year I say no, no, no, no
Je n'me prends pas pour Serge Lama	I don't take myself for Serge Lama[18]
Le champion de ces marathons	The champion of these marathons
De toute façon on sait déjà	In any case, we already know
Qu'il se prend pour Napoléon	That he takes himself for Napoleon
C'est pas demain qu'on me verra	You won't see me any time soon
Faire le pantin à l'hippodrome	Clowning around in the Hippodrome[19]
Si quelque part j'ai un royaume	If I have a kingdom somewhere or other
Je veux qu'ce soit à l'Olympia	I want it to be at the Olympia
Aznavour s'y voyait déjà	Aznavour[20] could see himself here
Quand il était pas plus haut qu'ça	When he was no taller than this
Et quand Johnny y est passé	And when Johnny[21] came through
On raconte qu'il a tout cassé	They say he wrecked everything
Au premier rang il y a Montand	In the first row there's Montand[22]
Qui pense déjà qu'la prochaine fois	Who's already thinking that next time
Il pourra tenir plus longtemps	He'll be able to stay longer
Et faire un an [à] l'Olympia	And sing a whole year at the Olympia

Moi aussi j'aime le music-hall	I, too, love the music-hall
Comme Chevalier et Charles Trenet	Like Chevalier[23] and Charles Trenet[24]
C'est pas ma faute si je suis né	It's not my fault if I was born
Dans les années du rock'n'roll	During the rock'n'roll years
Dans les années du rock'n'roll	During the rock'n'roll years
Oui mais	Yes but
Chanteur de rock'n'roll ou pas	Rock'n'roll singer or not
Ce soir je chante à l'Olympia	Tonight I'm singing at the Olympia

Translated with notes by Brian Thompson

Notes

1 Bruno Cocquatrix (1910–1979), French songwriter and music impresario who owned L'Olympia.

2 Luciano Pavarotti (1935–2007), renowned Italian operatic tenor.

3 Barbara, stage name of Monique Andrée Serf (1930–1997), French singer-songwriter.

4 Gilbert Bécaud, né François Silly (1927–2001), dynamic French singer, composer and actor, *Monsieur 100,000 Volts,* debuted at L'Olympia in 1954 and, as the headliner in 1955, attracted 6,000 the first night, triple the capacity.

5 Serge Gainsbourg, born Lucien Ginsburg (1928–1991), controversial French singer-songwriter, actor and director.

6 Claude Nougaro (1929–2004), French songwriter and singer from Toulouse, recorded his first live album, *Une soirée avec Claude Nougaro,* at L'Olympia.

7 Henri Salvador (1917–2008), French singer born in Cayenne, French Guiana, influenced the formulaion of the Brazilian *bossa nova* style and was known for his infectious laugh.

8 Jean-Loup Dabadie (1938–), French journalist, writer, song lyricist, award-winning screenwriter recently elected to the Académie Française.

9 Pierre Delanoë, born Pierre Leroyer (1918–2006), prolific French songwriter/lyricist who wrote some 4,000 songs for dozens of singers such as Edith Piaf, Charles Aznavour, Johnny Hallyday.

10 Julien Clerc, born Paul-Alain Leclerc (1947–), French composer-singer, starred in French version of *Hair.*

11 Miou-Miou, née Sylvette Héry (1950–), French actress with over 70 films to her credit, bore her second daughter, Jeanne – now an actress and comedian – to singer Julien Clerc.

12 France Gall, née Isabelle Geneviève Marie Anne Gall (1947–), popular French "yé-yé" singer, had a long career in collaboration with her husband, singer-songwriter Michel Berger, until his death in 1992.

13 Diane Dufresne (1944–), singer from Montreal, lived for several years in Paris singing in cabarets.

14 Michel Polnareff (1944–), French singer-songwriter popular from the 1960s through the 1980s.

15 Fabienne Thibeault (1952–), singer from Montreal, starred in *Starmania.*

16 Gilles Vigneault (1928–), Québécois
   poet, publisher and singer-songwriter,
   a national treasure.
17 Bobino, a legendary music hall in the
   Montparnasse section of Paris.
18 Serge Lama (1943–), French singer.
19 L'Hippodrome, famous theatre in Paris,
   with live stage productions and, later,
   silent motion pictures.
20 Charles Aznavour, born Shahnour
   Varenagh Aznavourian (1924–),
   Armenian-French singer, songwriter,
   actor and activist, named Entertainer
   of the Century by CNN and Time
   Online in 1998.
21 Johnny Hallyday, born Jean-Philippe
   Smet (1943–), French singer and actor, has sold over 100 million records.
22 Yves Montand, born Ivo Livi
   (1921–1991), Italian-born French actor and singer and international star.
23 Maurice Auguste Chevalier (1888-
   1972), French actor, singer, and popular entertainer.
24 Charles Trenet, born Louis Charles
   Auguste Claude Trénet (1913–2001),
   French singer and songwriter.

(Not so) Separate but Unequal: On the Circulation of Popular Culture Items between France and Quebec

GUY SPIELMANN

Any 'Atlantic crossing' implies a fascination and a critique of the other side of the ocean, as well as an implicit critique of the continent that one leaves behind. There is thus a dialogue that should not simply be seen as a dialogue between cultures, as an interaction between cultures, but as a questioning of these cultures ... (Bessière 387)[1]

While international exchanges in terms of art, literature, film, and other high-profile cultural productions tend to be well-documented but limited in quantity, the circulation of items belonging to popular culture tends to be as massive as it is surreptitious, especially since such items are often modified to fit the target culture in the most unobtrusive manner. Another feature of this type of relationship, its often asymmetrical character, makes the very term of "exchange" questionable, because of implicit "cultural imperialism" (Tomlinson); but does this apply to cultures that are not completely distinct because they share a common heritage and, to some degree, a common language, like the Québécois and the French? In order to answer this question, I will examine various types of evidence, such as television programs and comics (*bande dessinée* or "BD").

Research on popular culture, as I conceive it, does not imply a militant or political – namely, Marxist – agenda that some theorists claim as the inevitable corollary of cultural studies (see for example Frecero 9–10), arguing that artifacts or events usually qualified as "popular" necessarily express the point of view of an oppressed, exploited, or stigmatized group, or at least reflect the experiences and tastes that help define such groups. Besides, even if the asymmetrical nature of cultural exchange between France and Quebec might suggest a kind of neocolonial model, Quebec does not fall into the same category as former colonies, since its current French-speaking population is mostly descended from colonists, not colonized locals. Neither the way in which the Québécois, as a society, were arguably oppressed by their own powerful Catholic clergy, nor the way in which, as a minority group, they were oppressed by Anglo-Canadians really compares with the way in which France treated the people of Senegal, Algeria, or Vietnam. Nevertheless, the fact remains that books, films, songs, and other cultural artifacts from Quebec were not widely disseminated in France until after the end of colonization and, coincidentally, the onset of the Quiet Revolution.

My chosen corpus illustrates how the very notion of "popular culture" should no longer be taken for granted as a stable entity with fixed boundaries that could be dialectically opposed to "high culture," each carrying "a built-in educational requirement, low for the comic strip, high for the poetry of T.S. Eliot" (Gans 95). While the status of Eliot's poetry has not markedly changed, the comics genre has generated works of great narrative and representational complexity (e.g. Schuiten and Peeters's *Les cités obscures* series), as well as a level of critical analysis on a par with the most sophisticated literary scholarship (see Groensteen's doctoral dissertation, *Système de la bande dessinée*). In addition, *bandes dessinées*, unlike American comic books, are not always mass-produced and carry a sale price (at least $15 US per album) that sets them apart from disposable commodities.

Finally, in most artistic forms, postmodern æsthetics have blurred not only categorical distinctions, but also hierarchies, introducing meta levels of understanding that prevent us from ascribing a book, a painting, a show, a film, or any other artifact to a definite place, and negating the once-tenable claim of a fundamental, binary distinction between high and low culture (Gans 3–25).

The Demise (?) of Francophonie

This cautious attitude must extend to – and in fact begin with – a healthy diffidence towards the notion of francophonie, whose currency in North-American academic circles belies its status in France itself. In spite of the well-meaning official pronouncements that the "Organisation internationale de la Francophonie" is an egalitarian group of fifty-six participant countries, regions, and communities among which France holds no privileged status, there is abundant evidence that the creation and circulation of cultural goods remains de facto strongly hierarchical, if not outwardly neo-colonial. Naturally, this could be easily explained by the position of France as one of the largest economies in the world, and as producer of a much greater volume of books, films, comics, musical recordings, newspapers, and magazines than any other country where French is an official or vernacular language. However, the very modest attention given within France to francophone cultural products, in contradistinction to "foreign" products (i.e., not originally created in French), hints at a much greater complexity.

In March 2007, a group of forty-four writers led by Michel Le Bris issued in *Le monde* a manifesto titled *"Pour une 'littérature-monde' en français"* ("Towards a 'World Literature' in French") that proclaimed "the end of francophonie." The occasion was a "potentially historical" occurrence in the realm of major French literary prizes, which a few months previously had gone primarily to non-French writers. The radical, militant text dismissed francophonie as "the last avatar of colonialism" and announced a "Copernician revolution" that would relocate the center of the French-language literary universe "everywhere in the world." Beyond this sensational "death certificate for francophonie" ["acte de décès de la francophonie"], several points in the manifesto relate directly to our topic: the circulation of cultural artifacts in this supposedly centerless universe, the place of Quebec in it, and the status of "popular culture" productions, notably comics.[2]

Ironically, the French literary awards that prompted this manifesto are all bestowed by juries overwhelmingly comprised of established French writers and journalists, and to authors who are mostly published in Paris. What happened in 2007 simply reflected a very real interest in France for literature by "outsiders," who usually do not hail from francophone countries and regions. Curiously, this tract gave particular prominence to Québécois novelist Réjean Ducharme, who, though presented as "one of the greatest contemporary writers," has never received any French literary prize. In fact, before Dany Laferrière won the 2009 Médicis, the last Québécois recipient of a major award (the Prix Fémina) was Anne Hébert for *Les fous de Bassan* back in 1982 – but it was published in Paris by Le Seuil. Similarly, the previous Québécois laureate, some forty years earlier (1947), Gabrielle Roy, won for a Parisian edition by Flammarion of *Bonheur d'occasion*. The persistence of this situation forces us to take with a large grain of salt grandiose claims as to the "disappearance of the center": while indeed Parisian juries have been regularly bestowing prizes on foreign-born authors,[3] these people have in common having been published in Paris and having produced books that are fully compatible with a French mindset. Québécois authors, on the other hand, represent a political entity where French is the main official language, *and* which is not in a developing country, *and* which has its own full-fledged literary scene and economic network (of publishers, libraries, prizes, etc) in addition to its own potential readership numbering in the millions. This conjunction of factors distinguishes Quebec from all other members of francophonie, because of its independence vis-à-vis France. Should we consider it a coincidence that only one Québécois writer has received a major French literary prize since 1982, even while so many other foreigners have? This uneasy position, as we shall see, is far from limited to novelists and literature; it also prevails in domains of "popular culture" where we might not have expected the weight of tradition and of France's "genius" to exert any particular influence.

Television and film

On any given week, programs of nationwide open-access TV channels in France (TF1, France 2 and 3, M6, Arte[4]) include a large dose of foreign imports, most of them dubbed series and films from the United States. While the proportion varies according to the status (public or private) of each channel, it is so high that, in some time slots, there is often a single offering in a single genre that is *not* an import, so that viewers' choices are severely curtailed. However, because French audiences are gluttonous consumers of foreign fictions shown, with rare exceptions, in dubbed versions, such programs end up being perceived as more French, in a sense, than those from francophone countries, which are broadcast with their unfiltered original language track.

In addition, most Francophone countries are either economically unable to put out much original broadcasting, or, like Belgium and Switzerland, too geographically close to France to need a large amount of homegrown programming of their own. As a result, they mostly produce inexpensive, local-interest fare such as news, talk shows, and documentaries, a kind of "francophone" programming that hardly ever appears on French mainstream networks: it is ghettoized on a cable/satellite channel operated directly by the "Organisation internationale de la Francophonie," TV5 Monde,[5] a motley compendium of French-language programs with a predictably weak identity and viewership.

Remarkably, Quebec, the largest producer of television programs in French outside of France, does not contribute in a particularly conspicuous manner to the TV5 Monde grid; and until very recently, Québécois shows hardly ever aired on mainstream French TV. This is all the more intriguing as France imports much of its fiction programming from the US or from European neighbors. Dozens of American series have enjoyed

massive popularity in France, and often outperform competing native programs: in a typical scenario, a majority of the French prime-time audience
prefers to watch a dubbed US cop show over all other offerings, including
a first-run domestic drama.[6]

Similar-themed programming from the UK or Germany has earned
strong followings in France, whereas only half a dozen fiction series from
Quebec have been aired in their original form, including the cop shows
Fortier (2001) and *Pure laine* (2005), and the dramas *Masque* (1997) and
Nos étés (2005), none of which made a lasting impression on French audiences. By contrast, fifty-six English-language Canadian shows in a dubbed
version have been broadcast on various French channels.[7] This lack of
passion for Québécois TV shows mirrors the relatively unenthusiastic reception of feature films: an Anglo-Canadian journalist noted in 2006 that "In
recent years, most Quebec-made films that opened in France failed to win
large audiences, with two notable exceptions: *Les invasions barbares* and
The Last Seduction (Kelly, "*C.R.A.Z.Y.* beats the odds in France"). Paradoxical as it may seem at first glance, lukewarm appreciation has been the
norm, a phenomenon that demands explanation.

Studying the exceptions may provide our best lead towards better
understanding this puzzling situation. Since France manifestly consumes
more films and television programs than it can produce domestically, why
not turn to the "Belle Province," which is eager to export them? Lately,
this question has gained greater acuity, as the Quebec "Société de Développement des Entreprises Culturelles" (SODEC) initiated a new kind of trade
fair by bringing eleven production companies to Paris in December 2008,
in order to meet French distributors. The promotional copy for the fair
alleges that "The export of Québécois television programs has been on
the rise for the past few years ... There exists a new market for series in
France and the goal of the first *Vitrine TV-Québec* is to help professionals in this trade consolidate and develop their activities" (SODEC "Vitrine
TV-Québec"). Such an event reflects a concerted effort from Québécois
producers to break into the French market – the reverse being unneces-
sary, since TV channels in Quebec already import a large volume of French
TV programming – and the news that French networks had picked up a
number of series and sitcoms was greeted with a mixture of glee and surprise
in Quebec (Morissette).

Nevertheless, a fundamental ambiguity remains as to the exact terms of
these exports: "We all have in mind the great success encountered by the

adaptation of *Un gars, une fille*, but let us not forget the broadcast on French channels of series such as *Catherine, Fortier, Grande ourse, Pure laine, Minuit le soir*, among others" (SODEC "Vitrine TV-Québec"). Indeed, among all the shows listed here, *Un gars, une fille* definitely stands out because it proved a genuine audience pleaser and scored very significant ratings throughout its five-season run;[8] a missing but crucial detail, however, is that a completely new set of episodes was filmed with French actors, locations, and themes instead of the Québécois original (created by Guy Lepage, a former talk-show host). Nothing else was exported other than the concept of the show: short capsules about the conjugal life of a supposedly typical, but very quirky couple, that embodies in comedic form the eternal love-hate relationship between men and women, and whose originality resides mostly in its peculiar camera work and editing style.[9] As a result, the vast majority of its French viewers had no idea that this sitcom actually hailed from Quebec, since all traces of its origins were removed; hence the ambiguity of claiming it as an example of successful export, alongside other shows that aired in their original format and, as a result, did not do nearly as well. Indeed, the "European French" version of *Un gars, une fille* worked so perfectly and gained such visibility that Lepage capitalized on it to sell his formula to nineteen other countries worldwide, among which only one is francophone (Belgium) – another clue that the show had little Québécois specificity, and therefore that the favorable reception it enjoyed in France could hardly be taken as a harbinger of a "Quebec invasion" of French TV.

I would argue that, conversely, the French triumph of *Un gars, une fille* demonstrates how Québécois shows do not play well to French audiences unless they are "adapted" culturally and linguistically, which illustrates the elusive value of francophonie as an operational notion outside of academia, at least in the realm of popular culture: the francophone origin of a television program not only does not guarantee its eventual success in the French market, but it may rather prove a liability. Although this principle holds particular currency in France itself, French-made fictions sell very poorly abroad, and often, within the French market itself, cannot compete against American imports (Dufour, "Télévision, la crise des séries"); their conspicuous presence on Quebec TV simply reflects the need for French-language programming there.

No one knows for sure if the principle of exporting a formula, rather than an actual show, will turn into a solid trend; for now at least, Québécois producers appear to have opted for adaptation in their approach to the French market. M6, which has a track record of competing with larger, more established channels by airing unconventional, sometimes controversial programs, picked up *Les Bougon, c'est aussi ça la vie!*, a politically incorrect sitcom about a family of social parasites devoted to defrauding every kind of government agency – and "which opens the way for irreverent humor, a neglected niche on French television" (Fraissard). Even before it premiered, *Les Bougon* drew sharp criticism for its stark portrayal of working-class class characters as immoral, shiftless, petty crooks; a French critic described it as "the kind of program that is most unlikely to turn up on our TV screens: too trashy, too subversive" (Chevilley).

Far from being harmed by its sudden notoriety, the show was extolled by some European television executives as an example of much needed "bolder" programming; the management of TSR (the French-Language Swiss channel), stating that "La Belle Province is now on the cutting edge of TV fiction, in terms of production volume, of quality and of success," made known its intention of "paying heed to the audacity of Quebec, clearly in evidence these days through the French adaptation of *Les Bougon*" (Dufour, "La TSR mise gros sur les feuilletons"). Yet in an interview with *Le monde*, one of the writers expressed his disappointment that the French had considerably toned down Québécois humor in their adaptation (Séry, "Le bon filon").

Perhaps because of its controversial appeal, the show spurred unprecedented interest in Québécois series: the 2008 "Marché international des films et des programmes pour la TV, la vidéo, le câble et le satellite" (MIPCOM), held in Cannes within a few weeks of the *Bougon* October premiere on M6, was abuzz with announcements that French TV networks were eagerly shopping for more programs made in Quebec, such as *C.A.*, *Tout sur moi*, *Les sœurs Elliot et le gentleman*, *Les hauts et les bas de Sophie Paquin*, *Minuit, le soir*, and *Les Lavigueur* (Morissette). In most cases, however, these shows were not bought to be distributed in France in their original form, but remade with French actors in French locales and modified to reflect French more – a practice that illustrates how this "capacity of absorption" through which the center of the French cultural universe "used to force writers from abroad to shed their baggage and conform to the mold of [the French] language and its national history" is not nearly as outmoded as the signers of "Pour une 'littérature-monde' en français" would have us believe.

Why then choose shows from Quebec and not other countries? It could be argued that the French feel a certain kind of spiritual and cultural kinship towards their cousins across the Atlantic and that it is easier to rework material already in French; but the decisive factor seems to be the emerging "Quebec touch," a combination of effective story-telling, serialization, rhythm, and off-beat humor (Morissette), which is gaining worldwide recognition. The French simply happen to have quicker, more direct access to programming that is also much in demand elsewhere, even though, on the other hand, it is ultimately difficult to disentangle the sentimental from the practical reasons that lead producers from Quebec to seek distribution on the French market above others.

Novel as it may be, the recent peak of interest for Québécois programs has not yet brought about a revolution in the way they will be viewed on French TV, although some changes are already taking place. Several of the negotiations that occurred during the 2008 MIPCOM introduced a new possibility: rather than reshooting shows, the French could dub them with a "metropolitan" track. A Montreal journalist reporting this information wondered if the producers were upset at this prospect; but Pixcom's André Dupuy, who stands a good chance of selling several series to French networks (*Destinées*, *Le 7e round*, and *Au nom de la loi*), replied that the need for dubbing, though currently inevitable, might disappear over time, when buyers have supposedly gotten used to watching and enjoying these shows in their original versions (Morissette). Only time will tell if French audiences, who never much liked viewing Québécois shows either with their original soundtrack or with "metropolitan" French subtitles, eventually grow comfortable enough with what they still consider a nonstandard form of their language; until then, such programs are no different than imports from elsewhere.

A case in point is the remarkable success of Denys Arcand's *Les invasions barbares* (2003), which offers a prime example of puzzling evidence in the circulation of cultural products from Quebec to France. The most surprising of the thirty-seven awards that this movie won worldwide are the three "Césars" for best director, best film, and best writing ("Palmarès 2004"), not because it did not deserve them, but because, according to the rules of the "Académie des Arts et Techniques du cinéma," these awards are specifically meant for French films, directors, actors, writers, and technicians – there is a special category for best foreign film. Yet *Les invasions* is a film whose topic, location, director, and actors are all Québécois; only because its production funding was primarily (though not entirely[10]) French did it qualify to compete for a *César*; but when it also won the 2004 Oscar for Best Foreign Language Film, it was considered as "Canadian" by the US Academy of Motion Picture Arts and Sciences ("Oscars 2004"). Besides funding, another reason why this particular film could pass as French is that its linguistic specificity appears minimal, as the mostly urban, well-educated characters (Rémy, the hero, is a Montreal professor) speak a variety of French that remains fully comprehensible to all francophones. In addition, the erudite references in this witty, wry satire of a decadent society place *Les invasions* squarely in the league of intellectual cinema, not popular entertainment – and therefore, somehow, less identifiably Québécois.

The international exposure coming from the numerous awards bestowed upon this film gave its actors an opportunity to expand their careers, and the choices they made are telling: relative newcomer Marie-Josée Croze, crowned best actress at the 2003 Cannes festival for her portrayal of a junkie in *Les invasions*, resettled in Paris soon thereafter and was cast in a dozen French films within the next five years, but not in a single Quebec production (Kelly, "'I just wanted to live in Paris'"). Stéphane Rousseau, the other young lead, while not entirely turning his back on Quebec,[11] parlayed his new fame into multiple appearances on popular French talk shows (*T'empêches tout le monde de dormir*, *On n'est pas couché*, *On a tout essayé*, *Tout le monde en parle*), and teamed up with top French comic Frank Dubosc in a 2007 TV special, before landing parts in *Modern Love*, a French light comedy, and, more importantly, in the 2008 Gallic big-budget *Astérix aux Jeux Olympiques*. Yet, the French press, when mentioning his presence in *Astérix*, still routinely identified him as being from Quebec (e.g. Perrin 10), which proves that he has not completely blended in, despite having become a somewhat familiar presence on French TV. In her praise of another up-and-coming actor, Marc-André Grondin (who debuted in *C.R A Z.Y.* in 2006), a journalist for the mainstream cinema magazine *Première* noted that "he might just become the very first Québécois matinee idol to actually have a screen career in France. *Crazy*, isn't it?" (VLB 22)

By contrast, Rémy Girard, the central character in *Les invasions* and a favorite of Arcand's, who cast him in both *Le déclin de l'empire américain* (1986) and *Jésus de Montréal* (1989), has remained homebound, except for bit parts in south-of-the-border productions (in *Blades of Glory* and a Dunkin Donuts commercial); there is no evidence of his attempting (or being offered) a cross-over into French film or TV. The obvious difference is age, and the fact that Girard has become an iconic presence on Quebec television, appearing as Pogo in *La petite vie* (seven episodes in 1993–94), as Stan in *Les Boys* (1997–2008), and as Paul in *Les Bougon*.

From a purely Canadian perspective, this state of affairs may offer more advantages than drawbacks, as "the key difference between Quebec and the rest of Canada [is that] in Quebec, the film distributor can count on massive media support via the province's extensive stable of 'vedette' magazines and TV talk shows ... Given the linguistic restraints, Quebec's stars tend to stay and work at home" (Kelly, "Seducing the Canadian moviegoer"). True as this may be (or have been) from an Anglo point of view, the careers of Croze, Rousseau, and Grondin nevertheless exemplify a new pattern where ambitious Québécois actors must find validation in France in order to reach international stature, even if they do not necessarily try to branch out into English-language film; it is clearly not possible for them to earn this level of recognition as Québécois actors, in Québécois productions.[12] *Les invasions*, while very officially sanctioned as a French film, did not fully function as one in the sense that its success only afforded its young stars a stepping stone to recasting themselves as French actors, not de facto stardom in France.

In fact, *Les invasions* and *Les Bougon* provided two variations on the same main theme, the decadence of the Quebec welfare system: in one case, the character played by Girard is a victim of disintegrating public health care; in the other, he presides over a mafia-like family gang that specializes in abusing and defrauding this same system. While cynicism dominates both visions, the difference between the roles played by Girard is that Rémy belongs to the intellectual middle class, whereas the Bougons are definitely proletarian: critics have pointed out similarities between the series and *Married with Children* or *My Name Is Earl*, and a journalist for *Le monde* described *Les Bougon* as a French treatment of the "White Trash" stereotype, worrying that the complaisant, casual association of poverty and crime reflected a right-wing ideological subtext (Serisier). While such a political interpretation remains debatable, there is no question that *Les Bougon* puts forth a depiction of popular culture quite unlike what we see in the educated, sophisticated, and affluent milieu featured in *Les invasions*, and appeared on a channel that specializes in foreign imports and provocative, sometimes scandalous programming (M6). The presence of Rémy Girard in the leading part in both productions underscores the potentially dual nature of cultural artifacts, as if *Les invasions* and *Les Bougon* were two faces of the same coin, which get treated very differently when it comes to their circulation in France. The "low culture" side, while not rejected, is refashioned so as to filter out the Québécois elements.[13]

Bande dessinée

Bande dessinée (BD) provides another interesting litmus test because it enjoys a very high profile in France, both in terms of cultural status and of economic success, while its American counterpart, comics, is either treated as "entertainment" (i.e. a commercial property with little artistic merit) or remains bound to a niche market (graphic novels). The recent trend of adapting comics into major Hollywood movies has not fundamentally changed this value system: in North America, comics may now be respected for their money-making potential, but they are not quite yet fully put on a par with literature, as in Europe.[14]

In both France and Belgium, *bande dessinée* has long been considered as one of the liberal arts – *le 9e art* – a distinction first claimed in jest,[15] but later fully legitimized by the creation of state-sponsored museums and research libraries,[16] as well as by critical discourse in scholarly journals, dissertations, and monographs. This attention from scholars and intellectuals has coincided with huge sales, turning *bande dessinée* into a major cultural phenomenon: in the fall of 2008, for instance ("la rentrée," when the largest number of new books are launched in France), 956 new BD titles appeared (in addition to 446 manga and manhwa translated from the Japanese and Korean) from 160 different publishers, an output that dwarfed the 676 novels (including 463 French ones) scheduled to be released at the same time. Moreover, 23 leading BD titles had an initial print run of 100,000 copies, a remarkable feat in a country where 80 percent of new novels have a print run under 5,000, while only about 15 titles by established, best-selling authors reach the 50,000 mark ("La Rentrée BD").

By comparison, in August 2008 alone, Glénat put on the market 1.8 million copies of the latest installment in its leading BD series *Titeuf*. Although much criticism has been aimed at the popular draw of *Titeuf*, a series by Swiss-born Zep, whose target reader is between ten and twelve years old and which focuses on pre-adolescent sexual themes, other comics enjoy both large volume sales and widespread appreciation: *Tintin* and *Astérix* have inspired numerous articles, journal issues, museum exhibits, and erudite monographs, while selling in the hundreds of millions worldwide. As a result, *bande dessinée* has now completely caught up with traditional literary genres, to the point that Belgian critic Jan Baetens (2004) has argued that the trend of adapting literary classics, far from benefiting *bande dessinée* and raising its status, represents a serious threat to its integrity. Obviously, "Cartoons and cartooning break down distinctions ... between high and low art" (Garval and Goulet 159).

Be that as it may, the situation is dramatically different in Quebec, though not always in a visible manner. A striking, immediate difference between an American and a Québécois bookstore or public library is the greater space devoted to comics and BD in the latter: yet the importance of BD in Quebec cannot be analyzed merely as a transposition of a French cultural structure, because most of the titles available are actually imported from Europe. While French-speaking Canadians value BD relatively more than their English-speaking counterparts (and other Americans) value comics, this proclivity has not turned Quebec into a major international creative center of French-language BD – which, paradoxically, has a long and extremely rich history there.

In fact, Mira Falardeau, who wrote two monographs on the subject (1994 and 2008), has established that the very first BD published in the French language were contributed by Albéric Bourgeois to a Montreal newspaper, *La patrie*, in 1904 (Falardeau 2000) – just a few years after the comic strip now universally recognized as the originator of the genre, Outcault's *The Yellow Kid* (in the *New York World*, 1896), and long before anything comparable was done in Europe.[17] Falardeau notes that the vitality of comics production owed much to its tackling social and political subject matter, and that its cultivation of a homegrown type of humor made it a significant vector in affirming national identity (*Histoire de la bande dessinée* 39–40). After such an auspicious beginning, however, Québécois BD remained bound to local-interest themes, which ensured its popularity at home while making it all but unexportable abroad. Furthermore, this heyday proved short-lived: by 1910, comics from the US had flooded the Canadian newspaper market, leaving little space to the indigenous production,[18] which entered a fifty-year phase of stagnation (*Histoire* 41–2). Thus the situation of Quebec "at the crossroads of two of the world's largest comics markets" (Charbonneau 165) would prove both a blessing and a curse.

Only the Quiet Revolution would bring about what George Raby famously called "Le Printemps de la bande dessinée québécoise" (1971), a spring awakening that came too late. In the meantime, Franco-Belgian BD had grown into an extremely creative and productive field relying on a powerful network of publishers, distributors, and festivals, which had no need or want for input from Quebec but which was able to easily penetrate and dominate the latter's market. From the 1970s to the mid-1990s, indigenous creators expressed themselves almost exclusively through an impressive variety of magazines ranging from amateur, makeshift "fanzines" to professional publications that tried to emulate either a French or an American model (Falardeau, *Histoire* 91–116; Dubois; Viau). Most of these titles did not last for more than a few years, and many put out less than a dozen issues; more stable ventures like *Croc* (1979–95) and *Safarir* (1987–), while they managed to stay in print much longer, never cracked the European market: the French version of *Safarir* ran for a mere three issues in 1995, and its American avatar (retitled *Nut!*) for eight issues in 1997 (*Beyond the Funnies* 5). Again, this failure can be explained by a choice of themes and references, as well as a sense of humor strongly aimed at the Québécois public – but only to a degree. Among the hundreds of titles from France and Belgium available in Quebec, many rely on themes, references, and humor that are essentially European, yet they are perceived as possessing a kind of "universality," at least within the realm of francophonie.

Even the material form plays a part in this extremely asymmetrical circulation: Franco-Belgian BD production, in the main, uses the "album" format (forty-eight full color glossy A4 pages, with a hard-cover), which requires a large print run to be viable. On the other hand, the vast majority of the Québécois production (by houses like Fidès, 400 coups, Mécanique Générale, La Pastèque, Mille Îles, or Zone Convective) comes in a "graphic novel" format with more pages, various sizes, lower paper quality, and black-and-white or duochrome printing – a format typically reserved to limited runs for a niche audience. As a result, these titles are not widely distributed outside of specialized shops (and now online vendors), even in Quebec, where 95 percent of the stock in general-purpose bookstores comes from mainstream Franco-Belgian publishers (*Beyond the Funnies* 5).

Some recent developments provide useful clues in understanding more precisely this dynamics of exchange, both artistic and commercial, which bears a clear resemblance to what I described earlier for television and popular cinema. When Glénat, one of the major French BD publishers, opened a branch in Quebec (2007) with the avowed goal of recruiting local talent, its director explained quite frankly that he was not interested in the type of work being produced by Québécois authors, but that he wanted to scout promising artists who could adapt to the European market. His boss,

Jacques Glénat, was equally candid about the motivations for initiating a kind of farm system in Quebec, a "very interesting nexus of creativity" that is "unmistakably getting hotter" and that "a publisher must absolutely find ways to exploit" (Deglise). Apparently, the "Quebec touch" commands attention in the field of BD as in that of television, but not to the extent that the French will start massively importing Québécois productions in their original form. In the meantime a few artists from Quebec have already found publishers in France (e.g. Guy Delisle with Delcourt and Julie Doucet with L'Association), while, conversely, some French *bédéistes* have resettled in Quebec; but the most prominent case in the latter category exemplifies the unequal nature of the switch.

In 2006, a new BD series titled *Magasin général* provided an unprecedented focus on traditional Québécois society through its carefully documented chronicle of daily life in the rural setting of a small village, Notre-Dame-des-Lacs, in the 1920s. The five volumes in print so far (*Marie*, 2006; *Serge*, 2006; *Les Hommes*, 2007; *Confessions*, 2008; *Montréal*, 2009) were very favorably received and sell well in France. However, while the authors Régis Loisel and Jean-Louis Tripp do live in Montreal, they are both French and only recently settled in Quebec, after a long and – especially for Loisel – highly successful career in Europe. Moreover, the series was released by Casterman, one of the major Belgian publishers, with serialized previews in the Brussels newspaper *Le soir* and the French magazine *Bodoï*.

In other words, the most widely distributed *bande dessinée* title ever about Quebec has almost nothing Québécois about it, except for the participation of Jimmy Beaulieu, a BD author of his own right, but whose involvement was limited to the "adaptation of dialogues in Quebecois" ["adaptation des dialogues en québécois"] [sic]. It would seem then that subject matter from Quebec, and its linguistic expression, is deemed unsuitable for the French public unless it originates from a European creator, and preferably one with a stellar record (Loisel won the 2003 "Grand Prix de la Ville d'Angoulême," something like the Nobel Prize for comics). Perhaps even more remarkably, Loisel and Tripp were nominated for their work on *Magasin général* at the 2007 Joe Shuster Awards, a recently created competition specifically designed to recognize outstanding achievement in the creation of comic books by Canadian authors – a distinction that, to this day, no bona fide Québécois author has won.[19]

Further evidence of this paradoxical vision of national identity can be found in the collection of short stories that the "Festival de la bande dessinée francophone de Québec" (FBDFQ) commissioned to celebrate Quebec city's 400th anniversary *Québec, un détroit dans le fleuve* (Jimmy Beaulieu, Émile Bravo et al.). Rather than enrolling local talent and entrusting the project to any of the Montreal-based BD publishers (such as La pastèque, Mécanique générale, or Mille Îles), the FBDFQ gathered four Franco-Québécois writing teams and had the collection published in typical European "Album" format by Casterman in Belgium. In light of such circumstances, it is hardly surprising that the panoramic view of Old Quebec City gracing the cover was drawn by a Frenchman (Jean-Louis Tripp of *Magasin général* fame).

New media, new challenges

The evidence I have presented here shows just how difficult it may be to qualify the relationship between Quebec and France when it comes to cultural artifacts and practices that can be categorized as "popular." This very term takes on a peculiar meaning in Quebec, where nationalistic tradition dates back to the origins of the province (Balthazar 6), and where anything emanating "from the people" is believed to help forge collective consciousness (Bouchard 1), whereas elite culture appears undistinguishable from a French standard that serves as a benchmark throughout francophonie. Such reasoning can lead to highly problematic assumptions, for instance when scholars attempt to define the issues facing BD production in Quebec: "In order to be faithful to French Canada, should the language used in comics resemble that of France, that of the French Canadian intellectual elite, or the nonstandard variant spoken by underprivileged socioeconomic groups? This would hardly be at issue if French-language comics were made here, by professionals who are aware of the vernacular linguistic continuum, and could therefore balance standard and popular French in order to do justice to the Franco-Canadian idiom" (Guberman and LeBlanc 77). The authors here seem to believe that there is but one variant of French spoken in France, and that, somehow, "popular" language only exists in Quebec; moreover, they apparently do not know that, since the 1970s, dozens of purely Québécois authors have published hundreds of titles locally, in which all nuances of "l'idiome franco-canadien" are amply represented. As members of the Canadian cultural elite themselves, these academics obviously read newspapers, where comics are almost entirely imported from the US (*Beyond the Funnies* 7), but may never have come across examples of indigenous production, which are not readily available in university libraries or regular bookstores. Thus the issue may not lie with the comics themselves, but with the narrow view of "popular" culture and language by intellectuals who have no lived experience of either.

There is no better way to conclude this survey than to examine a truly exceptional Québécois success story in a medium that literally did not exist ten years ago. Michel Beaudet, an advertising executive specializing on humorous campaigns, imagined a sketch comedy format featuring plasticine puppets with superimposed human mouths and eyes against a fixed backdrop. Having recorded several demonstration skits in a makeshift basement studio, Beaudet pitched the idea to TV networks, but soon became frustrated and impatient at the complicated, lengthy process of getting his vignettes on the air; he shifted strategies and uploaded his short films on the internet as *Têtes à claques.TV* in August 2006, sending the URL to a few dozen acquaintances.

In a perfect example of "viral" information circulation, the site had half a million visitors within a month, and three million by November 2006, as the traditional media started running stories about what appeared to be a remarkable cultural phenomenon. Soon, *Têtes à claques* became the most visited French-language Canadian web site, and by February 2007 Bell Canada had acquired the rights to use the characters on its cell phone screens; a few months later, the French telephone operator SFR followed suit as the reputation of the clips continued to spread and Beaudet, now working with two associates, started selling branded merchandise and a DVD. Canal +, the main French pay channel, purchased all forty-five original vignettes and aired them in January 2008, only a month after Radio Canada. When Beaudet came to France to negotiate contracts with cell phone companies, he was interviewed in prominent papers like *Le monde* and *Libération*, an increase in exposure that brought the number of French visitors of *Têtes à claques.TV* to 800,000 monthly (Parent).

The most unusual dimension in the triumph of *Têtes à claques* is not its sheer scale, or the speed at which it happened – there have been many such cases in recent years – but the ease with which it gained a following in France as strong as its original viewer base in Canada, without a need for adapting, remaking, or repackaging. Among all artistic forms and products that have ever been brought from Quebec to France, none has even come close to achieving this level of recognition, even though most of the characters in the series express themselves in a definitely popular Québécois variant of French, including vocabulary (*ti-papoutes, tuque*), colloquialisms ("les p'tites poules vont capoter," "drette dans le schling") and "anglicismes" ("C'est pas beautiful, ça!" "Ostie que t'es wise!") that have absolutely no currency in France. Even references to familiar situations and objects from everyday Québécois life that remained opaque to French people – early on, thousands were wondering about the exact nature of pop tarts, an unknown delicacy in Europe that figured prominently in a vignette about Halloween – did not raise serious obstacles.

Though Beaudet and his team later produced a few clips especially for the European market, he has been completely unapologetic about the fundamentally Québécois flavor of the skits, including dialogues in a colloquial variant of French heavily laden with English words and structures. He was comforted – if somewhat surprised – by the fact that viewers in France did not want the dialogues dubbed, even though they sometimes could not understand them (Parent). When the DVD collection came out, however, the audio track offered subtitles in English, Québécois, and *français international*: an acknowledgement of the difference between two languages, but also a nod to the determination of viewers outside of Quebec wishing to watch the vignettes in their original form.

How could Beaudet achieve in a few months what his fellow writers, directors, and producers had not managed after years of efforts? As one French journalist noted, the stunning international success of *Têtes à claques*, like that of hidden camera bloopers produced by the Québécois production company, Just for laughs (Juste pour rire, an offshoot of the eponymous yearly festival held in Montreal), illustrate an incipient "globalization of laughter" and, more generally, a new model in the circulation of cultural goods (Séry, "La Mondialisation du rire"). Although he quickly received enticing offers to adapt his skits to traditional television and film formats, Beaudet decided to retain control of the production process and stay with his original on-line formula, while improving quality and pursuing new avenues such as dubbing the skits in English (Dreyfus).

By dealing directly with his audience, free of interference from the traditional media and outside the control of any power entity (*Têtes à claques* was launched without state subsidies or corporate sponsorship), Beaudet demonstrated, in effect, how Internet technology could make possible the development of popular culture under radically new conditions – a culture by the people and for the people, as it were. He also disproved the logic of television executives on both sides of the Atlantic, who consider that

French audiences could not possibly stand to watch an unedited Québécois show. For now, *Têtes à claques* remains an exception; but it may well be a harbinger of a new era when the circulation of popular culture items between France and Quebec will become an exchange, in the strictest sense of the word.

Notes

1 All translations are the author's, unless otherwise indicated.

2 For additional discussion of "littéra-ture-monde," see Jane Moss's article in this volume.

3 The Goncourt was awarded to Atiq Rahimi (Afghanistan), Amin Maalouf (Lebanon), and Tahar Ben Jelloun (Morocco); the Renaudot to Tierno Monénembo (Guinea) and Ahmadou Kourouma (Ivory Coast); the Fémina to Dai Sijie (China); the Interallié to Eduardo Manet (Cuba); the Grand prix du roman de l'Académie française to Vassilis Alexakis (Greece) and both the Goncourt and Grand Prix du Roman L'Académie française to Jonathan Littell (United States).

4 These channels drain the vast majority of viewers, as cable and satellite access remain marginal. Channels with a regional reach, such as Télé Monte-Carlo (TMC) or Radio-Télévision Lux-embourg (RTL), carry an even greater proportion of dubbed foreign programming, and free access to a greater number of channels through the quickly spreading digital broadcasting system (TNT) has only increased the overall ratio of non-French programming visible within France.

5 TV5 Monde is one of four "opérateurs directs de la Francophonie" (with the "Agence universitaire de la Francophonie" (AUF), Senghor University in Alexandria (Egypt), and the International League of Francophone Mayors). See the official web site of the OIF at

http://www.francophonie.org/oif /francophonie.cfm#operateurs.

6 For instance, on 12 January 2008, France 2 (the major public channel) ran three consecutive episodes of *FBI: Portés disparus* (*Without a Trace*) in its prime time slot, easily beating its main competitor TF1, which ran an original fiction piece made in France, *L'amour aller/retour* – a rather ironic twist, as it happens, since privately owned TF1 is the main provider of foreign, especially American, series.

7 According to the *Série télé* web site, going back to the 1970s, 47 German-made series have aired on French TV, 181 from the UK, and 1170 from the United States.

8 *Un gars, une fille,* which ran in Québec from 1997 to 2003 (131 épisodes over seven seasons) started airing in France in 1999; by early 2002, it had reached a remarkable 30 percent audience share, which was essentially maintained through its final season.

9 Even the format was not entirely carried over, as episodes were shortened from twenty-six minutes weekly to seven daily, giving the show a faster pace, a change further emphasized by choppy editing (most sequences last no more than ninety seconds).

10 Ten different production companies were involved, fewer than half from France – but these include Canal+, the private TV channel that has become a major player in French cinema.

11 He was featured as "Bo Bellingsworth" in *Le cœur a ses raisons,* a spoof of

American soap operas (four episodes, 2006–07).

12 A comparable occurrence of this phenomenon can be found in the field of popular music: although French audiences can prove extremely receptive to Québécois singers, even to the point of "naturalizing" them when it serves a national interest, recording artists from Quebec must struggle in order to achieve significant visibility, whereas their French counterparts immediately find a mass audience when they cross the Atlantic. See Brian Thompson's article in this volume.

13 French cinema in the US follows a similar pattern, whereby "art" or "independent" films, clearly targeted at an upscale audience, are screened in their original versions with subtitles, whereas those deemed to fall into the category of entertainment (mostly action movies and comedies), are remade in Hollywood, with American settings and actors, so as to reach a wider audience. Thus a promising French film is treated on the American market like a promising Québécois film or TV series on the French market: shown "as is" when perceived as art, repackaged when perceived as an entertainment commodity.

14 With perhaps a single exception: the Pulitzer-prizewinning *Maus* by Art Spiegelman.

15 By cartoonists Morris and VanKeer in *Le journal de Spirou* (1964).

16 The Centre national de la bande dessinée et de l'image opened in 1991 in Angoulême (where a festival had been held since 1974), and the Centre belge de la bande dessinée in 1989.

17 "Comics" are defined as a narrative expressed in pictures, with at least some text included in speech balloons – mass production, recurring characters and serialization being secondary criteria. Alain Saint-Ogan's *Zig et Puce*

(1925) was the first French series to fit this definition.

18 This situation still remains in newspapers (see Guberman and LeBlanc 78; *Beyond the Funnies* 7).

19 Conversely, Québécois authors published by a French or Belgian house are also eligible for these awards (see http://joeshusterawards.com).

Works Cited

Baetens, Jan. *"La bande dessinée 'littéraire': Une nouvelle chance pour la littérature, un danger pour la bande dessinée?"* In "Visual Culture," *Contemporary French Civilization* 28. 2 (2004): 252–71. Special edition, eds. Michael Garval and Andrea Goulet.

Balthazar, Louis. "La dynamique du nationalisme au Québec." In *Culture populaire et littératures au Québec*. Ed. René Bouchard. Saratoga, CA: Anma Libri, 1980. 5–18.

Beaudet, Michel. *Têtes à claques*. 5 April 2009. http://www.tetesaclaques.tv.

Beaulieu, Jimmy, Émile Bravo et al. *Québec, un détroit dans le fleuve*. Charleroi, Belgium: Casterman, 2008.

Bessière, Jean. "Présentation." "Traversées atlantiques." *Revue de littérature comparée* 78. 4 (October-December 2004): 387-9.

Beyond the Funnies: The History of Comics in English Canada and Quebec. Library and Archives Canada. 5 April 2009. http://www.collectionscanada.gc.ca/comics/index-e.html.

Bouchard, René. "Avant-propos." In *Culture populaire et litteratures au Québec*. Saratoga, CA: Anma Libri, 1980. 1–2.

– ed. *Culture populaire et littératures au Québec*. Saratoga, CA: Anma Libri, 1980.

Les Bougon, c'est aussi ça la vie. Dir. Alain Desrochers and Daniel Grou. Script by François Avard. Canada, Aetios Production / Radio Canada, 2004–06.

Les Bougon. France, CALT Productions / GMT / M6 Métropole Télévision, 2008.

Charbonneau, Olivier. "Les grandes industries mondiales de la bande dessinée." *Documentation et bibliothèques* 49. 4 (2003): 165–8.

Chevilley, Philippe. "Affreux, sales et méchants." *Les échos* (10 October 2008): 11.

Deglise, Fabien. "Bédé – la maison d'édition française Glénat se donne une base au Québec." *Le devoir* (Quebec), 3 April 2007. A2.

Dreyfus, Stéphane. "Michel Beaudet: 'Il est trop tôt pour adapter les *Têtes à claques* au cinéma.'" Interview. *La croix* (24 June 2008). http://www.la-croix.com/article/index.jsp?docId=2341731&rubId=25041, accessed 5 April 2009.

Dubois, Bernard. *Bande dessinée québécoise: Répertoire bibliographique à suivre*. Sillery (Quebec): Éditions D.B.K., 1996.

Dufour, Nicolas. "Télévision, la crise des séries; les séries TV françaises vont mal. Et pourtant, le genre se modernise. Analyse d'une crise paradoxale." "Samedi culturel." *Le temps* (Zurich), 3 November 2007. 2.

– "La TSR mise gros sur les feuilletons; la chaîne romande change sa manière de produire les séries …" "Culture." *Le temps* (Zurich), 17 October 2008. 1.

Falardeau, Mira. "La BD française est née au Canada en 1904." *Communication et langages* 126 (2000): 23-46.

– *La bande dessinée au Québec*. Montreal: Boréal, 1994.

– *Histoire de la bande dessinée au Québec*. Montreal: VLB éditeur, 2008.

Festival de la bande dessinée francophone de Québec (FBDFQ), 5 April 2009. http://www.fbdfq.com.

Fraissard, Guillaume. "Les Bougon, attachants anti-héros." "TV et Radio." *Le monde,* 12 October 2008. 2.

Freccero, Carla. *Popular Culture: An Introduction*. New York: New York University Press, 1999.

Gans, Herbert J. *Popular Culture and High Culture: An Analysis and Evaluation of Taste*. 1974. Revised ed. New York: Basic Books, 1999.

Un gars, une fille. Official French site. http://www.1gars1fille.com, accessed 5 April 2009.

Garval, Michael and Andrea Goulet. "Introduction." In "Visual Culture." *Contemporary French Civilization* 28. 2 (2004): 159–61. Special edition. Eds. Garval Michael and Andrea Goulet. "Visual Culture." *Contemporary French Civilization* 28. 2 (2004): 159–358.

Groensteen, Thierry. *Système de la bande dessinée*. Paris: PUF, 1999.

Guberman, Solange and Raymond LeBlanc. "La bande dessinée dans les quotidiens de langue française au Canada." *Présence francophone: Revue internationale de langue et de littérature* 27 (1985): 75–87.

Les invasions barbares. Dir. Denys Arcand. France, Astral Films / Canal+ / Centre National de la Cinématographie (CNC), 2003.

The Joe Shuster Canadian Comic Book Creator Awards. http://joeshuster-awards.com, accessed 5 April 2009.

Kelly, Brendan. "'I just wanted to live in Paris'; Marie-Josée Croze, back in Montreal promoting her latest movie, explains why she hasn't worked in Quebec since her stunning performance in *Les invasions barbares*." "Arts & Life." *The Gazette* (Montreal), 14 July 2008. D1.

– "C.R.A.Z.Y. Beats the Odds in France: Strong Opening. Quebec Films Rarely Do so Well There." "Arts & Life." *The Gazette* (Montreal), 10 May 2006. D5.

– "Seducing the Canadian Moviegoer: The Rest of Canada Could Learn from Quebec, Where 'Homemade' Is Not a Dirty Word." "Arts & Life." *National Post* (Canada), 27 April 2004. AL10

Le Bris, Michel et al. "Pour une 'littérature-monde' en français." "Le Monde des livres." *Le monde*, 16 March 2007. 2.

Lepage, Guy A. *Un gars, une fille*. Official Canadian Web Site. http://www1.radio-canada.ca/television/ungarsunefille, accessed 5 April 2009.

Loisel, Régis, and Jean-Louis Tripp. *Magasin général*. 4 vol. Charleroi, Belgium: Casterman, 2006–08.

Morissette, Nathaëlle. "La télé québécoise fait fureur à Paris." *La presse* (Montreal), 16 December 2008. http://www.cyberpresse.ca/arts/television-et-radio/200812/16/01-810755-la-tele-quebecoise-fait-fureur-a-paris.php, accessed 5 April 2009.

"Oscars 2004." Academy of Motion Picture Arts and Sciences Awards Database. http://awardsdatabase.oscars.org, accessed 5 April 2009.

"Palmarès 2004."Académie des Arts et Techniques du cinéma. http://www.lescesarducinema.com/#palmares, accessed 5 April 2009.

Parent, Marie-Joëlle. "Les *Têtes à claques* / Téléphonie française. 50 000 visites de plus dans leur site." *Le journal de Montréal*, 28 June 2007. http://www2.canoe.com/techno/nouvelles/archives/2007/06/20070628-123221.html, accessed 5 April 2009.

Peeters, Benoît and François Schuiten. *Les cités obscures*. 12 vol. Charleroi, Belgium: Casterman, 1983–2008.

Perrin, Élisabeth. "*Astérix aux Jeux Olympiques*. Delon: Ave César." *Le Figaro TV magazine*, 23–29 December 2007. 6–8, 10.

"Québec." *Séries télé*. http://www.serietele.com/serie-pays-8.html, accessed 5 April 2009.

Raby, Georges. "Le printemps de la bande dessinée québécoise." *Culture vivante* 22 (September 1971): 12–23.

"La Rentrée BD." *Livres hebdo* (22 August 2008): 1.

Serisier, Pierre. "*Les Bougon* - La face présentable de la misère." *Le monde des séries* (20 October 2008). http://www.lemonde.fr, accessed 5 April 2009.

Séry, Macha. "Le bon filon québécois." "TV et Radio." *Le monde,* 12 October 2008. 3.

– "La mondialisation du rire." "Analyses." *Le monde,* 2 January 2008. 2.

Tomlinson, John. *Cultural Imperialism: A Critical Introduction*. Baltimore: Johns Hopkins University Press, 1991.

Viau, Michel. *BDQ, répertoire des publications de bandes dessinées au Québec des origines à nos jours*. Laval, Quebec: Éditions Mille-Îles, 1999.

"Vitrine TV – Québec 1ère édition (1er et 2 décembre 2008 – Paris) Organisé par la SODEC en association avec Le Film Français." Société de Développement des Entreprises Culturelles (Quebec). http://www.sodec.gouv.qc.ca, accessed 5 April 2009.

V.L.B. [Véronique Le Bris.] "Les révélations: Marc-André Grondin." *Première* 383 (January 2009): 22.

Contributors

BONNIE BAXTER is a multi-disciplinary artist who has maintained a studio in Val-David, Québec since 1972. She has an extensive exhibition record both nationally and internationally, with work that ranges from Public-Art installations to large-scale pieces in print media, video, performance, and sculpture. She studied at Cranbrook Academy of Art in Michigan and received a MFA from Vermont College of Fine Arts. She has taught in the Print Media program at Concordia University since 1984. In 1982, she founded Atelier du Scarabée, where she has printed for noted artists such as Francine Simonin, Kitty Bruneau, and Jean Paul Riopelle. In 2005 the Musée d'art contemporain des Laurentides presented a ten-year survey of her work, which then toured across Canada and the USA. Bonnie has received grants from the Conseil des arts et des lettres du Québec and Canada Council for the Arts as well as awards at international print biennials in Bhopal, India, and Taiwan. In 2005 she was awarded the Prix à la création artistique en région, du Conseil des arts et des lettres du Québec. Her work is currently represented by Division Gallery in Montreal, Quebec.

ALISA BELANGER is currently a Chancellor Fellow in French and francophone studies at UCLA. She holds a Master's degree in French language and literature from McGill University, where she wrote a thesis entitled "Deuil et co-création dans l'œuvre de Denise Desautels." She has presented papers on Quebec Studies at several academic conferences, including ACQS, ACSUS, and CIEF. Her first publication, an "Introduction to Quebec Poetry" co-written with Dr Vincent Desroches, appeared in the January 2009 issue of *Contemporary French & Francophone Studies*. Her dissertation covers artist's books produced in Quebec and throughout the post-colonial francophone world. Beginning in the fall of 2010, she will be joining Georgetown's French Department as an adjunct.

NICOLE BROSSARD is a prolific poet, novelist, and essayist whose writings are central to the modern, post-modern and feminist traditions in Quebec. Her work has twice received Canada's most prestigious Governor General's prize, and her career was honored in 1999 with Quebec's Athanase-David award. She has received many other accolades and honors, most recently the W.O. Mitchell Prize in 2003 and the Molson Prize of the Canada Council for the Arts in 2006. Many of her works have been translated into English as well as several other languages. Her most recent works are the novel *La Capture du sombre* (2007) and the poetry collection *Ardeur* (2008). An anthology of her poetry spanning the forty years of her career, *D'aube et de civilisation*, also appeared in 2008.

ROBERT CHARLEBOIS is a Quebec author, composer, musician, performer, and actor. He is an important figure in French-language song. Born in Montreal, Quebec, he is best known for songs such as "Lindberg" and "Je reviendrai à Montréal." His lyrics, often written in "joual," are amusing and utilize plays on words. He won the Sopot International Song Festival in 1970. In 1999, he was appointed an Officer of the Order of Canada. In 2008, he was made an Officier of the Ordre National du Québec, the highest distinction given by the Government of Quebec.

MICHEL COCHET, a French actor and theatre director, has performed in many plays, including several with La Lune Bleue company. In 1997 he created his own troupe, La Compagnie du Zouave, with the goal of putting on plays by contemporary authors. He also co-directs the association A Mots Découverts, an artistic collective and experimental laboratory for theatrical writing. The plays he has staged include Philippe Sabres' *Soeurs secrètes* (2000), Larry Tremblay's *Le Déclic du destin* and *Les Mains bleues* (2000), and Bruno Allain's *Par la portière vue imprenable* and *L'anniversaire* (2005), among others.

PATRICK COLEMAN is professor of French and francophone literature at the University of California, Los Angeles. He is the author of *Rousseau's Political Imagination: Rule and Representation in the* Lettre à d'Alembert (1984), *The Limits of Sympathy: Gabrielle Roy's* The Tin Flute (1993), and *Reparative Realism: Mourning and Modernity in the French Novel 1730–1830* (1998). He has edited works of Rousseau and Benjamin Constant for Oxford World's Classics and co-edited several volumes of essays, including *Culture and Authority in the Baroque* (2005). He was editor in chief of *Québec Studies* from 2000 to 2004 and is working on a comparative study of French and English novels of Montreal.

LOUISE DUPRÉ, professor of literature at the University of Quebec at Montreal, is both a feminist literary scholar and the author of an impressive body of poetry, fiction, and dramatic texts. Her poetry collection *La peau familière* (1984) received the Prix Alfred-Desrochers, *Noir déjà* (1993) garnered the Grand Prize for poetry at the Festival international de Trois-Rivières, and her novel *La memoria* (1997) won both the Ringuet Prize of Quebec's Académie des lettres and the Prix de la Société des écrivains canadiens. In 1999, she was admitted to the Académie des lettres, and in 2002, to the Royal Society of Canada. Her most recent play, *Tout comme elle*, received the 2005–06 Critics' Prize from the Association québécoise des critiques de théâtre. Her scholarly works include *Stratégies du vertige* and, more recently, the co-edited collection *Sexuation, Espace, Ecriture: La littérature québécoise en transformation* (2002).

LOUISE FORSYTH is a specialist in the poetry and theatre of Quebec, on which she has given courses, directed theses, delivered scholarly papers and keynote addresses nationally and internationally, published articles and translations, edited special journal issues, published collections of essays, and edited anthologies. Her particular areas of expertise are the works of Nicole Brossard and Quebec women playwrights. She is also a specialist in the francophone theatre of Saskatchewan. She was head of the French Department at the University of Western Ontario, dean of Graduate Studies and Research at the University of Saskatchewan, and president of the Humanities and Social Sciences Federation of Canada. She has received a number of academic honors. She has recently edited *Nicole Brossard: Essays on Her Works* (2005) and *Mobility of Light: The Poetry of Nicole Brossard* (2008) and prepared the three-volume *Anthology of Québec Women's Plays in English Translation* (2006, 2008, 2010). The *Anthology* contains the complete text of twenty-eight plays (1966–2009), introductions to the volume, each play and playwright, and bibliographical material.

PAULA RUTH GILBERT is professor of French, Canadian, and women and gender studies at George Mason University in Fairfax, Virginia. She specializes in Quebec studies and French and francophone women writers, nineteenth-century French studies and the study of Paris, gender and violence, and gender/human rights and narrative. She has written or edited several books, including *The Aesthetics of Stéphane Mallarmé in Relation to His Public; The Literary Vision of Gabrielle Roy: An Analysis of Her Works; Traditionalism, Nationalism, and Feminism: Women Writers of Québec; Women Writing in Quebec: Essays in Honor of Jeanne Kissner; Doing Gender: Franco-Canadian Women Writers of the 1990s; Violence and Gender: An Interdisciplinary Reader; Violence and the Female Imagination: Québec's Women Writers Re-frame Gender in North American Cultures* (McGill-Queen's University Press, 2006), along with numerous articles. She is currently completing work on an edited collection of essays, *Confronting Global Gender Justice: Women's Lives, Human Rights*, forthcoming at Routledge, and a book-length study, "Narrating Female Lives: Human Rights Violations against Women and Girls." Her research has been supported by grants and fellowships.

KAREN L. GOULD is president of Brooklyn College in New York. She has also served as provost and senior vice president for Academic Affairs and professor of French at California State University, Long Beach, as dean at the University of Cincinnati and at Old Dominion University in Virginia. She is the author or co-editor of six books, including *Writing in the Feminine: Feminism and Experimental Writing in Quebec* (Southern Illinois Press, 1990), and more than fifty articles and essays on contemporary Quebec literature, francophone women writers, and the French *nouveau roman*, and is a former editor of the journal *Québec Studies*. She has served as president of the International Council for Canadian Studies and as president of the American Association for Canadian Studies in the U.S. and has been honored with the Canadian Governor General's International Award for Canadian Studies in 2003 and the Donner Medal in Canadian Studies in 2005 for her research and professional contributions to the field of Canadian Studies.

MARY JEAN GREEN is Edward Tuck Professor of French at Dartmouth College, where she also teaches in comparative literature and women's and gender studies. Founding editor of the journal *Québec Studies*, she has written extensively on Quebec women writers in her books *Marie-Claire Blais* and *Women and Narrative Identity: Rewriting the Quebec National Text* (McGill-Queen's University Press). Currently she is completing a book on the rewriting of history in fiction by francophone women, which will include a chapter on Régine Robin. She is a recipient of the Donner Medal of Canada and the Prix du Québec.

SUSAN IRELAND is a professor of French at Grinnell College. Her research interests include contemporary French fiction, Quebec women writers, the Algerian novel, and the literature of immigration in France and Quebec. She has published articles in these areas in journals such as *L'Esprit Créateur* and *Nottingham French Studies*. She is also an editor of *The Feminist Encyclopedia of French Literature* (1999) and, with Patrice Proulx, of *Immigrant Narratives in Contemporary France* (2001) and *Textualizing the Immigrant Experience in Contemporary Quebec* (2004).

LORNA IRVINE is Professor Emerita of English literature, cultural studies and women's studies at George Mason University in Fairfax Virginia. She is the author of *Sub/Version: Canadian Fictions by Women, Collecting Clues: Margaret Atwood's* Bodily Harm and *Critical Spaces: Margaret Laurence and Janet Frame.* She has published many essays and book chapters on a variety of Canadian writers and has frequently taught courses devoted to their work.

RACHEL KILLICK is Professor Emerita of nineteenth-century French studies and Quebec studies in the French Department of the University of Leeds. She has published a critical edition of Michel Tremblay's *Les Belles-Soeurs* (2000), was a guest editor for the 2003 *Globe* issue on "Le Québec au centre et à la périphérie de la francophonie," and most recently edited a collection entitled *Uncertain Relations: Configurations of the Third Space in Francophone Writings of the Americas and Europe* (2005). She served as director of the University of Leeds Center for Canadian Studies from 2005–08, in addition to serving as president of the British Association of Canadian Studies from 2006–08. She was awarded the Ordre des francophones d'Amérique by the Conseil supérieur de la langue française du Gouvernement du Québec in 2004.

CHANTAL MAILLÉ is a professor of women's studies at the Simone de Beauvoir Institute of Concordia University in Montreal. Her principal field of research is in women's participation in politics and on the women's movement in Quebec. She is the author of several key texts in this area, including *Cherchez la femme: trente ans de débats constitutionnels au Québec* (2002), *Malaises identitaires*, co-edited with Micheline De Sève and Diane Lamoureux (1999), and *Les Québécoises et la conquête du pouvoir politique* (1990). She is currently associate editor of the *International Journal of Canadian Studies*.

KAREN MCPHERSON is associate professor of French and francophone studies at the University of Oregon. She was president of the Conseil International d'Études Francophones from 2005 to 2007. Her research focuses primarily on French and francophone women writers. Her publications include articles on Nicole Brossard, Marie-Claire Blais, Simone de Beauvoir, and Maryse Condé. She is also the author of *Incriminations: Guilty Women/Telling Stories* (Princeton University Press, 1994) and *Archaeologies of an Uncertain Future: Recent Generations of Canadian Women Writing* (McGill-Queen's University Press, 2006).

FRANÇOIS MORELLI is professor at Concordia University and graduate program director of the Studio Arts MFA Program. He is best known for his hybrid sculptural/graphic installations and peripatetic performances. He develops found imagery and objects into web-like structures that sprawl and engage with architecture and social space. His intimate drawings and discreet sculptures, while focusing on the human figure, address its psychology, sexuality, and social relationships. His project *Home Wall Drawing (L'art de manger)* (2004) in France bartered twenty-two rubber stamped wall drawings in peoples' homes for home-cooked meals. *Table d'hôte* (2007) at the Hamilton Art Gallery used hand stamped porcelain plates to address the fragility of domestic space through ornamentation and pattern. *Hand to Mouth Drawing* (2008) involved belt head prosthesis with which he drew on the gallery walls.

JANE MOSS taught at Colby College for thirty years before becoming visiting professor and director of Canadian Studies at Duke University. After thirteen years as managing editor, she has become editor of *Québec Studies*. A past president of the American Council for Québec Studies and vice-president of the Association internationale des études québécoises, she currently serves as a councillor of the Association for Canadian Studies in the United States. She has published numerous articles and book chapters on Quebec and francophone Canadian theater and has been guest editor for special issues of *Québec Studies* and *Canadian Literature*. She was awarded the Prix du Québec in 2002 and was made an honorary member of the Société québécoise d'études théâtrales in 2005.

WERNER NOLD joined the National Film Board of Canada in 1961 and since that time he has served as film editor on many groundbreaking and historic projects, including *Pour la suite du monde*, *La vie heureuse de*

Léopold Z., La Gammick, Le Temps d'une chasse, and, perhaps most famously, the *Games of the XXI Olympiad,* a project that involved cutting 200 hours of footage into a feature-length production. In 1977, the year of the film's release, he was awarded the Queen Elizabeth II Jubilee Medal. In 1985, he received the Order of Canada. His work as a film editor has more recently been honored with a tribute by filmmaker Jean-Pierre Masse, *Werner Nold, cinéaste-monteur* (2003). He and Masse are currently completing a second project, *Le montage selon Werner Nold,* in order to preserve the memory and craft of this exceptional and exemplary figure in Quebec cinema.

MONIQUE PROULX is an author and screenplay writer whose works include seven novels and short story collections, and some dozen film screenplays and dramatic texts for television and radio. Her works have won numerous prizes, including two for *Sans Coeur et sans reproche* (1983), and four for *Homme invisible à la fenêtre* (1993). The film she adapted from her novel *Le Sexe des étoiles* (1987) was chosen to represent Canada for the 1994 Oscars, and garnered several awards domestically and internationally. Her most recent novel is *Champagne* (2008), which was a finalist for the 2008 Governor General's Award of Canada.

PATRICE J. PROULX is professor of French and women's and gender studies at the University of Nebraska, Omaha. Her research interests include contemporary Caribbean and Québécois fiction, francophone film, and the literature of immigration in France and Quebec. Her articles have appeared in such journals as the *French Review, Québec Studies,* and *L'Esprit Créateur,* as well as in a number of edited collections. She is an editor of *The Feminist Encyclopedia of French Literature,* and co-edited *Immigrant Narratives in Contemporary France* and *Textualizing the Immigrant Experience in Contemporary Quebec* with Susan Ireland.

MILÉNA SANTORO is an associate professor in the French Department at Georgetown University, with specializations in Quebec Studies and French and francophone women writers. She has published articles on Hélène Cixous, Jeanne Hyvrard, Nicole Brossard, Madeleine Gagnon, and Esther Rochon, among others, and has translated excerpts of works by Jeanne Hyvrard and Michèle Sarde. She produced and introduced a video of Quebec feminist writers entitled *La Théorie un dimanche: Sweet Suite* (ACQS and Le Conifère têtu, 2002). Her first book, *Mothers of Invention: Feminist*

Authors and Experimental Fiction in France and Quebec, was published in 2002 by McGill-Queen's University Press. Santoro served as associate editor for the *International Journal of Canadian Studies* for five years and is currently associate editor for the *American Review of Canadian Studies*.

GAIL SCOTT co-edited *Biting The Error* with Bob Gluck et al. (2004), which was shortlisted for a Lambda award. Her other books include her novel *My Paris* (1999); *Spare Parts Plus Two*, stories and manifestos (2002); the novels, *Main Brides* and *Heroine*; and the essay collections *Spaces Like Stairs* and *La Théorie, un dimanche* (with Nicole Brossard et al). Her translation of Michael Delisle's *Le Désarroi du matelot* was shortlisted for the Governor General's award in translation (2001). She is completing a fourth novel and teaches creative writing at the Université de Montréal. In the fall of 2008 she was Quebec's writer-in-residence in New York.

PATRICIA SMART is a Distinguished Research Professor Emerita of French at Carleton University and the author of *Les Femmes du Refus global* (1998), a finalist for the 1998 Governor General's Award. Her feminist study of Quebec literature, *Écrire dans la maison du Père*, won the Governor General's Award for 1988 and her translation of it, *Writing in the Father's House:The Emergence of the Feminine in the Quebec Literary Tradition* (1991), was awarded the Gabrielle Roy Prize of the Association for Canadian and Quebec Literatures. She is also the author of *Hubert Aquin agent double* (1973) and the editor and translator of *The Diary of André Laurendeau* (1991), a finalist for the Governor General's Award for Translation. She was an editor of *The Canadian Forum* from 1989 to 1998, was elected to the Royal Society of Canada in 1991, and received the Order of Canada in 2004. Her most recent book is a critical edition of Claire Martin's autobiography, *Dans un gant de fer* (2005).

GUY SPIELMANN is associate professor of French at Georgetown University in Washington, DC. He also held visiting positions in the Department of Drama at the Université Marc Bloch/Strasbourg II and in the Department of Performing Arts at the Université Paris X-Nanterre. His scholarly interests cover early-modern European performing arts broadly conceived, with a particular focus on stagecraft and non-literary genres (such as fairground theater and commedia dell'arte), and various forms of popular culture, notably comics. He has published over forty articles in a number of scholarly journals, as well as in numerous collected volumes. In 2002, his book *Le Jeu de l'Ordre et du Chaos: Comédie et pouvoirs à la Fin de règne, 1673–1715* was issued in Paris by Honoré Champion, followed by a critical edition of 18th-century "parades" (farces) with Éditions Lampsaque. This latter publication resulted from both text-driven research and stage production experience, as the theater group he founded in 2002, SapassoussakasS, has been giving "parades," shows, and workshops in Quebec, the USA, France, Tunisia, and the UK.

BRIAN THOMPSON wrote his thesis on "Vision and Blindness in the Novels of André Malraux," after his studies in Greek, German, and Comparative Literature at Harvard, Munich, and Paris. He has translated several books on philosophy and theology from German and French. His own publications are principally on Malraux, Mauriac, and "la chanson." He co-hosts a weekly radio show ("French Toast" on wmbr.org) and produces a 24/7 webcast, "L'Air du temps" (wumb.org), both on music from the French-speaking world. He is president of the AATF in Eastern Massachusetts (http://www.umb.edu/aatf) and founding president of a 501(c)(3) organization working with inner-city young people (earthen-vessels.org). He recently retired after teaching French at the University of Massachusetts at Boston for forty years.

Index

145–6; *La Médée d'Euripide*, 141–56; *Les mots pour le dire*, 141, 146–8; *Oedipe à Colonne de Sophocle*, 144, 155; *Le passé empiété*, 144, 150; *Peer Gynt*, 144; *La tempête*, 144, 154; *Les Troyennes*, 144, 154. *See also* Greek tragedy and mythology, theatre translation

Caron, Jean-François, 170–1
Carrier, Louis-Georges, 76
castles: in the air, 81; in Spain 81, 92n3; in Switzerland, 80, 81
castration, 129; fear of, 213
Catholic Church, 30–1, 39–40, 42, 44, 52, 69–70, 109, 113, 206, 211, 229
Centre de santé des femmes, 53
Centre des femmes, 53
Chagall, Marc, 231
chanson: bawdy, 287; folk, 286; patriotic, 287; political impact of, 290. *See also* song
chansonnier, 21, 288, 290–1, 298n3
Charlebois, Robert, 21, 259, 289, 290–2, 299n12; at L'Olympia, 292, 301–3
Chatelaine, 52
Chaurette, Normand, 161, 166–7, 171–2
Cherchez la femme, 50, 55
Chunnel, 8
cinematographic reworking, 216
civil rights movement, 54
Clauzel, Jacques (Éditions à Travers), 269
Clifford, James, 186
Cochet, Michel, 165, 174–6
collaboration, 12, 19, 20, 21, 79, 138, 144, 228, 234, 266, 268–70, 276, 278–80, 282, 283, 291–4, 297, 299, 303, 327. *See also* transatlantic
Collège Sainte-Marie, 76
Comité de lutte pour l'avortement libre et gratuit, 53
commodification, 3, 7–9, 13, 24n4, 306; gender and, 99, 101
conclusion: of *La capture du sombre*,

88–91; of *Prochain episode*, 87–91; tentative or inconclusive, 87, 88–91
Conrad, Joseph, 101
Conseil du statut de la femme, 53
Corbusier, Le, 101
Corti, José, 72
Council of Trent, 30
Counter Reformation, 30
Crémazie, Octave, 71, 167

Daillebout, Mme Louis, 38
Danis, Daniel, 17, 162, 165, 166–71
David, Gilbert, 168, 170
De Beauvoir, Simone, 14, 50, 51, 52, 53, 137; *The Second Sex*, 50, 51, 52, 53
De Calan, Madeleine, 52
De Decker, Jacques, 170
De Gaulle, Charles, 68
De Kooning, Willem, 231
decolonization, 54, 160
deconstructionism, 55
defeat, 27, 42, 68–9, 206
Delphy, Christine, 51
demoiselle sauvage, 209–10
Des Landes, Claude, 170
Des Rivières, Marie-Josée, 52, 53
Desautels, Denise, 20; *Black Words*, 277; collaborative practices, 276–80; *De la douceur*, 279; *Écritures / ratures*, 276; *L'enfant mauve*, 279; *Nous en parlerons sans doute*, 276; *Novembre*, 279; *Parfois les astres*, 278; *La passion du sens*, 277–8; *La répétition*, 276; *Le signe discret*, 276; *Théâtre pourpre*, 277; *Le Vif de l'étreinte*, 277
Deutsch, André, 73
difference, 13, 17, 55–7, 122, 124, 141, 142, 145, 150, 163, 269; cultural, 41–2, 138, 145, 163, 169, 208, 264, 314; and exile, 142, 144, 152; gender, 57, 87, 98, 151; not the same, 142, 152–3; outsider, 141–2, 144, 149–50;

thinking otherwise, 141–2

Dion, Céline, 292–3, 294, 297

displacement: of the self, 124, 210; Jewish displacement, 217

Djavann, Chahdortt, 133n4; *Comment peut-on être français*, 123, 127–32

Dorion, Hélène, 20, 266–7; *Carrés de lumière*, 272–4; *L'Empreinte du bleu*, 272; *Et ce n'est que vie*, 275; *Mondes fragiles, choses frêles*, 274; *Les Murs de la grotte*, 274; *Passages de l'aube*, 274; *Portraits de mer*, 274; *Voyages de Porphyre*, 274

Du dire au faire, l'egalité entre les hommes et les femmes dans l'espace francophone, 50

Dubois, René-Daniel, 161, 170–1

Dupin, Jacques, 232

Duplessis de Sainte-Hélène, Mère Marie-Andrée, 30

Dupré, Louise, 16–17, 120, 136–8, 278–9; *Tout comme elle*, 16, 138

Duras, Marguerite, 22, 137

Durham, Carolyn A., 143, 156

Edom, 74

English language, 309, 314; English-language writers, 70–1, 77; Mordecai Richler as, 70–1

epistolary genre, 16, 123–5, 127, 129, 134n12

exile, 6, 17, 18, 33, 76, 128, 144, 154, 190, 197, 216, 218, 219, 221, 228, 229, 231, 233, 246, 256n3, 288. *See also* difference

Fabre, Hector, 11

fallas, 75–6

Fanon, Franz, 54

Farhoud, Abla, 171n12

Feaver, Marianne, 234, 257n11

Fédération des femmes du Québec, 54

female reification, 213

feminism: black, 56; of *différence*, 56;

in Euripides 152; in Francophonie, 51; French, 50, 51, 55–8, 143; post-colonial, 56–8; Quebec, 14, 50, 51–7, 58; republican, 56; Western, 57

Les féministes et le garçon arabe, 56

Ferron, Madeleine, 52

festivals: important role of, 294–6

Fitzgerald, F. Scott, 71

flânerie/flâneur/flâneuse, 3–8, 11, 13–15, 18, 23–4, 98, 99–100, 102, 104, 127, 134n10, 181, 185–6, 187–8

Flinker, Karl, 238

Forestier, Marie (Mère Marie de Saint-Bonaventure), 30, 33, 36, 43

Fournier, Jacques (Éditions Roselin), 277–81, 282n1, 283n17

Fournier, Roger, 12

Fraisse, Geneviève, 51

France, 141, 148; French culture, 17, 31, 35, 38, 42, 122, 137–9, 148–9, 165, 193, 199, 201, 312, 316, 319; language of France, 124, 128, 130, 133n4, 151–2, 158–9, 168, 191, 193, 307–11, 313, 319; representations of: in *Adieu Babylone*, 197–8; in *Côte-des-Neiges*, 193; in *Les fruits arrachés*, 198–9. *See also* French language

Franco, Francisco, 69, 75

Françon, Alain, 166

Francophonie, 50–1, 57, 157, 167, 306–8, 310, 317; 12th Summit, 50

Fréchette, Carole, 162–4, 166–7, 171

French Canadian identity, 192, 193, 194–6; in *Les fruits arrachés*, 190, 198–9

French *coopérants*, 137, 138n3

French language, 124, 128, 130, 201, 310–11, 316, 319–20. *See also* France

Front de libération des femmes du Qué-bec, 50, 53, 54, 55. *See also* Quebec Women's Federation, 53

future, 86, 88–9; dystopian vision of 84, 91; and horizon, 84; revolutionary in

Prochain épisode, 89–90; utopian
vision of, 91

Gagnon, Madeleine, 51, 274
Galerie Esperanza, 236
Gallant, Mavis, 22, 71
Gallimard, 72
Garneau, Marc, 272
Garneau, Michel, 171
Gauvin, Lise, 16, 133n3, 158–9, 165,
  167–8, 171n14, 250, 257n22; *Lettres
  d'une autre*, 122–7, 129, 132; "sur-
  conscience linguistique," 158, 159,
  165, 167–8, 171
Gauvreau, Claude, 229
gays and lesbians, 55, 63, 86, 93n12,
  93n17, 106
Genet, Jean, 71
Germain, Jean-Claude, 160
Gheorghiu, Virgil: *La vingt-cinquième
  heure*, 108, 116–20
Giacometti, Alberto, 231
Giacometti, Diego, 241, 242
Giguère, Roland, 267
Girard, Rémy, 313–14
Godbout, Jacques, 159, 207
Goldman, Jean-Jacques, 293–4
Goncharova, Natalia, 231
Goodwin, Betty, 234, 277
Gracq, Julien, 69, 72
Graff Ateliers, 233
Grandbois, Alain, 269–70, 281
Grasset, 72
Greek tragedy and mythology, 17, 141,
  154; Antigone, 155; Clytemnestra,
  144, 146, 150; Electra, 146; Euripi-
  des, 141–56; Iphigenia, 146; Ismène,
  155; Jason, 153; Medea, 151–3;
  Oedipus, 155; Sophocles, 144, 155
Green, Julien, 69
Green, Mary Jean: *Marie-Claire Blais*,
  120n4
Guéhenno, Jean, 68
Guillaumin, Colette, 51

Haentjens, Brigitte, 16, 138
harem: the space of, 129, 131, 133n2
Harrisson, Sébastien, 171n2
Havercroft, Barbara, 112–13, 114
Hayter, William Stanley, 229, 231, 232
Hébert, Anne, 22; *L'Enfant chargé de
  songes*, 78n5; *Les fous de Bassan*, 84,
  307; *Le torrent*, 84
Hemingway, Ernest Miller, 71, 81, 98
Herman, Jean-Luc, 272–4, 277, 282n1
L'histoire des femmes au Québec, 51, 56
Holocaust, 180, 187, 200
horizon: and Nicole Brossard, 61, 84,
  87, 92n2; and Hélène Dorion, 273; of
  expectations, 151; and Werner Nold,
  205; and Gabrielle Roy, 219, 220
Hospitalières de Saint-Augustin (Augus-
  tinians), 30–1, 33–6, 40, 43
Hospitalières de Saint-Joseph, 29, 33,
  36, 38, 43
Hotte, Lucie, 107–8
Hugo, Victor, 8, 16, 92n6; *Les miséra-
  bles*, 8, 16, 108–12
Hungary, 68
Huston, Nancy, 22, 280

Ibsen, Henrik, 144
identity, 3, 5, 14, 70, 81, 123–4, 126,
  128, 133n4, 138, 142–4, 150, 159,
  167, 175, 186, 197–200, 202, 207,
  211–12, 214–15, 218, 220–1, 265n1,
  268, 286, 290, 297, 308; collective,
  11, 122, 124, 126, 160, 162, 211;
  cultural, 5, 291, 297; elusiveness of,
  19, 209–10; enigma of, 209–10; erosions of, 118, 219; exilic, 17; feminist, 56; francophone, 128, 159; and
  gender, 13, 221; instinctual or natural, 211; and repressive sense of self,
  149; social, 212. *See also* difference,
  France, French Canadian identity,
  Jewish identity, national identity,
  Quebec
Île aux Oies, 227, 252

immigrant. *See* immigration

musicals, 21, 292
Mouawad, Wajdi, 154–5, 171
Mouchetache Project, 246, 249–53
myth, 141, 143–4, 150

Nadar, 8
narrative, 143, 145, 150; storytelling, 141, 143, 151; voice, 143, 151
national identity, 57, 77, 81, 118, 122, 127–9, 132, 133n3, 133n6, 159, 200–2, 211, 267, 268, 316, 318. *See also américanité,* France, French Canadian identity, identity, Quebec
national question, 58
natural forces, 215
Nègres blancs d'Amérique, 54
New York, 62, 73, 180, 181, 185–7, 199, 229–32, 236, 238, 257n14, 258
Nold, Werner, 18, 19, 205–8, 234
Normand, Jacques, 287–8
Normandy, 69, 286
North. *See* Svalbard, voyage to the north
nous les femmes, 56, 58
nouveau théâtre québécois, 160, 162, 168
nouvelle dramaturgie québécoise, dramaturgie de la parole [theatre of language], 161, 163, 166–8
Nouvelle France [New France], 10–11, 13–14, 29, 31, 35, 37–9, 42–3, 54, 120n3, 286
Nouvelles questions féministes, 56

Occupation (France), 68, 181, 182, 183
L'Olympia, 21, 225, 292, 296, 301–3
Orwell, George, 69
otherness: of the artistic vision, 221; of dream, 214; and identity, 133n9, 214–15, 218, 221; of nature, 35, 214; "other voice" of women, 217, 221; outsider's perspective, 122–6, 132; of the personal and creative self, 221; of physical response, 216; and the self, 213, 221

Ouellette-Michalska, Madeleine: *La maison Trestler,* 84

Pan and Syrinx, 211
Paré, François, 159
Parenteau-Lebeuf, Dominick, 171
Paris, 3–18, 20–2, 24–5, 27, 60, 63, 65, 67–73, 76–8, 95–6, 97–104, 105, 122–3, 127, 129–34, 137, 139, 141, 151–2, 160, 162–3, 166, 174–5, 177, 179–84, 185–6, 188, 190–1, 193, 195–9, 201–4, 225, 228–232, 236, 241, 243, 246, 249, 254, 257nn19–20, 259–60, 266–8, 274, 277, 279–80, 287–8, 292–4, 296–7, 299n18, 301, 303n13, 304n17, 304n19, 307, 309, 313
Parizeau, Alice, 190–6
passage, *passeur/passeuse,* 3–22, 23 n1, 24, 25, 65, 80, 83, 87, 90, 99, 105, 154, 155, 163, 169, 177, 182, 191, 198, 201, 202, 210, 217, 220, 227, 228, 246, 252, 254, 255, 258, 261, 264, 265n1; Northwest Passage, 91
patriarchy: patriarchal logic, 101, 112; rejection of, 194–5; society, 97, 102, 109, 152, 194, 216
Patriot Rebellion, 69
Pednault, Hélène, 53, 145, 155
Perron, Carmen, 250
Perron, Maurice, 229, 250, 257
phantasmagoria, 4, 6, 8, 12, 23n4, 24n4, 25
Picasso, Pablo, 228
Place Ville-Marie, 9
Plamondon, Luc, 289, 292, 298–9n12
Pollock, Jackson, 231
Pool, Léa, 19, 210, 214–21; *À corps perdu,* 222n3; *Anne Trister,* 210; *La demoiselle sauvage* (film), 209, 210, 214–17, 220; *Emporte-moi,* 216–17, 222n11; *La Femme de l'hôtel,* 210; *Gabrielle Roy,* 217–21, 223; handling

of landscape, 215–16, 219–20; sound-track, 219
popular culture, 12, 13, 19, 21, 22, 154, 159–60, 168, 181, 206, 233, 267, 287, 290, 303n12, 305–10, 313–17, 319–22, 323n12
Portrait du colonisé, 54. *See also* Memmi, Albert
poststructuralism, 55
Poulin, Jacques, 22
Pour les Québécoises: Égalité ou in-dépendance, 53
power, 142; abuse of, 142; colonialism, 145, 148; systemic injustices, 142; vio-lence, 142, 145–8
present, 92n9; in relation to past and fu-ture, 89, 93n14; state of the world, 81. *See also présent recomposé* in *La capture du sombre*
Prochain épisode, 15, 80, 85–90, 92n2, 92n9, 93nn10–12, 93nn15–16, 93n18; allegorical frameworks in, 82, 83, 85; and Aquinian paradox, 85; and *La capture du sombre*, 80, 84–91; figure of K in, 85–7, 90, 93n10, 93n16; scene of lovemaking in, 85–7; spatial palimpsests in, 82; surfaces and depths in, 80, 92n2; suspension of time in, 80, 92n2
Promenades de la Cathédrale, 10
Proulx, Monique, 14, 16, 47–9
Proust, Marcel, 98
psychoanalysis, 55, 141, 143, 146–7
public order, 213

Quebec, 136–8, 141, 143, 149, 210, 217, 221; changing geopolitical reali-ties, 87; Eastern Townships, 136; iden-tity, 15, 21, 80, 182, 184–5, 196, 202, 269, 276, 291; independence, 54, 82, 83; inflected by gender, 87; literary history, 84, 92n8; in relationship to French-speaking Switzerland, 81–2, 84

québécois (language), 149, 290–1, 297. *See also* French language, *joual*, Quebec
Queylus, Abbé Gabriel de, 38
Quiet Revolution, 4, 21, 52, 87, 136–7, 230, 232, 316

racism, 54, 56, 98, 142–3, 183–4
Radio-Canada, 70, 76, 194
Rapley, Elizabeth, 30
Raynaud, André, 77n3
redemption, 15, 67, 68, 74–6
Refus global, 52, 229, 230, 257n23, 281
Révolution tranquille. See Quiet Revolu-tion
Ricard, Jacqueline (Éditions La Cour Pavée), 279–80
Richard, Zachary, 293, 297
Richler, Max, 68
Richler, Mordecai, 15, 67–77, 78n4, 78nn8–9, 78n15; *The Acrobats*, 68, 69, 73, 75–6; *Images of Spain*, 76; "A Sense of the Ridiculous," 71. *See also* English language
Rimbaud, Arthur, 48–9
Riopelle, Jean Paul, 19, 227–57
Riopelle, Yseult, 230, 255, 256
Robin, Régine, 18, 108, 122, 133n3, 179–88; *Berlin chantiers*, 187; *Cyber-migrances*, 180, 181, 182, 183, 185–8; *Le golem de l'écriture*, 180; *L'immense fatigue des pierres*, 179, 180, 185–7; *Mégapolis*, 185–6; *La Québécoite*, 180, 181–5, 186, 187
Romania, 68, 117
Ronfard, Alice, 144, 154, 156
Ronfard, Jean-Pierre, 149, 151, 155
Roy, Gabrielle, 19, 209–10, 217–21, 307; *Bonheur d'occasion*, 218–19, 221, 223n13; *La détresse et l'enchan-tement*, 218–19, 222n12; *Gabrielle Roy* (documentary), 217–21, 223; *Un jardin au bout du monde*, 219,

223nn14–15; "Où iras-tu Sam Lee Wong?" 219, 223n14
rupture inaugurale, 230
Russia, 68, 192
Ryngaert, Jean-Pierre, 160, 170

sacrifice, 32–3, 74, 75, 78n15, 153
Saint Augustine of Hippo, 69
Saint-Cyr-en-Arthies, 235, 243, 245, 246
Saint Jerome, 70
Sainte-Marguerite-Estérel, 234, 235, 236, 243, 246
Saint-Vallier, Mgr Jean-Baptiste de, 38
Sartre, Jean-Paul, 69; *Huis clos,* 113, 121
Sayer, Michael, 73
Schendel, Michel van, 70
Scott, Gail, 3–4, 13–15, 17–19, 27, 65, 97–104, 105–6, 139, 177, 225; *My Paris,* 97–104; *Spaces Like Stairs,* 101; as translator of France Théoret, 110–12; "A Visit to Canada," 97
Shakespeare, William, 144, 154; *The Tempest,* 154
Shakespeare & Co., 60
short story, 13, 19, 78, 98, 180, 183, 185, 186, 209, 211, 213, 222, 223n14, 318
Simone de Beauvoir Institute, 53
Simonin, Francine, 276
Sisters of Charity of Sacré-Coeur de Jésus, 136
Smart, Patricia, 13, 17, 93n10, 93n14; *Écrire dans la maison du père,* 93n14, 195
social and moral conformism, 221
social hierarchies, 209
socialization, 209
songs: bawdy, 287; folk, 286, 288; patriotic, 287; political impact of, 290–1. *See also* chanson
Spain, 69, 75, 81, 92n4, 192
St-Martin, Fernande, 52

Stein, Gertrude, 97, 98, 106
stereotypes, 142, 160, 166, 199; rejection of: in *Côte-des Neiges,* 193; in *La fiancée promise,* 200–1; in *Les fruits arrachés,* 199
Stratford, Philip, 77
subway. *See* metro
sugar lift, 238, 250, 257n13
suicide, 68, 73–4, 126, 131, 132, 211, 213–14
Sullivan, Françoise, 229, 256n5, 280, 281
Sulpicians, 38, 43
surrealism, 101, 230, 231
surveillance and control, 212
Svalbard (Norway), 90
Swiss Francophone literature, 210, 222n2. *See also* Switzerland
Switzerland, 15, 19, 20, 22, 23n2, 71, 164, 205–6, 208, 210, 211, 213, 216–18, 221, 286, 292, 296, 308; Aquin and, 80, 82–3; Brossard and, 83–4; female enfranchisement in, 222n8; in geopolitical context, 81, 92n4; as impossible place 82, 90; landscape of, 215, 216; literary significance of, 81, 92nn5–6; in relation to Quebec, 81–2, 84; in the Western imagination, 81. *See also La demoiselle sauvage, Emporte-moi* in Pool, Léa
Sylvestre, Anne, 293, 295

television shows, 308–12
Têtes à claques, 22, 320–2
Tétrault, Michel, 249, 250, 251; Galerie Michel Tétrault, 249
Théâtre des cuisines, 53
theatre, 17, 71, 137, 141–76, 286, 288, 304n19; translation, 141–156; translation theory, 144, 151, 153–4; theatricality, 144, 151–2; tragedy, 154
Théoret, France, 16, 107–20, 276; *Huis clos entre jeunes filles,* 108–9, 112–

21; *Journal pour mémoire,* 107–8,
120–1; *Laurence,* 108–12, 113, 120,
121
Thibault, Geneviève, 52, 53
time, 3–6, 14, 47–9, 96, 101, 103, 143,
159, 218, 227, 259–60, 264, 271,
280, 283n11; Brossard's course of,
83, 92n2, 92n7; imagined, 89; in
Robin, 187–8; suspension of, 80,
92n2
tourist, 47–8, 60, 75, 122, 211, 297;
European tour, 5; trade, 73
transatlantic, 1, 4–6, 8, 10, 12, 13–18,
20–3, 80–1, 84, 107–8, 118, 120,
122, 127, 138, 163, 169, 170, 172,
180–2, 186, 190, 191, 196, 197, 203,
204, 210, 217, 222, 228, 259, 265,
266–85, 286, 288, 289, 292, 294–7;
crossings, 16, 18, 20, 43, 67–8, 123–
4, 180–2, 185, 187, 190–1, 193–4,
195, 197, 200, 305; influences, 4, 8,
12, 13–17, 22, 50–53, 104, 137, 191,
193, 267, 287, 289, 303n7, 308; journey: in *Côte-des Neiges,* 191–6; in
Naïm Kattan, 197, 199, 200, 202,
203; of Werner Nold, 205–8; relationships: ambivalence of, 81; space,
122, 132. *See also* collaboration
Travers, Mary ("La Bolduc"), 287–8
Tremblay, Larry, 162, 164–5, 169, 171
Tremblay, Michel, 22, 133n5, 160–1,
166–7, 171n13, 182; *Des nouvelles
d'Édouard,* 78n5
Trenet, Charles, 287, 289, 296,
299n22, 303, 304n24

Un gars, une fille, 310, 318n8
Ursulines, 29, 30, 31, 33, 35, 37, 40,
42, 44

Vachon, Huguette, 243, 244, 247, 248,
250, 252, 257n13
Valencia, 69, 75–6
La vie en rose, 53

Vigneault, Gilles, 286–7, 289–94,
298n5–6, 302, 304n16
Ville-Marie (Montreal), 29, 33, 39, 43.
See also Montreal
voyage to the north: in *La capture du
sombre,* 86, 90, 91; in *Neige noire,*
90; in *Prochain épisode,* 88, 90

Web(site), 179, 181, 185, 186. *See also
Têtes à claques*
Weiner, Joyce, 73
West Island Rhodesians, 54
wilderness, 167, 211, 214, 257n24
Wilson, Scotty, 243, 257n19
witch, 213
Wittgenstein, Ludwig, 98
women, 6, 29–35, 62, 96, 138, 141–2,
145, 147, 149–50, 203, 222n8, 225,
281; femininity, 142, 144, 298n4;
feminism, 50–8, 125, 143; misogyny,
142, 152, 154; religious orders of,
30–1; selfhood, 14, 37, 43, 109, 119,
221; voices of, 87, 93n13, 97
world literature in French. *See littérature monde en français*
World March of Women, 51
writing: as practice, 15, 47, 71–2, 76,
98, 115, 145, 147, 152, 174, 213–14;
act of, 47; act of, in *La capture du
sombre,* 80, 83, 84, 91, 93n18; act of,
in *Prochain épisode,* 85–6; by women,
29–45, 47, 98–104, 115, 122–3, 129–
30, 141–55, 213–14, 218, 220–1;
words, 141–2, 146–50, 153

xenophobia. *See* racism

Yugoslavia, 68